Working i

Afte
of th
labo
but a
unde
the
hete

rang
and
emp
and
setti
voic
takir

B
have
and
soci

Chi
Mic

shop
ense
pool
ling
both
and

vide
tion
onal
sses
tical
kers'
iges

will
ents
lies,

of

Asia's Transformations
Edited by Mark Selden
Binghamton and Cornell Universities, USA

The books in this series explore the political, social, economic and cultural consequences of Asia's transformations in the twentieth and twenty-first centuries. The series emphasizes the tumultuous interplay of local, national, regional and global forces as Asia bids to become the hub of the world economy. While focusing on the contemporary, it also looks back to analyze the antecedents of Asia's contested rise. This series comprises several strands:

Asia's Transformations aims to address the needs of students and teachers, and the titles will be published in hardback and paperback. Titles include:

Debating Human Rights
Critical essays from the United States and Asia
Edited by Peter Van Ness

Hong Kong's History
State and society under colonial rule
Edited by Tak-Wing Ngo

Japan's Comfort Women
Sexual slavery and prostitution during World War II and the US occupation
Yuki Tanaka

Opium, Empire and the Global Political Economy
Carl A. Trocki

Chinese Society
Change, conflict and resistance
Edited by Elizabeth J. Perry and Mark Selden

Mao's Children in the New China
Voices from the Red Guard generation
Yarong Jiang and David Ashley

Remaking the Chinese State
Strategies, society and security
Edited by Chien-min Chao and Bruce J. Dickson

Korean Society
Civil society, democracy and the state
Edited by Charles K. Armstrong

The Making of Modern Korea
Adrian Buzo

The Resurgence of East Asia
500, 150 and 50 year perspectives
Edited by Giovanni Arrighi, Takeshi Hamashita and Mark Selden

Chinese Society, 2nd edition
Change, conflict and resistance
Edited by Elizabeth J. Perry and Mark Selden

Ethnicity in Asia
Edited by Colin Mackerras

The Battle for Asia
From decolonization to globalization
Mark T. Berger

State and Society in 21st Century China
Edited by Peter Hays Gries and Stanley Rosen

Japan's Quiet Transformation
Social change and civil society in the 21st century
Jeff Kingston

Confronting the Bush Doctrine
Critical views from the Asia–Pacific
Edited by Mel Gurtov and
Peter Van Ness

China in War and Revolution,
1895–1949
Peter Zarrow

The Future of US–Korean Relations
The imbalance of power
Edited by John Feffer

Working in China
Ethnographies of labor and workplace
transformation
Edited by Ching Kwan Lee

Asia's Great Cities. Each volume aims to capture the heartbeat of the contemporary city from multiple perspectives emblematic of the authors' own deep familiarity with the distinctive faces of the city, its history, society, culture, politics and economics, and its evolving position in national, regional and global frameworks. While most volumes emphasize urban developments since the Second World War, some pay close attention to the legacy of the *longue durée* in shaping the contemporary. Thematic and comparative volumes address such themes as urbanization, economic and financial linkages, architecture and space, wealth and power, gendered relationships, planning and anarchy, and ethnographies in national and regional perspective. Titles include:

Bangkok
Place, practice and representation
Marc Askew

Beijing in the Modern World
David Strand and Madeline Yue Dong

Shanghai
Global city
Jeff Wasserstrom

Hong Kong
Global city
Stephen Chiu and Tai-Lok Lui

Representing Calcutta
Modernity, nationalism and the
colonial uncanny
Swati Chattopadhyay

Singapore
Wealth, power and the culture of
control
Carl A. Trocki

Asia.com is a series which focuses on the ways in which new information and communication technologies are influencing politics, society and culture in Asia. Titles include:

Japanese Cybercultures
Edited by Mark McLelland and
Nanette Gottlieb

Asia.com
Asia encounters the Internet
Edited by K. C. Ho, Randolph Kluver
and Kenneth C. C. Yang

The Internet in Indonesia's New
Democracy
David T. Hill and Krishna Sen

Chinese Cyberspaces
Technological changes and political
effects
Edited by Jens Damm and
Simona Thomas

Literature and Society is a series that seeks to demonstrate the ways in which Asian Literature is influenced by the politics, society and culture in which it is produced. Titles include:

The Body in Postwar Japanese Fiction
Edited by Douglas N. Slaymaker

Chinese Women Writers and the Feminist Imagination, 1905–1948
Haiping Yan

Routledge Studies in Asia's Transformations is a forum for innovative new research intended for a high-level specialist readership, and the titles will be available in hardback only. Titles include:

1 **The American Occupation of Japan and Okinawa***
Literature and memory
Michael Molasky

2 **Koreans in Japan***
Critical voices from the margin
Edited by Sonia Ryang

3 **Internationalizing the Pacific**
The United States, Japan and the Institute of Pacific Relations in war and peace, 1919–1945
Tomoko Akami

4 **Imperialism in South East Asia**
A fleeting, passing phase
Nicholas Tarling

5 **Chinese Media, Global Contexts**
Edited by Chin-Chuan Lee

6 **Remaking Citizenship in Hong Kong**
Community, nation and the global city
Edited by Agnes S. Ku and Ngai Pun

7 **Japanese Industrial Governance**
Protectionism and the licensing state
Yul Sohn

8 **Developmental Dilemmas**
Land reform and institutional change in China
Edited by Peter Ho

9 **Genders, Transgenders and Sexualities in Japan**
Edited by Mark McLelland and Romit Dasgupta

10 **Fertility, Family Planning and Population Policy in China**
Edited by Dudley L. Poston, Che-Fu Lee, Chiung-Fang Chang, Sherry L. McKibben and Carol S. Walther

11 **Japanese Diasporas**
Unsung pasts, conflicting presents and uncertain futures
Edited by Nobuko Adachi

12 **How China Works**
Perspectives on the twentieth-century industrial workplace
Edited by Jacob Eyferth

13 **Remolding and Resistance among Writers of the Chinese Prison Camp**
Disciplined and published
Edited by Philip F. Williams and Yenna Wu

Critical Asian Scholarship is a series intended to showcase the most important individual contributions to scholarship in Asian Studies. Each of the volumes presents a leading Asian scholar addressing themes that are central to his or her most significant and lasting contribution to Asian studies. The series is committed to the rich variety of research and writing on Asia, and is not restricted to any particular discipline, theoretical approach or geographical expertise.

Working in China

Ethnographies of labor and workplace transformation

Edited by Ching Kwan Lee

 Routledge
Taylor & Francis Group

LONDON AND NEW YORK

First published 2007
by Routledge
2 Park Square, Milton Park, Abingdon, Oxon OX14 4RN

Simultaneously published in the USA and Canada
by Routledge
270 Madison Ave, New York, NY 10016

Routledge is an imprint of the Taylor & Francis Group, an informa business

Typeset in Times by
HWA Text and Data Management, Tunbridge Wells

British Library Cataloguing in Publication Data
A catalogue record for this book is available from the British Library

Library of Congress Cataloging in Publication Data
Working in China : labor and workplace transformations / edited by Ching
Kwan Lee.
    p.   cm. – (Asia transformations)
Includes bibliographical references and index.
1. Labor–China. 2. Working class–China. I. Lee, Ching Kwan. II. Series.
HD8736.5W68 2006
331.10951–dc22   2006007825

ISBN10: 0–415–76999–X (hbk)
ISBN10: 0–415–77000–9 (pbk)
ISBN10: 0–203–96698–8 (ebk)

ISBN13: 978–0–415–76999–0 (hbk)
ISBN13: 978–0–415–77000–2 (pbk)
ISBN13: 978–0–203–96698–3 (ebk)

Contents

Contributors

Cheris Shun-ching Chan is an assistant professor of sociology at the University of Pittsburgh and is currently a Global Fellow at the International Institute of UCLA. Her primary research interests include culture, economic practices, new religious movements, and the dynamics of globalization. She is currently working on her book manuscript, *Making Insurance a Way of Life in China: How Culture Matters in Creating a Market*.

Lei Guang is an associate professor of political science at San Diego State University. His research has focused on migration, migrants and the rural–urban divide in China.

Amy Hanser is an assistant professor of sociology in the Department of Sociology at the University of British Columbia. Her research has focused on service work, inequality and social change in urban China, with special attention to new constructions of gender and class in China's post-socialist context. She has also published articles and book chapters on consumerism in urban China and changing job search patterns among young women and men in China's cities.

Dimitri Kessler graduated from the University of Wisconsin, Madison with a degree in sociology in 2005. He wrote a doctoral dissertation to examine how conflicts of interest between governments, foreign and Chinese enterprises affect technology transfers to mainland China in the information industries. Currently, he is a researcher working with workers' rights NGOs and headquartered in Hong Kong. He is widely interested in issues of economic justice with a specific interest in issues of workers' rights and gender in mainland China.

Ching Kwan Lee is an associate professor of sociology at the University of Michigan. She is author of *Gender and the South China Miracle: Two Worlds of Factory Women* (University of California Press, 1998) and *Against the Law: Labor Protests in China's Rustbelt and Sunbelt* (University of California Press, forthcoming). Her research interests include labor, gender, development, social movement, and inequality.

Siân Victoria Liu received her doctorate in anthropology from the University of Chicago in December 2004. Her dissertation investigated the emergence of civil society in urban China, and interrogated the applicability of the "civil society" concept in nonwestern contexts. She is currently revising the dissertation into two books: an ethnography focusing on the relationship between changing domesticities and civil society in "working class" Beijing; and a research-based novel, exploring changing forms and meanings of Chinese family relationships during the last century. She recenlty returned from taking her two young children on their first expedition to China.

Ethan Michelson has been an assistant professor in the Departments of Sociology and East Asian Languages and Cultures at Indiana University-Bloomington since receiving his PhD in sociology from the University of Chicago in 2003. In addition to his ongoing research on a variety of dimensions of the Chinese legal profession, he is also studying social conflict in rural China.

Eileen M. Otis is an assistant professor of sociology at the State University of New York, Stony Brook. She is a recipient of the An Wang Fellowship from Harvard University's Fairbank Center. Her research on China's emergent service sector has received awards from the American Sociological Association's Sex and Gender and Asia/Asian America sections. Her work has also received the Cheryl Allen Miller award from the Sociologists for Women in Society. She is currently completing a manuscript entitled, "Serving the People: The Gender, Class, and Ethnic Organization of China's Globalizing Service Sector".

Andrew Ross is a professor of American studies and Director of the Metropolitan Studies Program at New York University. He is author of several books including *Fast Boat to China: Corporate Flight and the Consequences of Free Trade*; *Low Pay, High Profile: The Global Push for Fair Labor*; *No-Collar: The Humane Workplace and its Hidden Costs*; and *The Celebration Chronicles: Life, Liberty and the Pursuit of Property Value in Disney's New Town*. He has also edited several books, including *No Sweat: Fashion, Free Trade, and the Rights of Garment Workers*, and, most recently, *Anti-Americanism*.

Yan Hairong is an assistant professor of anthropology and East Asian languages and cultures at the University of Illinois at Urbana-Champaign. She has published articles on labor migration in *Cultural Anthropology*, *American Ethnologist*, *Dushu*, and *Taiwan: A Radical Quarterly in Social Studies*.

Tiantian Zheng is an assistant professor of anthropology at the State University of New York, Cortland, and coordinator of Asian/Middle Eastern studies. She obtained her PhD at Yale University in 2003. Her research interests include gender and sexuality, migration and prostitution, social inequality, STI and HIV/AIDS.

Acknowledgments

This collection grew out of a workshop on "Working in China" held at the University of Michigan on 5 June 2004. Funding for the event was provided by the Center for Chinese Studies, the Sociology Department, Office of the Vice-Provost for Research, the Institute for Research on Women and Gender, and the Rackham Graduate School, all of the University of Michigan. Three discussants – Robin Leidner, Heidi Gottfried and Stephen Collier – offered valuable comments on the papers. Above all, I am grateful to Mark Selden who has been a most incisive critic and enthusiastic supporter of this project.

1 Mapping the terrain of Chinese labor ethnography

Ching Kwan Lee

After a quarter century of market reform, China has become the workshop of the world and the leading growth engine of the global economy. Its immense labor force, accounting for some 29 percent of the world's total labor pool, is an important contributor to the nation's historic resurgence on the international scene.[1] But all too little is known about Chinese labor beyond the fact that some workers toil under appalling "sweatshop" conditions for extremely low wages. In reality, both the Chinese workforce and the Chinese workplace are far more diversified and heterogeneous than most existing scholarship has thus far documented. This book introduces the lived experiences of labor in a wide range of occupations and work settings. The chapters cover professional employees, such as engineers and lawyers; service workers as sales clerks in department stores, bar hostesses, domestic maids, and hotel workers; semi-independent workers, such as insurance sales agents and itinerant construction workers; and finally, blue-collar communities. The mosaic of human faces, organizational dynamics, and workers' voices presented in these ethnographies reflects the complexity of changes and challenges taking place in the Chinese workplace in the current era of globalization and market transition.

From political sociology to sociology of work

This book engages conceptual and theoretical issues at the intersection of labor studies and China studies. Scholarly interests are shaped by both developments in China and contemporary global intellectual currents. All the research in this book is based on fieldwork in a rapidly changing China undertaken by a new generation of scholars. One of the most salient analytical shifts the authors in this collection embrace veers away from political sociology and toward a sociology of work. In other words, the Chinese workplace is now treated as an organizational arena, where employment relations, labor processes, occupational culture, and identities are formed, and not merely as a political site for state-sponsored clientelism and ideological and political control. With this shift in perspective, researchers now broach questions of workplace practices, alienation, and exploitation, professional autonomy, managerial strategies, workplace culture, contestation over the labor process, and the constitution of interests and identities related to class, community, ethnicity, and gender–problematics that past scholarship has neglected in favor of an overriding concern with the politics of relations between state and society. This introductory chapter tries to map this dual transformation: a changing intellectual terrain against the backdrop of political economic restructuring in China.

The changing political economy of work

The *industrial* workplace and factory workers have dominated the field of contemporary Chinese labor studies, which, if broadly defined, includes studies of village life, agricultural production, and township and village enterprises. Since the founding of the People's Republic, state industrial work units, deemed the epitome of socialist modernity and a key nexus between state and society, attracted most scholarly attention. Nearly all seminal studies prior to the 1980s were concerned exclusively with the state sector, omitting the collective sector.[2] Andrew Walder's formulation of *Communist neo-traditionalism* has been particularly influential and has spawned many empirical studies and theoretical debates.[3] It holds that state control over urban society is accomplished by clientelist networks consisting of Party activists and management and ordinary workers in the workplace, and by a state-orchestrated system to keep citizens materially dependent on their work units. For several decades, the socialist work unit (*danwei*) has become a cornerstone of the urban social structure under Chinese socialism.[4] *Danwei*'s centrality was most evident in the Tiananmen uprising and numerous labor protests in the 1990s, when the *danwei* manifested its subversive potential, fostering employee defiance in moments of sociopolitical crisis.

Only recently has this singular focus on state industrial organization and state workers been broadened to include the private, international and joint venture sectors. Beginning in the late 1980s, with market reform and the mushrooming of foreign-invested factories, researchers have expanded their scope of analysis to incorporate migrant workers in non-state industries. Influenced by feminist theories and cultural studies, Chinese labor and workplace politics have come to be analyzed through the multiple lenses of class, gender, urban–rural, quasi-ethnic, or regional divisions. Studies by Anita Chan, Lisa Rofel, Gail Hershatter, Emily Honig, Dorothy Solinger, Ching Kwan Lee, Pun Ngai, Mary Gallagher and Jacob Eyferth, among others contribute to this tradition.[5] In these works, the world of labor is shaped by intra-class diversity based on gender, the urban–rural hierarchy, native-place-based localism, ethnicity, and the uneven effects of domestic and international market forces. Rofel's important study of the generational differences among women workers in state factories under reform, for instance, explicitly brings in a much needed gender sensitivity to understand the experiences of female workers under socialism. Lee updates Walder's theoretical analysis of labor dependence on the state, taking into account the recruitment of migrant workers in state factories and the gender inequality reproduced in state-owned factory reform.[6] Many recent studies also focus on the migrant workforce in private industries and expose the pressures on working conditions generated by global capitalism in conjunction with state authoritarianism.[7]

This book builds on and enriches these past studies both analytically and empirically. The first striking theme touched on in a number of chapters is the decline of state authority in the workplace. The ethnographic accounts collected here reveal that the state, or the Party for that matter, has repositioned itself toward the workforce and the workplace. Labor legislation and labor bureaucracy regulate employment relations and conflict resolution from outside, rather than from within the workplace (Guang, Chapter 4, this book; Lee, Chapter 2, this book). In private law firms (Michelson, Chapter 9, this book), foreign and domestic insurance companies (Chan, Chapter 12, this book), multi-national hi-tech companies (Kessler, Chapter 11, this book; Ross, Chapter 10, this book), and international hotels (Otis, Chapter 6, this book), employees are primarily subjected to managerial domination and the market forces of supply and demand, rather than the political-ideological control previously exerted by state-sponsored patron-client networks. The collapse of micro-political control, particularly evident in former working-class neighborhoods (Liu, Chapter 3, this book), is conducive to work-unit mobilization by aggrieved workers who are facing collective problems of wage and pension arrears (Lee, Chapter 2, this book). Even in karaoke bars (Zheng, Chapter 7, this book), the target of the state's anti-vice campaigns, government purification policies are routinely ignored by rent-seeking public security officials, who turn state regulation into a source of extralegal income. It is as shadow bar owners and patrons, not as agents of the state, that these officials exert tremendous influence on bar hostesses.

The secular decline of state political control over workers and the workplace occurs in the larger context of Chinese economic restructuring, labor and welfare reforms. First, the state sector has substantially contracted over the past 20 years. The percentage of industrial output accounted for by state-owned enterprises has dropped from a high of 75 percent in 1981 to only 28 percent in 1999.[8] The state industrial sector accounted for only 36 percent of total industrial employment contribution in 2003.[9] Moreover, the reform period also witnessed the rise of the service – tertiary – sector, which by 2003 accounted for 29.3 percent of total national employment, compared to 21.6 percent provided by the secondary industrial sector.[10] This changing economic structure has far-reaching consequences for state control over the workplace. Grassroots official unions confront a membership crisis as state employment has shrunk and union membership has fallen by 15 million between 1990 and 2000, to 103 million.[11] Non-state employers are unwilling to establish unions on the shop floors. Among private and foreign firms, the rate of union membership remained at just four percent and 33 percent respectively in 1999.[12]

Besides economic restructuring, labor policy reforms have also reshaped the legal context of work and employment. The gradual dismantling of the "iron rice bowl" or the permanent-employment system for state employees began with the introduction of the labor contract in the early 1980s and became universally mandatory in 1995, when China's first National Labor Law was implemented.

From that date, employment relations were to be regulated by the Labor Law, and labor conflicts would be resolved according to the 1993 Regulations for the Handling of Labor Disputes, involving a three-stage procedure of mediation, arbitration, and litigation.[13] Universalist laws, rather than managerial or Party policies, which were fragmented along the lines of business ownership, provide a floor of workers' rights and benefits. Mechanisms of the labor market also replace labor administrators in the allocation of labor. Together, the increasing importance of the law and the market frees workers from their past economic and political dependence on a particular work unit or official department.

Yet the "freedom" to choose and to change jobs comes at a high price. A panoply of new policies covering social insurance and welfare has overhauled the old work unit-based workers' entitlement system. Both employees and employers are now required to contribute to pooled insurance or housing funds managed by the government's social-security agencies, to cover employees' pensions, housing, and medical care. A central imperative underlying all these measures is to reduce the budgetary responsibility of the government and to shift the financial burden of welfare provision to individual employers and employees. Pension reform has gone the furthest, driven by recognition of the dire financial crisis faced by many state-owned enterprises and the sharp rise in the number of retirees in the past two decades. Nevertheless, many workers have fallen through the cracks of the new safety net, because of widespread unemployment, business bankruptcy, or managements' refusal to contribute.[14] In certain localities, employees in the state sector are caught in the transition between the old and the new systems, that is, when central budgetary allocation has stopped but local pooling of employer–employee contributions falls short of required pension payment.[15]

The Chinese workplace as contested terrain

Against this backdrop of a sea change in the political economy of work, what kinds of workplace relations and experiences can be found? A second common theme that emerges from the ethnographies collected here, besides the palpable decline of state and Party authority in the workplace, is the pervasive presence of conflict and cynicism, even alienation, in the workplace. This situation exists across a wide range of occupations; it seems that even after state political control recedes from people's daily working lives, new forms of conflict divide the workplace. Nor do most workers experience greater job satisfaction. To oversimplify, the Communist shop floor, as previous studies show, was burdened with employees with lackluster motivation, antagonism between political activists and ordinary workers, fear of persecution, the lack of opportunity for mobility, and cadre tyranny. In the reform period, on the other hand, labor discontents and workplace tensions reported in this book are primarily the product of layoffs, bankruptcies, insecurity of jobs and rewards, the failure of enterprises to pay wages over months and even years, the non-payment of benefits accumulated over a lifetime of labor, and the unsettled nature of legal and organizational frameworks regulating work relations and workers' rights. On the one hand, there is a shift from state to enterprise responsibility for securing welfare and wage payment. On the other hand, to many workers, the processes of the labor market are seemingly impersonal and lacking agents. Both trends have deepened workers' sense of powerlessness, particularly when the fledgling legal system has proven to be quite ineffective in defending workers' legal rights.

For instance, the legal profession that Ethan Michelson studies is plagued by job insecurity as well as financial and labor-market pressure. He has found that most Chinese lawyers are accorded very low social status, that they are merely self-employed "*getihu* with legal knowledge". They are paid entirely on commission and do not enjoy any social insurance or fringe benefits. Under constant pressure to screen out cases that are not financially profitable – that is, labor lawsuits – lawyers maintain confrontational relations with their clients. They are also alienated from their law firms, which are empty shells of workplaces, offering neither social support nor prospects for promotion. Michelson thus reaches the conclusion that even with legal reform and the rise of the independent law firm, one reason why Chinese workers' legal rights are not better protected is the weakness, low prestige, and instability of the legal profession. The denial of legal justice to a vulnerable and volatile segment of society prompts labor protests that Ching Kwan Lee examines in her chapter. She shows that the lack of effective legal institutional channels for workers to redress grievances and labor violations has pushed large numbers of workers to take their discontent to the streets.

Engineers in China's information technology industry who enjoy high, even inflated, salaries confront other problems. Dimitri Kessler's research in Beijing and Shanghai reveals that the shortage of young and experienced engineers, preferred by international companies, has led to intense competition among firms and dramatic salary hikes and high turnover in the IT-engineering labor market. High turnover makes control of proprietary information difficult, sparking anxiety among international managers, based on the widespread perception that Chinese engineers are technology thieves, driven by both nationalistic sentiments and personal interests. These forces in the labor market translate into shop-floor practices such as restricting engineers' access to companywide technology, isolating these engineers into narrow specializations and requiring elaborate documentation of their work processes. These control strategies in turn fuel yet higher mobility among engineers and aggravate workplace relations. Distrust, antagonism, and the lack of organizational commitment characterize China's high-tech workplace.

Andrew Ross, looking at China's new generation of knowledge workers in the greater Shanghai region, depicts the instability of the labor market, the insecurity of technical careers, and the unsettled rules of work in the information technology sector. Globally mobile multinational corporations come to China in search of cheap but skilled technicians and engineers while making a minimum commitment to the locality or workforce. This situation has created a mirror-image workforce – employees who seek to maximize short-term opportunities and who are keen on using job-hopping as their bargaining chip. Faithless employers meet rabidly individualist employees. For the moment, both find a common interest in bringing technical knowledge to China as other nations' corporations are eager to offshore so as to cut costs, while Chinese engineers are enthusiastic about moving China up the industrial chain and securing their own future careers. Yet, the harsh realities of a highly competitive industry, the fierce pressure to perform, and the mutual distrust between employers and employees combine to generate a great deal of tension in the workplace. Mutual cultural stereotyping and miscommunication are exacerbated when companies demand more flexibility and multitasking from their employees, or when managers try to translate an imported corporate policy into directives for an inexperienced local staff. In short, Ross finds that these conflicts derive from "the contentious nature of workplace relationships in a new industrial environment, where the rules of work are not yet established. What managers expect and what employees are willing to give is by no means a settled matter". Although these young knowledge graduates, earning an average salary of 1,550 RMB per month in 2003, have so far escaped the relentless downward wage pressure in the global "race to the bottom", this generation of Chinese workers, including its privileged segments, is beset by pressures not experienced by their parents.

Service workers experience particular forms of alienation. Selling life insurance is a new profession in China that has taken off since the overhaul of the work-unit welfare system. Cheris Chan finds that "apart from the daily embarrassment of being rejected, the commission-based sales system forces the sales agents to experience constant anxiety about their income". Sales work in general has always been accorded low status in Chinese society, but selling insurance also runs counter to the cultural taboo against talking and thinking about premature death. Life-insurance firms therefore take pains to instill among their agents a set of values and attitudes that they believe to be conducive to reassuring buyers. Among these are: the sacralization of money, the ethic of individual responsibility and self-reliance underlining the purchase of insurance, and a capitalist labor logic justifying commission-based unequal rewards. Yet, for vulnerable insurance workers, these psychological and attitudinal adjustments cannot overcome the stark reality of low income and high turnover. There is a great deal of ambivalence among sales agents about the relative merits of socialist and capitalist work ethics; this is especially true among those agents who had been laid off by state-owned enterprises before joining this new industry.

The contrast between a workplace infused with socialist ethos and one that is run along capitalist principles is driven home most forcefully in Amy Hanser's comparative ethnography of two department stores in Harbin. Despite a similar shift to "flexible" labor practices, the state-owned store retains certain institutional and cultural practices that enable workers to assert a degree of autonomy and dignity unavailable to workers in the privately owned department store. Throughout the 1990s, intense competition among manufacturers in a market increasingly saturated with consumer goods spurred the spread of the "factory-in-the-store" model in the retail industry. Manufacturers not only rent sales space from department stores but also pay salaries and commissions to salesclerks, though these are still hired, supervised, and controlled by store managers. In effect, salesclerks must now satisfy two sets of bosses, one from the store and the other from the factory, neither of whom consider them "fully-fledged employees". However, having worked on both sales floors as a uniformed salesclerk, Hanser discovered a more despotic labor regime in the privately owned store, where young female workers – 25 is the age-limit – do not enjoy any formal employment status and are assigned to different sales counters whenever a manufacturer leaves the store after a sales season. As workers *in* but not *of* the store, these clerks face a dual but fragmented management hierarchy and a highly atomized workplace community. Threats of fines and of deductions from pay for misbehavior or mistakes by members of a sales team generate constant anxiety and antagonism among salesclerks. On the other hand, in the state-owned department store, even as the same "factory-in-the-store" system was introduced in the 1990s and manufacturers now pay clerks' salaries, salesclerks legally remain employees of the store. Both managers and workers share an expectation of continuity and community – there is very little labor turnover, and children still fill the positions of their retiring parents. Enjoying a high degree of autonomy from store management and being able to assert their sales expertise *vis-à-vis* manufacturers' representatives, salesclerks in the state-owned stores are nevertheless motivated to work hard for team- and sales-based commissions. Intrastore competition exists, but it is mitigated by shifting workers to different work groups every few months.

In short, gone are the days when Chinese workers were given the institutional guarantee of welfare benefits, lifelong employment, and pension security. State ideology has also muted its past exaltation of the revolutionary sanctity of labor (*laodong*) or of the modern factory as the site of "modernity" and "liberation" for men and women. Available studies of workers' experiences under Chinese state socialism have stressed both the liberating and the oppressive natures of the socialist workplace. Earlier studies, based on interviewees with refugees, emphasized the negative impact of socialism on workers.[16] More recently, however, Lisa Rofel's perceptive study of three generations of women workers finds that women who entered the factory before and during the first decade after the Communist revolution applauded the liberation from patriarchy and domesticity that factory employment had offered them.[17] Another study on working-class memory narratives among workers coming of age in the 1950s and 1960s also underscores workers' pride, sense of community, and contribution to national development through labor.[18] For some, the nostalgic memory is mixed with more traumatic memories of fear, political violence, and cadre tyranny. The overall scenario of the pre-reform workplace was one of intimate connections between state power and everyday working lives. Against this background, the workplace ethnographies in the reform era seem to paint a very different picture. These days, employees have little to say about political control and more about economic insecurity and normative uncertainty.

Reconstructing worker identities and communities

The politics of work in reform China entails not just conflicts over fledgling institutional norms and workplace practices that threaten long-accepted worker rights, but also contestation over fluid occupational, gender, native-place, and class identities.

Gender identities and their implications for power relations among workers, employers, and consumers are explored in the three chapters on three service occupations – bar hostesses, hotel service workers, and maids. All three ethnographies point to the centrality of femininity as a worker's capacity and identity and as a tool for management control. Tiantian Zheng writes about sex workers' double marginality based on their rural origins and gender, which subject them to an extraordinarily abusive and violent work world; they are vulnerable to beatings, rape, and psychological and economic exploitation by madams, bar owners, gangsters, and local public-security officials. Her ethnography offers gripping details of bar hostesses' suffering and struggle for survival and it dwells especially on their ways to strategizing for upward social mobility by becoming madams themselves or by becoming the second wives of "good clients". The occupational trajectory of many sex workers migrating from farms to factories, dance halls, and karaoke bars, illustrates the narrow structure of opportunity that continues to constrain the chances of rural young women despite a quarter-century of market reform and increased geographical mobility.

Eileen Otis finds that young women working in the hotel industry in China are trained to practice a deferential form of femininity as part of what she calls a service regime of "virtual personalism". In her ethnography of a high-end luxury hotel catering to Western male business and political elites, Otis finds management's strategy of delivering customized luxury service by a combination of technology and femininity. On the one hand, intimate knowledge about customers' preferences is obtained and carefully constructed into individual files by frontline women workers through direct interaction with customers. On the other hand, young women selected to work for their bodies, voices, and youth are given intensive training about the national characteristics and cultural sensibilities of the hotel's international clientele, fashion, hygiene, and most important, self-transformation. Managers exercise intricate control over the women's walking posture, bearing, appearance, and facial expressions, as well as their perceptions and interactive skills. Interestingly, as female workers associate their learned femininity with professional pride and construe virtual personalism as "giving face" to their customers, inequality between clients and service workers becomes covert even as female subordination is enacted on a daily basis.

Becoming domestics (*baomu*), like becoming working women (*dagongmei*), has become a very common rite of passage among young migrant rural women in the reform period. Hairong Yan's chapter reveals the hidden injuries these domestic workers sustain in a low-end and morally questionable occupation. Employers, female domestic workers, and their rural families contest the meaning and status of *baomu* as an occupational identity. The occupation of domestics persisted throughout the Maoist period, when female domestic workers were addressed as *ayi* (literally, aunt) or *baomu* (dry nurse). At that time, some rural women took advantage of kin connections to find work with urban families for various lengths of time. The countryside was marked as a site of revolutionary virtue, commanding moral political values, and child care was more often the shared responsibility of kin and others. Domestics were treated as quasi-kin and given wide latitude and autonomy in the labor process of care work. This kind of social relation became unimaginable in the 1990s, when a new generation of rural women entered domestic service in urban households. Rural–urban hierarchies in the reform era defined rural society and migrants as backward and naïve, in need of education and modernization administered by their urban middle class employers. Discipline and control distinguish the labor process of domestic work today. At the same time, young domestic workers have to confront the moral anxiety of their fellow villagers about their sexual purity. Providing personal service in private homes and at close quarters is viewed with such suspicion that domestic workers speak of fear and rejection of the subordinate position of *baomu*.

Besides the politics of gender identity, other studies in this book examine the flexible meanings and experiences of "localism", "community", and "class". Lei Guang's analysis of the community of "guerrilla" migrant workers in the home-decoration business revises a conventional argument that native-place ties are the cornerstone of the migrant-worker community. Contradicting previous studies that emphasize such place-based identities among migrant workers, Guang offers a more nuanced and context-sensitive argument that localism is pivotal only in migrants' everyday social life but not in the realm of work. The organization of home-decoration work entails erratic and flexible team formation and mobile workplaces, requiring correspondingly fluid and open-ended social relations for different projects. "The rationale for the self-employed migrants to maintain bifurcated networks – one for work and the other for communal living – may have arisen from their ambiguous identities in the cities. As economic agents … they are very instrumental and want to keep rural relations out of the realm of work. … As social beings, on the other hand, these itinerant workers find themselves excluded from many elements of urban life and by default have to rely on place-based networks for communal living and social support in the cities", Furthermore, migrant workers have developed a moral economy of work that is very different from the one shared by China's state industrial working class. Devoid of any nostalgia for, or actual experience with, state paternalism, migrant workers' culture mixes elements of market-transaction logic with hard work, perseverance, and peasant familialism.

Changing meanings of class and community are also evident in working-class neighborhoods and in working-class protests. Siân Liu's ethnography of a Beijing working-class neighborhood emphasizes how public awareness of class positions has been replaced by "social positions", indexed by the types of job people hold and their access to and consumption of space. As people appropriate neighborhood public housing previously organized by the state through state-owned enterprises, the boundaries between public and private space are redrawn, and a decline of state power in categorizing and controlling the residents occurs. Liu's chapter documents the multifaceted and contradictory changes brought about by reform. On the one hand, the demise of the *danwei*, both as employer and mediator between state and family units, has devastating social consequences. Job loss, suicides, mental illness, marital and family problems, all seem to have proliferated. On the other hand, state-authored reform has inadvertent liberating effects. Laid-off workers who transform their apartments into unlicensed business offices or sublet their apartments to outsiders forge new social relations with migrant-residents who share with them semi-legal status. Many now pay scant attention to state propaganda notices on family planning and the theory of "Three Represents", usually posted on the walls of building or neighborhood notice boards. Residents are also reluctant to maintain public spaces, like keeping stairwells clean. For those who are doing well after leaving their *danwei*, private space has become the site of people's investment and identity formation. Interior decoration and home remodeling have become very popular, and the neighborhood is flooded with advertisements for such products as hardwood flooring, curtains, swinging doors, and mirrors, variously billed as "the most popular in Germany" or "American style" and "manufactured as in Europe". For Liu, the disappearance of the *danwei* occasions the renegotiation of discursive and practical appropriations of space and of communal life. The role of the *danwei* as the organizer of working-class community life and an extension of state control has substantially dwindled.

Ching Kwan Lee's chapter asks whether worker protests in China portend the rise of a working-class movement, and whether workers constitute "class" actors. She analyzes labor rebellions in the rustbelt province of Liaoning, where a large number of workers in faltering state factories have mobilized to demand payment of owed pensions and wages. She describes the prevailing mode of labor mobilization as "cellular activism", a process that entails localized and for the most part work-unit-based action and disruption, with an eye to generating pressure on local officials rather than creating lateral association among workers. In many cases the state tolerates cellular activism while cracking down hard on horizontal relationships such as an all-industry or all-city alternative union or struggle. She traces the roots of these cellular actions to the decentralization and differentiation of the political economy in the reform period. In terms of workers' insurgent identities, she finds that after decades of official indoctrination in Marxist and Maoist ideologies, such as the mastery of the working class and the superiority of socialism's lifetime job guarantee in contrast to the class exploitation under capitalism, veteran state-sector workers readily invoke class categories to understand their current predicaments. But since the state has abandoned the rhetoric of class and class struggles in the reform period, workers do not find "class" empowering in making claims on public and the government. On the other hand, as the state champions a discourse of legality and seeks to establish a law-based government, workers strategically incorporate demands for anti-corruption and the protection of workers' legal rights in their petitions and protests. But this incipient consciousness of legal rights is often challenged and shattered by the stark reality that workers enjoy few legal rights under the current political and judicial system in which the court is dominated by the new logic of capital. Their interactions with officials during petitions, protests, and litigations frequently result in disenchantment with the law and the legal system. What does provide an empowering and effective identity for workers making claims on the state is the notion of the underprivileged or "*ruoshi qunti*". Like the masses in Mao's mass line, these weak and disadvantaged groups appeal to a protective Party-state in opposition to corrupt and incompetent local cadres that deviate from the policies of the central leadership. Echoing the themes in many other chapters, Lee notes that worker identities are as unsettled and fluid as the institutions that enable and constrain their formation.

Overall, as a field of scholarly inquiry, labor studies on China have been given a new lease of life as a result of greater ethnographic access to the Chinese workplaces and a revival of the ethnographic tradition in mainstream Anglo-American sociology. The shift in the theoretical framework, away from political sociology to sociology of work, is informed by both the repositioning of the Chinese state's political and economic domination in the labor market and by the intellectual choices of researchers sensitive to agency, identity, process, culture, gender, class, and other principles of inequality shaping the domains of work and employment. As other ethnographers[19] have noted, in moments of great but uncertain transitions, when the planned economy and the Party-state recede and break down macro structures, these micro processes, practices, and agencies produce autonomous effects and assume inordinate significance. For this reason this book privileges ethnography in charting a new course of Chinese labor and workplace studies.

Notes

1 World Bank, *World Development Report*, 1996
2 Charles Hoffman, *The Chinese Worker*, Albany, NY: State University of New York Press, 1974; Martin King Whyte, *Small Groups and Political Rituals in China*, Berkeley, CA: University of California Press, 1974; Stephen Andors, *China's Industrial Revolution: Politics, Planning, and Management, 1949 to the Present*, New York: Pantheon Books, 1977.
3 Andrew Walder, *Communist Neo-traditionalism: Work and Authority in Chinese Industry*, Berkeley, CA: University of California Press, 1986.
4 Xiaobo Lu and Elizabeth J. Perry, *Danwei: the Changing Chinese Workplace in Historical and Comparative Perspective*, Armonk, NY: M.E. Sharpe, 1997; Yanjie Bian, *Work and Inequality in China*, Albany, NY: State University of New York Press, 1994.
5 Anita Chan, *China's Workers Under Assault*, Armonk, NY: M.E.Sharpe, 2001; Lisa Rofel, *Other Modernities: Gendered Yearnings in China After Socialism*, Berkeley, CA: University of California Press, 1999; Gail Hershatter, *The Workers of Tianjin 1900–1949*, Stanford, CA: Stanford University Press, 1986; Emily Honig, *Sisters and Strangers: Women in the Shanghai Cotton Mills, 1919–1949*, Stanford, CA: Stanford University Press, 1986; Dorothy Solinger, *Contesting Citizenship*, Berkeley, CA: University of California Press, 1999; Ching Kwan Lee, *Gender and the South China Miracle: Two Worlds of Factory Women*, Berkeley, CA: University of California Press, 1998; Ngai Pun, *Made In China*, Durham, NC: Duke University Press, 2005; Mary E.

Gallagher, *Contagious Capitalism: Globalization and the Politics of Labor in China*, Princeton, NJ: Princeton University Press, 2005; Jacob Eyferth (ed.), *Making Workers: Ethnographies of the Chinese Workplace in the Transition to and From Socialism*, London: Routledge, forthcoming.

6 Ching Kwan Lee, "From Organized Dependence to Disorganized Despotism: Changing Labor Regimes in Chinese Factories", (1999) 157 *The China Quarterly*: 44–71.

7 See citations in footnote 5.

8 *China Industrial Economics Statistical Yearbook 2004*, Beijing: China Statistics Press, 2005, table 2-4. The figures from 2000 to 2003, showing that "state-controlled or state-owned" sector at about 47% to 37%, are hard to interpret as these were double-counted as "others". The total percentage of all ownership types during these years exceeded 100.

9 *China Statistical Yearbook 2004*, Beijing: China Statistics Press, 2005, table 5-9.

10 Ibid., table 5-1.

11 Bill Taylor, Chang Kai and Li Qi, *Industrial Relations in China*, Cheltenham: Edward Elgar Publishing Ltd, 2003, p. 105.

12 Ibid.

13 Virginia Harper Ho, *Labor Dispute Resolution in China: Implications for Labor Rights and Legal Reform*, Berkeley, CA: Institute of East Asian Studies, 2003, China Research Monograph 59.

14 Mark Frazier, "China's Pension Reform and Its Discontents", (2004) 51 *The China Journal*: 97–114.

15 Ching Kwan Lee, *Livelihood Struggles and Market Reform: (Un)making Chinese Labor After State Socialism*, Geneva: United Nations Research Institute for Social Development, 2005, Occasional Paper No. 2.

16 Andrew Walder, *Communist Neo-traditionalism*, op. cit.; Martin King Whyte and William Parish, *Urban Life in Contemporary China*, Chicago, IL: University of Chicago Press, 1984.

17 Lisa Rofel, *Other Modernities: Gendered Yearnings in China after Socialism*, Berkeley, CA: University of California Press, 1999.

18 Ching Kwan Lee, *Against the Law: Labor Protests in China's Rustbelt and Sunbelt*, Berkeley, CA: University of California Press, forthcoming, Chapter 4.

19 Michael Burawoy and Katherine Verdery (eds.), *Uncertain Transition: Ethnographies of Change in the Postsocialist World*, Lanham, MD: Rowman and Littlefield Publishers Inc., 1999.

Part I

Remaking class and community

2 The unmaking of the Chinese working class in the northeastern rustbelt

Ching Kwan Lee

Workers' rage in Liaoyang

In mid-March 2002, tens of thousands of workers marched through Liaoyang, an old industrial town in China's northeastern rustbelt. Some carried a huge portrait of the late Mao Zedong that was mounted on four shoulder poles and accented by a red ribbon fastened in a knot at the top of the frame. While some people passionately sang the Internationale, an elderly woman cried aloud, "Chairman Mao should not have died so soon!".[1] Fueled by simmering anger at the corrupt local government and pressed by economic difficulties after their state-owned enterprises went bankrupt, workers from as many as 20 factories at one point demonstrated in front of the Liaoyang City Government building. They demanded payment of back wages, pensions, and unemployment allowances owed them for months, even years. But most shocking to the authorities, they insisted on the removal of business officials and the head of the local legislature, whose seven-year tenure as mayor had spawned rampant corruption and wreaked havoc with the lives of local people. Overseas human rights organizations claimed that it was the largest collective act of defiance since the bloody crackdown of the 1989 Tiananmen incident. But this time it was workers who formed the major active social group; no intellectuals, no students or private entrepreneurs joined their protests, and the official press censored the incident at both the municipal and national levels.

Liaoyang has the look of many old industrial towns in the northeastern province of Liaoning. A pervasive grayness and an air of morbidity beset what once was a proud and buzzing industrial center boasting a dozen major military factories and a nationally renowned chemical plant built with French technological assistance in the early 1970s. No inkling of such past glory can be found today on the faces of the many unemployed workers gathering in make-shift "labor market spots", holding in their hands or hanging on their necks placards announcing their skills to be sold: plumber, electrician, nanny, seamstress, etc. Abandoned brick workshops punctured by broken window panes lined the main road leading into this city of 1.8 million; one of these workshops was the Liaoyang Ferro-Alloy Factory, or Liaotie, the epicenter of the protests. For four years, the 3,000 employees of this state-owned enterprise had attempted in vain to petition the local government and to file lawsuits against the factory management for financial irregularities and non-payment of wages, pensions, unemployment allowances, and medical reimbursement. The columns near the main entrance were covered with posters and open letters. One open letter addressed to "All the People in Liaoyang" read:

> We the working masses cannot tolerate the corrupt elements who imposed an illegal bankruptcy on our factory. We must take back justice and dignity. We will not give up until we get all welfare, unpaid wages, and compensation … Our respected compatriots, brothers and fathers, we are not anti-Party, anti-socialism hooligans who harm people's lives and disrupt social order. Our demands are all legal under the Constitution and the laws. … Let's join forces in this action for legal rights and against corruption. Long live the spirit of Liaoyang![2]

Pointed and impassioned, these letters constituted a resounding denunciation of local government corruption, and official collusion with enterprise management. The panoply of worker compensation measures specified by central government policy remained empty but tantalizing promises. Liaotie workers' grievances were shared by many local workers throughout China's cities and especially across the Northeast. This vignette records events during the Spring Festival of 2002 in Liaotie's neighborhood. It was a harbinger of what would come a month later in the protests:

> It all began during the Chinese New Year [in Feb]. It was a particularly bad year for many. In my neighborhood, a couple who worked in our factory had only 182 yuan to spend for the Spring Festival. They had a kid and two elderly parents. How could you have a New Year with that little money? They could not even afford cooking oil and were not given any heating allowances. In the same residential area, we saw our cadres living in big apartments and coming home from their shopping spree with nicely wrapped gifts. They were celebrating bankruptcy! Some elderly workers were particularly upset, and they sang the Internationale during the New Year. I heard that several times. How the lyrics made good sense these days –"Arise, ye starving workers. Arise, ye oppressed masses of the world!"[3]

Nevertheless, as a disillusioned former party-secretary of one of the targeted factories explained to me, different groups of protesting workers participated, each group recalling its own unresolved "balance books". They came together in holding the local government responsible for their plight:

> First, there were laid-off workers who did not get their 180 yuan monthly allowance. Second, there were retired workers who complained that they were not getting the special allowance promised by the central government two years earlier. It was stipulated that for each year of job tenure, additional 1.8 yuan should be added to their monthly retirement wage. Third, there were

retired cadres whose career dated back to pre-revolutionary era complaining about unequal treatment of retirement. There was a policy for military personnel who were with the CCP before 1949 to get 1,800 yuan a month as pension, but those who surrendered to the CCP at the end of the anti-Japanese War were given only half of that amount. The latter group was of course furious ... Then, there were banners saying "We want to eat", "Return us our wages" ... People are nostalgic about the time of Chairman Mao when everyone had jobs, and society was stable and equal ... After devoting my life to political education work, I now feel my efforts have all been wasted. Since the early 1990s, after they started the director responsibility system, as party secretary I was sidelined, and he (the director) could rule and decide on personnel matters as he wished, with no restraint at all.[4]

While the Liaoyang episode could be considered extraordinary in its scale, its multi-factory participation, and its explicit political demand, it was also a radicalized version of several thousand similar incidents that have erupted each year since the 1990s. Police statistics on demonstrations, startling as they are, reflect only the tip of the iceberg. Between 2000 and 2002, in Liaoning province alone, more than 830,000 people were involved in 9,559 incidents, or an average of 10 incidents involving 90 people every day for nearly three years.[5] In 2003, the Ministry of Public Security counted some 58,000 "mass incidents" staged by 3 million people, including farmers, workers, teachers, and students, throughout the nation.[6] There has been a consistent surge in such incidents since 1993, when 8,700 such incidents were recorded, rising to 11,000, 15,000 and 32,000 in 1995, 1997 and 1999 respectively.[7] Labor strife has been brewing and intensifying among China's massive laid-off and retired proletariat as these people confront rampant nonpayment of wages and pensions. According to official trade-union statistics, the total number of workers in China's state and collective enterprises who were owed unpaid wages increased from 2.6 million in 1993 to 14 million in 2000[8] In Shenyang, the provincial capital of Liaoning, more than a quarter of retired workers were owed pensions, while another quarter of employed workers were owed wages.[9] With glaring holes in the new safety net, the estimated 27 million to 40 million workers eliminated from their work units in the state and collective sector since 1995 are plagued by a profound sense of insecurity.[10]

Drawing on field data collected in Liaoning, I analyze what I call *cellular activism*, the prevailing method of mobilization among Chinese workers engaging in protests in the rustbelt. Other scholars have documented cases of worker struggle in other parts of China that largely follow the same pattern.[11] In the following section, I examine the "critical case" of Liaoyang protests in the spring of 2002 as an exception that proves the rule, when, behind the façade of multi-factory participation, the protest organizers from one factory insisted on excluding other factories' workers from participating in planning meetings and meetings with the leadership. Interviews with key organizers of the Liaoyang protest reveal the underlying logic of such cellular activism. The massive multi-factory turnout was a chance incident that portended the specter of unintended radicalization rather than the result of workers' strategy or capacity for lateral mobilization. In the final part of the chapter, I seek to portray the insurgent identities that inform and constitute this particular mode of labor politics. While there is no lack of references to "working-class interests" and "citizens' legal rights" among workers in protests, the validity of these insurgent identities is negated by the workers themselves in the process of labor disputes. As workers confront the stark reality of unemployment, violation of their legal rights, corruption, and incompetence of the court and the local government, they come to embrace the new political identity of the "underprivileged".

Falling through the cracks of reform

The reform period witnessed the gradual dismantling of the socialist system for employment, marked by cradle-to-grave welfare and employment security for the permanent workforce in the public sector. At the same time, the central government attempted to construct a new social-security system and a labor rule of law. The 1990s witnessed the passage or revision of three important pieces of labor legislation: the 1995 Labor Law, revisions of the Trade Union Law in 1992 and 2002, and the Regulation for the Handling of Labor Disputes in 1993. The Bankruptcy Law of 1986 stipulated that priority would be given to payment and compensation to workers after the liquidation of business assets. During the 1980s and 1990s, welfare reforms affecting pension, housing, unemployment benefits, basic livelihood allowances, poverty relief, and more were enacted.[12] The scope of the crisis over non-payment indicates that all these laws and regulations are widely ignored.

While a full-scale analysis of the institutional gaps in welfare and legal reforms is beyond the scope of this chapter, two broad problems can be identified as the backdrop to the workers' situation and their protests. First, the general strategy of economic and fiscal decentralization pursued by the central leadership to spur local economic growth also means the decentralization of responsibility for welfare. Pension reform in public industries is an "unfunded mandate", and unequal provisions appear as economic conditions vary from one locality to another.[13] Liaoning, with an unusually high concentration of old, heavy and bankrupt state factories, is particularly plagued by insufficient pension funds pooled from ailing and unprofitable enterprises. Second, the ubiquitous violation of workers' most basic legal right to wage payment is also related to the failure of the judiciary to enforce the applicable laws and regulations, which is in turn the result of the judiciary's subordination to the government and the Chinese Communist Party. Not only are court budgets and judges' salaries beholden to the dictates of local governments, judges' appointment, promotion and authority also depend on the Party's approval and are subject to veto by Party officials. During the reform period, when local governments are vying for investors or are themselves business owners or partners, the courts are particularly hamstrung in enforcing laws that protect labor rights.[14]

Cellular activism

In the past decade and a half, workers' protests have largely followed the pattern of workplace mobilization; that is, protests are usually based in a single factory. Pensioners and laid-off workers would sustain months of non-payment before beginning to take action and launch collective petitions to both the business in question and the local government responsible for it. Under Chinese Communist rule, lodging complaints to the government is a well-established channel of political participation. Dating back to the Communist base area in the 1930s, petitioning the Letters and Visits Bureau is an institutionalized and legitimate means of making demands and expressing popular discontent with the government. When repeated visits to the local leadership fail to deliver heretofore unpaid pensions and wages, petitioners are prone to take their demands to the streets. Many incidents of workers blocking traffic, demonstrating outside government buildings, or marching through downtown streets have their origin in mass outrage against official failure to redress legal and legitimate grievances.

Shenyang: blocking traffic

At China's largest casting factory, Shenyang Casting Factory, several hundred retirees had staged some 20 protests in the period 1998–2000; they blocked city traffic to demand full payment of their pensions. One 73-year-old former party secretary from the production department was a central figure, who commanded tremendous respect and trust among his fellow retirees. He was owed a total of 2,400 yuan over a three-year period. Retirees had been paid only 60 percent of their total pension, while welfare subsidies provided by the factory, which made up the other 40 percent of the monthly payment, were not paid out at all. He and other workers were angry at such prolonged arrears, although they understood these were just a part of the problem of business insolvency:

> Our factory is in serious debt to everyone. In addition to our iron suppliers, it owes the social-insurance department hundreds of millions of yuan. More than once, I have seen police called in to investigate debt disputes … Worker action is legal, because pension is our lifeline money. Even the central government says that. And we don't have any ability to do business or find work in the marketplace. It is the responsibility of the enterprise and the supervising department. The "Three Represents" emphasizes the personal interests of the masses, doesn't it? We block city roads with only one goal in mind: give us our money, and we will go home.[15]

Regular participants in these blockage episodes all described them as spontaneous – that is, without mobilization by any specific individuals. There is, in fact, no need for formal organization, since the residential quarters of the work units provide ready organizational and ecological resources for action. This articulate foundryman, who retired in 1989, had participated in six of these protests; he gave a crisp account of the way in which these incidents typically unfolded:

> Every time the central government announced publicly that pensions must be paid in full, we became very upset. All of us have television at home, and we always watch. Who does not know about these announcements? Every day, elderly people gather in the elderly-activities room in our neighborhood, smoking and playing chess, poker, or mah-jong. Someone commented on our unpaid pensions and instantly suggested that we block the road. When we got angry, we just went instantly, or maybe on the morning of the following day, at eight or nine o'clock. Once we arrive at the destination, we did not say a word – no banner, no slogan, we just stood there. We just wanted to arouse public opinion, pressuring leaders of the Machinary and Electrical Works Bureau to talk to the factory director. There would usually be several hundred retirees – not that many when you consider that there are fifteen hundred retirees for the entire work unit. The traffic police would arrive several minutes after we began blocking. They did not intervene, they just asked politely which factory we were from. They said that they were just doing their job, and they urged us to do our best to move toward the sidewalk. Other police would come too, and they would even urge the traffic police not to push us too hard. They were afraid that elderly people would get hurt. Passersby on bicycles were very sympathetic and were merely curious to know which factory we were from. But people in buses or automobiles would swear at us, saying, "Those who should die, live". ... Very soon, local government officials would come, and we would tell them we were owed pension and had no money to see the doctor. Usually they were very patient. Once they promised to investigate or to see to it that we were paid the following week, we just disbanded and went home. The more workers were present, the higher the level of officials who would come down.[16]

Asked about the chosen strategy of blocking road traffic within Shenyang, rather than rallying or lying on the railroad tracks, the old man laughed and offered a simple explanation:

> Look, we are people in our seventies and eighties, our bodies are falling apart. We could barely walk. We could only stand still. Standing there on the road is painful enough, not to mention marches and rallies. My feet and legs are all sore. When we were young, in the Cultural Revolution, we could roam around town and demonstrate.[17]

While pensioners saw the disruptive impact of mass action on city life as their leverage and dared to increase the pressure on the local government by amassing more workers and escalating from minor roads to major roads when they did not obtain results, they were careful not to ignore the fine line between what they perceived as legal and illegal behavior, fearing for their personal safety:

We don't want to block railways. Those are major national arteries. We elderly workers are reasonable, and we have a good sense of state policy. In Liaoyang and Anshan, workers had blocked railways, and bad things had happened to them, public security officers were sent in. If any injury or death occurs, the nature of our action will be changed. ... First we approach our own factory, and if there is no response, we go to the superior department, and then to the city government. You have to follow the bureaucratic hierarchy of proceeding from lower to higher levels. Then, things will be easier.[18]

Retirees certainly felt strongly about the moral righteousness of their resistance; one 75-year-old retiree, a key figure in these protests, forcefully invoked Mao's authority as justification:

We only want to make one statement by blocking the road: superior officials must come to take a look! We only want our pension paid. Premier Zhu himself promised no arrears when he visited Shenyang. The central government has announced a new 49-yuan extra subsidies for us retirees. Our work-unit leaders made us sign a paper saying that they would pay us later, but so far nothing has happened. Pension is Chairman Mao's national policy![19]

According to retirees, the dynamic of their interaction with the government is that the bigger the incidents they manage to pull off, the quicker the response by the government, and more payment will follow. "Like squeezing toothpaste from a tube", an analogy they use jokingly that echoes the popular saying, "Big disturbance, big solution; small disturbance, small solution; no disturbance, no solution".[20] Most episodes of road blockage have led to various increases in the amount paid, say from 60 percent to 80 percent of workers' overdue pension. Yet, such increases may only last for a few months and then stop again, triggering another round of action, especially if the central government happens to re-emphasize the importance of guaranteeing pension. The target of pensioners' action is quite uniformly the local leadership: enterprise cadres and officials of the supervising government departments.

The central government did respond with a cash infusion and the quickening of social-security reform, paying particular attention to Liaoning, which was designated a pilot province for pension reform. Between 1998 and 2001, to quell the discontent and disruption caused by pension protests across the country, the central government pumped a total of 861 billion yuan to bail out the deficits caused by enterprise and local shortfalls. At the same time, the center also demanded universal pension payments through the banking system instead of through the enterprise. By the end of 2001, nationwide, 98 percent of pensioners received their pension through the bank rather than through their employer.[21] Pension protests subsided. "Now that they began regular payment, there is no reason for protests anymore", admitted one of the interviewees.

Tieling: protest in the valve factory

Many protests by laid-off workers were provoked by a long period of wage arrears before the firm initiated the formal procedure for bankruptcy. The key actors were workers who were still on the payroll; some even showed up on their shop floor regularly though they were not actually working or getting paid. Many did not bother to contact their work units, and these also ignored their workers; this situation is called "mutual disregard" or *liangbuguan*. Still, protests of wage arrears might erupt quite suddenly. The following incident occurred in China's largest industrial valve plant, in Tieling, an old industrial town about 80 kilometers from Shenyang. In its heyday in 1987, the factory boasted an annual profit of 10 million yuan, and a 4,000-strong work force. "There were so many workers that it took a quarter of an hour to get everyone through the gate at the end of the work day", one worker recalled proudly. The factory began to slide downhill in the early 1990s. Like other state-owned firms in this region, it was plagued by problems of market competition, debt, bad management, and the heavy burden of an aging workforce. At one point in 1992, all workers were required to make a "collective investment" in the firm, each paying 4,000 yuan to save the cash-strapped firm. Then, in 1998, the factory issued "stock", whose legal status has never been recognized by the local government. The company demanded that workers voluntarily convert their investment into stock; if they did not do so, they would risk losing repayment of their money. The general public was also enticed to buy the stock in what many considered to be the most established state-owned firm in Tieling. Yet the injection of this 20 million yuan investment was not able to reverse the company's decline.

On May Day, 2001, some 70 workers blocked the main entrance of the factory with a chain tied around the gate and formed a picket line to stop other workers from entering. The factory had not paid wages to the entire workforce for six months. A banner reading, "We Want to Eat, Return Our Wages to Us" hung at the gate. Even the security guards did not intervene, because they, too, were owed back pay. Most workers were sympathetic and did not force their way through. During the next three days while production was suspended, police cars were seen patrolling the streets surrounding the factory, and public security officers looked on, without taking any action to disperse the crowd. One key participant among the workers explained how his method had prevailed over other, more militant, tendencies among his co-workers and how he had convinced them to stay within the realm of legal behavior. He recounted how the incident had got off the ground:

> You don't need much organizing. I was taking a walk in the playground downstairs and ran into several coworkers who were talking about protesting against wage arrears the next morning. We wanted the director to come out and explain to us. Before that, a dozen of them had visited the petition office of the city government. We got checks for one month's pay after that. Then payments stopped again. ... There were at first twenty or so of us, gathering

at the gate. We were busy debating what to write on the banner. Someone cooked up something really clumsy and long-winded, not crisp enough to be slogans. I convinced them to go for a simple and clear statement, just "We Want to Eat, Return Our Wages to Us". On the sidewalk, we used eight plastic bags and wrote with black ink ... We waited there for the director to appear. Then, when we were told that he was heading for a meeting in Beijing, and that he'd said that he would not cancel his trip because of our protest, workers were infuriated. We immediately put an iron chain around the gate. Some workers yelled, proposing to set fire to company cars, others suggested blocking highways and city streets. I implored them to stay calm, and I reasoned with them. I said, asking for unpaid wages is righteous, but if we turn it into a riot, we violate the law. There are regulations against blocking traffic and against public disorder. It will change the nature of our cause. They [the officials] can then impose all kinds of caps on our heads.

This worker won the support of most of those who were gathering outside the factory. Thirty people were stationed at the gate until the evening. When the management informed the city government of the protest, a delegation of five officials from the Petition Office and the municipal Light Industry Bureau came to assuage the workers' anger, assuring them that the director had been instructed to take the first flight back tomorrow. They asked workers to elect their own representatives to negotiate with the director and to prepare a statement of demands. Worrying about future retaliation, a circumstance that had happened to other factories, the workers refused to appoint representatives, pointing out that there was nothing to negotiate because they had only one simple demand: that the enterprise pays them their wages. That night, these 30 workers took turns guarding the entrance. The director returned to the factory the following evening, appearing before a crowd of 100 workers:

He told us our enterprise is experiencing financial difficulty. His trip to Beijing was about something urgent, and he rushed back once that business was over. He was willing to follow the instruction of the government to pay a month's wages to us immediately, and that he would then come up with a more detailed repayment plan ... We were paid the following two months, but the payments stopped again after that. No one has ever seen any repayment plan.

The threat of police repression was intense and imminent, leading workers to set self-imposed limits on their actions. The sensitive political boundary between the factory and "society" has to be observed if a government crackdown was to be prevented. Workers felt protected as long as their activities remained confined to the work unit bound and the geography of workplace and residence allowed for easy communications among co-workers. But as was the case in Shenyang and Liaoyang, workers in Tieling were also divided in their interests. When rumors spread that the management of one of the workshops was close to completing a merger with a private firm from Shenzhen, headed by the sister of one of the premiers sitting in the Standing Committee of the Politburo, workers in that workshop were hopeful that they would soon be returning to work and to being paid their accumulated back wages. Such a deal would not benefit workers in workshops that had been "sub-contracted" to private and financially independent entrepreneurs, since they had severed their employment relations with the greater enterprise. For the rest of the unpaid workforce, the momentum to engage in further action diminished. When I visited these workers in January 2002, fliers were posted at the entrance of each residential building, announcing another protest scheduled for November to demand payment of eight months of wages in arrears. That mobilization failed because, by then, many workers were disillusioned and had been busy with whatever alternative jobs they had found. Finally, at the end of 2001, the central government policy of a one-off payment to workers in unofficially bankrupt enterprises resulted in a severance package of 400 yuan for each year the worker had been employed in that job. This policy did not provoke any protest.

In both Shenyang and Tieling, a confluence of factors produces this kind of cellular activism. First, the prevailing view among aggrieved workers is that their interests are workplace-specific and therefore the most effective unit of mobilization is the factory. During my fieldwork, I was often perplexed by the gap between workers' awareness of common predicaments and the absence of cross-enterprise action, especially in Tiexi, where residents claimed that the majority of companies had seen their retirees blocking the streets. Every time I challenged them to apply their theory of "big disturbance, big resolution" to joint action with other factories, I unvaryingly received the same reply: "It is no use coordinating with retirees from other factories, because some firms are more generous or stronger financially, and their workers get more subsidies. Some leaders take our interests to their hearts, while others don't care whether we are cold or hot". And indeed, factories had different subsidy packages for their retired employees, a practice that was encouraged by the government to increase the benefits of elderly workers whenever their firms could afford it. In the reform period, the problem of outstanding pension existed to different degrees across firms, depending on their profitability and corruption of their cadres. Retirees often launched bitter accusations of injustice, complaining about unequal retirement benefits across firms. In Shenyang, according to interviewees, in 2003, the casting factory paid their retirees an average of 600 yuan a month, but their counterparts in oil and chemicals or electric companies were paid more than 1,000 yuan.

At the same time, within companies, there are differences of benefits and interests that may look insignificant to outsiders but that are taken seriously by workers. Retirees' pension packages differed depending on the starting and termination date of their employment, with periodic raises given by the central government to pre-Liberation workers – that is, those who started working before December 1948, when the CCP liberated the northeast – or pre-PRC workers – those who began working before the establishment of the PRC in October 1949. Retirees were further separated by policies that gave preferential treatment to former workers involved in high- or low-temperature positions or in industries that involved occupational hazards and illness. Higher-paid retirees were looked upon with suspicion by lower-paid ones because they were able to maintain a more comfortable lifestyle even when they did not receive full payment.

Therefore, I use the term "cellular activism" to underscore not just the unrest based in a locality or a work unit, but also the intra-company divisions among workers who have coalesced into different "interest groups", to use their own terminology. Categorizations among "laid-off" workers – because of illness or because of financial difficulties or bankruptcy in a company – and among pensioners – marked by a specific cut-off date for the beginning of employment and of retirement – was refined according to the different entitlements and priorities in receiving payments. These differences, calculated by state policy, translated into what workers called "different interest groups" within work units. Sometimes, such division of interests percolates into workers' families and creates domestic tensions. I have seen hostility among family members who worked for the same enterprise but who found their interests at odds with each other under government policies. In another prolonged protest involving a textile mill in Tieling, management duly paid its pensioners but refused to settle laid-off workers' demands for severance payment.[22] When I was interviewing families with these two types of employees, I encountered cases in which the elderly parent and the middle-aged son had stopped talking to each other.

Workers attribute their plight to local political and economic forces. Since the mid-1980s, SOE reform has emphasized company and managerial autonomy, inter-firm competition, and a performance-based remuneration system, resulting in vast differences in firms' profitability and their workers' wage levels, housing, and medical and retirement benefits. Overall, decentralization and market competition have created a kaleidoscope of fine-grained social and economic differences across factories in the same locality. And despite the overhaul of the work-unit welfare system, Chinese workers' entitlements at work and after retirement continue to be closely tied to their work organizations. The availability of pensions, unemployment benefits, and industrial injury compensations still depend on the employing units' ability and willingness to contribute to insurance funds, pooled at the city or county level. This localized and workplace-oriented organization of workers' interests results in localized and cellular activism.

Besides the perception and constitution of interests, cellular mobilization thrives on the encompassing nature of Chinese factories. State-owned enterprises combine production and residence in the same communal space, where residential quarters for workers are geographically close to factories, forming self-contained, all-encompassing communities. They facilitate communication and the joining of interests, especially at the moment of mass layoff or dismissal.

In short, workers' cellular activism arises from the locality- and work-unit-based organization of interests and the readily available organizational resources provided by encompassing communities centered at the workplace. Workers' protests target local power holders because these are the only remaining access points in what is popularly perceived as a self-regulating market economy without agents. Workers seek to exert mass pressure and to leverage the existing bureaucratic hierarchy, rather than pursuing the risky path of lateral organization. Cellular resistance and hierarchical political orientation have material foundations in the concrete ways in which interests are constituted. It is not a less developed or myopic form of politics, nor an indication of traditional culture or conservative mentality.

Liaoyang: specter of class rebellion?

The specter of a working-class uprising that actually challenged the legitimacy of an organization was raised during the mass protests in Liaoyang, Liaoning, in the spring of 2002. The international media reported that some 20 factories were involved and that workers demanded the removal of local leaders, two features that distinguish the Liaoyang incident from ordinary worker protests. However, my interviews with core organizers of the protests show important similarities between the two. The situation of Liaoyang presents a case of prolonged cellular mobilization that evolved, through a "qualitative leap" – workers' expression – into an unintended radical episode. It began with workers from one factory, Liaotie, who had engaged in a four-year struggle with local officials. Liaotie as an enterprise had once been a pillar of the community, employing 7,000 workers in its heyday, the fourth-largest plant in Liaoyang. Since 1993, when Fan Yicheng was appointed director and party secretary, the firm's fortunes slipped, and as early as 1996, production was periodically suspended. Beginning in 1998, the workers repeatedly attempted to petition local and Beijing officials. Their complaints cited managerial corruption, illicit transfer and privatization of state assets, and unpaid wages, pensions, and medical reimbursement. All their efforts were in vain, and the local government took no action to alleviate the workers' plight.

In May 2000, two years before the mass protests, more than 1,000 Liaotie workers blocked the main highway from Liaoyang to Shenyang, demanding payment of wages and pensions. Armed police arrived and arrested three organizers. The following day, the workers regrouped and launched a siege of the municipal government building; they wielded a banner reading, "Arrears Guilty". They demanded a solution from the mayor, release of their leaders, and payment of overdue wages. One police source confirmed that at that time, some 2,000 people were still working at the factory but had not been paid for 16 months – not since 1998 – while 2,000 laid-off workers and 1,000 retired workers had not received their benefits for three to six months.[23] The leaders were later released but the workers were still not paid. The only gratification the workers could feel was that their action was reported by the overseas media, especially in broadcast news by the Voice of America, which was popular in Liaoyang.

The turning point toward radicalization came in late 2001, when the local government and the court declared Liaotie bankrupt. In an open letter titled "Government Eats its Word, Workers Demand Results", workers invoked the Chinese President's speech and the Bankruptcy Law in indicting their local leaders:

President Jiang Zemin has said, "Government officials and bureau cadres at all levels must care deeply for the masses, be responsible for them, and promote their interests." But the behavior of Liaoyang's leaders before and after the bankruptcy of the Liaoyang Ferro-Alloy Factory never complied with these instructions. ... The Enterprise Law and the Bankruptcy Law both formally require open and thorough investigation of the firm's accounts before an enterprise can be declared bankrupt. But our city officials have joined hands with company management to blatantly ignore the constitution of the People's Republic, the Union Law, and other laws; they ignore the strong opposition of all employees, enlist the threat of force by local public security and armed police; they have made four attempts to arrest and harass protesting workers and to coerce some workers' representatives to vote for bankruptcy in the workers' congress. Why do they act in this way? Do they dare to explain to the masses? On November 5, 2001, three days before declaring us bankrupt, all the machinery, raw materials, doors and windows were taken away. Whose fault is this?[24]

The letter went on to list some twenty additional economic demands, such as payment of all back wages, cost-of-living allowances – 182 yuan a month – retirees' enterprise welfare allowances, medical and housing subsidies, certified property rights in housing, and severance payments for laid-off workers.[25] When I visited this factory at the height of the rebellion in March 2002, open letters and posters depicting workers' grievances and demands were posted on the walls of the main building. Neatly typed and printed on 11.5" x 15" white paper, these posters were intended as calls to action, addressing compatriots (*tongbao*) and the masses (*qunzhong*) of Liaoyang. One informant described them as "black newspapers" (*heibao*) that he saw in public places in Liaoyang prior to the protest. Smaller flyers were posted in Liaotie's residential quarters, announcing the time and date of protests. One Liaotie representative related the ease and success of their mobilizing effort while denying that they were "mobilizing" (*dongyuan*) others – using a term that has the connotation of manipulation with subversive intent:

> Workers in this factory have relatives and spouses in other factories, spreading the news and solidarity across firms ... We did not mobilize other factories, but we used "Open Letters" as a way of encouraging more Liaoyang people to join us. We only posted flyers announcing the time and date of gatherings and petitions in our own residential neighborhoods. But anyone who wants to find out can come and see these flyers.[26]

He went on to explain that initial contacts among factories were made, ironically, in the municipal government. Prolonged official inaction toward these factory-based petitions inadvertently facilitated sustained contact by workers' representatives as they regularly visited the municipal government:

> All factories had their own workers' representatives because of all these years of petitioning the government. The government required that the workers

choose five representatives to present their case in petition, to avoid protesting crowds in public places ... The representatives from other factories sought out the specific dates and times of our action and spread the information to their own factories. People who wanted to come would know when to show up. All workers in Liaoyang had their grievances, but most of them were brave enough to be angry but did not dare to speak up. They look up to the Ferro-Alloy factory as a leader, because in 2000, our petition caught the attention of the foreign media, and so people knew that our action was effective in creating pressure. They joined us with high hopes, perhaps thinking that the action would catch society's attention.[27]

People's long-standing rage flared up in early March 2002, when Gong Shengwu, the chair of the Liaoyang People's Congress, a man notorious for his close association with Liaotie's corrupt director, proclaimed on Beijing television that there were no unemployed workers in Liaoyang.[28] The actual timing and site of the protest was passed on from Liaotie to other factories through workers' petition representatives in each factory as well as by word of mouth. Work units therefore arrived prepared with banners but they were at best only loosely, if at all, coordinated. The Liaotie workers had refused to include representatives from other factories in their core leadership group because they were fearful of police infiltration.[29] They held meetings in the neighborhood Elderly Activities Center and elected four echelons of representatives, a total of 40 people. Should the first echelon of leaders be arrested, the second would take over. Workers' representatives insisted that they did no more than disseminate the date and time of the protest and that they were surprised by the large number of people who showed up.

Besides the large number of factories involved, the most distinctive aspect of Liaoyang incident was that workers made political demands. Protest banners called for the removal of some enterprise officials, whom workers identified as "thirteen worms led by Fan Yicheng", as well as Gong Shengwu, their alleged patron in the government. This demand may have been the reason why the government cracked down more harshly than it did in other cases of worker unrest. But the bill of indictment for the two imprisoned leaders, who were given seven- and four-year prison terms respectively, makes it clear that their sentences were connected with their political background. The prevailing emphasis in the seven-page document is on their participation in the outlawed China Democracy Party and their association with such hostile foreign elements as the Voice of America and with labor-rights groups. Their "incitement and organization of the masses" was listed as the final item in the litany of subversion charges.

To quell the rebellion, the Liaoyang government promised to investigate and punish corrupt officials. It expediently paid ordinary workers some of their back salary, insurance contribution, and severance pay. In November 2002, the government arrested and indicted Fan Yicheng, the former director of Liaotie and a prime target of workers' anti-corruption demands, together with six other former Liaotie officials. Fan was sentenced to 13 years of imprisonment on smuggling charges, while other former officials were given four- to six-year prison terms for illegal business practices. The city's police chief was fired, and a top Communist Party official was demoted.[30] Official publications hailed these actions as an example of the Party's serious commitment to fight graft and official corruption.[31]

In short, the developing events of the Liaoyang protest highlight the logic, potential, and limit of cellular activism. Organizers consciously excluded outside workers from joining the leadership circle. Workers' demands, whether economic or political, were local and enterprise-based. In many of their open letters, the protesters pledged support for socialism and the central leadership. Of course, this expressed support can be interpreted as a tactic of self-protection, but the fact remains that there was no public challenge to the legitimacy of the regime, at most only lack of support of the legitimacy of the local government. The potential inherent in this form of cellular protest is that government inaction could fan the flames of networking across work units. But once workers were arrested, the support from other factories quickly collapsed. And once the government responded to some of Liaotie's demands and cracked down on the leaders, even the momentum for work-unit based action was impaired.

Insurgent identities

The above discussion makes clear the prevailing mode of labor mobilization in response to the non-payment of wages and pensions. It points out the ways workers' interests and capacities are organized and constrained. But extrapolating action from structural constraints forecloses the possibility that collective agency can be the source of structural change. The following discussion moves on to another, but related, dimension of labor contention: the impact of workers' cognitive and moral frames on the decision about the kind of action to take. An "insurgent identity", according to Roger Gould, refers to social identification that determines the way, in a given instance of social protest, an individual responds to specific normative and instrumental appeals. Once someone responds to an appeal, she acknowledges membership in the group whose boundaries are defined by the term of the appeal. In this sense, insurgent identities both affirm and forge the boundaries of social groups and make social relations more or less salient.[32] My argument is that Chinese workers' repertoire of insurgent identity consists of multiple and shifting elements that they can employ. Class discourses are invoked, but they have proven to be ineffective in bringing about results, since the state has de-emphasized class rhetoric. Similarly, workers are eager to use the law to defend their rights, but their experience with the judicial process often results in popular disenchantment with the law as a channel of redress. Many then shift their tactics, when they present themselves as victims of injustice and supplicant of state protection or as "the underprivileged", who mix claims of moral economy with legalistic demands, they find that their actions generate the most desirable, albeit still limited, responses from the local government.

Repression of class rhetoric

"The working class takes leadership in everything" was a popular slogan under Mao, and now workers bitterly and self-mockingly describe their situation by turning that claim into "Everything leads the working class". In petition letters and protest banners, workers seldom invoke the term "class" (*jieji*), which, with its connotation of antagonism and struggle, was jettisoned by the regime at the beginning of the reform era. Nevertheless, workers talk about "workers' personal interests" (*gongren de chexinliyi*), workers' treatments and rewards (*gongren de daiyu*), and particularly workers as *zhurenweng* (masters), the Chinese socialist notion of the working class as owners of their enterprise. This is a firm-based class identity that defines a corporatist, particularistic, and localized social membership. Arguably, it has resulted from the prolonged lack of labor mobility, the structure of wages and benefits by seniority, and the recruitment of immediate and extended into the same firms. Today, workers assert their claim to the surplus accumulated for many years and banked in the enterprise. The workers assert that their families' contributions and their acceptance of low wages allowed the enterprise to expand. The collective wealth, the workers maintain, now squandered by corrupt cadres, should belong to workers. In one instance, at a rally, workers' representatives in a Tieling steel window-frame factory alluded to the widespread outrage caused by the demolition of the factory, stating that "every inch of soil and grass on the premises" was the result of their labor, performed with sweat and blood.[33] In another instance, when Liaoyang workers' representatives explained why they were so persistent, they made reference to a "strong working class tradition", a phrase by which they meant, "We saw the enterprise grew from one with only RMB 2000 fixed asset to one with RMB 30 million in 1989, the heyday of factory profit". Workers' ownership rights over the fruits of their labor were embodied in the welfare provisions sponsored by the state. That is also the reason why, in the Tieling textile mill, protesting workers argued with great resolve that "The shopping mall is our child, for supporting our lives when we get old".

Elsewhere, class exploitation is a cognitive tool that plays a framing role in protests, but again in a subterraneous, rather than publicly and socially articulated, manner. I have heard workers' representatives framing the loss of welfare benefits under reform as "exploitation" and dehumanization; these indictments of the present draw on the workers' "class" experiences. One woman worker offered this reflection, without my provocation, on how she came to understand the meaning of "exploitation" (*boxue*). For her, as for many others I interviewed, it was the denial of their basic human needs that constituted class exploitation:

> In the past, we had many welfare services. For female comrades, the most important were the nursery, the female sanitary room and sanitary napkins, the mess hall, the shuttle, and the barber shop. When this new director came, he abolished all these ... I now understand what "exploitation" really means. We workers are very pitiful now. In the past, no matter how bad production

became, if you needed housing, they gave you a place to live. But for years, not one single apartment building has been built.[34]

Therefore, if class subjectivity has any empowering consequence for protesting workers, it resides in the specific notion of collective ownership of any enterprise and welfare deprivation seen as exploitation. However, chronic unemployment and retirement of many from the state sector has, in their expression, "pushed them into society". Instead of retaining working-class status, they were now "orphans", without an organization to depend on. Class is neither a socially recognized and valorized nor an empowering subjectivity that workers embrace or constitute in protests, despite their private adherence to the class rhetoric.

The disenchanted citizens

If the state has abandoned the language of class and class struggle, it has vigorously adopted the rhetoric of the law and legality as the basis of government. That is why, in all the accounts of mobilization analyzed above, we find a constant invocation of the law and government regulations in workers' interactions with local officials. But does this circumstance imply that Chinese workers think of themselves as citizens with rights? How do they understand the relation between themselves, the law, and the various levels of government? Discussions with workers' representatives reveal a more cynical and ambivalent orientation toward the law. First, workers are too keenly aware of the lack of legality to envision themselves as citizens with guaranteed legal rights. When I suggested to them that they were fighting for citizens' legal rights, I encountered cynical comments, such as, "Workers' thinking is not that advanced!"; "Legal rights? What is legal, where is the law?"; "There are laws, but no one implements them"; "The law is just, but its implementation is not". Such disillusionment is often amplified in the process of petitioning the government; it easily turns into a process of discovery of deep pockets of local corruption and power collusion. This process is most apparent in the case of the textile-mill struggle. In a group discussion, workers' representatives deplored the fact that the lawyer who was assisting them was warned by officials from the local court to quit the case, which he did, leaving the workers without professional legal counsel. They were also frustrated by officials' tactics in delaying the investigation until it was too late to apply legal procedures. One of their demands to the provincial government was to have an investigative team look into the company management's allocation of apartments to local municipal officials. It was delayed for so long that when they finally heard from the provincial Party Disciplinary Inspection Committee, they were told that those transactions fell outside the time frame of the law. Elsewhere, workers realized that the police were in close communication with enterprise management and would show up ahead of them to stop their march to Shenyang.

Nevertheless, "legal right" is the only rhetorical instrument workers believe available for their engagement with officials, whom they see as their only hope. One Tieling workers' representative put it most clearly: "Because you are talking to the government, you have to talk about laws and regulations. Otherwise, they can ignore you". To the workers' dismay, even when, in their action, they invoke and abide by the law, there is no guarantee that the authorities will respond. During the Liaoyang protests, one representative brought along a copy of the Constitution and cited her rights of assembly when the police interfered.[35] Workers attempted to protect their rally from being crushed by filing an application, hoping that the police would observe the law. In the end, disillusioned, they concluded that:

> [t]here is no one you can reason with in such a big country. Anything the ordinary people do is allegedly illegal. We filed an application for a rally after March 11, giving the Public Security Bureau everything that is listed in the law: the route, the time, the organizers, and then they said that they did not approve it because it was handwritten and not typed! So, the next time around, we submitted a typed application for the April 16 march. They still rejected it. The PSB chief said to me that he would impose any number of charges on me to stop me from leaving Liaoyang. If I tried to get to Hong Kong, he would detain me by charging me with something like an outstanding fine of 250 yuan.

In short, the more experienced these workers' representatives are in dealing with the government and using the law, the more they find the rule of law elusive. They keep adopting the language of legality and citizenship as a procedural necessity, not out of a sense of empowerment or entitlement. It is not to deny that workers do aspire to having their rights protected by law and enforced by the government.[36] But even among the most legally savvy, daring, and thoughtful representatives, the civic citizenship they have in mind is one that dovetails with the regime's project of "rule by law" rather than a "rule of law" system. There is no criticism of the lack of popular participation in legislation, no demand for independent workers' organizations, no questioning of the adequacy and rationale of law and policy set by the central authority.

The underprivileged masses

The most common, empowering, and effective self-identification used by workers is "the masses", *qunzhong*, and sometimes more specifically, "weak and disadvantaged groups", *ruoshi qunti*. Enshrined in Mao's "mass line", the masses – whose spontaneity, willfulness, and voluntariness, and not just obedience, were to be cultivated and harnessed – participated in constructing and defending socialism under the leadership of the Party. Hailed as a core contribution of Chinese Communism to Marxism-Leninism, and put into practice as early as the Yanan period, the mass line instructs cadres to approach and incorporate mass opinion and effort as a component in policy making and implementation. On their part, the masses are expected to make active efforts to keep the political system functioning smoothly, to "struggle resolutely against all illegal manifestations in order to support the interests of the state and the people".[37] Yet the masses are to be led by the Party, the vanguard of the working class.

In the reform period, the collective identification of the masses still occupies a prominent place in official propaganda, most significantly in Jiang Zemin's theory of the "Three Represents", one of which is representing "the fundamental interests of the broad masses". At the same time, the notion of "*ruoshi qunti*", or the underprivileged, has also gained currency and is often invoked by workers who are seeking state protection. Found in official media and scholarly discourse since the late 1990s, the term was mentioned by Premier Zhu Rongji in a 2002 government report in which he urged officials to take seriously the government's responsibility to better protect weak and disadvantaged groups from the adverse effects of market reform. A more precise definition of the term was then given by a director of the Labor and Social Security Ministry, who referred to four sub-groups: unemployed workers, migrant workers, the elderly and the handicapped, and retirees with small pensions. Since then, a deluge of commentaries in the national and local press, supported by social scientific analyses of leading academics, shed light on the existence of subordinate groups. The general opinion reflected in the speeches of provincial and local government officials and union functionaries is that the government should protect these groups through the law and the construction of a national safety net.

Not surprisingly, both identities – the masses and the underprivileged – can be found in workers' banners and action strategy. In the Liaoyang protest, there were banners demanding "Serious Implementation of the Three Represents", "Liaotie Workers Want to Meet with Honest Official Bo Xilai" – Bo is the governor of Liaoning – and "Punish the Thirteen Corrupt Official Worms". In several of their open letters, workers deplored their demotion "from worker aristocracy to weak and disadvantaged group (*ruoshi qunti*)". In their letter to the Party's Central Disciplinary Committee, which by and large echoed other open letters, Liaotie workers emphasized the interests they shared with the Party and the state, and they noted that they were targeting those who sabotaged the common project of the state and society. The following excerpt shows how workers reasoned as supplicants and appeal to the center as the masses:

> From the time when Chairman Mao promoted "Serve the People" to General Secretary Jiang Zemin's "Three Represents", the core principle of the Party has been to serve the interest of the broad masses ... The worker-masses (*gongren qunzhong*) love our motherland, love the Communist Party, and support the construction of socialism with Chinese characteristics ... But they hate all those corrupt elements, those big and small vampires and parasites, who go against the law for their own selfish interests, to try and topple the socialist flag, destroy the basis of socialist economy. Yet, their goal will never be realized. The Party and the government and the broad masses are determined not to let them harm state policy or people, and will bring them to the trial of history.[38]

In Tieling, workers repeatedly expressed their approval and trust in Premier Zhu Rongjie's policy of guaranteed livelihood allowances to unemployed and laid-off workers. Even though workers are vehement in accusing company managers and their conspirators in the local state bureaucracy of being "enemies of the people" or "worms" in society, their faith in the moral and political integrity of the central state has largely remained unwavering. Time and again, workers declare their conviction that "*guojia*" or "*zhongyang*" – Central Committee of the Communist Party – has designed good policies to protect workers; the problem is local failure to implement them. When I asked what made them trust the center, one said, "You can see that on television, central leaders always emphasize the need to guarantee laid-off workers' livelihood. But when it comes to the local level, things are distorted, and good policies are not always implemented". Thus, the mere promulgation of protective laws and regulations buttresses the legitimacy of the regime in the eyes of the populace who limit their critique to local agents responsible for the laws' implementation.

The finding that, to date, the political subject of rustbelt workers in protest is one of "*qunzhong*" or "*ruoshi qunti*", appealing to a protector central authority, in no way warrants the projection of an unchanging political subject. For one thing, workers' continual appeal to the central government as its protector results from the stark reality, or at least the general perception, that there is no alternative to this single, unshakable national authority. One protesting worker complained tellingly, with palpable frustration, "Where else can we turn but to the government?". In many of my interviews, workers expressed in unmistakable terms that every leader has to be careful with the potential power of the masses, which may cause instability. The image of people's power surfaces with poignancy among the most articulate of the workers' representatives, who have privately contemplated a more radical break with their docile politics of supplication. The following offers a glimpse into their thought:

> It's a pity that the student protests were abruptly suppressed. Students had foreseen what we did not: the problem of corruption is still with us today … We, the masses, understand that reform will bring with it waves of instability; that much we understand. But you [cadres] cannot ask us to sit and watch while you pocket tens of thousands of dollars. It is not easy for us, the masses, to summon the courage to confront the cadres. Only when we have no alternative are we forced to challenge the government [that is, the enterprise]. We only want to get a verdict of justice from the officials … During the revolution, why could a small Communist army defeat Chiang's Kuomindang? It's because it had the support of the people. Without the people, where would there be any cadres or nation? … I joined the army at nineteen, and seven years later, I came back to join the factory. I gave my youth to the state. After thirty-some years of job tenure, at fifty-three, with young and elderly dependents at home, you make me a laid-off worker. How can I get any balance inside? Cadres can go to the office any time they like, and they can have ladies sitting around the dinner table. Yet, we cannot even get our livelihood allowance on time![39]

Overall, workers' public assertiveness in defense of their interests has so far been met with a mix of bureaucratic delay, non-response, occasional doling out of emergency funds, and threat of police suppression. Across the country, every single day, frontline cadres and persistent workers engage in a protracted war of petition and bargaining, however asymmetrical their respective power. The lack of response and the threat of punishment may mollify some people's will, and they give up asking. But the tension between workers and the government may also accumulate and threaten to sow the seeds of either collective mobilization on a larger scale or social violence.[40]

Conclusion

Chinese workers in the rustbelt protesting against the nonpayment of wages and pensions typically pursue cellular mobilization and embrace the insurgent identity of the underprivileged. To date, these protests have been somewhat effective with regard to workers' economic demands – most workers reported obtaining some of their owed pensions and wages. However, labor activism has not brought about any significant changes with regard to rampant corruption, the lack of accountability, and of rule of law.

I have tried to show that this mode of labor contention has roots in the decentralization of economic authority and welfare responsibility, economic differentiation caused by market competition, the ecological and social organization of Chinese enterprises, and the changes in state discourse. In its organization and identity, workers' political stance of being the underprivileged is embedded in a hierarchical political community and imagination. Lateral organizational capacity or associational power based on membership in a class or a citizenry are conspicuously absent, if not frustrated in the process of protest. But by offering the cases of Liaoyang and workers' representatives' own reflections, I have also emphasized the potential for unintended and deliberative transformation. Cellular activism may evolve into broad based, multi-unit protests against the same local officials, and class interests and citizens' legal rights are still part of the identity repertoire among Chinese workers. The politics of the underprivileged, championed in part by rustbelt workers, is therefore potentially expansive and explosive.

Notes

1 Interview in Liaoyang, August 5, 2003.
2 Fieldwork in Liaoyang, March 25, 2002. This open letter was dated March 5, 2002 and undersigned by "Bankrupt and Unemployed Workers of Liaoyang Ferro-Alloy Factory".
3 Interview in Liaoyang, August 5, 2003.
4 Interview in Liaoyang, March 25, 2002.
5 Murray Scot Tanner, "Protests Now Flourish in China" *International Herald Tribune*, June 2, 2004.
6 Josephine Ma, "Three Million Took Part in Surging Protests Last Year", *South China Morning Post*, June 8, 2004.

7   Pei Minxin, "Rights and Resistance", in Elizabeth Perry and Mark Selden (eds), *Chinese Society: Change, Conflict and Resistance*, London: Routledge, 2003: 29.

8   Research Department, All China Federation of Trade Unions, *Chinese Trade Union Statistics Yearbook, 2001*, Beijing: China Statistical Press, 2002: 67 and 90.

9   Research Department of the All China Federation of Trade Unions, *Chinese Trade Union Statistics Yearbook 2001*, Beijing: China Statistical Press, 2002. (In Chinese) John Giles, Albert Park and Cai Fang, "How Has Economic Restructuring Affected China's Urban Workers?", (March 2006) 185 *The China Quarterly*: 61–95.

10   There are various estimates of the size of the unemployed population. Li Qiang, a leading sociologist on unemployment surveys, put the figure at 27.258 million in 2002. "Urban Unemployment in China and Its Countermeasures", to be included in a collection of papers on Xiagang, edited by Thomas Gold *et al.* The Institute of Labor of the Ministry of Labor and Social Security gives an accumulated total of 25 million laid-off workers and 12.83 million unemployed between 1998 and 2001. See *The Blue Book of Chinese Employment 2002*: 25 [in Chinese], eds. Ru Xin, Lu Xueyi and Li Peilin, Beijing: Social Science Documentation Publishing House.

11   William Hurst and Kevin O'Brien, "China's Contentious Pensioners", (2002) 170 *The China Quarterly*: 345–60; Feng Chen, "Subsistence Crisis, Managerial Corruption and Labor Protests in China", (2000) 44 *The China Journal*: 41–63; Feng Chen, "Industrial Restructuring and Workers' Resistance in China", (2003) 29(2) *Modern China*: 237–62; Stephen Philion, "The Discourse of Workers' Democracy in China as a Terrain of Ideological Struggle", PhD Dissertation, Department of Sociology, University of Hawaii, 2004.

12   A summary of the major labor and welfare reforms and their impacts on workers' entitlements can be found in Ching Kwan Lee, *Livelihood Struggles and Market Reform in China*, Occasional Paper Series, United Nations Research Institute for Social Development, forthcoming.

13   Mark W. Frazier, "China's Pension Reform and its Discontent", (2004) 51 *The China Journal*: 97–114.

14   See the analysis of the labor rule of law by Virginia Ho, *Labor Dispute Resolution in China: Implications for Labor Rights and Legal Reform*, Berkeley, CA: Institute for East Asia Studies Monograph, forthcoming.

15   Interview in Shenyang, December 25, 2002.

16   Interview in Shenyang, July 4, 2003.

17   Interview in Shenyang, December 24, 2002.

18   Interview in Shenyang, December 24, 2002.

19   Interview in Shenyang, December 24, 2002.

20   Interview in Shenyang, December 25, 2002. See also Elisabeth Rosenthal, "Workers' Plight Brings New Militancy in China", *The New York Times*, March 10, 2003, p. A8.

21   Zheng Chenggong, *China's Social Security System: Transformations and Assessments* [in Chinese], Beijing: China People's University Press, 2002: 96.

22   Ching Kwan Lee, "The Revenge of History: Collective Memories and Labor Protests in Northeastern China", (2000) 1(2) *Ethnography*: 217–37.

23   *South China Morning Post*, "Angry Workers Besiege City Hall", May 17, 2000, and "PRC Police, Steel Workers Clash Over Unpaid Wages", *FBIS-CHI-2000-0516*. Also, "An Open Letter to Provincial Governor Po Xila", March 5, 2002.

24   Open letter dated March 8, 2002. This letter was posted near the entrance of the factory even after the mass rally on March 18, 2002.

25   In a letter to the Liaoyang People's Government, dated June 25, 2002, signed by more than 100 Liaotie workers, workers explained in detail their economic demands, including reasons why they did not accept the government's proposal to transfer severance compensation to workers' social-security accounts. They wanted both, and they wanted them to be issued separately.

26   Interview in Liaoyang, August 5, 2003.

27 Interview in Liaoyang, August 5, 2003.
28 John Pomfret, "With Carrots and Sticks, China Quiets Protestors", *The Washington Post*, March 22, 2002, P. A24.
29 Interview in Liaoyang August 5, 2003, and personal communication with Philip Pan, a *Washington Post* reporter.
30 Erik Eckholm, "Two Promoters of Worker Protests in China Get Prison Sentences", *New York Times*, May 10, 2003.
31 (2003), no. 5 *Dang Feng Yue Bao* (Party Discipline Monthly): 18–22.
32 Roger V. Gould, *Insurgent Identities: Class, Community and Protest in Paris from 1848 to the Commune*, Chicago, IL: University of Chicago Press, 1995.
33 Ching Kwan Lee, "The Revenge of History", 2000, op.cit.
34 Interview in Tieling, June 1999, textile mill.
35 It was reported in *Ming Pao*, May 2, 2002.
36 Some even thought that workers' legal rights might be realized as China joined the World Trade Organization, which would, they imagined, allow Chinese workers to migrate and work overseas! In an interesting discussion in Tieling, representatives of the textile mill talked glowing about workers' rights in advanced capitalist societies. Citing examples of acquaintances who had worked, ironically, illegally in the United States and Hong Kong, they were envious of workers in these countries who can use the law to protect their rights when they were injured or denied pay. Following the footsteps of many residents in this city, the son of one of the worker representatives was about to leave China to work as an undocumented worker in South Korea!
37 James R. Townsend, *Political Participation in Communist China*, Berkeley, CA: University of California Press, 1967: 75.
38 A letter addressed to "To the Comrades of the Central Disciplinary Committee", dated June 15, 2002, and signed by "All Former Liaotie Workers".
39 Interview in Tieling January 31, 2002.
40 The Beijing leadership has been so alert to the rise of social violence perpetrated by workers and peasants that a high-level interdepartmental steering group was said to have been set up in 2003 by the Hu-Wen leadership to handle quasi terrorist social violence, like poisoning, assassination, explosion, hijacking, and arson. Willy Woo-Lap Lam, *CNN* "Beijing Faces Winter of Discontent", posted September 30, 2003.

3 "Social positions"

Neighborhood transitions after *danwei*

Siân Victoria Liu

A neighborhood in flux

In Beijing's Liujiayuan-Tangjiayuan residential neighborhood (*xiao qu*), China's economic reforms have caused sweeping and unplanned changes. By the summer of 2000, reforms of the state-sector work-unit system had resulted in high levels of unemployment for the roughly 30,000 occupants of this working-class Chaoyang District neighborhood. Previously, these residents had constituted a relatively homogenous group of state-sector workers, employed by the various industrial work units (*danwei*) in the area. While my initial impression of the Liujiayuan-Tangjiayuan neighborhood was of a working-class enclave – a community of mostly factory workers living in the public housing (*gong fang*) assigned by their *danwei* I soon learned that vast numbers of neighbors were suffering the effects of the loss of their state-sector occupations.

In order to survive, many laid-off workers turned to local markets, opening small neighborhood shops, becoming peddlers or vendors of newspapers and other goods. Some even sublet their assigned apartments to the unregistered migrants who had traveled to Beijing in search of work, thus initiating a successful and lucrative – although illegal – housing market. State-sector workers and their families paid low fixed rents to the municipal Facilities Management Company (FMC) – typically between 100 and 300 yuan a month. However, in Beijing's tight housing market, they could charge sub-lessees a market rate of between 1000 and 3000 yuan a month to live in these same *gong fang* apartments. Most of these workers then left the neighborhood and moved in with family or friends elsewhere in the city, so that all the money they collected in rent was disposable income – a necessity for these former workers and their families, whose social-welfare provisions for such essentials as healthcare and education were typically lost along with their *danwei* jobs.

Thanks to the prevalence of sub-letting at Liujiayuan-Tangjiayuan, workers and former workers now find themselves living next door to migrants working as taxi drivers, restaurant workers, students, migrant laborers, shopkeepers, forgers, newspaper vendors, prostitutes and others who have as yet not found work. At the same time, approximately one-third of the residential population are reinventing themselves as local entrepreneurs, abandoning their previous state-sector identities.

Some former workers have invented the new occupation of *zhongjie* (apartment brokers), mediating the lucrative new sub-letting market.

Some external and structural trappings of work-unit life remain: for example, Neighborhood Committees (*juweihui*) still nominally maintain (albeit skewed and incomplete) demographic records and "elderly support centers" (*yang lao zhongxin*); *gong fang* tenants still pay their monthly rents at the on-site FMC office; and workers still gather for long leisurely evenings with their colleague-neighbors to chat and play mahjong. Yet social and economic changes in the wake of the disintegration of the work-unit system mean that the formerly homogenous and stable sociality generated by the system that assigned housing according to the work unit is giving way to the production of new kinds of socioeconomic practices and ideologies; these are instead associated with market-mediated "social positions" (*shehui diwei*), which new neighbors gauge and assume. Laid-off workers who have become local entrepreneurs are facilitating social change, by virtue of their roles of shopkeepers, peddlers, and apartment brokers, in establishing socioeconomic relationships between new neighbors. And, as Li Zhang[1] has noted, contestations over housing and local space inform sociopolitical identities, relationships, and alliances, all of which are involved in the construction of social positions.

Neighborhood residents' construction of social positions strikes at the heart of the transformation of post-*danwei* neighborhood life. In this chapter, I focus on the sizable group of workers-turned-entrepreneurs, whose changing identities from state-sector workers to self-employed entrepreneurs evidence significant social, economic, and political transformations, extending far beyond the boundaries of this neighborhood. First, I examine the concept of "social position" in the context of transitions from worker to entrepreneur, and I discuss the ways these residents' entrepreneurial strategies and sub-letting schemes are producing new post-*danwei* identities and relationships among neighbors. Second, I turn to reconfigurations of neighborhood space, in order to examine the ways in which these markets are implicated in redrawing boundaries between private and public space, and the consequences of these boundaries for the state. These aspects of social positioning indicate profound socio-spatial transformations in neighborhoods after the demise of *danwei*, and these transformations in turn are shifting the relationships between subjects and state and informing large-scale socioeconomic change.

Evading state categories to produce social positions

In Liujiayuan-Tangjiayuan, and throughout Beijing, the term *shehui diwei* has become a typical expression people use to talk about their places in urban society. During the course of fieldwork, I heard this term almost daily, especially when people talked about their economic and social aspirations – although use of its socialist predecessor, referring to sociopolitical "class" (*jieji*), was notably absent. In practical usage, "social position" refers to physical occupation of space, the type of job a working subject performs, and the social status indexed by these characteristics, linking work, space, and social "face" as inextricable socioeconomic categorical constructs. It connotes the pursuit of status associated with a growing prominence of "middle class" or bourgeois values, concerning the status conferred by work and home, as consumerism and marketization become increasingly widespread in neighborhoods after *danwei*.

For workers-turned-entrepreneurs, not only socioeconomic practices and relationships, but also access to and valuation of space are in flux. As workers lose their state-sector jobs and must find other sources of income, the divisions and relationships between home and workplace are challenged and reconfigured. This change is particularly prominent as laid-off (*xiagang*) workers open small shops or concessions at their homes or sub-let their apartments, thereby transforming the home into the source of income as they appropriate "public housing" neighborhood space for their own economic purposes. This evidences a shift in the meanings of "public" as outside space and "private" as the inside spatial realm. Drawing new boundaries between public and private space reveals new tensions between residents and the state.

This practical concept of "social position" emerges alongside the state's increasing inability to access and effectively categorize the population. The beginning of my two years of fieldwork in Liujiayuan-Tangjiayuan coincided with the advent of the nationwide 2000 census, China's fifth. As Lavely[2] notes, rural to urban migration, illegal economic strategies, and a growing group of unregistered persons led to massive evasion of the census. Discrepancies between census reports and the household register (*hukou*) revealed that China's bureaucracy could no longer produce high-quality population data. Liujiayuan-Tangjiayuan residents told me that official fears of evasion were realized. According to residents, while legal occupants who illegally sub-let their apartments were suddenly no longer present to be counted in the neighborhood, they also evaded enumerators at their new, unregistered, addresses. Afraid of having their illegal occupations discovered by the state, huge numbers of sub-lessees who lacked Beijing registrations, as well as those with unlicensed local businesses, including many workers-turned-entrepreneurs, also chose to evade census enumerators.

"I just didn't open the door when the officials came", one young migrant resident told me. "If they caught me, they would send me back home, to Anhui [Province]", another young man said. "I don't know anyone who got a temporary residence permit (*zhanzhuzheng*) … it's too expensive and hard to get, but without one, the police will arrest us". A local newspaper vendor who had not applied for a vending license claimed, "I said that I was visiting friends and don't live here". Difficulty, born of bureaucratic red tape and corruption, and expense were universally cited by neighborhood residents as reasons for noncompliance with bureaucratic rules governing residence and business.

According to neighborhood residents, only those who still worked for the state sector or who were retired could afford to respond honestly to the census. Participants in the illegal sub-letting market and the proprietors and employees of local unlicensed businesses found themselves unwilling or unable to be categorized by the state. As Lavely notes, the state census was complicated by issues of unemployment, migration, unregistered businesses, and housing-tenure issues. These same issues are prompting neighborhood residents to produce new social categories, relationships, and understandings of space – the new "social positions" of a post-*danwei* world.

The crisis of *danwei* loss

Work units had provided workers with jobs, incomes, housing, food, access to education and healthcare, and a place in China's socialist cosmology, as the vanguard of the revolution.[3] They had institutionalized workers as a group and even documented workers' autobiographies in personal dossiers.[4] They had provided China's urban workforce with social positions: not merely with the occupation of work, but also with housing and a high social status dependent on the particular work-unit connections and roles.[5] The loss of a work-unit job, therefore, equated to a loss of social position – work, housing, and status – constituting a crisis for these workers and their families, reaching from the practical economic dilemmas they faced, to the more conceptual issues tied up in their subjective identities and social status.[6]

I first encountered this crisis on one of my first days of fieldwork. While sitting in the Jiang neighborhood shop, I was startled and concerned when a neighbor, Wang, clad in a heavy army-issue overcoat, entered. "I am going to kill myself", she sobbed. "There is no way out for me now that we have lost everything – our *danwei*, our money ...". Chatter among the few customers inside the shop's cramped quarters quickly quieted as we listened, appalled – and embarrassed – by Wang's ceaseless, muted weeping and her repeated mutter that she was going to kill herself. Ding, one of the shop's proprietors, comforted Wang. Later, she told me that Wang had been cheated out of her family's savings. After losing their *danwei* jobs, she and her husband had decided to raise capital and become entrepreneurs, opening a small neighborhood shop. Unfortunately, she had been swindled into sinking their life savings into stolen goods, which had been confiscated by the police, leaving them with nothing.

As I later learned, this was not the only case in which loss of state-sector employment led to suicide threats. Neighbors frequently whispered gossip about various residents who had committed suicide after losing their state-sector jobs. Apparently, lacking capital and connections, several men living in the neighborhood had decided to end their lives – one at the eve of Spring Festival in 1999, by jumping out of the window of his fourth-floor apartment. In another tragic case, after losing his state-sector job, Shao began drinking heavily. His wife, unable to cope with the situation, ran away, abandoning their baby daughter. One morning, Shao didn't get up: he had drunk himself to death. His mother, a retired worker relying on a pension, came with a friend to take care of their daughter in his apartment.

As the Spring Festival approached, other neighborhood residents seemed to find a morbid entertainment in sharing stories about impoverished former workers who had also killed themselves. In one popular often-told tale, a worker who had lost his *danwei* job was racked with guilt because he did not have enough money to buy meat for his family's New Year meal. His young son, distressed by his father's sadness, stole meat at the local market, and was caught red-handed by the butcher. The butcher called the police, who arrested the child. His father, guilt-stricken and horrified by his inability to provide for his family, and his family's descent into crime, killed himself on New Year's Eve. In these stories, the loss of a *danwei* job is blamed not merely for a person's suicide, but also for the destruction of morality and family. This destruction of the family, divided as a result of *xiagang* and morally degraded through, in these cases, alcoholism and theft, violently illustrates the loss of identity and the breakdown of society that laid-off workers perceive and experience, as a way of life under the *danwei* system disintegrates. These depressing stories apparently pervade China's northeastern rustbelt, where state sector unemployment is rife.[7]

Degraded social positions of workers

Danwei jobs gave workers safe, established social positions. In the context of rapid urban marketization, however, state-sector workers as well as workers-turned-entrepreneurs considered workers' social positions to be inferior.[8] Residents tended explicitly to blame the government for their low social status, standards of living, money troubles, and the "youthification" (*nianqinghua*) programs that marginalized this mostly middle-aged group. At the Jiang shop, operated by two laid-off workers, I was surprised by the frequency and virulence of residents' comments about the government. "The government doesn't care about us workers", was a common refrain at the shop. "We should blame the government!" neighbors often ranted. One woman who had been laid off told me that, although workers used to enjoy high status, these days, "workers have no social position".

Residents frequently bemoaned the difficulty of maintaining a standard of living now that they were no longer part of *danwei* life, and they talked openly of their money worries now that they had been laid off. A local laid-off worker told me that after losing the income from her insolvent *danwei* several months ago, she had not been able to find any other work. When I asked about any retraining programs the *danwei* might have instituted, she laughed, saying, "work units don't have such programs" – a claim that other local workers corroborated. She also told me that it was impossible to apply for any emergency money (*jiujijin*) from the *danwei*, as apart from the fact that she didn't think that the *danwei* had any funds left to give to workers in difficulties, she was unable to provide all of the documentation the work unit's trade union – an official bureaucratic institution – required in order to process such a request. For example, the trade union required her family's proof of income before it could issue emergency funds, but she was unable to document the irregular – and frequently under-the-table – monies that her husband and son had received from their work units.

Others I talked with about the problems of workers also worried about the loss of status associated with the scarcity of steady income. Li, a local worker, told me, "Workers have no self-esteem, because they are not an important economic or social class to the government". Compounding this problem, in 2000, the government reinvigorated an ongoing propaganda campaign to promote the "youthification" of enterprises and industries. Frequent articles in Beijing newspapers spoke of the need for young people to rejuvenate the nation's economy with their fresh ideas, superior training, and energy. When I asked the laid-off workers of the Liujiayuan-Tangjiayuan neighborhood about the "youthification" campaign, most concurred that they could not compete with youngsters in winning private-sector jobs and that their only option, therefore, was to become small-scale self-employed entrepreneurs or to sublet their *danwei*-assigned apartments to migrants. According to Ding, those who had worked for the state sector could not compete for private-sector jobs because they were "too old to learn new skills, and did not even understand the concept of economic competition" – a concept that she said "the national government needs in its cultivation of the private sector".

Li told me, "At my work unit, workers did not compete with each other or even work particularly hard". He explained that workers in the state sector are all paid exactly the same, regardless of how hardworking they are, according to age gradients designating income, and that although the management would hold meetings to encourage a sense of "competition" in workers, these meetings were "useless". Li's comments indicated his respect for economic competition in the private sector – as well as his dissatisfaction with a government that had enabled workers to become "lazy" and obsolete.

Reshaping the social positions of workers-turned-entrepreneurs

While workers and former workers bemoaned the institutionalized "laziness" they perceived to have crippled the state sector, numerous retired or laid-off workers of all ages had already "jumped into the sea" (*xia hai*) of the market economy, vigorously refashioning themselves as local entrepreneurs. These self-employed entrepreneurs depended on local customers – their neighbors – for the survival of their new businesses. According to Ding, Jiang, Wang, Su, and other local business people, they also depended on themselves and their personal abilities (*nengli*). Many operated small shops and public telephone stands out of the windows of their ground-floor apartments, licensed by new bureaucratic offices that had sprung up throughout the district, a process requiring Beijing *hukou*. Others sold newspapers or other goods, roaming through the neighborhood as licensed or unlicensed peddlers. Some residents had even opened a hotel – completely illegally.

According to neighborhood entrepreneurs, those who successfully made the transition from the state sector to self-employment had some kind of capital, typically borrowed from their families. For example, Su, a long-term resident who had been forced into early retirement, told me that several years ago, after he retired from his factory *danwei*, her husband Wang used money loaned by family members to open his neighborhood shop selling beverages and ice cream. While Wang opened his shop, Su decided to sell newspapers for a living.

Su said that working for oneself conveys a higher social position. Even though her sales earned her only about 10 yuan each day, she regarded work as a necessity for life. She was contemptuous of other retired workers who chose to pursue leisure rather than some other "worthwhile, money-making" occupations. Su said: "I keep working because I want to live. If [you] don't have anything to do all day, [you] will die. I don't make much money selling newspapers, maybe only a few yuan a day, but I like to keep working ... Many of my comrades at the work unit are already dead because they retired and didn't have anything to do but die. It is important to keep working if you want to live".

Su's statement illustrates that state-sector workers who have become entrepreneurs value work for its own sake, and they respect such attributes as resourcefulness and managerial capabilities. Moreover, it shows that those who are still actively making money perceive their status to be tied up with their money-making capabilities – that their status is associated with their active engagement with often unpredictable and competitive markets rather than with the daily planned tasks of *danwei* occupations. Conversely, to these entrepreneurs, occupations in which money is not actively pursued equate to stagnation in the social system of the socialist era. Among this class of long-time state-sector workers, it indicates the transition of values: from the material and social benefits work could provide through the welfare state's *danwei* system to the value of personal enterprise. It also suggests the valuation of money as a substance able to command and actualize consumer desire, quantifying the social status associated with jobs.

Ding, co-owner of the Jiang shop and operator of an illegal apartment brokerage (*zhongjie*) business, agreed with Su's statement of the value of work. She added, "Not everyone can become an entrepreneur – it takes talent". In 1997, Jiang and Ding had opened a small concession stand within Liujiayuan, using capital raised by asking relatives for loans. According to Jiang, opening a shop was a major step for his family as they made the transition from laid-off state-sector workers to entrepreneurs. "We are becoming middle-class", Jiang said. "Our social position is getting better". His statements reflect his equation of class status with social position, rather than with sociopolitical category.

Along with other neighbors who were workers-turned-entrepreneurs, Jiang imagined his own entrepreneurial efforts within the larger context of global capitalism rather than simply a local effort to avoid economic disaster following the loss of his job. Interestingly, Jiang and his neighbors frequently spoke of China's accession to the World Trade Organization with hope and optimism. Although many newspaper reports and official testimonies concluded that WTO transition could cause problems for China's workers, Jiang stated, "When China joins the WTO, workers in China will be equal to the workers everywhere else in the world – with workers in America. The Chinese government will have to respect workers. After the WTO, the government won't be able to put obstacles in the way of people trying to be entrepreneurs – the WTO means equality for Chinese workers."

Other neighbors agreed, claiming that "the Chinese Communist Party is too restrictive" and that "after China joins the WTO, China's regulations will have to be in accordance with the rules of the world, so the government won't be able to do whatever it wants". These statements reveal the perception of social solidarity between state-sector workers and small-scale entrepreneurs, commonly marginalized in urban China. Jiang's comment indicates that, to him, workers and now entrepreneurs are exploited by a despotic state – and that these categories of people should have the right to rely on supposedly "fair" global market forces for their success.

In practical form, this social solidarity was evidenced by local economic alliances. For example, Jiang and Ding, along with other local shopkeepers, would often be approached by neighbors seeking credit or loans. In one case, Jiang and Ding extended credit to a young rural migrant woman living in a basement room in their building of which Ding had orchestrated the sublet. This young woman explained to them, politely calling them "Uncle" and "Aunt", that she did not have enough money for toilet paper and instant noodles. Jiang and Ding agreed to give her these items as long as she would pay them back when she was able. In another example, during December 2000, a young man working as a barber, a neighbor and frequent customer at the shop, approached them to borrow money. He explained to Ding, also calling her "Auntie", that he would not be paid until the end of the month and did not have enough money to survive until then; Ding offered him an interest-free (as was typical) loan of 200 yuan on condition that he paid it back at the end of the month. I witnessed numerous such transactions, and in only one case was there a default on a loan. Although small-scale and non-lucrative, these financial relationships created networks of social solidarity and economic dependence that served to further buttress the social positions of benevolent local entrepreneurs.

In other cases, Jiang and Ding would defer payment or accept payment in kind, particularly from peddlers, many of whom are migrants. These people have established social relationships with Jiang and Ding, deferentially calling them "older brother" and "older sister", regardless of actual seniority. Indeed, if Jiang and Ding do not have a social relationship with a person, they refuse to extend credit. Ding explains, "My shop is a business and I cannot give gifts!". These interactions reveal an emerging "market-based" morality as relationships with new neighbors are forged through idioms of kinship and the medium of monetary exchange. They also show how workers-turned-entrepreneurs are able to enhance their social positions by becoming patrons of those less well off, creating local communitarian networks of financial dependence.

The new social position of the *zhongjie*

The apartment brokerage business offers another example of the efficacy of local socioeconomic relations. Between 2000 and 2002, three *zhongjie* businesses opened in Liujiayuan-Tangjiayuan. To gain access to apartments for brokerage, the proprietors of these businesses depended on their social relationships with legal residents, especially with those who had lost their *danwei* jobs and might be considering sub-letting their apartments in exchange for disposable income. Typically, *zhongjie* are not paid by landlords; their incomes come from finders' fees assessed from potential and actual sub-lessees. By cultivating local friendships, *zhongjie* were able to establish trusting relationships, thereby persuading potential landlords that they would be able to find good tenants, while concealing their practice from officials and police – the essential basis for their businesses.

Many legal residents who had decided to sub-let their apartments told me that *zhongjie* were indispensable. For example, Zhang, a middle-aged apartment lessee in Tangjiayuan who decided to sub-let his assigned apartment after losing his state-sector job, told me that finding good tenants is a problem: the best way to find desirable tenants for an apartment is to rent to people already known to the landlord. "But I can't do it this way as I don't have any social connections to people who might want to sub-let my apartment", he explained. "I don't personally know anyone who wants to sub-let, and my friends and neighbors here aren't interested [in sub-letting it] and don't have these social connections either". According to Zhang, this situation meant that he needed some other way to connect with potential sub-letters, a need that he said was fulfilled by *zhongjie*.

In order to run this business successfully, *zhongjie* must convince potential clients of their reliability and expertise in responsibly forging reliable ties with would-be tenants. On the other hand, *zhongjie* also had to be able to screen and assess potential sub-lessees, to find safe tenants for these apartments. For *zhongjie*, this activity involves new kinds of skills and knowledge in terms of contractual paraphernalia and information brokering. Besides these kinds of knowledge, *zhongjie* must set themselves up as a certain kind of local "insider" in order persuasively to produce identities as moral experts with the knowledge and bureaucratic skills rendering them worth dealing with – and worth paying.

Ding was aware of the issue of her social position in the operation of her business, and she explained it in several ways. She told me that she, like most migrants, was a relative newcomer to the neighborhood. She started her apartment-finding business in 1998, after moving here from Harbin, in China's northeastern Heilongjiang province, after losing her industrial *danwei* job. At the same time, she emphasized that she "belonged" in the neighborhood, as a legal *hukou*-possessing occupant. Her subject positions as a former worker, an entrepreneurial migrant, and a woman in a working world that tended to privilege men enabled her situationally to manipulate her identity, comprising a status-laden social position as a successful neighborhood entrepreneur. (Ding also claimed that, as "everyone knew", women were better than men at "creating good relationships".) Each of these subject positions was marginal in relation to state categories but empowering in the neighborhood. Ding explained that her dual identities as unemployed worker and as migrant meant that her loyalty to her local clients on both sides of the *zhongjie* business, rather than to officialdom, was clear and public. "People trust my ability because I know how to make good social relationships", she stated. She also justified her expertise at walking the fine line between legality and illegality by claiming, "Police always tell you what you can't do. But when you have to find a place to live, it's not a police matter. That is a matter for the common folk".

Ding told me that advertising, authoring, and brokering contractual agreements and the assessment of newcomers' "character" were all specialized kinds of knowledge necessary for the operation of her *zhongjie* business. When she started her business, Ding began to solicit sub-lessees by inviting inquiries through advertising at her shop; she would then circulate this information to her neighbors. "My business is successful because I have a very good personal reputation as a smart business person and a good judge of character", Ding stated. "When I am meeting potential sub-lessees, I look to see what their social positions are – accent, age, clothing, what they do for a living ... these are all clues. I can tell who will be reliable and pay rent without causing any trouble". Now the most successful local *zhongjie*, she facilitates sub-lets of apartments throughout the neighborhood and earns thousands of yuan each month.

Social positions of absentee workers-turned-landlords

Those who decided illegally to sub-let their apartments for disposable incomes are typically former workers, elderly or middle-aged. This occupation involves leaving the neighborhood, residing elsewhere, and, in the local social scheme, becoming an absentee landlord. These people have a relatively high degree of social status, as they collect money at market rates. Although non-residents, many frequently come to the neighborhood, to visit friends, collect rent, keep an eye on their tenants, and even to muster customers for their new enterprises among their former colleagues and neighbors. An elderly lady who had returned to her sub-let Tangjiayuan apartment to collect rent and visit friends told me, "Each month I make over one thousand yuan, simply by leaving my apartment alone. I moved in with another old lady so ... I don't have any expenses. I can finally relax".

Other workers who still lived in the neighborhood spoke of these new landlords as having found an easy source of income. However, the vast majority of younger and middle-aged residents who sub-let their apartments use the rents they collect every month in order to fund other businesses or enterprises. For example, Liu, a former worker in his thirties who sub-let his apartment to me, used the money he made from this transaction to pay for driving classes and to buy a stake in a car. He now works as a driver, renting his services out to businesses – an occupation with a high prestige quotient, associated with the value of mobility, the cost of cars, and the bureaucratic red tape involved in the process of applying for a drivers' license. Similarly, Zhao, assigned the apartment downstairs from mine, had become a taxi driver. These people were in the process of remaking themselves yet again, utilizing all of their resources in the enhancement of their social positions.

Earlier, I discussed the case of Wang, the former worker who threatened suicide after being swindled out of her savings. This case can serve as a meaningful footnote to the situation of former workers, in the context of transitions in post-*danwei* neighborhoods. Wang's pitiful condition and terrible threats of suicide made Ding lend her an interest-free 3,000 yuan. "I wanted to help my sister (*meimei*)", said Ding. "She lacked the capacity to help herself. How could I let a neighbor – a fellow worker – kill herself?". Ding persuaded Wang to sub-let her apartment, and promptly orchestrated its sub-let to a migrant family from Anhui province.

This example shows that in the context of the emerging markets at neighborhoods after *danwei*, even the really marginalized – the seemingly totally down and out – can exploit their resources to attain a new, viable social position. It also shows that those who are successful in reinventing themselves as workers-turned-entrepreneurs, such as Ding, can effectively utilize both their financial capital and their morally conditioned social connections to enhance their social prestige, power, and positions in the post-*danwei* world. After leaving the *danwei*, the relationships of former workers to their neighbors reveal the aspirations of workers-turned-entrepreneurs, to improve their social positions through local, moral, socioeconomic relationships that foster social solidarity among all those struggling with the demise of the *danwei* system. The flip side of this, an increasing antagonism between neighbors and state, can be illustrated by an examination of changing meanings, after *danwei,* of public and private space in this neighborhood.

Demarcating public and private neighborhood space

Prior to 2000, residents' relationships to their homes were overwhelmingly mediated by their local work units. In fact, the very expression "public housing" described the relationship of work units to residential neighborhoods. Those who had been assigned to live in these homes did not own them. These residences were "public" by definition, in the sense that they were assigned and overseen by work units or, in some cases, municipal or county authorities. They were also public conceptually, by virtue of their connection to *danwei* community hierarchies that superseded the claims of individual householders. As the term "public housing" implies, work-unit-assigned housing did not correspond to a bourgeois sense of a private home; rather, *danwei* housing was equivalent to a kind of communal, community lifestyle in which local sociality mirrored work-unit hierarchies and relationships.[9] However, in neighborhoods such as Liujiayuan-Tangjiayuan, where sub-letting is endemic and local markets are entrenched, "public housing" no longer neatly describes any kind of public, *danwei* community life.

Two kinds of inscribed discourses, which I will discuss below, can illustrate the strengthening boundary between public and private space. These are state-authored propaganda and interior decoration. In Liujiayuan-Tangjiayuan, communal spaces are papered with state propaganda, notices, and bulletins. These artifacts inscribe public space, insinuating officialdom into post-*danwei* landscapes and implying the continuing domination of these neighborhoods by state-sanctioned regimes of public order. Yet, while these visual marks of public space proliferate, residents' understandings of them have changed. In practice, residents have appropriated public housing as private, personal space; and their understandings of and responses to propaganda only emphasize and illustrate this practical and conceptual rift. While propaganda marks space as public, new popular discourses and practices of interior design show how public housing is being transformed into private, bourgeois homes. This transformation is uncomfortable for the state in that it indicates that the post-*danwei* neighborhood is no longer transparent or accessible to state scrutiny.

Public space and neighborhood propaganda

Propaganda posters, placed outside and within residential spaces, show the interest of the state in promoting conformity to national, municipal, and district-wide directives. Such propaganda used to be disseminated through work units. However, the recent withdrawal of *danwei* from neighborhood life means that the state now directly interfaces with neighborhood residents. Neighborhood propaganda is overwhelmingly concerned with public-health issues, family planning, such "moral crimes" as drug use and pornography, and public safety.

The most obvious and prolific propaganda notices, placed high up on each of Liujiayuan-Tangjiayuan's 49 residential buildings by the city government, urged residents to adhere to China's one-child policy. These red or blue plaques contain messages in pithy couplets, such as "Family planning: the benefits last from one spring to one thousand autumns". The most popular couplet was that on the building in which I lived. It stated, "Family planning depends on you, depends on me, and depends on him/her" (*Jihua shengyu kao ni, kao wo, kao ta*). Although a traditionally patterned couplet, it was the source of many bawdy jokes among residents, who would make salacious comments concerning the three subjects mentioned in the couplet, along the lines of wondering what three people were doing together in the bedroom "planning" their "family."

The bare, dirty cement stairwells of each unit were crowded with advertisements for products and services, notices from such neighborhood services as trash collection, and state-authored propaganda posters. Many private moving companies – a significant recent innovation spawned by the widespread practice of sub-letting – had pasted advertisements throughout the stairwells, as did local department stores, cellular phone shops, and dealers in products for interior decorating, such as hardwood flooring, bathtubs, and bathroom fixtures. The trash collector had painted a reminder to residents up the stairs of many of the buildings as well, urging "comrades" to put refuse in the rubbish chutes. The terminology used in this notice, referring to people as "comrades", was viewed by residents as an amusing nostalgic reference to a time past, when people would communally care for the appearance and upkeep of the building – not a compelling incentive for people to cooperate with these directives. In fact, residents would wait for the FMC to clean up trash and messes in the unit areas rather than cleaning them themselves. As my upstairs neighbor said, "Why would I waste my time, waste my money cleaning up the unit stairs? I pay a sanitation fee, and it is the FMC's business, not mine".

Numerous black-and-white official notices concerning family planning and sexually transmitted diseases were taped on the walls of each unit's first floor as well as throughout the communal areas of the neighborhood. Brightly colored posters urging adherence to the national census of November 2000, depicting happy, prosperous families, were left up long after the census was over. As my earlier discussion indicates, residents did not find such propaganda compelling.

Other propaganda posters concerned public safety, security and crime; one contained a list of telephone numbers of the various police departments in the district – including separate phone numbers for emergency services and the departments responsible for controlling pornography, drugs, and gambling. The caption to this poster read, "Handle well society's public security, enable the residents to live and work in contentment".

Propaganda asserts these issues to be matters of public order. By placing this propaganda within residential spaces, Chinese officialdom reveals its concerns about what residents are doing within the closed and invisible spaces of their apartments. The focus on reproduction, sexual behavior, and reproductive health issues – family planning, sexually transmitted diseases, reporting pornography – indicates the state's preoccupation with the new opacity of the boundary of the private residence, now that *danwei* no longer mediate the relationship between subjects and state. Although the work-unit system had in place a number of controls on family and personal life, including birth planning and control, and medical problems and care, the state lacks developed channels by which to monitor and infiltrate these aspects of intimate life. While work units required personnel to tender petitions for everything from marriage to moving residence to having a baby,[10] the state can no longer control the actions of subjects who illegally occupy or misuse – in unlicensed businesses – public housing.

Propaganda about reproductive health and morality issues placed within residential buildings is as close as the state can come to infiltrating the enclaves of people's homes and to demanding that subjects attend to these issues of national uniformity and importance. This, as already noted, equates to asserting issues of sexual behavior and deviance as matters of public order. By so doing, the state is implicitly denying occupants' rights to perceive and practice sexuality as a "private" matter. As Farquhar[11] shows, regarding sexuality as a kind of "modern Chinese experience" presupposes a certain kind of subject, one who regards sentiment – and bodily practices of sentiment – as personal and private. This suggests a more problematic, personally experienced contention between emerging categories of private and public, subjects and state.

The case of prostitution can illustrate this conflict. As neighbors told me, some migrant newcomers to the neighborhood did indeed work as prostitutes – "working from home" in their apartments. I had personal experience of this fact, as the sound-insulation of these apartments was poor; lascivious sounds emanating from the apartment directly above me, sub-let by nattily dressed young women from the northeast, indicated their profession. Instead of describing prostitution as a moral crisis, or as a public-health issue, neighbors were critical of prostitution for the unwanted attention it drew from police. "I don't want prostitutes to live here because it means that police will come here more often", a neighbor explained. "Police are always causing problems for us, so I don't want any other reasons for them to come here ... the police could make problems for me here, too". The prostitutes upstairs declined to comment.

The fairly regular appearance of new propaganda images and slogans meant that residents frequently noticed and commented on the fresh material, in spite of the inevitable routinizing effect of constant exposure. Propaganda marks the stairwells and buildings – the communal areas of these buildings – as public, state-controlled arenas. However, as consumerism and marketization burgeon in neighborhoods, residents increasingly regard their "public housing" apartments as private, personal spaces that are and should be beyond state control.

Private space and interior design

In recent years, in Beijing, interior decorating has become extremely popular. As Lei Guang notes in this book, migrant laborers are increasingly involved in the innovation of local home-decoration markets. When asked, most residents told me that they liked to make their homes look attractive: they had more money now to spend on decorating, and more materials for home decoration were now available in Beijing. "It's fashionable to decorate our homes", a middle-aged entrepreneur told me, echoed by his neighbors. Examined in a social context, this "fashion" of the moment equates to a fundamental transformation from work unit life to a market-driven desire for self-expression, by way of the decorative transformation of one's home.

Many of the apartments that laid-off workers had chosen to sublet in Liuijiayuan-Tangjiayuan, as a way of making some much needed money, were undecorated – even unfinished, to my sensibilities – as were the apartments still occupied by state-sector workers. Most apartments had bare, uncovered cement floors, with extruding electrical wiring, and bare dangling bulbs as the only lighting fixtures. Whitewashed walls appeared undecorated, and the bathrooms and kitchens lacked showerheads and hot water. Yet, as I will explain, although I mistook these conditions for poverty, research indicated that they did not merely index the socioeconomic status of residents, but also revealed a different, premarket or socialist, *danwei* way of conceiving of interior design and decoration.

At work-unit apartments that I stayed at in Chuiyangliu, in Beijing's Chaoyang District, Dongying, Shandong province, and Harbin, Heilongjiang province, I noticed a remarkable uniformity in residents' treatment and understanding of the boundaries between communal and home space. According to my sensibilities, all of these apartments were distressingly cramped, unattractive, uncomfortable, and unfinished. All had bare cement floors, poor paint jobs, and visible wiring on the ceilings. However, families residing in these work-unit buildings did not carry out the business of living within the boundaries of their apartments but tended to utilize the communal spaces of the buildings for activities and storage. For example, during the winter months, they typically stack cabbages and other vegetables in the stairwells, leave shoes and outerwear outside the doors of their apartments, and use the hallways for communal and neighborly food preparation.

People I talked with were quite shocked by the suggestion that they lived in the squalor of urban poverty. Workers for these work units had not experienced reduction or stagnation of salaries, or faced massive layoffs, as had residents of Liujiayuan-Tangjiayuan. According to these workers and their families, their purchasing power, and quality of life, had not diminished in recent years. Rather, worker residents told me that they had indeed decorated their apartments; they had purchased balloons, commissioned expensive "glamorshot" posters of their children for their walls, and decorated the windows with brightly colored shadowcuts and plastic stick-on butterflies. They had also stuck luridly colored Western-style pictures of puppies, children, and European mountain scenes, cut out of calendars, onto their walls.

In contrast, the apartments of workers who had left their work units and become neighborhood entrepreneurs tended to look very different. Most of these former worker residents invested in improving the interiors of their apartments, adding hot water and such bathing facilities as showers and bathtubs and finishing the walls, ceilings, and floors with tiling, laminate, or wood. They also decorated in less expensive ways, hanging locally purchased curtains at their windows and placing family snapshots around their apartments. Some embellished their apartments with trendy features, such as the "television window" – a tiled mosaic-like large decorative panel applied directly to the wall, meant to serve as a frame for the big-screen TV these entrepreneurs aspired to or already owned. They also ceased to use the public spaces of their buildings for food storage and preparation, restricting living activities within the boundary of their apartments. These changes suggest that different sensibilities were at work here: that "work-unit space" and "market-economy space" were associated with different aesthetic standards and different ideas of function and use.

Work units typically provided facilities for employees – and even their families – to bathe at the workplace, thereby eliminating the need for bathing facilities in the home. Work-unit cafeterias, with subsidized prices for workers, reduced the amount of time workers spent in their kitchens preparing food: this same amenity also meant that hot water, refrigerators, and other kitchen appliances and enhancements were not as significant to the needs and qualities of workers' home lives as they became to those who had left their work units. However, the reasons for residents' choice to design or redecorate their homes extended beyond the fact that some – especially those who had become entrepreneurs – simply had more money, as well as functional ideas of the "need" for certain facilities in the home for those who no longer had access to the communal facilities of the work unit. As many residents told me, these home improvements indicated "middle-class social positions".

Privatizing space and becoming "bourgeois"

According to Tang,[12] interior design relates to the production of a subjectivity that recognizes its own interior wants and needs and that, through consumption, manages to externalize these internal desires. As a consumer culture takes over urban China and conspicuous consumption becomes a cultural norm, the interior of the home – even in the case of public housing – has come popularly to signify a private domain. The business of interior design "cashes in" on residents' recognition of and desire to realize their personal preferences.[13] Liujiayuan-Tangjiayuan residents focused on the idea that they were realizing their personal preferences in an external form by redecorating and designing their living spaces. For example, Jiang, a worker-turned-entrepreneur, told me that decorating his home was the first time in his life he had been able to choose, furnish, and design his living space "just as I want it".

The articulation of a private space, bounded against public communal state-controlled realms, is implicit in interior-design projects. Residents told me that they regarded their homes as their own space; one former worker stated, "My home is for my family. It is not the business of police or the government or officials … it is for family business". A young migrant woman working for a local restaurant told me, "All migrants living here without registrations have to keep our homes away from police and … the government …We have to make sure that our private matters [*sishi*] are kept private". By not using the communal spaces of the building for food preparation or other daily chores, occupants are bounding their personal or familial "private spaces" against public areas. Moreover, by designing the interior of an apartment according to their own desires, subjects are personalizing their space, imprinting their own ideas upon it. The refusal of residents to clean up or transform the communal stairwells of the residential buildings indicates the scope of the contrast between the ways personal living spaces and communal spaces are practically viewed, valued, and dealt with. As residents pay nominal fees for the service of stairwell maintenance, their relationship to communal space is now market- rather than work-unit-based. Hetherington[14] claims that this basis is characteristic of bourgeois subjects, who laboriously divide their private, interior homes from communal space.

Interior decoration in Liujiayuan-Tangjiayuan indicates the emergence of a bourgeois sensibility, in which a sense of identity is not granted or authored by work-unit affiliation but is rather produced through the intersections of interior personal space and market consumerism. For example, arranging framed photographs on the walls and tabletops of the home has become popular among neighborhood entrepreneurs. As Halle[15] points out, the placement of family photographs in the home, particularly those that are displayed in movable frames on surfaces, indicates the pervasiveness of certain values: that the family members depicted in photos and responsible for their display are the makers of social value; that the family interior is asserted as an important social sphere; and that mobility and flexibility, through the ability to move photographs around and replace them with others, have become principles indicating the conceptual importance of and possibility for both social and personal advancement.[16] In the Chinese context, the differentiation between the relative lack of these photos in *danwei* homes and their pervasiveness in entrepreneurs' homes evidences a correlation between aesthetic sensibilities and social position. In the neighborhood, family photos, with their interlinked connotations of the values of agency, family interiority, and mobility, indicate the identification of these subjects with "social position" corresponding to the values of a bourgeois middle class.

These bourgeois boundaries are sometimes explicitly disputed by the state. For example, residents frequently gossiped about police undisputedly entering apartments, particularly in the search for pornographic materials, even when the apartments in question were legally rented by married couples. "The husband–wife relationship is a private matter", a taxi driver who lived in Tangjiayuan told me. "Police should not interfere with this. This is a human right!". By invoking the expression "human right", this neighbor was recognizing the political implications of demarcations between public and private and was articulating them in global-political terms. The assertion of space as interior and private in this social context is, therefore, also a contestation of tenacious official regimes of space and public order, that reveal a deeper fault line over the emergence of a "private" subjectivity and that sometimes results in overt conflict between occupants and the state.

"Social positions": space, sociality, and subjectivity

The definition of residential space as private indicates the emergence of a post-socialist subjectivity among former workers and new entrepreneurs. A sharply drawn boundary between neighborhood space – between communal space, which had been treated as a communitarian extension of the household, and private space, demarcated by locked doors for personal privacy and distinct standards of decoration and cleanliness – indicates also that, in neighborhoods, the meanings of social positions are changing after *danwei*.

As discussed, "social position" has become a popular idiom for discussing status, work, and spatial location as the work-unit system retreats before advancing marketization. After the disintegration of the *danwei* system, workers – and their migrant neighbors – are remaking themselves as the complex of positional relationships that defined them has been disarticulated through reforms. Now that work, space, and status are no longer mutually constituted according to state-sanctioned, sociopolitical, *danwei* categories, neighborhood occupants are defining their social positions by engaging with markets through personal identity articulated within the distinctly private realm of the home, with reference instead to consumer desire and interior choice. As the loss of *danwei* jobs means that work, socially and spatially, increasingly becomes a non-state "inside" or private matter, sociality in the neighborhood has been discombobulated by the coming of stranger-sub-letters. As a bourgeois concept of the home gains ground in the neighborhood, however, occupants are increasingly able to retreat within the personal spaces of their bounded homes, which they have divided from other social spaces. Practically speaking, residents' "social positions", in terms of the relationships between private space and social status, have become connected to emerging class identities as marketization continues. Despite alienation from the state – and even from each other, a common understanding of social position, identities, and morality is coming about through mutual participation in local markets.

Along with the break between public and private domains comes the production of subjects who are "turning away" from the state, in that they understand their "social positions" in relation to work, spatial location, and "middle class" social status rather than in terms of state-authored hierarchies – as under the work-unit system. As the example of the census shows, the state is obviously still implicated in producing meaningful social categories and regimes of value, including those in which wealth and education are prized. However, neighborhood residents' understanding of their social position depends much more on their explicit assessment of their own location in emerging class structures. They cement and display their social locations through a variety of techniques of self-representation that have little if anything to do with the state. Instead, their understanding of class and identity is now closely entwined with their engagement with the market. This change also indicates that subject formation has radically altered, from the public, *danwei* production of "work-unit subjects" to the privatized, marketized formation of a more independent citizenry, aware of the rights and responsibilities of economic self-determination. Although small-scale workers-turned-entrepreneurs may seem a diffuse and marginal group, the social positions they pursue and assume evidence paradigmatic shifts in the ways people understand themselves and relate to one another and the state after leaving the *danwei*.

Notes

1 Li Zhang, *Strangers in the City: Reconfigurations of Space, Power, and Social Networks Within China's Floating Population*, Stanford, CA: Stanford University Press, 2001: 117.
2 Lavely, William, "First Impressions from the 2000 Census in China", (2001) 27(4) *Population and Development Review*: 755–69.
3 Liu, Jianjun, *Danwei Zhongguo*, Tianjin, China: Tianjin Renmin Chubanshe, 2000: 4–5.
4 Lü, Xiaobo and Elizabeth J. Perry, *Danwei: The Changing Chinese Workplace in Historical and Comparative Perspective*, Armonk, NY and London: M.E. Sharpe, 1997.
5 Dutton, Michael, *Streetlife China*, Cambridge: Cambridge University Press, 1998: 58–60.
6 Ibid.
7 Lee, Ching Kwan, "The 'Revenge of History': Collective Memories and Labor Protests in Northeastern China", (2000) 1(2) *Ethnography*: 217–37.
8 Lee, Hong Yung, "Xiagang, the Chinese Style of Laying Off Workers", (2000) 40(6) *Asian Survey*: 914–37.
9 Dutton, Michael, *Streetlife China*.
10 Lü, Xiaobo, and Elizabeth J. Perry, *Danwei*: 3–4.
11 Farquhar, Judith, *Appetites: Food and Sex in Post-Socialist China*, Durham, NC: Duke University Press, 2002: 31.
12 Tang, Xiaobing, *Chinese Modern: The Heroic and the Quotidian*, Durham, NC: Duke University Press, 2000: 308.
13 Ibid.
14 Hetherington, Kevin, "In Place of Geometry: The Materiality of Place", in Kevin Hetherington and Rolland Munro (eds), *Ideas of Difference: Social Spaces and the Labor of Division*, Oxford: Blackwell Publishers, 1997.
15 Halle, David, *Inside Culture: Art and Class in the American Home*, Chicago, IL: University of Chicago Press, 1993.
16 Ibid.: 115–18.

4 Rural "guerrilla" workers and home renovation in urban China

Lei Guang

When I first interviewed Cheng Gong in Beijing in 1995, he had just turned 19 but was already a veteran migrant in the home-renovation industry among a growing number of new arrivals from the vicinity of his native village in Laomei county, Anhui Province.[1] He left his village for Beijing in 1993, a year before graduating from one of the best local high schools. His dropping out was traumatic for his parents; they had hoped that he would be the first in the family to go to college and then find employment with the government or get a job in a city.

But he was not to follow the traditional path to the urban workplace. Instead, his trajectory in search of work started with an abbreviated apprenticeship with a village carpenter, who first took him to Beijing in 1993. During the next several years, his itinerant employment involved all manner of irregular construction work, except for a short stint in insurance sales in Beijing after a falling out with the master carpenter, and a brief police detention. Since 1996, he has worked steadily in Beijing in the field of renovation, a niche industry dominated by migrants from rural areas. After registering a small renovation company in 1998, nowadays he shows up at the construction site more often as a contractor/supervisor than as a manual worker. He still does physical labor from time to time, especially when there is a shortage of hands. Most migrants from his county are still stuck in the guerrilla-worker mode. They form roaming groups of renovation workers moving from one apartment complex to another. "We in the home-renovation business are 'guerrilla workers', with no fixed place and schedule of work." Cheng Gong once said, "Everything is good when we have work to do. When we don't have any work, we couldn't do anything but wait."[2]

These self-styled guerrilla workers have emerged as a significant labor group in urban China today. The work gangs are made up of laid-off urban workers, poor retirees, and migrants from the rural areas.[3] Some scholars have used the term "casual labor" (*sangong*) to refer to the same population, whose number is significant but hard to gauge.[4] In this chapter I focus on these mobile migrant workers who are unwilling – because of the cost of obtaining permits – or unable – because they do not have urban employers – to obtain legal papers for their work in the cities. Compared to the legal migrants who have work and residence permits, these guerilla workers represent an under-studied group. I first interviewed some of these workers at their temporary residence in Beijing in 1995. I located them through their families and acquaintances back in several Laomei villages where I did my dissertation fieldwork. The fact that I grew up in the same area and speak the local dialect facilitated my initial access to them; but tracking them over the years in Beijing was more difficult because they were so mobile. Contacting their families back in the village or their acquaintances in Beijing helped me to keep in touch with many of them over time.

Remarkably for a mobile group of migrant workers, some have stayed in the same line of work in Beijing for over 10 years. My main informant, Cheng Gong, has been working in construction in Beijing since 1993. Most of the migrant workers active in such areas have no legal status in the city, and the official regulations on employment – on minimum wage, work conditions, unemployment insurance, etc. – do not apply to them. They have urban clients but no urban employers. Their employment is irregular, and their income is intermittent. They perform an array of work and services at mobile sites – in people's homes: renovation work, domestic service, etc., or on public streets: bicycle repairers, small vendors, fruit sellers, etc. – rather than in such traditional workplaces as factories. As a result, they experience minimal state control at their workplaces.

How do we locate these workers and their experience in the increasingly complex labor formation in China today? How does the Chinese state relate to these itinerant workers? How does "migration" – the passage from a village community to an urban competitive setting – affect the social relations among the fellow migrant workers in the course of and outside of work? In this chapter I address these questions by focusing on the non-traditional workers and on the political and economic conditions that give rise to their itinerant identity and shape their experiences in the cities. I will draw on my interviews with one group of itinerant construction workers in Beijing who came from nearby villages in Laomei county, Anhui province. The interviews are supplemented by participant observation at their work sites and by the analyses done by other Chinese researchers on casual labor and construction workers.

Locating guerrilla workers in China's labor formation

The emergence of guerrilla workers is part of the trend of increasing diversity in China's urban labor force and industrial relations during reform. For several decades before reform, the state-owned and collective units more or less monopolized urban employment opportunities, so much so that the Chinese word for proper work – *gongzuo* – is still largely associated with formal employment in the public sector today.[5] Reform, however, has fundamentally restructured work and labor relations by allowing private enterprises to exist and by permitting the migration of labor between places. By the late 1980s and 1990s, there co-existed in China at least three realms of "work", each associated with a distinct political economy or production system: the realm of public-sector employment linked to a rapidly changing state/collective economy (*gongzuo*), formal private-sector work at the private/foreign enterprises (*gugong* or *dagong*), and finally, self-employment and largely informal jobs in the urban areas (*dagong*). For our purposes, informal jobs are those not regulated by the state authorities or carried out by legally incorporated organizations, such as state enterprises or formal private corporations in regard to recruitment, work conditions, and remuneration. Informal work is structurally heterogeneous and ranges from casual wage labor to unlicensed self-employment activities.[6] Here is how a Chinese researcher describes these workers: "... a considerable number of migrants do not have an employer but rely on their own efforts for jobs. They make up approximately 25 percent of the rural migrants in the cities. Not employed by any urban unit, they are primarily into the production and sales of small commodity items or they are scattered in a variety of commercial or service activities ... They constitute a most complex social group among the migrants."[7]

Although the term *dagong* is commonly used for private-sector employment of all kinds, not just informal work, workers in the formal private companies often want or have legal and contractual protection, whereas informal workers fall outside state regulations. Thus, not only do these three realms of work vary systematically in their institutional embodiment – *danwei*, corporations, or contingent labor groups – but workers in these institutional settings relate to the state authorities and market forces in different ways. For example, the labor bureaux and other government agencies are much more likely to intervene in a state-owned enterprise than in a private or foreign-owned company to help resolve a financial crisis or mediate labor disputes. For the private sector, market-mediated employment is now the norm, although this is not to say that the state's retreat has led to any greater freedom for the workers.[8] Compared to both these sectors, the urban informal sector is largely populated by migrant workers – who are now joined by large numbers of laid-off urban workers. They are not only exploited economically as workers but are also treated as disfranchised rural outsiders in the cities. They thus encounter the urban state authorities as the dispenser of monetary fines, corporal punishment, and other coercive regulations aimed at "civilizing" them or keeping them out of the cities.[9] As a consequence, these informal-sector migrants often engage in semi-clandestine work to make a living.

It is worth noting that rural workers have long been part of the urban labor force in all three areas of work mentioned above.[10] But in recent years, the large-scale infusion and settling of the migrant workers in cities made them an even more important part of China's working class. The construction industry in particular has attracted large numbers of rural workers. Government statistics show that, nationally, over 70 percent of the construction workers held rural household registration, and more than one-fifth of these rural workers were migrants in 2002.[11]

Take Beijing's construction sector as an example, the state-owned companies in the city started sub-contracting rural construction teams since the early 1980s. In 1997, Beijing's No 1 Construction Company alone employed 214,460 rural workers – twice the number of its regular urban employees – from several dozen rural base areas.[12] More rural workers work for independent and privately owned companies that are loosely affiliated (*guakao*) with the state construction companies. They do not show up in the companies' official roster of workers, although they typically work for these companies. Finally, there is the category of "unaffiliated" rural construction workers, whose number is the hardest to ascertain. One estimate put the number of such unaffiliated construction workers (*lingsang gong*) at 100,000 or more for Beijing in the mid-1990s.[13]

Guerrilla workers belong to this last category of irregular and unaffiliated workers. They are a sub-set of the rural migrants who participate largely in the informal economy in the cities. For the most part self-employed or employed by fellow migrants, they maintain fixed living quarters but have mobile work sites. Most have migrated to cities via informal networks of kin, village, or friends rather than bureaucratic channels or employment agencies. Once in the cities, they tend not to be affiliated with any formal organization but continue to rely on kinship or village ties in their everyday associations. For many of these migrants, non-affiliation with an urban work organization often translates into illegal existence in the cities. Given their weak economic situation, their inability or unwillingness to obtain legal papers from the city authorities makes them more vulnerable.

As I have mentioned earlier, all my interviewees work in the field of home renovation in Beijing. Like most other cities in China, Beijing has experienced a boom in home renovation since the late 1980s as more and more city residents acquired ownership of their apartments under housing reform. With a fraction of the money they spend on purchasing a home, the Beijing residents could now upgrade their once austere apartment – with bare walls and cement floors – into well-decorated living spaces. In recent years, interior renovation and design in the city is further fueled by the housing-construction boom and by the swift development in the real-estate market that has led to a more frequent turnover in homeownership. This is a national trend not confined to Beijing or other big cities. For the country as a whole, the home renovation industry was already a 300 billion yuan industry in 2000, having grown a hundredfold in 10 years from the 1990 level. In 2001, over 300,000 home-renovation businesses nationwide employed a total of 5.5 million workers, most of them rural migrants.[14]

Since home renovation involves small-scale, customized, low-profit, and labor-intensive operations, it is largely neglected by established construction or commercial-renovation companies. In the beginning, its menial status also made urban residents reluctant to engage in such work. As a result, home renovators consist predominantly of rural migrants. In Beijing, many home renovators come from such rural provinces as Anhui, Jiangxi, Jiangsu, Henan, and Hunan. When I visited Cheng Gong in 1995, he told me that about 200 people from his county alone lived on the same street and relied on home renovation for a living. In 2002, according to Cheng Gong, 60 percent to 70 percent of the migrant renovators hailed from the Anhui province, half of them from his native county.[15]

Three characteristics distinguish the home renovators from the formal-sector workers commonly studied by researchers. First, these guerrilla workers differ from traditional workers in that they do not inhabit a fixed workplace – such as a factory – that constitutes the spatial and institutional underpinning of stable labor relations and production politics. Since they work in individual homes, their work sites are scattered and frequently changing. A contractor puts together a team of workers for a particular project, only to disband it at the end of the project and reconstitute another team for the next. The word "guerrilla" aptly describes this work situation insofar as it designates a shifting band of people moving from place to place in search of work. There is little, if any, sustained interaction among these workers *as* workers. The lack of socialization at work sites, however, forms a sharp contrast to their constant association outside the work in kinship or home-village groups.

Second, given their mobility and the informal nature of their employment, the guerrilla workers encounter government authorities primarily outside the context of work – that is, at the site where they live ordinarily: their rented residence, public streets, and recreational sites. For example, because of their non-citizen status, they are often treated as "people of three nos" (*sanwu renyuan*) rather than part of a city's regular workforce. Their most frequent encounters with the state authorities are generally with the police and other city administrators rather than with factory managers or labor inspectors. Until very recently, state power was primarily imposed to stop them from coming to the city or to expel them from its limits, both of which actions have engendered resistance from the rural migrants.

Finally, since they are not, and never were, part of the formal state or private-sector economy, their ethical principles regarding work – what is fair and not fair, etc. – or what I call the moral economy of work, are unlikely to derive from their prior experiences in the state socialist institutions or from socialization with fellow workers on the shop floors of privately owned factories. They display a profound indifference to socialism, and therefore China's pre-reform past does not form a benchmark of comparison in their critique of their contemporary situation.[16] Their sense of fairness is often shaped by the contrast with their rural experience. For example, they are more likely to protest against the closing of the city gate which leads to their exclusion from the urban labor market, than that of the factory gates which causes the layoff of urban workers. Their "rural origins" and migrant identity exert great influence on their work and life experiences in the cities. Let me elaborate on each of these three characteristics below.

Bifurcated networks: the organization of work and migrants' everyday association

Migration researchers everywhere acknowledge the importance of kinship networks and native-place ties in the migration process. Such networks are an important source of information about jobs at destination sites, a reliable supplier of financial and logistical assistance for the needy, and an organization of mutual emotional support for the sojourners. Migration via informal networks is thus not particularly rooted in the Chinese culture or its agrarian tradition. The wide use of kinship or localistic ties in the case of Chinese rural migrants has less to do with the villagers' familial values than with a labor policy that has closed off channels of mobility for the rural population.

According to some Chinese researchers, about 43 percent of the first-time Chinese rural migrants utilized kinship ties (*qingyuan*), and another 23 percent took advantage of connections based on territory (*diyuan*) in the mid-1990s.[17] Not only are such networks important in transporting rural labor to urban areas, but they also continue to exert a significant influence on the urban labor market *after* the migrants arrive in the cities. Ching Kwan Lee describes the continuing role of localistic networks in supplying new job information, loans, and emergency aid among migrant women already working in Shenzhen's factories.[18] Zhao Shukai finds that kin and fellow villagers tend to concentrate in the same or similar professions, live in the same area – e.g. Zhejiang village – and frequently socialize among themselves.[19]

But does localism infiltrate the workplace, thus affecting the very organization of work itself? By the organization of work I refer to such matters as the recruitment of workers, assignment of work, authority relations in the workplace, and the like. The answer to this question seems to be positive, at least in the context of a fixed workplace or stable institutional setting. For example, many state construction companies subcontract work to teams of rural workers from specific regions (*chenjianzhi shuru*), thus building localism into their very operation. In the private sector, as Ching Kwan Lee has pointed out, localistic networks permeate the workplace and form the basis of a despotic factory regime.[20] Localism seems to characterize the informal sector as well. Itinerant operators in the same market or on the same street can often be traced to the same rural origin.[21]

Given the preponderance of evidence on the importance of localism among the rural migrants, I expected to find close-knit kin or fellow villagers banding together *for* renovation work and *at* construction sites. I also expected that there was going to be relative stability to the composition of construction teams, because they supposedly draw their members from a steady pool of relatives and co-villagers. Such, however, did not turn out to be entirely the case. What I found was that, while rural migrants frequently socialize with their kinsmen and fellow villagers, they often part company at work and sometimes deliberately avoid village acquaintances on renovation projects. My findings about the weakness of localistic ties at work are not consistent with Lee's argument about the importance of localism at the workplace. Lee describes factory scenes, whereas I am talking about the itinerant workers without a fixed workplace. Not all migrants are guerilla workers. To the extent that some of the migrants work at itinerant jobs, I am saying, such localism does not extend to their workplace relations.

I once asked several migrants from Laomei county to rank in order the people with whom they associated most (*lianxi zui duo*) in Beijing. What I got in each case was two separate maps of people's names in concentric circles, with the innermost circle being the respondent's closest associates. One map included almost exclusively kin and fellow villagers with whom the person shared an intimate social life; the other included some close kin or co-villagers, but also quite a few workmates from counties or provinces other than the one the migrant is from.

Migrants from the same region live in proximity in the city and socialize with each other for many reasons. Since many were brought to the cities by their fellow kinsmen or villagers, it is not surprising that they should come to live in the same place after arrival in urban areas. They share the same dialect, similar tastes in food, and common aspirations, all of which facilitate rooming or cooking arrangements among the migrants, most of whom are men and singles. Besides, government regulations of the rental market tend to push migrants to certain areas, usually on the outskirts of the city proper, where rental regulations are least stringent. They are further drawn to each other because of the hostilities they face from other groups, including the locals: if others know that we are many, one interviewee once told me, they will not intimidate us easily. Finally, the migrants' living quarters are a hub of information about jobs, and they may also be a recruiting ground for newly arrived workers.

But if the migrant's everyday association is a relatively steady one, their association at work tends to be quite erratic, flexible, and not strictly reflective of kinship or village ties. For example, Cheng Gong experienced an almost complete reshuffling of workmates between 1997 and 2004, but his social circle included many of the same people at these two points in time. Part of the reason for the fluidity of workmates has to do with the nature of renovation work. Each home renovation site – typically an apartment – is a rather cramped space. It can accommodate a small band of people – usually about five or six, including at least one carpenter, a tiler, a painter, and sometimes an electrician and/or plumber. Each job usually lasts for about four to five weeks. Small teams with short-duration jobs make for a very flexible labor arrangement. Unless another job comes along, the most recently assembled team will have to disband and allow its members to seek new combinative arrangement with others. Thus, work teams are assembled and disassembled on a regular basis; no amount of kin or native-place loyalty will hold a work team together for long if no jobs are available.[22]

The migrant workers take other considerations into account. While visiting some of the construction sites, I was sometimes struck by the *mix* of workers from different localities.[23] I once asked Cheng Gong why he included several out-of-county workers on a job he contracted, while many migrants from his own county or even his own villages were out of work at the time. His answer boiled down to the fact that the out-of-county workers caused less trouble for him at work and were easier to manage:

Laomei people are not good at detailed work. They don't put in a lot of effort and tend to be on the lazy side; besides, they are not trustworthy. They seek every opportunity to talk to the homeowner and ingratiate themselves into his or her favor. ... They may "steal" (*qiang pao*) your prospective jobs. Finally, Laomei workers are hard to manage. Since we all come from the same area, you can't criticize them too much; and relations easily go bad if things are not handled well. So, even though many Laomei workers don't have a job at this point, I am not willing to use them because every one of them is a potential competitor. But these workers from Dongzhi [a different county in Anhui province] are different. They are honest and do quality work. They usually just work for others, and do not want to contract work themselves. So I'm more comfortable with them.[24]

It is rather common for these itinerant workers to avoid people from the same village or even distant relatives when they can get away with this behavior. One reason, as the above interview reveals, is that migrants wanted to "partner" or work with the "best" persons suited for the job, not necessarily with those they are most intimate with in their everyday associations. One migrant told me that his brother, who worked as a renovator in the same city, was very unhappy about not getting work from him because he favored someone else; but he said he couldn't help it, because he and his brother simply did not work well together. Avoiding unnecessary entanglements that may result from their rural connection is another motivation for the migrants. One migrant working in a Guangzhou factory told me that he was reluctant to introduce people from his hometown to work in his factory. "It is a lot of trouble. My hometown people think that everyone can make big money in Guangzhou; yet they are not prepared for the sacrifice. They would rely on you again if they cannot adapt to life here. If something unfortunate happens to them, their families would come to my family in the village, which would cause more trouble for me".[25]

As it has been alluded to in the above interview, labor control is another issue that weighs on the mind of some migrants, especially ones who have accumulated some capital and are in a position to employ other migrants. Researchers have found that many established companies diversify workforce in terms of their hometown origins in order to neutralize the power of workers from any one given region and thus exert maximum control over the entire labor force.[26] Similar considerations may apply to these construction sites, but rural migrants dividing work among their fellow villagers have an added concern about the rural ramification of their practices in the cities. One migrant-entrepreneur explained why he had *not* employed more fellow villagers in a furniture business he once operated in Zhengzhou: " ... after they get back in the village, my co-villagers would complain about not getting paid adequately. So I'd rather hire outsiders ... You can be very assertive with them. I can fire them if they are not doing a good job. They will work extra hours if I want them to ... And I don't need to care too much about my 'face'."[27]

This sentiment resonates with many self-employed migrant workers I have interviewed who work in home renovations. They understand the negative side of mixing work and life insofar as social ties may interfere with work arrangements and discipline, and they fear that harsh work relations may strain neighborly ties or even brotherly love.[28] Many migrants therefore resort to keeping the two spheres of life and work as distinct from each other as possible. But neglecting fellow villagers in assigning work may carry its own social liabilities for some migrants back home. They will have to balance the accusations of neglect by fellow villagers against possible indictments of unscrupulousness. These migrants thus experience ambivalence and contradictions in maintaining bifurcated networks.

Ultimately, the rationale for such dualistic networks – one for work and the other for communal living – may have arisen from their ambiguous identity in the cities. As economic agents in the cities, they can be very effective and would want to keep rural relations out of the realm of work as much as they can until just before that process can hurt their reputation back in the village. The fact that they are self-employed may impart some further entrepreneurial ambition that makes them keep their distance from kin and fellow villagers. As social beings, however, the itinerant workers find themselves rejected by urban life. Their circumstances in the cities thus make them turn towards their fellow villagers for communal living and social support.

This is not to say that migrants do not in any way rely on their kin or village networks in the organization of work. This is far from being the case. Such networks are important sources of information for the migrants about potential jobs; a core group of close relatives and co-villagers usually stay and work together as a team. Migrants also rely on each other to survive financial difficulties when they are out of a job for long or not paid right away by their clients or bosses. Kin or village-based social networks are particularly crucial for newly arriving migrants. But because, over time, the competitive logic of work makes it harder and harder to maintain the intimacy of relations, tensions will start to arise among these migrants. Some migrant entrepreneurs strive to maintain a balance: they search for workers who are unrelated to them but who are from broadly the same region.[29]

Cheng Gong's story in Beijing illustrates a migrant's negotiation between the dual networks. When I first met him in Beijing in 1995, he was still a novice migrant, living with close friends from his village in a place called Xiju in Beijing. He was very much dependent on them for work as well. "Quite a lot of us from Laomei lived in Xiju then … We from the same area like to live at close quarters so we can take care of each other. Proximity made it easy for us to exchange information and to find people to work on renovation projects."[30] Two years later, in 1997, he moved out of Xiju, which then was packed with Laomei migrants, to a different part of the city, Qinghe, which had fewer of them. He said that he had grown tired of the "bad atmosphere" (*huai fengqi*) in Xiju, where migrants from the same home towns were preying on each other, sometimes strong-arming one to extend loans (*qiangxing jieqian*). It bears noticing that, in 1996 to 1997, Cheng Gong had a couple of "good" years contracting home-renovation jobs from Beijing residents. In late 1997 and early 1998, he registered his first small renovation business, using help from several city homeowners he had befriended over several previous jobs. In 2002, he was still working closely with several kin and friends from Laomei, but he was pleased that he "no longer tried to find work partners or subcontractors based on kinship or hometown considerations".[31]

Cheng Gong's story and the above discussion show that networking is an important aspect of the migrants' life and work in the cities. But one should be careful not to reify the migrant networks to the point of attributing to them primordial relations between them. As we have seen above, the rural migrants construct, straddle, invoke, and shift between two kinds of networks, depending on whether they are novice or seasoned migrants, on that stage of their career, and on their entrepreneurial or plebeian orientation.

The application of state power and resistance of itinerant workers as migrants

The productive units in China's formal economy have traditionally been organized hierarchically, with large state-owned enterprises at the top and private or individual firms at the bottom. The level of state intervention varies according to the position of the enterprises in this hierarchical system. However, the informal sector – of which our itinerant construction workers are a part – largely escapes the gaze of the state as a domain of work, except when a campaign is mounted to "formalize" work in a given area or when a disaster draws the sudden attention of state officials. Even when these occasions arise, the state's attention on the informal workplace may be merely fleeting. Official statisticians rarely bother to collect data on unregistered firms; labor inspectors do not usually know their way to the work sites of informal laborers.

As I have already described, rural home renovators in Beijing rely on face-to-face contact with urban home-owners to solicit jobs. Once someone gets a job, he will assemble a team of workers to carry out the project before moving on to the next one. By virtue of their unaffiliated status, this work is largely unregulated by the state authorities in spite of a plethora of formal rules and regulations governing the construction industry. In this sense, itinerant renovators are "free" to devise their own ways of soliciting work and performing it among themselves.

Migrants are quick to exploit the absence of state power by engaging in illegal or semi-legal operations. To lend some legitimacy to their operation, for example, they often use fake company names when negotiating with homeowners; sometimes they make promises about guaranteeing their work that they have no intention of keeping. Once when I was visiting a group of itinerant workers at their residence in Beijing, my attention was caught by a stack of advertising flyers that they were about to distribute to new apartment owners. These flyers, which bore the names of non-existent companies, described these companies and included references to the companies' many years of construction experience, local registration status, a range of completed projects, promotional discounts for veterans' families and people with disabilities, and so on. Except for the contact numbers listed on these flyers, none of the information was true, according to my interviewees.[32] They assured me that all these claims were simply advertising gimmicks. Once they did get the job, they said, they had to work hard until they finished it. After all, they rely heavily on word of mouth for referrals.

Migrant renovators further exploit the vacuum of state power by engaging in questionable sub-contracting and organizational practices during the renovation process. The official regulations grade construction companies according to size and technical capacity for undertaking construction projects. Low-grade companies are allowed to sub-contract work *from* general contractors, but they are not permitted to sub-contract work *to* others or to share the work with them.

Since most home-renovation companies run by migrants do not measure up to even the lowest grade for construction companies, they are legally forbidden to sub-contract work to other individuals or business entities. But as it turns out, sub-contracting or shared contracting is the norm rather than the exception among migrant home renovators. One migrant renovator describes sub-contracting in the home-renovation field as rampant. Another explains the common arrangement: "Some of us specialize in distributing flyers and finding jobs. They then contract the jobs to us. ... We call these people 'agents' (*jingji ren*). They must have a telephone. We all want to become 'agents' because we could then make about 10,000 yuan on each job. Hard manual labor, on the other hand, at most brings in 1000 to 2000 yuan per month."[33]

To the extent that the state authorities want to exert control over the migrant renovators, they have sought to formalize the home renovation industry by registering renovation workers with established companies. After the mid-1990s, the municipal authorities in many cities began to promote the establishment of large and organized renovation supermarkets (*jiazhuang shichang*). They then encouraged migrant renovators to register with these supermarkets. For example, in 2004, one gigantic supermarket in Beijing, EasyHome (*juran zhi jia*), had 29 renovation companies registered in its northern branch alone.[34] While the government has tried to steer more and more homeowners to the mega-sized supermarkets for renovation jobs beginning in the late 1990s, many migrant renovators continue to rely on the method of street-corner or door-to-door solicitation. Even today, guerrilla renovators account for a significant portion of the home-renovation business. A recent report estimated that in 2004, 70 percent of the renovation business in Shanghai was still performed by the so-called street guerrillas.[35] One reason is, no doubt, the cost: the guerrilla renovators still offer the cheapest service to the urban consumers. Moreover, even in cases where registered companies contract the job, the actual work is likely to be left to a team of unregistered guerrilla workers.

In unusual moments of disaster or crisis, the state may briefly intrude into the migrants' work space, but even under such circumstances the officials' attention span is likely to be short and their focus narrow. One migrant told me the story of how the police and labor inspectors descended on the scene of an accident when one migrant worker fell to his death from a high-rise building during work. The police and the labor inspector asked perfunctory questions and took notes. But as soon as they ruled out homicide and came to the conclusion that they were dealing with a work-related accident, they essentially left it to the migrant contractor to negotiate an outcome with the deceased worker's family. They neither had the intention of broadening the scope of their inquiry into the work condition or safety regulations of the renovation company, nor were they particularly interested in the outcome of the settlement between the contractor and the deceased worker's family.

So far, I have described the relative absence of state power over the realm of work in the case of itinerant home renovators. In contrast to their laissez-faire approach to regulating migrants' work, however, urban state officials liberally exercise disciplinary power over migrants outside work and at the site of their everyday living. Throughout the 1980s and 1990s, self-employed itinerant workers faced harassment in the hands of police and other quasi-security personnel – such as the city-image patrol, or *jiucha dui* – mostly at their place of residence or on urban streets.[36] The following accounts were typical of many migrants' experience:

On the insecurity at the place of residence:
We go back to our rooms at about 7 p.m. and hit the bed right away. We lock our doors from the outside. That is because the "community security team" (*zhi'an dui*) usually inspect temporary residence permits between 7 and 9 p.m. If we don't go to bed and they see light or hear our voices in our rooms, they will demand to see our residence permits. If we are caught, we will be fined 50 yuan.[37]

On the hazards of soliciting work:
There're simply too many restrictions on us passing out flyers [for renovation work]. Urban dwellers think too many flyers harm the city image, so the old ladies guarding apartment gates often chase after us. ... I would hold my breath and pray (*tixin diaodang*) while entering the gate because I do not want the gate security to see me. I act as if I were a thief. It is true that they would treat me like a thief too if they were to catch me.[38]

On arbitrary detention on the street:
A fellow worker and I just got off the bus and were taking a break on the curbside when two plainclothes policemen approached us and asked for our temporary residence permits. We said we didn't have them on us. ... Because I didn't have any money on me to pay the fine that day, I was sent to a detention camp in Changping [near Beijing] for two days ... On the third day, a group of us were taken to the railway station and put on a train bound for Suzhou, Anhui province.[39]

Today the urban state seems to have passed its most repressive phase and relaxed many of the restrictions it had imposed on rural migrants in the 1980s and 1990s. At the peak of state control in the 1990s, however, rural migrants were among the most heavily regulated subjects in Chinese cities. This was especially true of the self-employed guerrilla workers who were not affiliated with any formal municipal organization. The city police routinely raided residential areas to round up migrants without residence permits. The civil-affairs officials regularly repatriated out-of-work migrants to the rural areas. Quasi-security personnel – the city-image patrols and gate keepers for apartment complexes – frequently punished migrants for transgressive actions. Numerous studies have documented the fact that city-image patrols were among the most hostile to the migrant workers in the informal sector.[40] Even as migrants largely elude the intrusive state in their workplace, they are under the constant gaze of state officials on urban streets as roving subjects.

Since state power is directed less to regulating their work than to controlling their existence in the cities, migrant workers experience the state simultaneously as an irrelevant institution at the site of production and as an omnipresent coercive apparatus intent on preventing their "reproduction" in the cities. The state thus stands between a migrant's ambition to make a living in the cities and his access to stable work there; but it does not so much restrict his exploitation or self-exploitation at the workplace. One Chinese survey conducted in 1995 was quite telling in the information it revealed about the migrants' knowledge of formal government organizations in the destination localities. It showed that while 9 percent of the migrants knew about the location of labor unions or women's associations and 28 percent were aware of the existence of government labor service or job agencies in the destination localities, 32 percent had some interaction with the local police and 60 percent knew about the location of the nearest police station.[41]

The state's heavy-handed regulation of the rural workers' presence in the cities has generated much resistance from them. Migrants engage in a variety of tactics to blunt the state's power or frustrate the implementation of its policies. One common way is to ignore various permit requirements and bypass the government authorities altogether in obtaining work in the cities. "We home renovators work for ourselves, so we don't have a work unit to sponsor us." One migrant said, "It is very troublesome to get these permits. So I would rather not get them and risk being fined when caught."[42] Virtually none of the home renovators I interviewed in Beijing beginning in the mid-1990s bothered to apply for a temporary residence or work permit, partly because of the cost and partly because of their unaffiliated status making them ineligible for such a permit to begin with. Their unaffiliated status thus prevents them from obtaining the minimum legal status, which differentiates them from ordinary migrant factory workers.

Besides widespread non-compliance, these migrants resort to other strategies, such as leveraging the influence of their local connections. "Most important is your relationship with the landlord," one migrant told me, "if the landlord has influence in the local area, your life [as a migrant] is going to be much easier."[43] Another migrant explained why the best person to rent your room from is someone who has a family member in the local police. "Some landlords have family members or know someone in the local police station, so we get advance notice about evening inspections by the police. We will then just stay away during that time. Because these landlords' houses are the safest, the rents on them are generally expensive as well."[44]

Occasionally, the migrants would find power in numbers. Their communal living arrangement in the city often makes collective resistance possible if not always effective. One migrant worker explained the advantage of living close to each other on the same street: "Others will not be able to pick on us when there are so many of us at one place". Consider the following description of an encounter between the Beijing police searching for an alleged criminal and a multitude of Anhui migrants thronging forward in a suburban residence: "As soon as the police appeared on one end of the [urban] village and were ready to charge in, all the narrow lanes were suddenly filled with agitated migrants. Like disturbed bees from bee hives, all of them came out of their rooms and filled the street as if a collective calamity had occurred. They did not show any signs of open resistance, yet the human wall made it difficult for the police to inch forward."[45]

Migrant renovation workers and their moral economy of work

Michael Piore once made the following observation about the migrants: the separation of the migrants' work and their home social community creates a unique environment, in which they become rather uninhibited about pursuing purely economic ends at their place of destination. It is with this observation in mind that Piore called the temporary migrant a "true economic man, probably the closest thing in real life to the *Homo economicus* of economic theory".[46] On the surface, the itinerant workers we have analyzed would fit his description of uprooted, asocial migrants. The fact that our renovators often do not enjoy the state's legal and contractual protection may make their work even more of a self-help situation, one in which each person focuses on his own gain.

But given what I have described about the bifurcated networks for the migrants, the claim that they are the true economic men is a partial one at best. It fails to consider the importance of social networks to the renovators' urban lives; and it ignores their constant effort at mobilizing social connections and constructing networks in the city of destination. For the migrants, to be economically rational requires immersion in social relations. Even their instrumental approach to work associations should be seen from the perspective of migrants straddling different social worlds in the village and in the cities.

Moreover, treating migrant workers as purely economic beings misses the harshness of the urban existential condition that shapes their interest and drives their competitiveness in the city. When they have work to do, migrant renovators may be marginally better off economically than the urban laid-off workers. But their livelihood depends on their getting jobs regularly. Unemployed migrants cannot count on the city government to bail them out the same way it does urban workers. Moreover, regardless of the economic situation, rural migrants inhabit a social position that is inferior to that of registered urban dwellers. They are still treated as sociocultural outsiders and non-citizens in the cities, and they are excluded from the formal redistributive economy.[47]

Given their social and economic positions in China's urban political economy, migrant workers have evolved distinctive views of work that differ from those of the traditional state-sector workers. Such views mix elements of market transactional logic with a low sense of entitlement and a familial or relational ethic that governs the accumulation and use of monetary gain. Migrants seek urban employment primarily for economic reasons, but they experience work in the cities *socially* through a set of norms and expectations about their entitlement to work, the remunerative standard and work conditions. I call such patterned attitudes or social norms their moral economy of work.[48] It is shaped by the migrants' self-understanding about work and "proper" employment relations.

We can sum up our migrant renovators' moral economy of work as consisting of three main elements: work competitively, expect little, and take care of the family. In my interviews with the Laomei renovators in Beijing, I find little trace of nostalgia about the urban-centered employment system under state socialism that had once excluded them. While many urban workers readily invoke or incorporate the old socialist discourse or ideals in their critique of the reform,[49] none of the migrant renovators I interviewed refers to what they do in the city as *gongzuo* or proper employment that is reminiscent of the socialist labor system. Even a veteran renovator like Cheng Gong, who has worked in the city for many years and has registered his own renovation businesses, prefers the term *dagong* in describing his employment status. For him and other migrant workers, *dagong* denotes the image of temporary work where formal employment relations, complete with tenure, minimum wage standards, and regulated work condition, do not obtain.

In the world of *dagong*, there is no unemployment to speak of because rural migrants are not included in the relevant government regulations. Even though more migrants experience long periods of unemployment than do urban workers, the former are not entitled to government assistance because of their non-resident status.[50] As a consequence, migrants generally view themselves as being different from urban workers. Ironically, this sense of difference leads some to regard discontinuous employment as a form of "freedom": "We are different from the urban dwellers," one migrant said. "They have guarantees (*baozhang*), but we have the freedom (*ziyou*). They go to work in the morning and come home in the afternoon. Our situation is different: we work when there are projects for us to do but play when there is none. We're not under any constraint [to work every day]."[51]

Another migrant expressed similar views about the "freedom" of working in the cities, although these views were obviously tempered with anxiety about the prolongation of such "freedom": "I pretty much played the whole time during the first month [of my arrival]. About thirty to forty of us lived in this place, but ten of us did not have any work to do. So we played poker and slept. For a whole month, I bore a very heavy burden on my mind. I felt rather depressed (*kumen*). But I could not go back to Suzhou [his last stop before coming to Beijing]. One reason was that I didn't have any money on me. Another reason was that I'm a man of family, so I can't just go from one place to another like this and waste my money on the trip."[52] This sense of resignation, mixed with a quiet determination to find work on their own, is the prevalent sentiment expressed by many informal-sector migrants whom I interviewed over the years.

Because of such sentiment, the guerrilla workers generally show little sense of solidarity with the urban laid-off workers, another social group that has experienced serious economic hardship. Many migrants feel that the urban workers have simply failed to seize the opportunity that was available to them but was denied to the rural migrants. While they are generally sympathetic to the plight of laid-off workers, they believe that the latter still fare better than the migrants in the cities. Sometimes, one even detects a feeling among the migrants that laying-off of urban workers is not wholly unjustified:

The Northerners[53] are generally not as eager for work as the outsiders. Absolutely not. They are also no match for the latter when it comes to work effort, the ability to absorb hard labor, and perseverance. They tend to be conservative in their thinking and are not flexible about what they can or cannot do ... True, most of the workers were laid off involuntarily, but from a rural person's perspective, I don't think it is that unfair. They may blame their situation on changes in the enterprise system or government policy. But from an individual standpoint, unemployment is also a process of winnowing out the incompetent [*yousheng lietai*]. Aren't there still many people who are not laid off? ...Why can't they seize unemployment as an opportunity? ... I don't care about what their living conditions are like, but they still live a better life than the villagers. After all, they are from Beijing, have many local connections, and are generally better educated than we migrants. There is no work that migrants can do but the laid-off workers cannot.[54]

If the migrants regard work as a privilege or an opportunity to be earned through hard labor, their sense of entitlement regarding security, work conditions, and remuneration starts from an extremely low baseline. Migrant renovators work with the expectation that their employment will last only as long as their current project. Continuous work depends on luck and on decisions made by whoever gets the next renovation contract. There is some stability to the composition of work teams that are continuously employed on renovation projects, but most migrants join teams and leave them in a casual, matter-of-fact fashion.

Rural migrants endure the worst working conditions in construction. But their tolerance of the hardship is often predicated on the timely payment of wages *and* on expectations of eventually returning to their villages for recuperation. Here is how some Chinese researchers have described a meeting between them and a group of construction workers: "Both Xu and You, leaders of two migrant construction teams, cry 'bitterness' on behalf of the migrant workers. They said that their men work 'harder than peasants'. Meals are bad, and living conditions at construction sites are abysmal. But migrants can tolerate all this as long as wages are paid on time and there is money to be made. The two leaders were indifferent to the various stipulations in the 'Labor Law'. They stated that their workers care most about earning money, and the 'Labor Law' provisions are 'too fashionable' [*shimao*] for peasants. Xu added: 'Although it's hard work now, but after they earn the money, they could go home and rest for two or three months at one stretch'."[55]

Making money is always a struggle for the migrant renovators. Even in Beijing, a place considered by many Anhui migrants as full of generous people, 30 percent of the homeowners did not pay the renovators or paid less than promised for various reasons, according to one migrant I interviewed in 1996. He further mentioned that "about twenty percent of us migrants do not make any money at all".[56] For the migrants, success in money-making is not strictly calculated according to the monthly ledgers of earnings and expenses on a given renovation job. Rather, it is measured by the amount of savings one could bring to the families in the villages. To make money, itinerant workers have to both earn money *and* depress urban consumption. The village, not the city, is the final point of accounting of a migrant's income and thus his success. The goal of a successful migrant, therefore, is to spend the hard-earned money on building a house, contracting a marriage, contributing to a family member's education, or starting a business in the rural areas.[57]

Such a rural and familial orientation gives rise to a kind of remuneration ethic among the migrant workers that is distinct from the ethic that obtains under a formal wage-labor system. It is almost always the case that migrant renovators are paid different amounts for identical jobs because of the particular contracts entered into by migrant contractors and urban homeowners. Because the workers are typically not paid on fixed calendrical schedules, timely payment usually means dividing up the money at the end of the renovation project, after the homeowner and the contractor have settled their accounts. In some cases, workers are paid only on the eve of returning home for the summer harvest or Spring Festival holidays. "When people are going back, you have to let them have their money so they don't go home empty-handed", one migrant contractor said, emphasizing the importance of getting money into the hands of migrants on the eve of return trips.[58]

Many migrants commonly associate *dagong* with temporary work *and* erratic pay, and so they generally consent to payment delays as long as they get paid before home visits. To tide them over long periods of time when they receive no payment, migrant workers take small loans from the contractors or team supervisors. Such an arrangement limits the migrants' consumption in the city and, in a perverse way, helps them to save the money they will bring back to their rural families. There is no doubt that it also gives the renovation supervisors and contractors more power and control over ordinary workers.

Conclusion

In this chapter I have described a new kind of workers – the guerrilla workers in home renovation that have appeared in urban China during the reform. These workers are not only distinguished from regular urban workers by the informal economy in which they are positioned, but also by their history of migration from rural to urban areas. Grasping their rural origins, and their continuous circulation between country and city, is the key to understanding their lived experiences as workers in the cities. As Theodor Shanin, an astute observer of peasant politics, once pointed out, "[rural] labor migrants cannot be fully understood as a group without bringing into the picture their origins ...". That is because "[T]he dream of return, rich and successful, into one's own village, has been the grand utopia, around which strategies, norms and claims were structured by the migrants".[59]

My study points to three main conclusions. First, it identifies the bifurcation of social relations among the informal-sector migrants along the two divergent lines of work and everyday association. The guerrilla renovation workers I have examined are *doubly* embedded in the village- and kin-based relational networks and in the competitive urban underground economy. Much as they try to maintain a close-knit social circle of relatives, friends, and co-villagers in order to weather the hostilities of urban life, they also display an instrumentalist side in the selection of work partners. They invoke, define, or avoid socially-obligatory networks, depending on their socioeconomic position and career cycle.

Second, this study suggests that for China's informal sector migrants, the politics of state-worker relations is primarily located in the place of their everyday living rather than at the site of production. This is because, until very recently, the Chinese state has restricted rural workers' access to urban space. Rural migrants in China thus protested against the closing of city gates during the reform but protested less against the shutting down of the old state factories that employed urban workers. Rural migrants circumvented state restrictions on their mobility and refused to obtain the necessary legal papers for work in the cities. It was not a coincidence that in the 1980s and 1990s, millions of rural migrants took to the informal sector that was least controlled by the state.

Finally, I show that itinerant rural workers have developed a distinctive perspective on work and entitlement that is different from the view shared by China's traditional urban workers. The key to understanding this difference is to grasp the migrants' past exclusion from the urban economy and their recent rural origins. Their past experiences lead them to harbor no illusions about securing permanent employment in the cities, they treat urban informal work as the source of accumulation for *rural* ends. The emergence of heterodox labor groups such as the guerrilla workers necessarily complicates China's labor politics today.[60] It is time for us to look beyond the industrial employees of the state, collective, and private enterprises.

Notes

1 Laomei is a fictitious name for a county located in the central part of Anhui province.
2 Interview with Cheng Gong, March 7, 1997.
3 Qiang Li and Zhuang Tan, "Chengshi nongmingong yu chengshi zhong de fei zhenggui jiuye", (2002) (6) *Shehuixue yanjiu*, pp. 13–25, Yihong Jin, "Fei zhenggui laodongli shichang xingcheng he fazhan zhong de jige wenti", (2000) (10) *Zhongguo laodong*, pp. 7–10.
4 Daming Zhou, "Guangzhou wailai sangong de diaocha yu fengxi", (1994) (4) *Shehuixue yanjiu*, pp.47–55, Xiang Mou, "Zhujiang sanjiaozhou dushi wailai sangong yanjiu", (2002) (6) *Chengshi wenti*, pp. 44–8.
5 Barbara Entwisle and Gail E. Henderson (eds), *Re-Drawing Boundaries: Work, Households, and Gender in China*, Berkeley, CA: University of California Press, 2000.
6 A standard definition of the informal economy refers to work, other economic activities, and sometimes entire sectors that are unregulated by the relevant state or societal institutions. See Alejandro Portes, Manuel Castells, and Lauren Benton (eds), *The Informal Economy: Studies in Advanced and Less Developed Countries*, Baltimore, MD: Johns Hopkins University Press, 1989. On the rural migrant workers and the informal economy in China, see Qiang Li and Zhuang Tan, "Nongmingong", Yihong Jin, "Fei zhenggui laodongli shichang xingcheng he fazhan zhong de jige wenti", (2000) (10) *Zhongguo laodong*, pp. 7–10.

7   Weiding Huang, *Zhongguode Yinxing Jingji*, Beijing: Zhongguo shangye chubanshe, 1996: 67–8.

8   Anita Chan, *China's Workers under Assault*, Armonk, NY: M.E. Sharpe, 2001, Ching Kwan Lee, *Gender and the South China Miracle: Two Worlds of Factory Women*, Berkeley, CA: University of California Press, 1998.

9   Dorothy Solinger, *Contesting Citizenship in Urban China*, Berkeley, CA: University of California Press, 1999, Li Zhang, Strangers in the City, Stanford, CA: Stanford University Press, 2001, Shukai Zhao, "Criminality and the Policing of Migrant Workers", (2000), 43 *The China Journal*, pp. 101–10.

10   Marc Blecher, "Rural Contract Labor in Urban Chinese Industry", in Josef Gugler (ed.) *The Urbanization of the Third World*, New York, NY: Oxford University Press, 1988, Anita Chan, *China's Workers under Assault*, Armonk, NY: M. E. Sharpe, 2001, Andrew Walder, "The Remaking of the Chinese Working Class, 1949–1981", (1984) 10(1) *Modern China*, pp. 3–48.

11   State Statistical Bureau, *Zhongguo laodong tongji nianjian*, Beijing: Zhongguou tongji chubanshe, 2003: 59.

12   ACFTU, *Zhongguo Nongmingong Wenti Diaocha*, Beijing: ACFTU zhengce yanjiu shi, 1997: 84.

13   Yue Yuan, *Luoren: Beijing Liumin De Zuzhihua Zhuangkuang Yanjiu Baogao*, Beijing: Beijing Horizon Market Research and Analysis Company (1995): 34–5.

14   Bianjibu, *Zhonghua renmin gongheguo nianjian*, Beijing: Zhonghua renmin gongheguo nianjian she, 2002, vol. 22: 545. The entire renovation industry, including both commercial and home renovation, had a total output value of 550 billion yuan in 2000. It had 350,000 commercial and home renovation companies and employed a total of 8.5 million workers (21 percent of employment in the total construction industry) in 2001.

15   These figures are clearly exaggerated. But there are no accurate statistics on the renovators. Here I cite his figures simply to underscore the significant presence of Anhui migrants in the home renovation business.

16   Ching Kwan Lee, "The Labor Politics of Market Socialism", (1998) 24(1) *Modern China*, pp. 3–33.

17   Ying Du and Nansheng Bai, *Zouchu Xiangcun: Zhongguo Nongcun Laodongli Liudong Shizheng Yanjiu*, Beijing: Jingji kexue chubanshe, 1997: 86–9.

18   Lee, *Gender and the South China Miracle*: 84–8.

19   Shukai Zhao, *Zongheng Chengxiang: Nongmin Liudong De Guancha Yu Yanjiu*, Beijing: Zhongguo nongye chubanshe, 1998: 61–3.

20   Lee, *Gender and the South China Miracle*: 116–23.

21   Zhao, *Zongheng Chengxiang*: 65.

22   The personnel composition of some teams is quite stable, not so much because they include fiercely loyal kin or fellow villagers, but because they manage to get steady work.

23   Localities have elastic boundaries. Depending on the context, one's local acquaintances may include people from the same village, township, county, or province. So the question of whether one is from the same "local" area as another cannot be ascertained on the basis of geography, but depends on perceived, (inter-)subjective understanding of the parties in question. If one person is not regarded as a *laoxiang* or *jiali lai de* by another person, the two are not from the same locale, even if their rural residences are within the same region in some geographical sense (for example, the same province) Lee, *Gender and the South China Miracle*: 84. The same is true for kinship, another socially-constructed category. "Fictive kinship" is a case in point. As Ole Bruun has noted in his study in a study of family business in Chengdu: "The distinction between the categories of household members and strangers or between relatives and nonrelatives … is often vague and frequently nonexistent. Kinship terms are often applied to close friends of the household – uncle, little sister, big brother, and so on. In

the case of close cooperation, such terms are so commonly used that an outsider finds it impossible to distinguish between relations of true kinship and those of friendship … ": Ole Bruun, *Business and Bureaucracy in a Chinese City*, Berkeley, CA: Institute of East Asian Studies, 1993: 58.

24 Interview with Cheng Gong, March 7, 1997.

25 Interview with a migrant worker, July 28, 1996.

26 Zhao, *Zongheng Chengxiang*: 65.

27 Interview with a migrant worker, February 4, 1997.

28 For example, one villager I know decided that her two sons from two different marriages should not migrate and work together because she was afraid that the two half-brothers "may not get along and would lose their brotherly love for each other".

29 Weibing Gong, *Laodong Li Waichu Jiuye Yu Nongcun Shehui Bianqian*, Beijing: Wenwu chubanshe, 1998: 68.

30 Interview with Cheng Gong, May 1, 2004.

31 Interview, December 8, 2002.

32 For a detailed description of such "fake" advertisement, see Lei Guang, "The Market as Social Convention: Rural Migrants and the Making of China's Home Renovation Market", (2005) 37(3) *Critical Asian Studies*: 391–411.

33 Interview with a migrant worker, July 2, 1996.

34 See http://juran.com.cn for description of branch markets (accessed on June 17, 2005). By 2005, it has opened four branches in the city. Its northern branch on the fourth ring road (si huang) alone boasted retail space of 56,000 square meters and sales revenue of 1.5 billion yuan in 2002.

35 "Lai zi Shanghai jiazhuang shichang de neimo diaocha", www.ijiajia.com/news/article.php?id=308 (accessed on May 18, 2004). The article is attributed to *Jiefang ribao*, February 14, 2004.

36 For a more detailed look at urban policing and control of rural migrants, see Zhao, "Criminality and the Policing of Migrant Workers".

37 Interview with migrant workers, August 5, 1996.

38 Interview with a migrant worker, July 2, 1996.

39 The incident occurred in 1994 and was related to me by a migrant in an interview on May 19, 2004.

40 Daming Zhou, "Guangzhou wailai sangong de diaocha yu fengxi", Xiang Mou, "Zhujiang sanjiaozhou dushi wailai sangong yanjiu".

41 Zhao, *Zongheng Chengxiang*: 76–7.

42 Interview with a migrant worker, July 3, 1996.

43 Interview with a migrant worker, January 24, 1997.

44 Interview with a migrant worker, July 2, 1996.

45 Yuan, *Luoren*: 111.

46 Michael J. Piore, *Birds of Passage: Migrant Labor and Industrial Societies*, Cambridge: Cambridge University Press, 1979: 54.

47 See Lei Guang, "Rural Taste, Urban Fashions: The Cultural Politics of Rural/Urban Difference in Contemporary China", (2003) 11(3) *positions: east asian cultures critique*: 613–46.

48 I take the central idea of moral economy to be that humans are interpretive animals and that their actions – work or protests – are guided by a collective sense of what is legitimate or fair in the society rather than by any pre-social or asocial interests. In using the term moral economy I stress the sociopolitical considerations under which seemingly economic transactions take place. For more on the notion of moral economy, see James C. Scott, *The Moral Economy of the Peasant: Rebellion and Subsistence in Southeast Asia*, New Haven, CT: Yale University Press, 1976, Edward P. Thompson, "The Moral Economy of the English Crowd in the Eighteenth Century", in Dorothy Thompson (ed.), *The Essential E. P. Thompson*, New York, NY: The New Press, 2001.

See also William James Booth, "A Note on the Idea of the Moral Economy", (1993) 87(4) *American Political Science Review*, pp. 949–54.

49   See C. K. Lee's discussion of three types of reactions to the economic reform – socialism betrayed, transformed, and liberated, which are shaped by different memories of Chinese socialism. Ibid. See also Marc Blecher, "Hegemony and Workers' Politics in China", (2002) 170 *The China Quarterly*, pp. 283–303.

50   According to Qiang Li and Zhuang Tang, a higher percentage of migrants experience job loss than urban workers. In 2002, 45.4 percent of the migrant workers in Beijing went without a job for three months or more, up from 33.5 percent for 2000. See Qiang Li and Zhuang Tan, "Chengshi nongmingong yu chengshi zhong de fei zhenggui jiuye": 22.

51   Interview with a migrant worker, July 2, 1996.

52   Interview with a migrant worker, July 5, 1996.

53   In this case, northerners refers to Beijing residents. Anhui migrants also use the word northerners to refer to people from northern China in general who are stereotyped to be less industrious and flexible than southerners. Depending on context, the term may also refer narrowly to urban state-sector workers in the North.

54   Interview with Cheng Gong, May 19, 2004.

55   Yuan, *Luoren*: 35.

56   Interview with a migrant worker, July 5, 1996.

57   Rachel Murphy, *How Migrant Labor is Changing Rural China*, Cambridge: Cambridge University Press, 2002.

58   Interview with a migrant worker, July 3, 1996.

59   Teodor Shanin, "The Peasants Are Coming: Migrants Who Labor, Peasants Who Travel and Marxists Who Write", (1978) 19(3) *Race and Class*: 281, 85.

60   On historical fragmentation of the Chinese labor, see Elizabeth J. Perry, *Shanghai on Strike: The Politics of Chinese Labor*, Stanford, CA: Stanford University Press, 1993.

5 A tale of two sales floors

Changing service-work regimes in China

Amy Hanser

Introduction

In the basement locker room where workers at the high-end, privately owned Sunshine Department Store change into their uniforms, a large sign painted on the wall declares: "If you don't work hard today, tomorrow you'll work hard looking for a job [*jintian bu nuli gongzuo, mingtian jiu nuli zhao gongzuo*]". To my surprise, I found the very same slogan at the state-owned Harbin No. X Department Store, where a large, red-lettered sign hangs above a case holding employees' timecards. No doubt these two signs suggest new workplace realities in China's department stores, a part of the service sector once dominated by state-owned enterprises offering workers secure employment and stable, if relatively low, wages. What is work like in these new service work environments, and does the appearance of the same sign – the same threat, really – in a private store and a state store suggest a convergence of labor regimes as well?

Ostensibly, these two stores were organized along the same employment model. Like many large retailers in China, both stores had adopted the "factory-in-the-store" system. Retailers contract out floor space to merchandise suppliers, and suppliers pay salesclerks' wages and commissions. In some stores, like Sunshine, salesclerks no longer have any legal employment relationship with the store itself, and manufacturers pay salesclerks directly, in cash, once a month. This model of employment has made many of China's department stores exemplars of flexible labor arrangements.

But as I endeavor to show in this chapter, not all sales floors are equal. The comparison between a state-owned department store and a new, privately-run luxury one illustrates how short-term and uncertain service sector employment has become. Changing employment practices have also deprived young workers laboring under new service-work regimes of the institutional and cultural resources that enable older workers to assert their dignity and demand respect in the workplace. The contrast between the Harbin No. X and Sunshine Department Stores reveals how new labor regimes that lay claim to greater efficiency and better service come at a significant cost to workers.

Of course, pre-reform Chinese workplaces were no workers' paradise. The highly politicized workplaces of Maoist China were often despotic, and workers were caught in webs of intense "organized dependence" that forced them to rely on their work units to meet almost every need (Walder 1986). While the introduction of market forces and the retreat of politics from everyday economic life have loosened the grip work units once held on their workers, the reform era has nevertheless produced equally despotic work settings, if differently so. Industrial workers in both state-run and private factories are now disciplined by piece-rate pay scales, strict controls over the shop floor, and other manifestations of managerial power (Lee 1998, 1999; Rofel 1999; Zhao and Nichols 1996). The growing power of management and its greater flexibility and autonomy with regards to labor issues is a broader trend that crosses ownership forms and has become an increasingly standard characteristic of Chinese businesses (Gallagher 2004).

Like the shop floors of China's industrial workplaces, the sales floors of the country's service sector have also been reconfigured by economic reform. New business practices of department stores are emblematic of these changes and show the degree to which the "flexibility" of labor relations can aspire. This chapter explores the consequences of new work regimes for sales clerks and demonstrates how the maintenance of pre-existing employment practices in older work units serves to insulate some workers from these changes.

This chapter is based upon data gathered in China between 2001 and 2002, when I conducted participant observation in two large department stores in the northeastern city of Harbin: the private, luxury Sunshine Department Store and the state-owned Harbin No. X Department Store – both names are pseudonyms. In each site I spent over two months working as a uniformed salesclerk. I supplemented this ethnographic work by observing in a number of other service-work settings in the city. I also conducted interviews with workers, store managers, merchandise suppliers, and other industry experts and conducted archival research on institutional changes to China's retail sector. Ultimately, my comparison of sites will show the identical signs at Harbin No. X and Sunshine belied two dramatically different worlds of work.

Department stores and flexible labor: the factory enters the store

What exactly is the "factory-in-the-store" business model? How did it arise, and how has it come to dominate department store labor relations? The answers to these questions frame the ethnographic material that follows and require a brief detour into China's two-plus decades of economic reform.

The factory-in-the-store system provides great flexibility and control for employers. For department stores, the system shifts many costs onto the shoulders of the manufacturers and suppliers of merchandise. Suppliers not only provide merchandise, but they also pay the set-up and maintenance costs of a sales area, rent storage space, and pay the salaries and commissions of the clerks who are selling their goods. Merchandise is sold on a *koulü* ("percentage deduction") basis, with the store taking a cut of sales – usually 23 percent to 25 percent on clothing, less for such items as household appliances. In this way, stores stock and staff their sales floors with steeply reduced overhead costs.

The factory-in-the-store system also creates more flexible employment relations. Clerks work in these stores as long as their manufacturer-employer operates a sales space, which given the seasonal nature of the clothing industry, may be as short as three or four months. When a manufacturer leaves, whether permanently or for a season or two, sales clerks must wait for reassignment to another position in the store. Store managers still maintain control over who works in the store, and suppliers generally hire their sales clerks from store-generated lists of potential workers. Store managers also monitor daily work performance and fine workers for misbehavior.

While this business practice holds obvious advantages for retailers, why did manufacturers and merchandise suppliers go along, and how did factory-in-the-store arrangements proliferate? Ironically, the origins of system currently found in almost all large department stores lie with state-owned retailers and not with new entrants in the market. Enterprise reforms begun in the early 1980s led to the rapid expansion of direct links between retailers and manufacturers (Department of Commerce 1989: 119–21; Naughton 1995: 116). Industries supplying goods to urban retailers saw large numbers of new entrants in the 1980s, a result of both preferential government policies and the shift from a planned economy (Naughton 1995). As competition heated up among manufacturers in a progressively more saturated consumer-goods market, factories anxious to get merchandise to market preferred to avoid state wholesalers and go directly to stores to promote their products, a trend that only accelerated through the 1990s (Guo *et al.* 1992; Yang and Zhu 1998).

This competition spurred new business arrangements between factories and state-owned stores. During the 1980s and early 1990s, the most important such arrangement was commission sales (*daixiao*), whereby manufacturers supplied stores on a sell-first, pay-later basis, with stores earning a percentage of sales (Li 1987; Wang 1984; Wu 1989). Less common were factory-in-the-store arrangements, used to introduce trial merchandise; in these cases, manufacturers paid clerk wages (Department of Commerce 1989: 122; Wang 1984; Wu 1984). "The factories were knocking on *our* doors, wanting to get their goods into our store," one sales department manager explained. Interviews revealed that by the mid-1990s, in Harbin, most major retailers were operating on a commission-sales basis.

The early 1990s were boom years for large urban retailers. Existing stores made major investments in expansions, and new department stores were constructed at a rapid pace (Li *et al.* 2001; Wang and Jones 2001). In Harbin, between 1993 and 1995, the city center's four large state-run department stores were joined by at least six competitors – representing state, private, and joint-venture investments – and another three had opened by 1997.

But by the mid-1990s, department stores both old and new, state-owned and private, faced greater competition, shrinking market shares, stagnating profits, and for some, burdensome, outstanding loans. In many cases, expansions proved over-ambitious and excessive, and anticipated profits were slow in coming. The mid-1990s marked a turning point as overinvestment in the retail sector and changing consumption patterns caused profit margins among large state retailers to shrink from 25 percent to 30 percent to a scant 3 percent to 5 percent (Wang and Jones 2001: 32).

In this intensely competitive environment, privately-owned department stores began to shift their operations from commission sales to the factory-in-the-store model. "Bringing the factory into the store" (*yinchang jindian*) shifted many operating costs to manufacturers. These department stores maintained control over their sales spaces by tracking the sales performances of brands in the store and evaluating the merits of manufacturers petitioning to enter. Borrowing a retailing practice pioneered – albeit on a small scale – in large state-owned department stores, private department stores expanded the model to serve as their primary mode of business. Competitive pressures among retailers pressed more conservative – usually state-owned – department stores to adopt the factory-in-the-store model in the late 1990s.

When I conducted my field research in 2001–2002, interviewees estimated that 60 percent to 70 percent of all merchandise in the average Chinese department store was sold on a factory-in-the-store basis. By 2000, all of Harbin's major department stores, regardless of ownership structure or organizational history, used this procedure to procure the majority of their merchandise – often over 80 percent. Many expect the factory-in-the-store model – often referred to today as factory-store "cooperation", *hezuo* – to remain stable and dominant. As one informant emphasized, it has simply "become accepted practice" (*bei shehui renke*) in China's urban department stores.

Clerks now find themselves answerable to two sets of bosses – store managers and "factory" ones. Indeed, the ability to more closely monitor sales clerks' behavior was one of the most attractive aspects of *yinchang* arrangements for suppliers. "Manufacturers were happy to" pay salesclerk salaries, one department store manager insisted, "because it meant they have a lot more control over the people selling their goods." Merchandise suppliers concurred, noting that paying salesclerks wages makes them "easy to manage" (*hao guanli*). Said one, "If someone isn't doing her job, you fire her ... before, we couldn't do that". On the sales floor, manufacturers and suppliers have become a daily presence, checking up on sales, managing inventories, and even supervising sales activities. Yet even though store clerks now often have two "bosses", in many stores they are not considered full-fledged employees by either set of bosses, and department-store sales work is less and less likely to provide health insurance or other benefits. For salesclerks, the rise of the factory-in-the-store system has also ushered in a new system of flexible employment. A proliferation of bosses has not been accompanied by stronger ties to the workplace.

What is more, despite the pervasiveness of the factory-in-the-store model among Chinese department stores, "factories" have not entered all stores on the same basis. As the following discussion will show, the different employment practices in private and state-owned stores mediate the implementation of the factory-in-the-store model. Numerous factors, including government pressure and financial support, enable state-owned stores such as Harbin No. X to avoid the more despotic versions of the new business model. A more secure set of employment relations insulate state-sector workers from the vagaries of a seasonal and fluctuating labor market, and these workers are able to maintain high levels of authority, autonomy, and ultimately, dignity on the sales floor. The contrast between two department-store sales floors highlights the despotic direction in which employment relations have shifted in China's urban service sector.

Sunshine Department Store: the despotism of the modern service regime

When I took up a post selling cashmere sweaters in the upscale Sunshine Department Store, I found myself in a tightly managed ship. A glistening structure rising from Harbin's bustling streets, Sunshine dominated a downtown shopping plaza. The privately owned-and-operated retailer explicitly catered to Harbin's wealthiest consumers: its target market was the top three percent income bracket in the city (Wang 2001: 11), and the goods arrayed across Sunshine's marble floors were the trappings of a luxurious lifestyle. Having first opened its doors in the early 1990s, Sunshine was considered a model of modern managerial practices. It was generally acknowledged as the city's most exclusive, and probably most successful, department store.

The store was also an exemplar of flexible employment practices, with important consequences for its workers. Sales clerks at the store labored in a kind of limbo: though they were not full-fledged store employees, they had to navigate the managerial demands of two sets of bosses, store and "factory". At the same time, a system of individualized responsibilities for salesclerks had accompanied the entry of the "factory" into the store. The result, I suggest, was a workplace characterized by fragmented managerial authority and atomized work relations among workers.

Work under a flexible labor regime

Sunshine had adopted the factory-in-the-store system on a sweeping scale. Sunshine's ability to attract a moneyed clientele meant that the names of manufacturers and clothing distributors wanting to enter the store filled a lengthy waiting list. This, in turn, enabled Sunshine's management to be the first in the city to implement extensively the factory-in-the-store model, in the process shedding the bulk of the store's labor costs.

Even so, Sunshine maintained a tight control over its sales staff. Job seekers first had to meet the store's basic employment requirements: local residence, a high-school education, age 25 or younger, height of 1.6 meters or more, attractive appearance, and for most positions, being female. Potential sales clerks were then filtered through the store's personnel department, which maintained a "human talent warehouse" (*rencai ku*) from which they generated lists of potential salesclerks for merchandise suppliers. Suppliers selected workers from these vetted lists, negotiating wages and commissions directly with their clerks. At Sunshine, monthly wages were paid in cash, handed directly from the supplier's sales representative to the clerks who worked under him. Not only did Sunshine sales clerks not enjoy a lifetime "iron rice bowl", but they had no formal employment relationship with the store at all.

Being a legal employee of the "factory" introduced greater employment uncertainty into sales clerks' lives. Many manufacturers sold their goods at Sunshine on a seasonal basis – winter clothing, such as cashmere sweaters and fur coats, might be displayed for only five months of the year. There was also turnover among the manufacturers within the store, with anywhere from 10 percent to 30 percent being removed from the sales floors every year because their sales were not up to the mark. When a sales clerk's supplier left the store, she would be placed back into the store's "warehouse" to await a new job assignment. Although I have no systematic information on these employment gaps, a month's wait was common. A sales clerk's movements in and out of the "warehouse" could continue, until she reached the age of 30, the standard age at which clerks were retired from the sales floor.

Few clerks actually remained at the store long enough to confront the upper age limit. While the personnel manager I interviewed declined to specify how many positions, on average, the store needed to fill every month, she did acknowledge that turnover was high. Although outright firing was rare – only a handful per month – the manager named many reasons workers left the store. The average worker might stay two years. Some left to continue their education, while others hoped to start their own – small-scale – retail businesses. Many also left to have children. By the time they would be ready to return to the labor market, these young women would frequently be over 25 and ineligible for working at Sunshine again.

Sunshine sales clerks were also likely to find themselves without any of the benefits that employment in a large organization in urban China usually provides. The merchandise suppliers did not view these young women as their full-fledged employees, given that they actually worked *in* the department store and were frequently on the payroll for only part of the year. As a result, sales clerks were rarely provided with health insurance or other benefits, unlike the local sales managers and sales representatives also employed by the "factory". And because stores like Sunshine do not technically employ these sales clerks, they also do not take on responsibility for health insurance or other forms of social welfare for these workers.

That Sunshine sales clerks were workers *in* but not *of* the store became clear to me as the Chinese New Year approached. One day, boxes of beer and cooking oil suddenly appeared at one end of the basement locker room where workers changed into their uniforms. These were New Year's gifts to store employees – a standard workplace tradition in China – and were to be distributed to managers, floor supervisors, and store cashiers, all of whom drew salaries from the store, unlike sales clerks. So while managers often claimed that sales clerks were part of the "Sunshine family", being an actual store employee clearly had its benefits.

More bosses on the sales floor

Generally speaking, these flexible labor arrangements did not translate into a looser hold over workers. Rather, the tenuous nature of the employment relation was coupled with greater managerial authority on the sales floor. In fact, workers now found themselves answering to *two* sets of bosses instead of to one. Sales areas at Sunshine were domains controlled by both store and merchandise supplier, and, as a result, both department-store managers and manufacturers' sales representatives were a daily presence in sales clerks' work lives. "Bringing the factory into the store" had also resulted in a push-and-pull relationship for sales clerks, who constantly balanced the often-competing demands of store and manufacturer. Sales clerks were truly caught in the middle, not full-fledged employees of either "boss" and yet subject to the demands – and reprimands – of both.

Although Sunshine had effectively shed the costs of employing a sales force, its managers continued to exercise great control over clerks. The store issued uniforms – rented by manufacturers – and established detailed regulations regarding the workers' appearance – no dyed hair, no heavy makeup, fingernails clipped to a specified short length; workers could be fined for violating these requirements. On one occasion, a co-worker spent her shift cowering in her sales area because she feared that she would be fined because of the color of her shoes; the soles of her shoes were yellow rather than the store-mandated black. And even though sales clerks had no direct financial relationship with the store, they were nevertheless subject to fines for misbehavior, which they might be expected to pay on the spot. Store managers also set parameters for service interactions that included standardized greetings, product introductions, and farewells. Sunshine also required sales clerks to sign a "service contract" that outlined the store's service expectations, and clerks attended store-sponsored training classes, meetings, and other events. Management was also committed to "quantifying" (*lianghua*) responsibility in the store and issued each sales team an individual sales goal.

On the sales floor, store managers monitored day-to-day selling activities. A manager's approval was needed for merchandise returns and other routine matters, and the floor manager and her two assistants would regularly inspect sales areas for compliance with store policies and standards. Upper-level store management would conduct periodic inspections of the store, each manager wearing white cotton gloves in order to test for dusty surfaces.

It is hard for me to convey how much anxiety all this close supervision caused me when I first arrived at Sunshine. I found Sunshine highly regimented, and opportunities for mistakes and shortcomings abounded. A workday at Sunshine began in the dimly-lit basement locker room, where clerks jockeyed for space as they changed into their uniforms. We would then climb up the unheated stairwells to our sales floors. The doors to each floor were briefly unlocked from 8:15 to 8:30 a.m. The doors were again locked between 8:30 and 8:45, when each floor manager held her daily "morning meeting" (*zao hui*) for sales clerks. Because a partial roll call was conducted each morning, locked-out, tardy clerks risked discovery and a fine of 10 yuan. Promptly at nine, the theme from Bizet's '*Carmen*' would be broadcast over the store's public-address system. As customers entered the store, clerks would stand at military-style attention along the aisles, their feet neatly pressed together to form a '*Y*' and their hands delicately folded. Unsuspecting sales clerks who dared to chat with one another across the aisles might find themselves soundly scolded by stern-faced managers inspecting this "morning greeting" (*zao ying*).

The Sunshine sales area where I worked was also the domain of Goat King, a cashmere-sweater company. Like department-store floor managers, Goat King managers and sales representatives were a daily presence, though they were less concerned about service than about sales. Sales reps were primarily responsible for supplying us with merchandise, but our main sales rep, Little Wei, would closely supervise Goat King sales clerks, insisting that displays of sweaters be rearranged to his specifications. A bit like a cross between a bully and a mischievous boy, Little Wei would bang his hand on the counter when sales were slow and yell at the sales clerks, "Why don't you sell something!" In a bad mood, Wei would threaten all sorts of fines – for lateness, for slowness, for bookkeeping mistakes – though by the next morning, he would usually have forgotten these threats. And unlike the three store managers assigned to our floor, our Goat King sales rep would spend large amounts of time hovering about the sales area. At Sunshine, it often seemed that we sales clerks were never free from some kind of surveillance.

Too many bosses spoil the sale

I joined a three-person sales team in the Goat King cashmere sweater sales area. Zhang Xin, in her mid-twenties, was the senior salesclerk, having worked at the store for several years. Married and in the early stages of pregnancy, Zhang expected to leave Sunshine the following spring. Wang Lihua, a single woman in her early twenties, had worked in Goat King's Sunshine sales area the previous winter; given the high turnover at the store, this made Wang a veteran salesclerk. Finally, there was Xiao Hong, also single and in her early twenties. She worked for Goat King in another store the previous year, but at Sunshine she was considered a rookie. Zhang and Wang each earned a base salary of 500 yuan a month, Xiao 450 yuan, and the three split a one percent commission on monthly sales. Goat King set this pay arrangement, and a sales rep from the company handed wages, in cash, directly to the clerks once a month. With commissions figured in, wages ranged from 1200 to 1400 yuan a month – compared with a reported average monthly wage of 580 yuan in Harbin (*Statistical Yearbook of Harbin* 2001). For such respectable wages, these young women labored long hours, rotating three daily shifts – morning, day, and night – without any scheduled rest days.

The issue of whether or not to offer special promotional discounts illustrates the clash of managerial edicts created by the factory-in-the-store, two-boss system. Often, a department store offers discounts of 10 percent to 20 percent in the hopes of drawing customers away from competing department stores. But manufacturers, who compete against other brands *within* a single store – and usually have sales spaces in other department stores as well – are often loathe to cooperate. When manufacturers contract space with a store, most of these agreements include a clause that prohibits the manufacturer from offering discounts elsewhere in the city unless he also offers them at the store specified in the contract. As a result, manufacturers worry that a promotional sale, and a consequent cut in profits, in one store could result in a forced reduction in prices everywhere. These divergent interests complicate decision-making about discounting, and at Sunshine it was not always clear to salesclerks where "the store" and "the manufacturer" stood on these issues. In the resulting confusion, sales clerks could easily find themselves caught in a tangle of contradictory commands and vacillating instructions.

For example, as the Chinese New Year approached, Sunshine managers reminded sales clerks of a special promotional sale at 20 percent off. I was working with Wang Lihua that morning, and we both assumed that Goat King would participate in this holiday promotion. When our sales rep, Little Wei, arrived later that morning, Wang informed him of the storewide sale. Wei was both surprised by and unhappy at the news; he immediately called the manufacturer's local office to confirm that we would offer the discount. Later on, Goat King's manager Song arrived and told Wang Lihua to offer the 20 percent discount for the time being; then he left.

In the early afternoon, Wei reappeared. He snooped around the neighboring sales areas and then returned, informing us that we were no longer to offer the special discount. Wei was irritated and restless, bossing us around for a while and then slipping off. We sales clerks were despondent; because we were not offering an extra discount when other brands were doing so, Goat King's sales were bound to suffer – and sales commissions along with them.

Then, in a seeming reversal of managerial edict, in mid-afternoon our junior sales rep, Ming, okayed a 20 percent discount to help Zhang Xin close a sale. A short while later, Zhang confidently offered another woman a 20 percent discount. But later in the day, manager Song came and explained that the situation had changed. We were not to openly offer 20 percent reduction, but if it seemed that the sale would not close, we could gradually relent to a 15 percent, and even 20 percent, discount. Manager Song made a point of explaining that if a customer seemed to be randomly asking about prices, we should respond that there was no discount.

Manager Song disappeared, and head manager Li, in charge of Goat King's Harbin sales operations, arrived. He was fresh from negotiations with the store's top management, which seemed to have altered Goat King's position. He instructed us to grant everyone the special discount, but still, he reminded us, to try to be as discreet (*hanxu*, meaning "veiled" or implicit) as possible. He offered no explanation as to how exactly one would do this.

Late in the day, near the end of my shift, I was standing in the Goat King sales area with Xiao Hong when a couple clad in fur coats arrived to look over our sweaters. As they considered the selection, the man asked whether or not we could offer him a discount. When Xiao Hong hesitated, he asked me. Uncertain of my ability to be "discreet", I hastily referred him back to Xiao Hong, who then fumbled and offered a 20 percent discount, explaining apologetically that we did not want others to know that we were offering such a discount. The couple left without making a purchase, leaving Xiao Hong and me to wonder how one both does and does not offer customers a discount.

Fragmentation and atomization on the sales floor

These frequent confusions unsettled sales clerks, not simply because they created uncertainty, but also because Sunshine clerks were held responsible for their mistakes, often monetarily. What is more, sales clerks' "responsibilities" and managerial surveillance, coupled with pressures to sell, produced a fragmented, atomized workplace. The factory-in-the-store model at Sunshine had also generated high levels of within-store competition among sales teams and even created tensions within teams of sales clerks.

There was, for example, a great deal of competition among sales areas selling similar merchandise. My fellow sales clerks were often preoccupied with comparing their sales figures with those in other cashmere sales areas in the store, and they constantly calculated and recalculated daily and monthly sales figures and commissions. The store strongly encouraged this preoccupation by posting monthly sales rankings on each floor's bulletin board. The clerks also checked on other Goat King counters across the city, and they regularly visited neighboring sales areas in an attempt to pry sales figures out of other clerks. One morning, I arrived early at the sales area to discover a clerk snooping around the Goat King counter looking for our sales figures from the previous day; she quickly retreated when she saw me. On other occasions, sales clerks would deliberately fail to direct customers to other sales areas and even steer them away from competing sales areas. Although sales clerks would come to one another's aid in various circumstances, this rarely involved helping another sales area make a sale.

The factory-in-the-store model challenged workers' loyalty to the store in other ways. The clearest example was that of "private collection", or *sishou*. The term refers to the acceptance of payment directly from a customer to a salesclerk. The money would then be passed to the manufacturer, bypassing the store entirely and denying it its share of the sale. Store management viewed the practice as a serious threat to profitability, and guilty sales clerks were punished harshly. The instructor of my Sunshine salesclerk training class warned us that hidden cameras – the existence of which I later came to doubt – could catch us in the act of *sishou*. She also reminded us that most manufacturers would deny any knowledge of a salesclerk engaging in private collection of payments, leaving the clerk to bear the punishment – a hefty fine and immediate and dismissal. The subtext to these warnings was that a clerk should take care not to align herself too fully with her "factory".

More insidious were the tensions that could crop up within a sales team employed by a single merchandise supplier. Clerks were not only fined for misbehavior or violations of store policies but could also be charged the actual cost of their mistakes. This practice introduced pressures within a supposedly cohesive group of salesclerks, because if individual responsibility could not be determined, all members of the group would have to split the cost of the mistake. Even when blame could be assigned to one person, this system produced stress for workers. For example, if a salesclerk granted too large a discount in order to make a sale, the manufacturer might deduct the extra discount from her pay. Little Wei threatened this procedure when Zhang Xin granted a 15 percent discount to a customer purchasing only two sweaters – usually it would take purchase of three or more sweaters to earn such a high discount. An even greater concern was the loss or theft of merchandise. Theft-prevention was entirely the responsibility of sales clerks, and the cost of a lost or stolen item would be deducted from monthly wages. Given that the cost of a sweater easily amounted to a month's wages, the possibility of lost merchandise was a source of great anxiety.

As a result, my co-workers engaged in what seemed to be endless counting of the merchandise in our sales area – sometimes as often as three times in one day – in order to ensure that not a single sweater had gone missing. Once, Xiao Hong arrived at work looking pale and wan; she explained that she had hardly slept the night before. Her last count of merchandise the previous evening had come up one short, and she spent the night worrying about the consequences of a lost sweater. It turned out that the miscount resulted from a recording error, not a lost sweater, but sorting out the situation consumed much of Xiao Hong's and Zhang Xin's energy that day. These fears about stolen merchandise complicated my relations with my co-workers at the Goat King counter. When I first arrived, Zhang Xin and Wang Lihua in particular saw me as a burden and potential liability because they feared that they would be penalized for merchandise I had lost. It was only after I had established myself as trustworthy in this regard that they relaxed with me.

The result of such tensions was that the sales team at Sunshine was far less cohesive than workers at Harbin No. X. The many forms of "responsibility" and competition one the sales floor resulted in numerous divisions among workers. High turnover among clerks meant that there were no extensive and long-standing social networks, such as those among sales clerks at Harbin No. X. In addition, clerks might jockey among themselves for the sales positions within the store that offered greater sales volumes or higher commissions. But perhaps the strongest indication of fragmentation among workers was the way in which the threat of fines and deductions from one's pay led to scapegoating within sales teams. To my indignation, it was the exceedingly kind Xiao Hong, as a newcomer, who was the target of such tactics by her co-workers Wang Lihua and Zhang Xin. These factors all combined to create a fragmented and atomized workforce.

Harbin No. X Department Store and enduring work unit practices

By contrast, at the Harbin No. X Department Store, factory-in-the-store labor relations had not yet replaced the employment practices of a traditional, socialist work unit. The store itself was a prize of the revolution, nationalized even before the formal founding of the People's Republic in 1949. Physically, the department store was vast, a massive ring of eight towering floors of cement, covering an entire city block. Each day, Harbin No. X opened its doors to a highly operatic broadcast of the store song, steeped in revolutionary fervor and sung in CCTV military chorus style, entitled "Soar, Harbin No. X!". Although composed for the opening of the store's new building in the early 1990s, the song was infused with the language of the Chinese revolution and extolled the contributions of China's workers to a glorious future.

Nevertheless, economic pressures had led this state-owned department store to adopt a semblance of the factory-in-the-store model. At Harbin No. X, however, the implementation of this system consisted neither of the flexible salesclerk employment nor of the fraught, atomized work relations found at Sunshine. Instead, pre-existing employment practices tempered the entry of the factory into the store and fostered a sales floor work culture characterized by a very different set of values – stability, work security, and high levels of worker autonomy and authority. The resulting service work regime was strikingly different from Sunshine's despotic sales floors.

The durable iron rice bowl

Despite numerous organizational reforms, Harbin No. X retained many institutional practices rooted in China's pre-reform era. Economic reforms had, of course, dramatically altered the way the store engaged in the business of retailing. Through the course of the 1980s, the store shifted to commission sales, even operating a few counters on a factory-in-the-store basis. Starting from the 1980s, workers were shifted from flat monthly wages to group, and then team, commission systems. The early and mid-1990s were boom years, and with loans from the local government, the store constructed a massive new structure. But, as noted above, the mid-1990s was also a turning point in China's retail sector, and suddenly Harbin No. X faced intense and growing competition from emerging private retailers.

By the late 1990s, store profits shrank and financial pressures grew. Store ownership was converted to stock, though the government retained a formal 33 percent stake in the enterprise and in practice controlled the 33 percent interest retained by the store itself – the remaining shares were owned by staff and management – giving the local government *de facto* control over the store. Also in the late 1990s, the store formally shifted to a factory-in-the-store system; manufacturers now paid salaries to sales clerks, though all workers remained legal employees of the store. Other attempts to reduce operating costs included changes to health and retirement benefits in 2001, when store workers were enrolled in social welfare programs sponsored by the city government and into which they made individual monthly contributions. As a result, the store no longer shouldered the full social-welfare burden for its workers.

At the same time, Harbin No. X was a strikingly different work institution from Sunshine due to a number of factors. Continued links to the local party-state meant that despite mounting financial woes, managers felt confident that the store would not go bankrupt. Managers also believed that, given the high rates of unemployment in Harbin, the city government would not allow the store to add to the pool of the unemployed. Managers even expressed the view that the store had a *duty* to employ people (*cf* Guthrie 1998), and both workers and managers believed that the employment relationship was a fairly permanent one. Store managers claimed that they were unable to fire workers unless the individuals engaged in illegal activities, and they could not recall a single instance of having let a worker go.

There were many other examples of strong work-unit ties to the workforce. Wages, for example, were deducted from manufacturers' earnings but issued to workers by the store. In the slow summer months, when Harbin No. X experienced cash-flow problems, workers were paid regularly, whereas the store was slow to hand earnings over to manufacturers. And as one "factory" sales manager complained to me, state-run stores like Harbin No. X assigned salespeople to a supplier with little or no supplier input. "Even if you ask to have someone removed from your sales area, it takes forever for that to happen ... if it happens at all!" Workers "belonged" to the store, and suppliers expected Harbin No. X managers to side with workers in supplier-worker disputes. Even more telling, none of the sales clerks I worked with had any plans to leave Harbin No. X to find other work; they considered the store a stable *danwei*.

Workplace stability and community

This employment system supported a set of work relations on the sales floor that differed markedly from those generated by the more flexible – and despotic – system found at Sunshine. In many ways, Harbin No. X exemplified Brantly Womack's (1991) concept of "work unit socialism", where workplace relations are characterized not only by "loyaltism and clientelism", the instrumental and despotic elements identified by Andrew Walder (1986), "but also skill, seniority, family relationships, personality, need and so forth" (Womack 1991: 325). The socialist work unit was a stable community, shaped by an "expectation of continuity" (Womack 1991: 328) and characterized by strong, long-term relationships and a sense of collective interests.

My assigned position at Harbin No. X was on the Ice Day down coat counter, in the women's department. As at Sunshine, I joined a team of three sales clerks: Big Sister Zhao, in her early forties; Big Sister Lin, in her late thirties; and Little Xiao, in his late twenties. My co-workers earned a one percent sales commission on their monthly sales, an amount divided equally among the sales team; this commission could double, triple, even quadruple the basic monthly wage of 400 yuan. Despite the common perception of state-sector workers as lazy and inefficient (Rofel 1989), my co-workers actively pursued sales commissions, and on the sales counters I worked I never witnessed workers restricting sales upon reaching a collectively recognized sales limit, what has been termed in the literature on American department stores a "stint" or a "good book" (Benson

1986; Dalton 1974). My co-workers rotated two shifts – 8:30 a.m. to 4 p.m. and 8:30 a.m. to 7 p.m. – working two days then resting a day.

My sales team formed just a small part of a much larger community in the store. My second day on the Ice Day counter, a disheveled elderly lady stopped to chat with Big Sister Zhao. After learning a little about me, the woman exhorted me to "be careful walking home from the bus stop ... and don't go home too late at night. I'm an old lady, I have experience, you should listen to me". After she left, Zhao explained that the woman was a retired store clerk who stopped in from time to time to say hello. Over the next couple of months, I encountered other retired workers who visited the store, people with whom my co-workers were quite familiar. The department store was, I began to see, a durable community.

The store had no employee turnover to speak of. In 2000, the store had added just 27 new workers to a workforce of almost 3,000. These new additions also represented a form of continuity, for they were all the children of retiring workers who filled their parents' positions. Workers might *leave* the store, of course, but such workers were likely to go on leave – without wages – in order to maintain entitlement to the store's social-welfare provisions.

In the same way, sales departments formed stable groups. Over time, workers could expect to work with or near almost every other worker, and they kept close tabs on each other even after they were no longer assigned to the same counter. For example, after I left the store, I returned periodically to visit with old co-workers. Because the layout of the sales floor changed seasonally, my co-workers were regularly redistributed across the women's department. I quickly learned, however, that I needed merely to locate one co-worker and I could easily find everyone else. "Little Xiao, he's downstairs selling discounted winter coats", Xu Li-mei, who had worked at a neighboring counter, would report. "Big Sister Zhao is over by the stairs, and Fang Dong is in a boutique by the escalator – but she's not here now, she's working the late shift today".

This sociability was part of the proverbial fabric of life at Harbin No. X, and lax managerial supervision granted workers the freedom to cultivate this sense of community. Workers were subject to fines – for being late, for a messy work area, for chatting with one another – but in practice, such penalties were infrequently exacted. So on slow days, workers utilized their relative freedom to move around the store to visit co-workers. Little Xiao would slip off for a lengthy lunch with some mates, and Big Sister Zhao would play an afternoon session of cards in the break room. During trips to the toilet, workers claimed that they needed "a partner" along to chat with and on the way back to the sales areas, would frequently take "the scenic route". Workers would also use "spare" time to run errands, for themselves as well as for co-workers, cementing bonds among themselves in more practical ways.

Sales clerks also knew a great deal about one another's personal lives. For example, one afternoon a store worker on maternity leave visited our sales area with a baby in her arms. Later, Little Xiao informed me that her husband – also a store worker – was 12 years younger than her. "So?", I replied. "I think that's great. No one would care if it was the man who was older". "But when she's in her fifties, she'll be an old lady (*lao taitai*) and her husband won't even be forty yet!", he said. Little Xiao then launched into a lecture on love, marriage, and responsibility. What I found instructive, in this case and many others, was how much workers knew about each other's lives. Even if workers were unfamiliar with co-workers' lives outside of work, they at least expected to be able to recognize them. So when a man claimed that he should get a discount since he was a store employee, Big Sister Lin exclaimed with surprise, "How is it I don't recognize you?".

Worker autonomy and authority

This stable community was one in which workers enjoyed high levels of authority and asserted their sales expertise. Management was rarely present on the floor, and when a manager did pass, he or she was likely to focus on superficial and incidental problems, such as a forgotten bucket of soapy water or a messy work area. A combination of trust in workers, disinclination to assert themselves with workers, and perhaps some degree of laziness on the part of managers resulted in a high level of autonomy that gave workers the freedom to organize their work activities as they saw fit, producing a highly efficient, if idiosyncratic, self-organization of work. The rhythms of work were similar to those Christopher Warhurst (1998) observed in a factory on an Israeli kibbutz where he identified high levels of worker self-direction and autonomy as a key element of an "alternative socialist work setting". While Harbin No. X's salesclerks were certainly not free from managerial control, they claimed many of the privileges that Warhurst ascribes to the socialist labor process. Workplace autonomy extended far beyond the freedom to circumvent formal store rules and even beyond flexibility in dealing with customers – the kind of autonomy we might expect with service work (Leidner 1993; Sherman 2003). Most importantly, sales clerks' self-direction allowed them to cultivate a sense of competence and to assert their authority and expertise on the sales floor.

In a technical sense, sales clerks at Harbin No. X, like those at Sunshine, had two bosses – store management and representatives of manufacturers. But in striking contrast to the clerks at the Sunshine Department Store, Harbin No. X sales clerks repeatedly asserted themselves with manufacturers' sales reps. Harbin No. X workers recognized that they depended on their manufacturers for access to the best and most popular merchandise, and so the issue of merchandise stock was one about which they were constantly exerting pressure and expected both store managers and manufacturers and suppliers to defer to their authority. It was, for instance, a regular practice for sales clerks to make lists of the merchandise we hoped our manufacturer would re-supply us with. If they were dissatisfied when new shipments arrived, clerks might hassle the "*daili*", or sales rep, when he arrived on his daily rounds. On one occasion, Big Sister Zhao was particularly stern with our sales rep, an affable, middle-aged man from the company headquarters in Jiangsu province. Zhao informed him that on the previous day – her day-off – she had visited a wholesale clothing market in Harbin and discovered a wholesaler selling a style of Ice Day coat that our counter had never carried and another style of which we had only received a single box. Big Sister Zhao even quoted the prices of the coats and their product numbers. The sales rep seemed somewhat surprised but asked her to write down this information for him, assuring her that he would try to get us these goods. Zhao did not conceal her annoyance at his oversight.

Later that day, several boxes of merchandise arrived. When the sales rep returned the following day, Big Sisters Zhao and Lin enthusiastically informed him that the new styles were selling very well. The sales rep handed over a master list of prices that included the new items. Big Sister Zhao examined the list closely and found a number of items that we lacked; she immediately grilled the sales rep about these. He defended himself by explaining that not all the products had been sent to the Harbin sales region.

This sense of authority enabled workers to assert themselves in other ways, such as resisting attempts to impose new routines or work practices on them. For instance, Ice Day coats were all labeled with a cardboard tag. At the base of each tag was a detachable stub listing the coat's color, style, and size. This was a system to track the best-selling coats, but because the procedure was new, we frequently forgot to rip off the stubs. One afternoon, one of our sales reps pressed Big Sister Zhao and Little Xiao about this, asking, "How can we calculate your wages if we don't have the tabs?".

"You have to pay us!", exclaimed Zhao. "What do you expect us to eat if we are to sell your coats, the northwest wind (*xibei feng*)? You can't live off the northwest wind, you know!".

Little Xiao joined in. "Sometimes we are simply too busy to have a chance to rip off the tags". Zhao added, "Some customers dislike it (*you fan'gan*) when we rip off the tags, they don't like it".

The harried sales rep eventually left for another sales counter, and though we all made a greater effort to collect the tabs, no one seemed anxious about doing so.

Negotiating competition

As at Sunshine, sales clerks at Harbin No. X competed with each other, especially because sales were made, and paid, on a factory sales-counter basis. However, the specific features of this state-owned department store meant that competition took on a form peculiar to Harbin No. X. The sociability and stability of the workplace reinforced a sense of mutuality among workers, particularly as they might expect to be working with a different configuration of co-workers every three months or so. As a result, competition itself was contentious. Sales clerks at the state-run retailer negotiated the tensions produced by intra-store competition by trying to balance competitive pressures and a sense of fairness and collective interest.

The competition that did occur at Harbin No. X was more subtle than that at Sunshine. It took me a long time to notice that the daily exchange of sales figures among clerks was, in fact, a form of competition between workers selling different brands of merchandise. This seemed to be the only overt form of competition acceptable among sales clerks, and it was done freely. Underlying the exchange of sales information, however, was disgruntlement with pay disparities. For example, as the down coat season progressed, my Ice Day co-workers expressed dismay when they learned that the Snow Lion salespeople would be earning twice as much as the result of higher sales volume. "We'll earn something like 800 yuan, and they'll earn 1600!", Little Xiao lamented.

The norms of this workplace – its sociability and durability – meant that clerks were uncomfortable with such inequalities. Clerks working at counters with strong sales might try to de-emphasize disparities by drawing attention to their sales on days when their business was slow. For instance, one day "Snow Lion" Wang, whose counter was doing brisk business overall, called out as he passed our counter, "Just six coats [today]!". Six coats was a poor showing.

Throughout the winter season, competition nevertheless heated up between the clerks on my counter and those on neighboring counters. Big Sister Zhao repeatedly noted with irritation that other sales clerks passed information back to their manufacturers. The brand-based competition among sales clerks – driven as much by the competitive practices of manufacturers, who would copy one another's best-selling styles, as by the commission-based pay system – demonstrated how the factory-in-the-store had fragmented workers' interests in this store as well. Competition ratcheted up a notch with the arrival of some new Ice Day coats that appeared to be modeled on Winter Weather's best-selling men's coats, at the next counter. The very next day, Ice Day's sales picked up considerably, while the Winter Weather counter was quiet. That same day I was the unwitting catalyst for bringing all this subterranean competition out into the open.

The incident began when two male customers stopped at the Winter Weather counter. One wanted a small size, and I mistakenly thought that Tao Jin, the Winter Weather salesclerk, had told them that she did not have any small sizes. I hesitatingly mentioned to the two men that Ice Day had the same coat in small sizes. I immediately regretted these words, and a chill settled over the two counters. Big Sisters Zhao and Lin received the customers, pulling out the coats for them to try on.

It turned out that all along Tao Jin had been looking for the coat in the right size; she was now holding that coat, but the men had already moved over to our counter. She angrily tossed the coat aside, and suddenly I realized I had "stolen a customer" (*qiang ke*). After a few minutes, the man who was looking to buy a coat went back to the Winter Weather counter to look at that merchandise. While he went to look in the mirror, I slid next to Tao Jin and apologized.

"I thought you didn't have the size in stock", I told her. "I didn't mean to *qiang ke*".

"That's okay", she said a bit too brightly. "It's perfectly normal to do so. Go ahead and steal (*Ni qiang ba*)".

By this time, a little crowd had gathered at the Ice Day counter, attracted by the man who was trying on the disputed coat. The original customer bought a coat from us, as did a woman. I was intensely embarrassed about the *qiang ke* incident, which made the two segments of counter space feel like two opposing camps.

Tao Jin was known for her fiery temper. She soon passed through our counter area, and she joked with me, "Feeling guilty, huh?". Then she added airily, addressing Zhao and Lin, "I told her it doesn't matter, if you want to steal, then go ahead and steal (*qiang jiu qiang ba*); besides, you can learn how to do it from Zhao!".

"What do you mean?", Zhao shot back angrily, but Tao Jin had already begun to pass out of earshot. Zhao called out to no one in particular, "Those two men originally saw our coats on display, but they didn't know where to find them, it was *our* coats that they liked in the first place". Big Sister Zhao was very angry; she started to busy herself with this and that and then left the counter. I felt even worse; I seemed to have started a small feud between Tao Jin and Zhao. Big Sister Lin chatted with me cheerfully, clearly feeling the need to lessen the tension at the counter.

The necessary target for redirecting all this negative energy soon arrived in the form of an elderly beggar. He stopped when he saw me and made a pleading bow. Without thinking, my hand went straight to my pocket, though I had no money on me. Tao Jin immediately flew over, yelling at the man, "She's a foreigner, don't you beg from a foreigner, how humiliating (*diu lian*)!". Big Sister Lin shooed him away as well, saying, "This is a business place, you can't beg here, it's a bad influence, a bad influence (*yingxiang bu hao*)!". The man persisted. Lin started to look fierce. "Do we have to go get store security?". By this time Zhao had returned, and joined forces against the old man, saying, "So healthy (*shenti nemme hao*), why doesn't he try to earn his living?".

Finally the man left, but discussion about him continued, providing a neutral topic on which everyone could agree. I started to note things down, and Lin asked me, "Are you going to write about the old man?". "Yes", I replied, embarrassed. She called out this news to Tao Jin, and they agreed, "You get such people wherever you go". Tension still hovered over the counter and did not dissipate until late afternoon, but the elderly beggar had relieved some of the accumulated bad feelings.

Clearly, I unwittingly broke an informal but critical sales clerks' rule at Harbin No. X. However, the rift-mending that followed the customer-stealing incident is as instructive as the outburst it produced. Workers were clearly anxious to re-establish equilibrium among themselves. In the face of divisive pressures introduced by the factory-in-the-store system, sales clerks endeavored to maintain the wholeness of their work community.

Conclusion

In China, the factory has entered the department store. In such settings as Sunshine, sales clerks find themselves "between" two sets of bosses, both in terms of authority on the sales floor and in a more material sense. When conflicting instructions result in mistakes, the salesclerk is usually expected to accept the responsibility – and the penalty – for the error. It is the salesclerk, the member of the triad with the least power, who is most likely to be reprimanded by either set of managers. What is more, because their employment relations with manufacturers are often seasonal and always mediated by the department store, sales clerks are not considered full employees of either. They receive none of the health insurance or other social benefits that manufacturers offer their sales managers and sales representatives – or that stores offer their own managers – and that stores offer their fully vested staff. Salespeople belong neither to the store – which pays them no wages – nor to manufacturers – in terms of where they physically labor.

But as this tale of two sales floors suggests, the dominance of the factory-in-the-store retail model has left some workers in privatized stores more vulnerable than those in state stores. At Harbin No. X, not only did employment practices insulate workers from the most negative aspects of flexible employment, but workers themselves maintained a work culture that preserved a sense of workplace community and worker expertise and competence. Harbin No. X was unlike the private Sunshine, where competition was divisive and always legitimate and where workers were inexorably drawn in.

At Sunshine, worker strategies were fragmented and individualized, and labor arrangements were deeply antithetical to collective action. Sales-floor dynamics created fractured, competitive, and even distrustful relations among sales clerks. In this setting, workers would largely resist with their feet, leaving to seek employment elsewhere. But, as Ching Kwan Lee points out, when "some 30 percent of both urban and rural labor is considered 'surplus'" (2002: 198), it is managers who have leverage over workers. At the very least, it is clear that changes to the organization of service work like those found in department stores have been, in many ways, a recipe for worker disempowerment.

How is it, then, that two such different labor regimes co-exist? At Sunshine, market competition, profitability, and new notions of service produced a despotic labor regime. By contrast, managers at Harbin No. X were uninterested in regulating workers. The reasons for this range from high levels of trust in sales clerks – due in part to the maturity and long tenure of the sales clerks and to the fact that many managers, especially older ones, had worked their way up from salesclerk positions – to strong ties between the store and the local party-state. For Harbin No. X's top management in particular, the sales floor was relatively unimportant compared to relations with local municipal leaders, and the attention they devoted to the local state bureaucracy was both a symbolic and a material orientation – a confirmation of the store's glorious past as well as its financial lifeline in the present.

Does the presence of two service-work regimes also suggest that a more humane organization of work could be competitive in Chinese department stores? Workers at Harbin No. X were no less efficient than were clerks at Sunshine – indeed, at one point my Harbin No. X co-workers learned that our Ice Day down coat sales were the best in the city – but the high degree of autonomy and lack of standardization at the store meant that sales clerks there were perceived as undisciplined and even lazy. Workers at the state-run department store had little patience for "modern" service models requiring scripted displays of deference by sales clerks increasingly expected by China's well-heeled customers. In fact, when I returned to the store in 2005, the store's numerous financial woes – including large outstanding loans, pension burdens, and loss of customers to cheaper, small-scale private merchants (*getihu*) – had prompted store managers to adopt increasingly despotic sales-floor practices. In the end, salesclerk autonomy and assertiveness are probably too closely associated with failing businesses and "bad" service to survive very far into the twenty-first century.

References

Benson, S. P. (1986) *Counter Cultures: Saleswomen, Managers, and Customers in American Department Stores, 1890–1940*, Urbana, IL: University of Illinois Press.

Dalton, M. (1974) "The Ratebuster: The Case of the Saleswoman", in P. L. Stewart and M. G. Cantor (eds) *Varieties of Work Experience: The Social Control of Occupational Groups and Roles*, New York, NY: Halsted Press: 206–14.

Department of Commerce (1989) *Chinese Dry Goods Business* (Zhongguo baihuo shangue) Beijing: Beijing University Press.

Gallagher, M. E. (2004) "'Time is Money, Efficiency is Life': The Transformation of Labor Relations in China", (2004) 39 *Studies in Comparative International Development*: 11–44.

Guan, Xinlin (1998) "Guanyu xiaoshou huikou ruogan wenti tanjiu" (An exploration of certain problems associated with sales commissions), (1998) *Finance and Trade Economics* (*Caimao jingji*) September: 54–7.

Guo, Zhijun, Wang Xilai, Cui Xun and Wu Xiaohui (1992) " Guoying shangye pifa qiye de xianzhuang ji duice" (The current situation of staterun commercial wholesale enterprises and relevant policies), (1992) *Finance and Trade Economics* (*Caimao jingji*), April: 46–51.

Guthrie, Douglas (1998) "Organizational uncertainty and labour contracts in China's economic transition." *Sociological Forum* 13: 457–94.

Lee, C. K. (1998) *Gender and the South China Miracle: Two Worlds of Factory Women*, Berkeley, CA: University of California Press.

—— (1999) "From Organized Dependence to Disorganized Despotism: Changing Labour Regimes in Chinese Factories", (1999) 157 *The China Quarterly*: 44–71.

—— (2002) "From the Specter of Mao to the Spirit of the Law: Labor Insurgency in China", (2002) 31 *Theory and Society*: 189–228.

Leidner, R. (1993) *Fast Food, Fast Talk: Service Work and the Routinization of Everyday Life*, Berkeley, CA: University of California Press.

Li, Shaomin, He, Xiaofeng and You, Youming (2001) *Zhongguo gongshang jingying* (China's Industrial and Commercial Operations), Beijing: Beijing University Press.

Li, Xianghua (1987) "*Peitao yingyong xiandai guanli fangfa tuijin guanli jinbu: shenyang shi tiexi baihuo shangdian tuixing xiandaihua guanli de diaocha*" (Making use of the full set of modern management techniques to advance management improvements: A survey of the implementation of modern management at Shenyang City's Tiexi Department Store), (1987) 58(2) *Shangye yanjiu*: 20–1.

Naughton, B. (1995) *Growing Out of the Plan: Chinese Economic Reform, 1978–1993*, Cambridge: Cambridge University Press.

Rofel, L. (1989) "Hegemony and Productivity: Workers in Post-Mao China", in A. Dirlik and M. Meisner (eds), *Marxism and the Chinese Experience*, Armonk, NY: M.E. Sharpe: 235–52.

—— (1999) *Other Modernities: Gendered Yearnings in China After Socialism*, Berkeley, CA: University of California Press.

Sherman, R. E. (2003) "Class Acts: Producing and Consuming Luxury Service in Hotels", Ph.D dissertation, Sociology Department, University of California, Berkeley.

Statistics Yearbook of Harbin (2001) Harbin: Heilongjiang People's Press.

Walder, A. G. (1986) *Communist Neo-Traditionalism*, Berkeley, CA: University of California Press.

Wang, Guisen (1984) "Zuohuo shengyi, tigao jingji xiaoyi: huaibei shi xiangshan baihuo shangdian de diaocha" (Enlivening business, increasing economic efficiency: A survey of Huaibei City's Xiangshan Department Store), (1984) *Caimao jingji* January: 50–2.

Wang, S. and K. Jones (2001) "China's Retail Sector in Transition", (2001) 20 *Asian Geographer*: 25–51.

Wang, Yanhong (2001) "Sectoral position analysis", unpublished manuscript in the author's possession.

Warhurst, C. (1998) "Recognizing the Possible: The Organization and Control of a Socialist Labor Process", (1998) 43 *Administrative Science Quarterly*: 470–97.

Womack, B. (1991) "Transfigured Community: Neo-Traditionalism and Work Unit Socialism in China", (1991) 125 *The China Quarterly*: 313–32.

Wu, Huiqiang (1984) "Nanfang dasha de san xiang gaige" (The three reform projects at Southern Mansion), (1984) 28(2) *Shangye yanjiu*: 24–7.

Wu, Minqing (1989) "Duo qudao jiejue shangmao qiye liudong zijin duanque de wenti" (Many channels solve commercial trade enterprises' problems with shortages of liquid capital), (1989) *Caimao jingji* January: 63.

Yang, Wenjie and Yuhong, Zhu (1998) "Guoyou pifa shangye zou chu kunjing zhi lu" (The path out of difficulty for state-owned commercial wholesale enterprises), (1998) 5 *Caimao jingji*: 51–2.

Zhao, M. and T. Nichols (1996) "Management Control of Labour in State-Owned Enterprises: Cases from the Textile Industry", (1996) 36 *The China Journal*: 1–21.

Part II
Gendering service work

6 Virtual personalism in Beijing

Learning deference and femininity at a global luxury hotel[1]

Eileen M. Otis

China's ascendancy as an economic superpower has been fueled, not only by a low-cost factory labor, but also by its rapidly expanding consumer market.[2] The world's factory is emerging as a global retail and service magnet; major international retail, fast-food, and hotel chains proliferate in China's urban centers. Whereas the Mao era's centrally planned economy minimized consumer services, currently the tertiary sector represents over one-third of China's gross domestic product, expanding thirty-fold between 1980 and 2000.[3] To make way for department stores, fast-food restaurants, boutiques, supermarkets, beauty salons, and hotels, municipal governments rezone urban residential neighborhoods as commercial districts, transforming the urban landscape.[4]

By spawning millions of new consumer service jobs, the booming service sector has also transformed the urban occupational landscape, particularly for women.[5] Retail and service managers typically employ youthful, attractive women to enhance the allure of products and services. By the time they reach their late twenties, these workers are jettisoned from the frontlines of labor, considered by management to be too old to appeal to male customers. Hence, workers dub service jobs a "youth rice bowl" (*qingchunfanwan*).[6] Today, a generation of working-class women whose mothers toiled in factories and farms in the service of socialism serve the emerging elite and middle class, as well as a growing contingent of global, professionals. The oft-repeated slogan, "the customer is god" reflects the new forms of deference female service workers enact.

How are vast economic disparities between workers and customers translated into asymmetries of respect, attention, and care on the service shop floor?[7] Why do women workers participate in the manufacture of interactional inequalities and how do they cope with them? Understanding the production of relational inequalities between customers and workers on the service shop floor requires taking into account the transformation of women workers' bodies, identities, and sexualities in the workplace. This transformation of women workers is enabled by an organizational foundation that combines new global work repertoires with a legacy of employment practices. The labor regime produced by this synthesis is termed virtual personalism. Virtual personalism cultivates a brand of deferent, class-inflected femininity which fosters deep and invisible customer control. Workers draw upon local cultural schemas and hotel service repertoires to create emotional distance from customers and to level symbolic inequalities. Paradoxically, these strategies to recast the service relation tended to foster compliance to customer service.

To understand the ways in which new gender and class inequalities are formed, sustained, and challenged in China's new service workplaces, I conducted six months of ethnographic research at the pinnacle of China's new consumer-service sector: a five-star luxury hotel catering to Western, male business and political elites, called here the Beijing Transluxury (hereafter, BT).[8] At the BT, workers confront some of the most dramatic gender and class inequalities found in China's new consumer-service sector. At the BT, I worked as a volunteer English teacher for six months in exchange for research access. I interviewed 55 individuals attached to the BT, including waitresses, hostesses, security personnel, butlers, housekeepers, and managers.[9] I also shadowed the work of these personnel. I regularly chatted with employees and managers informally during lunches in the staff canteen. I participated in multiple training seminars and hotel events.[10]

As capital of the fastest-growing economy in the world, Beijing has become a global city that hosts a substantial contingent of affluent, international professionals, who consume high-end goods and services.[11] Seeking a foothold in this market niche, the BT management trains local, working-class women to provide state-of-the-art service for an a predominantly male, globetrotting clientele. At the BT, workers personalize service by using customer-preference data that are stored by workers on computer files.[12] The service regime creates the effect of a personal relationship between the guest and the service provider, but staff members are rarely personally acquainted with guests; personalism is virtual.[13] Virtual personalism addresses a long-standing problem faced by firms serving large markets. In her study of the rationalization of service sector work, Robin Leidner notes that consumer service firms "want to treat customers as interchangeable units but they also want to make the customers feel that they are receiving personal service".[14] By creating flexible, deferent workers with access to consumer preference data stored on computers, virtual personalism reconciles these two apparently contradictory objectives. With access to guest background information a staff member who has never before encountered a guest can tailor service to the customer's individual preferences. As a labor regime, virtual personalism is founded on a deep level of control by the customer that is largely invisible. Furthermore, by requiring staff members to record and store information about customer preferences the hotel chain frees itself from long-term dependence on the knowledge workers acquire about customers. Without this dependency, the employer can more easily substitute new workers for old.

Management prepares workers to minister to the minute personal preferences of customers by training its frontline workforce in the art of deference, linking performances of deference to femininity. Through ongoing training, women workers undergo an intensive process of self-transformation;[15] they simultaneously develop an acutely feminized bodily awareness and a hyperconsciousness of customer preferences. If, as Joan Scott argues, gender is a "primary way of signifying relationships of power",[16] then service requirements for bodily performances create, elaborate, and invite gendered modes of interaction and domination. Unlike the middle-class American flight attendants of Hochschild's classic study, who applied emotional sensibilities from their middle-class homes to exchanges with customers in the aircraft cabin, BT managers to do not condition workers to adopt the sentiments from their private lives on the shop floor, even though employees did smuggle in their own interpretive frames while enacting service. Rather, like a Pygmalion tale,[17] BT's management trains women workers to exhibit deferential, class inflected forms of femininity through disciplining their bodies, comportment, facial expressions, and modes of perception. The systematic linkage of service protocols requiring deference to femininity naturalizes inequalities between customers and workers by grounding them in gender hierarchies.

Paradoxically, a set of retooled Mao-era practices in the form of benefits and workplace community undergirds the acquisition of new feminine dispositions. These practices, adapted to a global commercial workplace by the BT, provide a familiar foundation on which the deep work of feminine self-transformation required by the personalized service regime can take place. The practices ameliorate the profound inequalities workers confront, creating a material and communal basis for workers to sustain a sense of dignity in the face of new and profound inequalities.

Of course women staff members are not blank slates, and workers carry their own experiences and norms for understanding the service relationship into the service workplace. I found that the version of femininity workers actually enact on the shop floor can also help to mitigate their experience of inequality as they use their femininity as a resource to elevate their own dignity and self-respect. Female frontline staff import cultural schemas of "face-giving" onto the shopfloor to maintain emitonal distance from customers. Furthermore, the service repertoires acquired by staff members allow them to interpret the process of self-transformation as engendering an elevation of the self above the customer, socially and morally, even as subordination is performed. At first glance, this self-elevation might look like worker resistance to subordination. However, workers' claims to social and moral superiority reinforce compliance to work protocols that require deference.[18]

From comrade (*tongzhi*) to "miss" (*xiaojie*): gender, post-socialism, and service

Gender is a central axis of the new inequalities that have emerged in post-socialist societies. The economic and political restructuring of post-socialist economies disproportionately impacts women, who confront shrinking welfare spending and lay-offs, and are systematically excluded from real power in the political arena.[19] The growth of new economic sectors also shapes women's experiences of post-socialist, market transitions. Whereas socialist societies minimized consumption to conserve resources for building industrial infrastructure, post-socialist societies are experiencing a mushrooming of consumer-services, with profound consequences for women workers.[20] The trend is reflected in China's workplaces. In Mao-era

China consumer service work was minimized and expressions of femininity in the workplace were muted. Today, consumer services proliferate, and pronounced expressions of deferential femininity facilitate consumption.

After 1949, the Chinese Communist Party (CCP) integrated the majority of urban women into manufacturing labor, adopting Frederich Engel's supposition that women's labor-force attachment would bring about a gender-egalitarian society. To ease women's entry into the predominately male world of work, the Party promoted a proletarian class identity to be shared by all workers, muting expressions of gender inequality and difference.[21] Even though manufacturing industries tended to be sex-segregated, it is unlikely that managers controlled labor through elaborating ideologies of femininity; they were more likely to suppress such ideologies.[22] In general, men and women working in the same enterprise earned comparable wages and benefits.[23] To buttress women's identification as workers, the Party celebrated the brawny women of the "Iron Girls' Brigades", whose competence at technically and physically challenging jobs – such as construction and steel work – challenged deep-seated assumptions about women's inherent inability to perform such tasks.[24] Workplaces eliminated overt gender distinctions by requiring all workers to wear baggy, unisex clothing.[25] The most pronounced inequalities were not defined by gender, but by political criteria, which ranked individuals by class background and level of workplace activism.[26] By emphasizing proletarian identities shared by women and men, while minimizing expressions of sexuality in clothing and appearance, the party facilitated women's presence on what had been in the decades preceding the Mao era, a predominately male-populated shop floor.

But gender inequality persisted, even as the CCP drew women into the workplace and declared their liberation.[27] The Party celebrated a working-class identity anchored in a model of masculinity, at the same time stigmatizing expressions of traditional femininity in dress and comportment for their association with bourgeois, commercial culture.[28] According to Evans, "Feminine pleasures and feminine beauty were … used as a metaphor for moral degeneration or ideological impurity".[29] At the same time, women continued to take primary responsibility for housework, but rarely did the Party formally acknowledge women's labor in the home.[30] Underscoring the presumed incompatibility of femininity and factory labor, in the 1950s, the Party launched the "Let's Be Pretty" campaign, drawing women out of the workforce to relieve cities from growing unemployment. The campaign prioritized men's attachment to the labor force over women's, encouraging women to return to the household, where they might were encouraged to the "feminine" pursuits of fashion and beauty.[31]

While consumer-service units employed a disproportionate number of women,[32] the small service sector eliminated expressions of femininity and deference.[33] Service work was not commodified and did not require forms of emotion work[34] characteristic of capitalist consumer service. The socialist shortage economy required consumers to compete for access to scarce goods; workers acted as gatekeepers – often surly ones – and it was the burden of the customer to gain their cooperation. Symbolic markers of collectivist ethics were apparent in service outlets. Workers addressed customers in the egalitarian language of "comrade" (*tongzhi*) that emphasized the equal treatment of all and special treatment of no one.[35] In fact, workers developed a reputation for their willful inattention to customers. An older woman I interviewed captured the spirit of service work in the Mao era as she reflected on her pre-reform employment in a state-owned retail store, "at that time we didn't even have to smile, we could yawn out loud and tell the customer to shut up, and no one cared".

Exiled from production in the Mao era, today managers cultivate femininity and deference in their workers to serve a competitive consumer market. Employers strive to distinguish their product through the attention offered by female interactive service workers. In the process, management and customers wield unprecedented power over frontline service workers. No longer sporting the professional white lab coat worn by Mao-era service workers, at restaurants, hotels, and department stores female hostesses now wear tight-fitting, thigh-exposing "*qipaos*". Sexual innuendo infuses the terms that designate service workers: customers use "server" (*fuwuyuan*) and "miss" (*xiaojie*) interchangeably to address workers. Purged during the Mao era, *xiaojie* has reemerged to designate consumer-service workers.[36] *Xiaojie* is also a commonly used euphemism for sex worker. Indeed, the term conflates legitimate and illicit service work.

Once banned under the Mao era, today sex work is increasingly commonplace, despite its illegality.[37] The routine sex work in hotels, bars, restaurants, and beauty salons affects the service staff, who are readily categorized as sex workers.[38] Ching Kwan Lee and Pun Ngai both found that factory workers deliberately avoid service work for its threat to female respectability.[39] The BT protects workers from stigmatizing association with sexual commerce. Furthermore, affiliation with a high-status employer and a workplace that offers relatively generous benefits and perquisites are sources of pride for workers. Together, these components of the workplace prop up workers' status and respectability enabling them to share a modicum of guest status while even sometimes rendering themselves as the customers' moral and social betters.

The Beijing Transluxury Hotel

The lobby of the BT transports the guest from the bustle of the streets of Beijing to an asylum of calm and exquisite comfort. The space contains the requisite markers of "luxury" present at most high-end hotels: a spiral staircase, spotless marble floors, and crystal chandeliers. Silk upholstered chairs and ottomans grace the lobby. On most afternoons, a quartet performs on the balcony overlooking the lobby. Workers pass by, look you in the eye, smile and offer an affable, yet dignified, "Good afternoon".

The BT, a 300-room boutique hotel, which opened in the late 1990s, taps into the global economy through an equity joint-venture with a United States-based transnational corporation, here called "Galaxy". Among the most internationalized and largest hotel corporations in the world, Galaxy owns properties in dozens of countries,[40] employing well over 100,000 people worldwide. Beijing is one of the 10 largest metropolitan areas in the world, and the capital of a country whose economic growth outpaces the world's other major economies. Indeed, Beijing is a strategic city for global capital. Galaxy has partnered with a high-ranking, central Chinese government agency to establish the BT. The BT targets an affluent, predominately male Western business market by offering highly customized services. The hotel wields considerable commercial power stemming from Galaxy's internationally recognized brand name and its access to high-end Western markets through a global partnership of hotels, airlines, credit cards, and car-rental agencies. Extensive advertising in the United States, Europe, and Asia also enhances its customer base.[41] The BT counts national presidents, royalty, celebrities, and business executives among its clientele. Executive managers from the United States, Norway, Germany, Australia, and New Zealand oversee BT's operations. The remaining managers and staff at the BT are Beijing residents.

The BT's female frontline workers are urban residents. Their ages range from 17 to 28. Most are unmarried and daughters of factory workers living with their parents, to whom they turn over their salary in exchange for a monthly allowance. Nearly all of these workers are vocational-high-school graduates. They sign two-year renewable labor contracts with the hotel. At the BT, all the local mid-level managers offer the same rationale for placing women in frontline work: the clients are men. One manager explained, "when girls make a mistake, they can just smile. As they smile, the customer will be halfway to forgetting any mishap." Women learn how to deploy disarming smiles in the process of hotel training and work.

At the BT, management enfolds workers in an exclusive, yet temporary, community that projects the prestige of the firm and its clients onto the staff while integrating many customary, albeit retooled, elements of the Mao-era workplace. The exclusive community is premised on relatively generous benefits, entertainment activities, managerial "care", participation in corporate culture, and protecting of workers from the stigma of prostitution. Together these advantages redress the low occupational status of frontline service work.

The BT welcomes workers into its global corporate culture. Each staff member receives a small card, to be carried at all times, reading, "I am the Transluxury". The card pronounces the Transluxury to be "more than a hotel; it is familiar surroundings for exceptional lives". Management invites workers into the "community of the exceptional", attempting to reflect the prestige of Galaxy and its clients onto them. The exorbitant sums firms spend on name recognition and branding can serve not only to appeal to consumers but also to impress, intimidate, and control potential workers. In general, retail businesses from the United States enjoy a cachet among China's urbanites. Aware of the allure of working for an American company, the BT's management reinforces the prestige of attachment to a United States firm. In departmental meetings, managers weld employee and hotel status; as a hotel restaurant manager insisted to workers, "Your reputation is directly linked to this hotel. If people don't think much of this hotel, they won't respect you".

Frequent ritual events bolster workers' sense of status. Regular presentations by regional corporate managers attempt to dazzle staff with slide shows of

Galaxy's hotel properties, including castles and palaces around the globe. For staff members who enjoy scarce opportunities to travel abroad and little exposure to the architectural grandeur of Europe, the images met with excitement as they spark hopes for mobility and travel. During one meeting, when an image of the BT appeared onscreen amid slides of Galaxy hotels in Rome, Paris, New York, and Singapore, the otherwise reserved staff cheered and applauded. By juxtaposing the BT with other world-famous hotels, the slide shows encourage staff members to imagine their participation in an organization that reaches far beyond the boundaries of the nation. At the same meetings, regional managers outline Galaxy's strategy to dominate Asia's hotel market, sharing profit statements, and describing high-powered client networks and marketing strategies as if the staff members were themselves corporate shareholders.

In addition to including workers in a status-enhancing corporate culture, the BT offers quite decent remuneration. Entry-level wages at the BT equivalent to 150 US dollars per month, but slightly below the average wage for all work sectors in Beijing.[42] With bonuses, entry level earnings exceed average salaries for formal workers in the hotel industry in Beijing. Workers receive a 20 percent bonus when the hotel meets its profit goals, which it often does. In addition to wages, the BT provides a number of fairly generous benefits that reflect continuities with Mao-era workplaces. The union branch and the local enterprise management together determine employee benefits within the broad guidelines stipulated by the 1994 Labor Law. The human resources department distributes welfare benefits – retirement, health care and the like – while the union organizes most other perquisites, services, and activities. Part of the state-sponsored All China Federation of Trade Unions, the hotel's union branch combines its traditional Mao-era mandate – to transmit Party policy to the workplace in a top-down fashion,[43] with a new mandate to support enterprise management's profit-making objectives. In the words of the union chairman, "through its activities, the union helps to realize management goals". Because the BT's local co-owner is a high-ranking central state agency, it serves as a highly visible model for the state's treatment of workers. Furthermore, its privileged ranking in the state administrative hierarchy lends it access to relatively abundant resources and a legacy of generous workplace benefits. Partnering with a large global corporation also avails the hotel of considerable resources.

These benefits, distributed through the workplace, can be viewed as a legacy of the supports offered by the Mao-era work unit, which provided cradle-to-grave welfare for workers.[44] However these contemporary benefits are scaled back and retooled for markets, offering no long-term guarantees. In the Mao era workers received comprehensive benefits like housing, medical care, food, education for their children, and entertainment that supported them throughout their lifetime and were distributed through the work unit. At the BT, in the context of a two-year labor-contract system, benefits are no longer guaranteed for a worker's lifetime. Instead of receiving housing, as in the Mao era, workers receive housing subsidies. Retirement benefits and unemployment insurance are portable, based on the reality of workers' limited tenure at the BT. Staff members receive health insurance and subsidies for parental funeral expenses only during their period of employment at the BT.

Other benefits of the workplace exhibit some limited continuity with Mao-era practices. The hotel provides employees free meals in the staff canteen. On special occasions, like the Moon Festival, workers receive consumer items, such as cases of cooking oil, fruit, or soda – items that were called "worker protections" (*laobao*). At Chinese New Year, workers enjoy a cash bonus delivered in red envelopes. In the Mao-era workplace, managers selectively distributed perquisites to reward "activist" workers for maintaining shop-floor control and party loyalty.[45] At the BT, middle managers have little discretion over the distribution of benefits, which are shared equally among workers and distributed by the workers' union.

Like the Mao-era work unit, the BT organizes a substantial amount of workers' leisure time, promoting camaraderie between staff and management. Activities include soccer, ping-pong, and karaoke competitions, singles' parties, and collective weddings. The BT arranges monthly department-level outings and birthday parties, as well as holiday celebrations, each accompanied by lavish buffets in the canteen. Local Chinese managers and staff together attend plays and concerts, compliments of the workers' union. In short, management invests staff members with a stake in the success of the hotel by projecting corporate and guest prestige onto workers, organizing social activities that builds community among workers, and providing generous benefits as well as profit-contingent bonuses.

Some benefits support managers in the task of maintaining new "hygienic" practices. On International Women's Day, the union distributes a gift of makeup to female staff and invites a makeup specialist to teach application techniques. Workers receive a monthly gift of free hosiery, to be worn with their uniforms. Haircuts are highly subsidized, and managers frequently insist that workers trim their hair before work. Each staff member is assigned a locker, given access to showers, which they are required to use daily, and provided with uniforms that are cleaned and pressed daily.[46] A medical clinic provides workers with various forms of birth control, including the "morning-after pill". Female middle managers personally distribute birth control to sexually active female staff and advise women on their sexual activities in accordance with the national birth-planning policy, encouraging norms of monogamy. On national holidays, managers distribute Western-imported strawberry-flavored condoms.

The American general manager actually objected to the distribution of commodity items to hotel staff, in his view a debilitating vestige of the socialist "iron rice bowl". Voicing an opinion I found to be typical of the Western managers, the general manager propounded, "The system perpetuates a lack of responsibility. So if all I give you is X amount to survive on, and I promise you that your other needs will be taken care of, then in effect you take seventy-five percent of what you and I are responsible for as Westerners for ourselves, and you take it away from the individual. They don't understand what it's like to have to be responsible, to have to provide for themselves".

By dismissing the socialist work unit as serving merely to coddle workers Western managers failed to grasp that the ideological content of these practices diverges dramatically from that of the Mao era. Rather than sustaining an egalitarian ethic at the BT, the practices provide a material and organizational foundation that enables local managers to train women workers to enact deferent forms of femininity as part of global labor repertoires. The practices introduce a semblance of familiarity and credibility to the global workplace and its alien work requirements.[47] In spite of the recalcitrance of individual Western managers, the reproduction of socialist-era practices persists. Typical of joint-venture partners, Galaxy relinquished discretion over personnel issues after encountering implacable resistance by the local partner to any alteration in the structure of benefits.[48]

At the BT, middle managers train workers to be highly sensitized to the needs of customers. These local managers enforce detailed standards of appearance, comportment, and interaction among staff members. In doing so, they are required to adopt a "personal and positive approach" as specified on managerial evaluations. I found that in order to enforce rules regarding the bodily appearance and hygiene of workers, managers develop a measure of intimacy and ease with staff, fostering friendly, if manipulative ties. The BT is the first work experience for most of its female frontline staff members; managers spoke to me of employees as undergoing a rite of passage into adulthood, often referring to the workers' neophyte status when they discussed training. One manager often pointed out that "I'm teaching them to become human beings". Middle managers' performance evaluations are based in large part on how effectively they coach, counsel, and build confidence among employees; that is, managers must adopt a caring and paternalistic approach to training workers.

The BT attempts to minimize organizational hierarchies, and this approach, in turn, optimizes conditions for managerial care. On the frontline of service, it can be difficult to distinguish between managers and workers. A restaurant manager explained, "I'm their supervisor and their assistant". Restaurant managers frequently carry drink orders to guests and convey dirty ashtrays to the dishwasher. Behind the scenes, managers engage in tension-releasing jesting with staff. In the words of yet another restaurant middle manager, "Sometimes we all joke around, managers and staff together". Managers are required to dine in the canteen alongside staff; I frequently overheard managers commiserate with workers over their shared antipathy toward irritating customers. Instead of formally reporting instances of worker misconduct to the personnel department, most local middle managers maintain an informal record of infractions, and iron out problems with workers personally.[49]

Managers also pool workers' tips, using the money to purchase items in bulk – combs, brushes, small food items, makeup for women, razors for men – which they personally distribute to workers. Managers even intervene in family affairs to assure workplace commitment, siding with staff members in their family disagreements. The cafe manager phoned a waitress's mother, "I told the mother that work at the hotel is hard and tiring … she should understand that the child can't do a lot around the house". Workers generally responded positively to managerial care, calling managers "older sister" (*jiejie*) or "older brother" (*gege*). A waitress commented that "our manager is so amiable, she's like my old mother". Managerial caring is crucial to the self-transformation of workers, a transformation which requires an intensive and intimate process of altering bodily dispositions.

If culture, benefits, and managerial care enhance receptivity to transformative service routines, the elimination of overt sex work at the hotel keeps employees' dignity intact. Sex work is commonplace in China's service environments such as hotels, and frontline service work carries the taint of association with the sex industry. The BT deploys its video surveillance system and security personnel to obstruct sex work on the premises. By scouring the hotel of sexual commerce, management protects the reputation of the hotel and its high-profile clients.[50] Consequently, workers are rarely propositioned by guests, and the BT's sterling reputation rubs off on staff members. Unlike staff at other hotels and service environments, BT employees reported that their family and friends respected their work, in large part because the local work unit and Galaxy were above reproach. Together, the cultural, material, managerial, and sexual dimensions of this global workplace form the foundation for a virtual personalistic service regime that enables workers to perform deference with dignity.

Training workers in virtual personalism

For female staff members, maintaining access to the relatively generous and prestigious work unit requires remaking the self into a deferent and feminine frontline worker, one who is highly attentive to guest preferences. As a component of deferent femininity, workers also learn to customize services. The BT attempts to build long-term relationships with customers by constructing records of their preferences. Employees glean information about consumers' preferences at the point of interaction with guests. They use this information to build individual computer files containing lists of preferences amounting to, in some cases, 50 pages of information.

For example, room attendants act like detectives, taking note of where guests leave their TV remote, wastebasket, and shaver, so as to place these items accordingly upon each visit. Female frontline staff in the restaurants and at the front desk memorize the names and titles of each guest, their partners and children, and even their favorite dishes and drinks. Frontline staff members take note of special requests. If a guest asks for a hypoallergenic pillow, a blanket be folded in a particular way, or a chair to accommodate a bad back, the information is noted in the file and the item is provided without prompting upon the next visit. If a guest orders a specific brand of spirits or of mineral water, the details are noted in the file, so that the brand might be provided automatically upon the next visit. If a guest prefers a Fuji to a Macintosh apple, or roses to irises, that preference will be noted in the file. Staff members are warned to note special conditions as well. For example, when a vocalist stayed at the hotel, the hotel sent her a complimentary bouquet of flowers; she immediately sent it back, complaining that her throat was sensitive to the pollen; the sensitivity was noted in her record so that the mistake would not be repeated.

Virtual personalism is encapsulated in the hotel's advertising slogan, "We know you intimately". Through the virtual personalistic service regime, guests become hypervisible to a relatively invisible retinue of female frontline workers. Virtual personalism taps the consuming potential of guests by placing favored items within easy reach, dismantling any barrier to consumption. For example, butlers are advised to place specific brands of spirits preferred by customers in their minibar, which, the butler training manager noted, "the guest always uses". With intimate knowledge of customers stored in the computer files, there is little need for staff members themselves to form personal ties with customers. Furthermore, when staff members depart after their contracts expire, their knowledge of customer preferences remains stored in the BT's computer files. To optimize clients' consuming potential, the regime of virtual personalism renders workers subject to deep and invisible levels of customer control. At the BT this control is enabled by teaching women workers to enact new forms of deferent femininity.

At the BT virtual personalism involves remaking workers' bodies and selves to appeal to the hotel's upper-class male clientele. This process begins at hiring, continues through training, and is sustained by managerial evaluation and control. From the first day a female job applicant steps into the hotel, managers screen her for her body, youth, and appropriately modest femininity. In one interview, I observed the applicant timidly proffer vague responses to the manager's questions and take a call on her cell phone mid-interview. After the interview, the manager declared to me in a sober manner "I will hire her for her body". When I was asked to screen applicants for their skills in the English language, the personnel manager instructed me to assess the attractiveness of each candidate using a code system.[51] I found that management also avoids hiring women who look to be of "questionable morality"; the personnel department rejected an applicant whom the manager described as a "fox fairy".[52]

Hotel staff training and evaluation focuses intensively on bodily dispositions, emphasizing that a worker's every movement, utterance, gesture, facial expression, and bodily pose is a vehicle to communicate with the guest and an opportunity to leave the guest with a positive impression of the BT. New staff members attend one week of training seminars, for which they are paid. In addition, management requires workers to train continually throughout their tenure at the BT by attending seminars, after-work department meetings, and individual consultations with managers. Through a battery of intensive, hotel-wide training exercises, BT management focuses staff perception so that staff members may observe and respond to the minutiae of customer activity. Staff members learn to notice and value customer preferences. Customers themselves might not be entirely conscious of these preferences.

During an introductory training session, the local training manager asked new employees to describe in detail what they saw on an ostensibly blank paper he distributed to them. The trainees insisted that they saw nothing but a white sheet of paper. The trainer then distributed a piece of pink paper with a small hole in the middle. Trainees moved the circle to the specks on the otherwise clean sheet, to reveal tiny lines that materialized with the aid of the punctured pink paper. The trainer explained, "When a guest has a special request or need we should remember, you reduce the scope from this big – hands held out wide – to this small – points to the punctured hole in the paper. Our guests have their idiosyncrasies, and these need our focus".

Management train staff members to respond to the cultural proclivities of the hotel's international clientele. To make themselves accessible to the predominately Western clientele, frontline workers are to adopt English names – the only names they are allowed to use at work. A training module entitled, "Needs and Expectations of International Visitors" stereotypes national characteristics, specifying tailored responses to each. According to the list, Germans, who can be abrupt and demanding, expect efficiency and formality, as well as precise and quiet service. Americans appreciate humor and informal conversation but can be expected to make detailed requests and expect special treatment, as well as specific explanations should anything go awry. Eye contact or any behavior that suggests familiarity offends Japanese customers. Should there be a mishap, Japanese prefer a quiet, sincere apology to an explanation. Staff members are also taught to read guests' moods and to adjust their behavior accordingly. Workers are trained to listen to the customer, offer a demonstration of empathy, inquire further into the details of problems, and solve them with dispatch, following up to make sure that the customer is satisfied. In this effort, the staff member must always be cognizant of specific cultural traits.

Training managers help staff members gain insight into the subjectivities and basic motivations of guests. Invoking Abraham Maslow's hierarchy of needs,[53] the local training manager links the fulfillment of workers' basic material needs to the "self-actualization" of customers. During one training session, the local trainer pointed to a wall poster depicting the Maslowian pyramid and expounded:

> On that chart, we have a pyramid with five levels. The very bottom level is basic needs: food, shelter, water. ... The next level is belonging. Then there's self-esteem. ... Self-esteem is a two-way street, self-respect and respect for others happen at the same time. Why smile? To show respect. [The customer is] spending so much money, you must give him respect. *One person's smile is really powerful. Our profit comes from your smile.* One step from there, self-actualization, is to realize your dream. Why do we smile? Why do we communicate? *To give guests self-esteem. They are paying for their self-esteem and respect.* If we don't have profits, we don't have salary. More than fifty percent of that profit comes from your smiles.

In what emerged as an uneven economy of self-esteem, Maslow's hierarchy does not reveal the path to the trainee's self-actualization; rather, it is used to channel the smiles of employees to fulfill the self-esteem needs of guests in the interest of profitability. Through fulfilling the needs of male customers, women workers might meet their own more basic needs. Hence, Maslow's hierarchy of needs is recast as a class and gender hierarchy: those with material resources purchase attention and those struggling to satisfy physiological and security needs manufacture respect. On the other hand, the discussion suggests that customers lack innate self-esteem and must therefore purchase it. The discussion positions employees as minor psychoanalysts, who can but pity those who must purchase respect. At any rate, staff members are explicitly trained to treat their smiles, gestures, and emotions instrumentally in this relationship. But when employees smile, they can feel a little smug in the knowledge that their own self-esteem is not tied to wealth.

In addition to adjusting employees' subjectivity, managers exercise intricate control over frontline workers' behavior, disposition, and appearance. At the beginning of each shift, female workers line up military-style in their departments as middle managers inspect their appearance, scrutinizing their hair, makeup, and fingernails, but also inciting them to smile, to make eye contact with customers, and to comport themselves in a feminine fashion, chastising workers who "walk like men", swaggering back and forth. The employee handbook prescribes precision control over workers' bodies in public areas of service: "Do not lean or squat, do not spit, do not place hands in your pockets, do not pick your nose, do not talk loudly or shout, do not hold hands, do not clear your throat, do not scratch any part of your body". During my second month of fieldwork, a staff member was dismissed for spitting on the marble floor in the lobby.

The handbook sets specified parameters for standards of appearance. The topic of women's hair merits 19 guidelines. Women's fingernails are not to exceed ".5 centimeters beyond the fingertip", and their earrings are not to be larger than 1.5 centimeters. Watches must be of a "conservative style". As for makeup, female workers must use it to "create a natural appearance". Lipliner, tattoos, and second earrings are prohibited. Lectures by the personnel department address the most personal points of hygiene, specifying appropriate underwear, specifically warning hostesses not to wear long underwear beneath their thigh-revealing dresses. Staff members are told how often to change their socks, how to avoid dandruff, and how to brush their teeth. They are to wear shoes with soles that make no sound when walking on the marble floors.

When advising workers, local managers emphasize the proper facial expression. The training manager explained, "Facial expression is the key element of communication. If you don't believe it, try speaking with a straight face … If you speak with a straight face, people can hear it. But if you speak with a smile, you'll look prettier". During formal evaluations of staff, managers offer intensive feedback that can last over an hour. For example, an assistant manager instructed a waitress on the nuances of smiling: "Your biggest problem is that you don't smile enough. I am not saying that you have to smile all the time. But if you have eye contact with a guest, then you have to smile. Of course, don't always smile. If they have a complaint, don't smile. You should listen to the guest attentively and try to think about how to use your smile flexibly. Your smile is a tool". In another evaluation a manager scolded a waitress: "In these two months, I've seen you talking to guests without any facial expression. It's a habitual problem. You can't even feel it when you frown. When guests ask for something, you just frown when we don't have the item. ...You should be aware of the way you stand and the impression that you make".

Local managers present a continuous stream of suggestions for enacting proper and deferent femininity, conveyed as manifestations of their care. But when workers fail to meet standards of femininity they are met with a certain moral disapproval. When managers correct workers' comportment or facial expressions, they often imply that workers were not adequately "pretty" or feminine which, in turn, reflects poorly on a woman's moral character. Managers believe that the adjustments in workers' disposition will aid staff members in their jobs, make them better people, and ensure their long-term survival on the labor market.[54]

Putting virtual personalism into practice

How do frontline workers manage the gaping inequalities confronted in interactions with customers? I found that the very service regime that requires subordination is also used as a shield to fend off a subjective experience of subordination. Service repertoires bound up with new forms of femininity lend workers a sense of control and sometimes serve as a badge of rank, elevating workers socially and morally above customers. When workers initially enter the super-luxury environment, they are acutely conscious of being subject to panoptic surveillance by powerful video cameras, managers, and customers. For working class staff members, who had never before ventured into a luxury hotel, "luxury" itself exercises a kind of discipline. A hostess expressed a typical reaction to her first weeks of employment at the hotel: "When I first got here, I felt this place was huge, I thought, wow, it's so luxurious! I didn't dare touch a thing, the cups are crystal, the ashtrays are crystal, the cutlery is silver. I felt so nervous. I feared I would do something wrong".

In an unfamiliar environment, service protocols offer a reassuring refuge. A waitress described a heightened awareness of being subject to evaluation for the mundane activity of carrying coffee: "if you do something awkwardly, then [guests] will already form their impression of you. If you take a guest a cup of coffee in a cultured way, then everyone will think, this girl is all right. But if you are flustered, just to look at her you can tell she's afraid ... that girl can't carry things! I hope that when guests see me they'll think, this girl is not bad, she can carry anything".

Protocols lend workers self-confidence as they navigate what can be an intimidating environment. Vicki Smith finds that working-class employees value the training they receive on the job in interactive skills for their utility in managing workplace and personal interactions.[55] At the BT, the skills that require subordination paradoxically become the means by which workers mitigate inequality. Indeed, workers begin to master the class dispositions of their Western elite clientele as they become purveyors and even guardians of the cultural protocols.

These skills can lend workers a sense of superiority over customers, which in turn, reinforce workers' willingness to acquire and deploy service protocols, fostering cooperation with the service regime. The femininity cultivated by service protocols aids workers in maintaining respectability as they perform for customers and managers. A female butler explains, "When I was trained as a butler, [I learned that] a gentleman is a gentleman, and a lady is a lady. So I use that as a starting point, and I feel more sophisticated than before". Through hotel training seminars, staff members absorb Western etiquette, and they develop expectations of ideal guests who embody this etiquette. According to most of the workers I interviewed, the ideal customer proffers "pleases" and "thank-yous", responds to greetings, leans away from the table when being served, knows what and how to order, and may even leave a tip. The manager of the Chinese restaurant opined, "We expect a certain kind of guest, when we train, the videos and the materials feature Western aristocrats. Sometimes the guests don't live up to the image".

Frontline workers muster warm greetings, using the guests' titles and names but guests frequently ignore these gestures of familiarity. I empathized with workers who summoned the confidence to greet guests only to be repeatedly ignored. Many shared the reaction of one hostess: "Sometimes, you're really warm and enthusiastic, but guests just ignore you. Then I think … he's got money but no quality (*suzhi*)". Roughly equivalent to the accusation of lacking "class", "quality" is a measure of an individual's education, ethics, sophistication, manners, and poise. Such a judgment takes on a moral cast in its assumption that some individuals are more deserving – of wealth, attention, and respect – than others. I found a tendency among workers to evaluate Chinese guests particularly harshly; having limited exposure to Western etiquette, these guests are more apt to respond inappropriately to service protocols. By construing themselves as "higher quality" than some guests, in terms of their manner and bearing, workers also suggest that they are also more deserving, socially and morally.

As some guests fail to prove themselves worthy recipients of female staff members' service, employees begin to refer to their own learned femininity as elevating themselves socially and morally above the customer. A cocktail waitress's polite disdain for customers epitomizes the power women invest in their professional modes of femininity: "The quality of the guest's manner doesn't have anything to do with me. I do whatever I have to do. I try to teach them through my smile, so that they can improve their breeding". She continues: "Today, there was a guest who seemed very rich. He made a huge mess … cigarettes everywhere. I put a clean ashtray in front of him, so that he knows. So it's very subtle". Workers evaluate customers' lapses in courtesy through the service perceptions and protocols acquired at the hotel.

To mend the gap between expectations of "high quality" and the sometimes déclassé reality, frontline staff guide guest consumption, showing customers how to order properly and how to use new utensils; they also provide service before customers ask for it. In the process they symbolically invert the server–guest authority relation. Staff members describe their panache in handling awkward moments. A waitress preened: "There was a couple who was very picky. At the end of the meal, he said that it was too expensive. So I said, there is such a pretty lady having dinner with you, you care about the expense?". In response to a customer's request for a date, a cocktail waitress asked, "Can I bring my boyfriend?".

I was surprised to discover that employees found the virtual personalistic service regime beneficial for its concealment of customer authority in the service interaction. Staff members preempted customers' requests by drawing on data in their computer file as well as through anticipatory service; responding to guest needs as they were expressed in telling facial expressions and gestures. The vocalization of requests by customers is a public reminder of the workers' subordination. Workers disdained the occasional customer who barked, "miss" from across the room. A hostess bemoaned, "It's like the old times: landlords hollering at the servants". By silently anticipating customers' requirements, preemptive service veils the authority relation between staff and guests. A waitress at the Western café exuded accomplishment in preempting customer requests: "You must rely on observation. The third day the guest comes, I can just bring him tea before he asks. *He doesn't need to say a thing!*". A butler described the control she maintains over a customer by reading his identity and mood: "You look at his appearance, his manner and bearing, and his first words, how he speaks; I can just look at someone and tell what kind of mood that person is in". Anticipatory service transfers the imperative to serve from vocalized directives to silent gestures. In the process the customer silently and often invisibly consumes the efforts of staff members.

Construing virtual personalism as "giving face" (*geimianzi*) also enhances workers' dignity as they enact subordination. The multitude of gestures, facial expressions, demonstrations of empathy, and forms of proactive customized service are understood by workers as so many means of "giving face". I found that through "giving face" staff members normalize workplace hierarchies, smuggling into work cultural schemas compatible with virtual personalistic protocols.[56] "Giving face" refers to a conferral of status; it is a bestowal of social honor involving routine enactment of deference. Female staff construe work practices as so many methods of tapping into customers' wealth through the art of giving "face". A waitress in the Italian restaurant links preemptive service and "face": "We have an Italian guest who comes often … he comes, smokes a cigarette, he eats bread, and then drinks Qingdao, then he orders saffron risotto. When this man comes, he doesn't need to say a thing, we bring him an ashtray, a glass of Qingdao, for the friends he brings, this gives him face. 'Look at me, I come to this five-star restaurant and everyone recognizes me'".

Rather than eliciting contempt, the unseemly amounts of money guests spend at the hotel convince staff of the profitability and value of their service. As a waitress explained: "If I offer guests enough face they will feel that coming here is worth the price". A female butler claimed, "If the guest pays a hundred yuan this is one *fen* [1/100th of a *yuan*] of my own salary, so giving him face is very important". Conceiving of face-giving gestures as a way to siphon the wealth of the customer tempers the experience of inequality, especially when workers feel that "face" is a free and inexhaustible resource and that they are directly benefiting from customers' expenditures through the redistribution of profits via bonuses and perquisites. Staff members link profit directly to their own status-enhancing capacities. While the language of face-giving normalizes the production of social hierarchy, it also links social hierarchies to *performances* of subordination. By emphasizing the performative dimension of service inequalities, the schema of face denaturalizes workplace hierarchies.[57] One female butler inverted the status-giving hierarchy, claiming that "I don't give the customers face – they give me face by paying my salary".

While face involves extreme displays of deference, it is a semi-ritualized deference that keeps customers at arm's length. As a form of emotion work,[58] face is not conditioned by an underlying notion of individual authenticity. Workers repeatedly claimed that their work did not involve displays of emotion or sincerity (*ganqing*), which are reserved only for more intimate social relationships. In their view, service work – by definition – requires not emotional authenticity, but "face", a conscious performance of deference. Construing service as "giving face" allows workers a degree of emotional and strategic distance from customers. At the same time, "giving-face" suggests an implicit critique of customers as individuals whose self-esteem requires the deference of workers. In interpreting deference through the schema of face, workers view customers' status, in part, as a product of their own performance of subordination. Silencing service hierarchies, keeping guests at arm's length, using smiles and charm to train and defuse customers are evidence that women use gendered-work repertoires to rank themselves favorably *vis-à-vis* customers and to maintain dignity.

Conclusion

How are vast economic disparities between customers and workers manufactured into asymmetries of respect, attention, and care in the global service workplace? Workplace practices that synthesize local organizational legacies and global service repertoires form a basis of legitimacy upon which women frontline workers transform their bodies and identities to conform to a modest, class-inflected form of deferent femininity. I find three striking anomalies in the ways femininity is mobilized as part of hotel luxury service. First, the inculcation of deferent femininity at this global, luxury hotel is, in part, grounded in a foundation of collectivist organizational resources that in the past were linked to a worker identity grounded in masculinity. The state enterprise that co-owns the Beijing Transluxury has absorbed foreign capital while embedding global luxury-service repertoires in retooled socialist work institutions that are familiar and credible to workers. The meanings and forms of labor associated with retooled socialist practices allow mid-level local managers to exercise intimate control over workers' appearance, behavior, and attitude. Managers immerse women workers in new, hyperfeminizing service protocols of deference that magnify the individual preferences of customers. If the Mao-era workplace muted femininity to ensure workplace discipline, today femininity is organizationally mobilized to produce profit. Like a Pygmalion tale, managers train young women to walk, and talk and act like – deferent – ladies.

The second anomaly is that feminized workers provide personalized service without personally knowing the customer. This service technique, called here virtual personalism, is based on a separation of knowledge and execution; knowledge about customers is gleaned at the point of service interaction and stored in a centralized computer system so that any employee may use it at any time in the course of serving the guest.[59] The hotel uses the collective knowledge of employees stored in computer files, and minimizes reliance on personal relationships between customer and employee. As a result, the high-tech regime extracts from service workers a potential source of value and power in the form of their individually accumulated knowledge of customers. Since personalism is virtual, workers are left without the kind of autonomy and influence over their relationships with guests characteristic of jobs in which workers develop genuinely personalized knowledge of the customers.[60] The personal knowledge that interactive service workers accumulate about customers is a source of profit in the service workplace; the BT, and other luxury service employers, extracts and centralizes that value, systematizing it so it may be provided at any time, by any worker. By enabling customized service virtual personalism attempts to redress the dehumanizing effects of routinization on customers of large firms. But if the virtual personalistic regime magnifies the individual preferences of customers, it renders the individual identity of the worker increasingly irrelevant.

The third anomaly is that staff members find the regime of virtual personalism and its attendant forms of femininity useful in maintaining a sense of dignity and even, at times, construing themselves as morally and socially superior to the customer. Designed to perfect service subordination, virtual personalism is inventively deployed by workers to rank themselves favorably *vis-à-vis* their affluent clientele. Thrown into a Western super-luxury environment, workers wield skills associated with virtual personalism as an effective means to navigate a novel and intimidating work context. Female frontline staff members critically evaluate customers through the lens of Western etiquette acquired at the hotel, often using feminized repertoires to elevate themselves socially and morally above customers. Furthermore, the anticipatory service required by virtual personalism conceals authority relations with customers. Finally, in the absence of scripts to guide and routinize interactions with customers, workers draw explicitly on their own cultural schema of "face-giving" to normalize hierarchical interaction and keep customers at arm's length. The schema ultimately denaturalizes inequalities by emphasizing the performative dimensions of shop floor inequality.

The boundaries of distinction drawn by workers make full use of the etiquette and protocols they acquire at the hotel to bolster their status.[61] But their sense of superiority does not undermine service delivery. On the contrary, precisely because workers use the protocols and skills acquired at the hotel to elevate themselves *vis-à-vis* customers, their sense of superiority tends to generate compliance to the regime of virtual personalism. The more skilled workers become at executing etiquette, protocols, and deferent femininity properly, the better able they are to make self-elevating distinctions. The femininity learned at the hotel not only schools employees in the art of deference, but becomes a resource for their own status-enhancement on the shop floor.

If the transition era requires the acquisition of new forms of capital for success,[62] working-class women employed in frontline work in China's consumer service sector wield little beyond "feminine capital", the skills and aptitudes they acquire in the workplace that are deeply bound up with new forms of femininity. The BT inculcates and maximizes that capital among young women by immersing them in hyperfeminizing protocols of deference. But this feminine capital is only valuable when it is attached to young, female bodies. As they approach their late twenties, female service workers are considered by management to no longer be attractive to the male clientele. In response to the limited tenure on the job and the limited life of their feminine capital, women workers repeatedly spoke of feeling an impending "sense of crisis" (*weijigan*) in their lives. Most female workers are uncertain of their prospects once they are deemed too old for work at the hotel. As their contracts at the BT expire, it remains to be seen if find new occupational fields where they can put their capital to use.

Notes

1 Generous support for the research and write-up of this project was provided by a University of California Pacific Rim Research Project Fellowship, a UC Davis Humanities Dissertation Fellowship and a Harvard Fairbank An Wang Postdoctoral Fellowship. I am deeply grateful to those who supported this project in its entirety, providing extensive and careful advising: Vicki Smith, Fred Block, G. William Skinner, Nicole Biggart, and Elizabeth Rudd. I thank Ching Kwan Lee for her incisive comments on this chapter. Thanks also to Hairong Yan for illuminating feedback. I also gratefully acknowledge the helpful comments I've received from the following scholars: Joan Acker, Maria Charles, Maxine Craig, Shao Dan, Tom Gold, Gail Hershatter, Emily Honig, Joya Misra, Seio Nakajima, Estee Neuwirth, Sean O'Riain, Rhacel Salazar Parrenas, Winnifred Poster, Carlos Rojas, Preston Rudy, Beverly Silver, Eva Skuratowicz, Bindi Shah, Mayfair Yang, Emily Yeh, and Li Zhang. My thanks also go out to the staff and management of the "Beijing Transluxury" for all of their assistance in support of my fieldwork. A version of this chapter was presented at the conference, "The Next Great Transformation? Karl Polanyi and the Critique of Globalization", UC Davis, 2002.
2 Davis, Deborah. S. "Introduction: A Revolution in Consumption," in Deborah S. Davis (ed.), *The Consumer Revolution in Urban China*, Berkeley, CA: University of California Press, 2000: 1–24.
3 The sector expanded from 12 billion to 371 billion dollars, growing from 21 percent to 33 percent of GDP in the same time period. See *China Labor Statistical Yearbook*, Beijing: China Statistics Press, 2001:. 5.
4 Li Zhang, "Contesting Spatial Modernity in Late Socialist China", in press, *Current Anthropology*.
5 For analyses of gender and service work see also Yan, Chapter 8, and Zheng, Chapter 7, this book.
6 Eileen M. Otis, "Serving the People: Gender, Class, and Ethnicity in China's Emergent Service Sector", University of California, Davis, unpublished PhD dissertation, 2003.
7 Arlie Hochschild's class study of interactive service work describes inequalities in emotional displays enacted by service workers as part of an "emotional economy",

with differences in what types of and how much emotion work is owed to different kinds of people determined by structures of gender and class inequality. Arlie Russell Hochschild, *The Managed Heart: Commercialization of Human Feeling*, Berkeley, CA: University of California Press, 1983: 84.

8   This name is a pseudonym, as are all names used in this chapter unless indicated otherwise.

9   These interviews, which lasted between 45 minutes and two hours, were recorded with the consent of the respondents; they were conducted in the hotel training room and outside the hotel in coffee shops, in my apartment, and in workers' homes. The analysis does not include front-desk workers. Unlike other frontline workers, who graduated from vocational schools, most of the front-desk staff, whose jobs required considerable fluency in English, were college educated. This analysis focuses on the shared service training and task characteristics that run through all of the interactive jobs performed by staff members I interviewed.

10 I attended three training seminars for new staff, multiple department training seminars and meetings, an executive council meeting, a family-planning seminar, informal outings, departmental parties, and a singles party organized by the hotel. I stayed at the hotel for two nights and patronized the restaurants and bars on a number of occasions.

11 For an analysis of this trend in global cities, see Saskia Sassen, *The Global City: New York, London, Tokyo*, Princeton, NJ: Princeton University Press, 1991.

12 Similar efforts to customize service are becoming commonplace in luxury hotels throughout the world. See Carol Jones, George Taylor, and Dennis Nickson, "Whatever it Takes Managing 'Empowered' Employees and the Service Encounter in an International Hotel Chain", (1997) 11 *Work, Employment, and Society*, September: 541–54; Charles G. Partlow, "How Ritz-Carlton Applies 'TQM'", (1993) 34 *Cornell Hotel and Restaurant Administration Quarterly*, August: 16–24.

13 Gutek *et al.* describe three types of relationships between customers and service providers: the "service relation" refers to a personalized, durable relationship with a single person. The "encounter" refers to a one-time interaction and the "pseudo-relation" refers to customer loyalty to a company in the absence of interactions with a single worker. Virtual personalism comes closest to pseudo-relation but is distinctive for its simulation of a service relation. See Barbara A. Gutek, Cherry Bennett, Anita D. Bhappu, Sherry Schneider, and Loren Woolf, "Features of Service Relationships and Encounters", (2000) 27 *Work and Occupations*, August: 319–51.

14 Robin Leidner, *Fast Food, Fast Talk: Service Work and the Routinization of Everyday Life*, Berkeley, CA: University of California Press, 1993: 178. Furthermore, Gutek *et al.* (2000) find that customers prefer services that involve ongoing personal interaction. See Gutek *et al.*, 2000, op. cit.

15 See Robin Leidner (1993), op. cit.; Cameron L. Macdonald and Carmen Sirianni, "The Service Society and the Changing Experience of Work", in Cameron L. Macdonald and Carmen Sirianni (eds), *Working in the Service Society*, Philadelphia, PA: Temple University Press, 1996: 1–26.

16 Joan Wallach Scott, *Gender and the Politics of History*, New York, NY: Columbia University Press, 1988: 42. Pei-Chia Lan argues that gendered bodies are disciplined to carry messages about the organization and preserve symbolic domination. Pei-Chia Lan, "The Body as a Contested Terrain for Labor Control: Cosmetics Retailers in Department Stores and Direct Selling", in Rick Baldoz, Charles Koeber, and Philip Kraft (eds), *The Critical Study of Work: Labor, Technology, and Global Production*, Philadelphia, PA: Temple University Press 2001: 83–105.

17 The main character of a classic Greek myth, Pygmalion sculpts an image of the perfect woman from stone; an image which eventually comes to life. The tale is modernized in George Bernard Shaw's *Pygmalion*. In Shaw's version, set in early twentieth century London, a professor of phonetics teaches a low-class, cockney flower-girl to

speak and comport herself like a duchess. See George Bernard Shaw, *Pygmalion: A Romance in Five Acts*, London: Penguin Classics, 2003.

18 Research reveals the diverse and context-specific ways in which hotel workers struggle to position themselves favorably within organizational hierarchies. See Amel Adib and Yvonne Guerrier, "The Interlocking of Gender with Nationality, Race, Ethnicity, and Class: The Narratives of Women in Hotel Work", (2003) 10 *Gender, Work, and Organization*, August: 413–32; Rachel Sherman, "Producing the Superior Self: Strategic Comparison and Symbolic Boundaries among Hotel Workers", (2005) 6 *Ethnography*: 131–58. Adib and Guerrier demonstrate the centrality of gender as it intersects with other categories of identity. Sherman's analysis of hotels in Northern California does not find gender to be a salient factor in the ways workers position themselves and highlights an array of other factors.

19 Lynne A. Haney, *Inventing the Needy: Gender and the Politics of Welfare in Hungary*, Berkeley, CA: University of California Press, 2002; Elizabeth Rudd, "Reconceptualizing Gender in Postsocialist Transformation", (2000) 14 *Gender & Society*, August: 517–39; Wang, Zheng, "Gender, Employment, and Women's Resistance", in Elizabeth Perry and Mark Selden (eds), *Chinese Society: Change, Conflict, and Resistance*, New York, NY: Routledge, 2000: 62–82.

20 Gal, Susan and Gail Kligman, *The Politics of Gender after Socialism: A Comparative-Historical Essay*, Princeton, NJ: Princeton University Press, 2000. Eileen M. Otis, "Reinstating the Family: Gender and the Family-formed Foundations of China's Flexible Labor Market", in Lynne Haney and Lisa Pollard (eds), *Families of a New World: Gender, Politics, and State Development in a Global Context*, New York, NY: Routledge, 2003: 196–216; Dorothy Solinger, *Contesting Citizenship in Urban China: Peasant Migrants, the State, and the Logic of the Market*, Berkeley, CA: University of California Press, 1999.

21 These practices can be viewed as a method to combat the forms of dishonor women workers encountered on the shop floor. In the pre-revolutionary Republican era, women laboring in factories suffered social stigma because the work put them into contact with non-kin males. See Lisa Rofel, *Other Modernities: Gendered Yearnings in China after Socialism*, Berkeley, CA: University of California Press, 1999.

22 By contrast Ching Kwan Lee shows how conceptions of femininity are constructed and used in processes of labor control in reform-era factories. See, Ching Kwan Lee, *Gender and the South China Miracle: Two Worlds of Factory Women*, Berkeley, CA: University of California Press, 1998.

23 Zheng, 2000, op cit.

24 Emily Honig and Gail Hershatter, *Personal Voices: Chinese Women in the 1980s*, Stanford, CA: Stanford University Press, 1988.

25 Some women adorned unisex factory garb by tailoring and belting it as well as adding touches of fabric. Such expressions of female difference might have constituted small acts of resistance. See Hung-yok Ip, "Fashioning Appearances: Feminine Beauty in Chinese Communist Revolutionary Culture", (2003) 29 *Modern China*, July: 329–61.

26 Jean-Francois Billeter, "The System of 'Class-Status'", in Stuart R Schram (ed.), *The Scope of State Power in China*, London: School of Oriental and African Studies, 1985: 127–69; Andrew G. Walder, *Communist Neo-Traditionalism: Work and Authority in Chinese Industry*, Berkeley, CA: University of California Press, 1986.

27 Judith Stacey, *Patriarchy and Socialist Revolution in China*, Berkeley, CA: University of California Press, 1983; Margery Wolf, *Revolution Postponed: Women in Contemporary China*, Stanford, CA: Stanford University Press, 1985.

28 Mayfair Yang, "From Gender Erasure to Gender Difference: State Feminism, Consumer Sexuality, and Women's Public Sphere in China", in Mayfair Mei-hui Yang (ed.), *Spaces of their Own: Women's Public Sphere in Transnational China*, Minneapolis, MN: University of Minnesota Press, 1999: 35–67.

29   Hariet Evans, *Women and Sexuality in China: Female Sexuality and Gender Since 1949*, New York, NY: Continuum, 1997: 135.

30   Honig and Hershatter, 1988, op. cit.; According to Wang Zheng, "Housewife, by definition not a participant in social production, became a scorned urban social category and increasingly a historic relic". See Zheng, 2000, op. cit.: 63.

31   Hariet Evans, 1997, op. cit.

32   Wang Zheng, 2000, op. cit.

33   For example, Yan describes urban restaurants in the Mao era as having, "ill-tempered workers who acted as if they were distributing food to hungry beggars instead of paying customers". See Yan Yunxiang, "Of Hamburgers and Social Space: Consuming Macdonald's in Beijing", in Deborah Davis (ed.), *The Consumer Revolution in Urban China*, Berkeley, CA: University of California Press, 2000: 201–5.

34   Arlie Hochschild defines emotion work as altering or managing emotions so as to produce a particular state of mind in the customer. Emotion work is sold on the market for profit. Hochschild, 1983, op. cit.

35   According to Vogel, "Part of the ethic underlying the concept of comrade is that there is an important way in which everyone in the society is related to every other person … The other side of the concept is that one should not have special relationships with certain people which would interfere with the obligations to anyone else": 55. See Ezra Vogel, "From Friendship to Comradeship: The Change in Personal Relations in Communist China", (1965) 21 *The China Quarterly*: 46–60.

36   "Misses" are also referred to as a pink-collar class. See Zhang Zhen, "Mediating Time: The 'Rice Bowl of Youth' in Fin de Siècle Urban China", (2000) 12 *Public Culture*: January: 93–113.

37   Gail Hershatter, *Dangerous Pleasures: Prostitution and Modernity in Twentieth-Century Shanghai*, Berkeley, CA: University of California Press, 1997.

38   Tiantian Zheng, Chapter 7, this book.

39   Ching Kwan Lee, 1998, op. cit.; Pun Ngai, "Becoming *Dagongmei* (Working Girls): The Politics of Identity and Difference in Reform China", (1999) 42 *The China Journal*, July: 1–19.

40   International Labour Organization, *Facts on the Hotel, Catering and Tourism Industry*, Geneva: International Labour Organization, 2001.

41   In a single year Galaxy invested tens of millions of dollars in award-winning advertising campaigns to build brand identity.

42   On the whole, the hotel industry pays just slightly below the average wage in all sectors in Beijing. The average annual employment earnings in Beijing in 2000 were (in United States dollars) $1,939 for all sectors, compared to $1,920 in the hotel sector. See *China Labor Statistical Yearbook*, Beijing: China Statistics Press, 2001: 95 and 119.

43   Anita Chan, "Chinese Trade Unions and Workplace Relations in State-owned and Joint-venture Enterprises", in Malcolm Warner (ed.), *Changing Workplace Relations in the Chinese Economy*, New York, NY: St. Martin's Press, 2000: 34–56.

44   Walder, 1986, op. cit.

45   Walder, 1986, op. cit.

46   These particular practices are found at many luxury hotels.

47   In fact, evidence suggests that some of China's work units continue redistributive practices in altered form. See Connie Barbara Francis, "Reproduction of Danwei Institutional Features in the Context of China's Market Economy: The Case of Haidian District's High-tech Sector," (1996) 147 *China Quarterly*, September: 839–59.

48   Margaret M. Pearson, *Joint Ventures in the People's Republic of China: The Control of Foreign Direct Investment under Socialism*, Princeton, NJ: Princeton University Press, 1992).

49   Managers can file formal complaints, or "misconduct slips" in worker dossiers. However, the human resources department discourages the use of formal mechanisms for discipline.

50 I do not claim that BT customers do not engage sex workers. But when they do so, they are required to be extremely discreet.

51 I felt extremely uncomfortable in this role and was reluctant to make judgments that would affect the future of potential workers. Hence, I gave every candidate the highest score.

52 The personnel manager described her "wild long hair and big earrings", concluding that she was "too sexy".

53 A psychologist, Abraham Maslow described human motivation by reference to a hierarchy of needs. According to Maslow, more basic social and material needs lower in the hierarchy must be satisfied in order to meet higher-ranking "growth" needs, which lead to the realization of human potential and self-fulfillment. See Abraham Maslow, "A Theory of Human Motivation", (1943) 50 *Psychological Review*: 370–96.

54 The extensive effort to alter workers' dispositions suggests that in some service contexts, consumption and production do not occur entirely simultaneously. In the present case service requires substantial "behind the scenes" work to alter workers' bodily dispositions. Consumption on the "frontline" of service work can involve substantial "production" of workers selves in training processes which occur behind the scenes of the service workplace.

55 Smith finds that positive valuations of interpersonal skills acquired on the job can be a key component of eliciting worker cooperation and cannot be understood outside of the race, class, and gender identities of workers. See Vicki Smith, *Across the Great Divide: Risk, Uncertainty, and Opportunity in Flexible Workplaces*, Ithaca, NY: Cornell/ILR Press, 2001.

56 Leidner finds that forms of routinization can protect workers from customers by limiting interactions to a set of pre-formulated scripts. Giving face can have similar effects by linking service to a set of cultural scripts for managing hierarchical interactions. See Leidner, 1993, op. cit.

57 For a discussion of the performative dimensions of class, see Julie Bettie, *Women without Class: Girls, Race, and Identity*, Berkeley, CA: University of California Press, 2003.

58 Hochschild, 1983, op. cit.

59 Braverman found that work systems undergoing rationalization processes are characterized by the increasing separation of the conception of the labor process from its execution. See Harry Braverman, *Labor and Monopoly Capital: The Degradation of Work in the Twentieth Century*, New York, NY: Monthly Review Press, 1975.

60 Barbara A. Gutek *et al.*, 2000, op. cit.

61 According to Michele Lamont, symbolic boundaries are a process of identity construction that positions individuals and groups within social and moral hierarchies. See Michele Lamont, *The Dignity of Working Men*, Cambridge, MA: Harvard University Press, 2000. Lamont does not focus on gender processes involved in the formation of symbolic boundaries, nor does the work examine how boundaries are constructed within organizational practices.

62 Gil Eyal, Ivan Szelenyi, and Eleanor R. Townsley, *Making Capitalism Without Capitalists: Class Formation and Elite Struggles in Post-Communist Central Europe*, London: Verso, 1999.

7 From peasant women to bar hostesses

An ethnography of China's karaoke sex industry

Tiantian Zheng

Introduction

The heavy thud of techno-music drums rumbles from the entrance of a karaoke bar. Three tall and beautiful young women dressed in identical red cheongsams bow elegantly to all entering customers and usher them inside the bar. The entryway spills out into an expansive lobby of glossy marble and ceiling-high mirrors. Over 100 seductively dressed women are gathered on the left side of the lobby. They sit on three rows of benches, like the audience at an invisible performance. In fact, however, they themselves are the ones being observed. A camera installed on the ceiling provides a live feed to monitors installed inside each private room. Customers can select their escorts from the comfort of couches in these suites. Madams will bring these selected escorts to the customers' private rooms for their companions of the night. The stairs leading to the private rooms on upper floors are lined with two teams of waitresses, all of the same height and with the same hair style, dressed in the same dark embroidered mini skirts, their breasts half exposed and their hips scarcely covered. They greet customers in chorus, "Good evening!".

The upper stories are divided into five sections (A, B, C, D, E) of 10 karaoke rooms each. A dressing room for hostesses also serves as a hideout during police raids. None of the activities inside the karaoke rooms can be seen from the outside. Each karaoke room is equipped with a complete set of karaoke equipment, including a 29-inch TV set that continuously plays excerpts from erotic Western videos. Each karaoke room is provided with an air-conditioner, rosewood furniture, beautiful window drapes, wallpaper, carpeting, magnificent dim ceiling lights, a big couch, and an end table. There is a space between the TV and the end table where clients can dance with hostesses. They can dance either to each other's singing or to the dance music chosen from a song booklet. The couch can be unfolded into a bed at the request of clients. Many karaoke rooms have adjunct secret bedrooms separated by a curtain camouflaged in the same texture and color as the wallpaper. This is designed to prevent discovery in case of a police raid.

In the dimly lit karaoke room, an 18-year-old hostess was sitting next to her client, singing a song titled "Why Do You Love Other Women Behind my Back?"

(*weishenmo ni beizhe wo ai bieren*)" in a provocative voice. As she sang, her fingers were nestled in her client's crotch, she fondled him, leaned her whole body over him, and coquettishly asked him, "My husband (*laogong*), why do you make love to other women behind my back?".

These paragraphs describe an upscale karaoke bar, one of the three principal karaoke bars where I conducted my research in the port city of Dalian, in Liaoning Province. In 1984, following the promising results of more liberal economic policies in Shenzhen, Zhuhai, Shantou, and Xiamen, the State Council granted Dalian the status of "special economic zone" (SEZ) in 1984. By the late 1990s, municipal propaganda boasted that Dalian had developed into the "Hong Kong of the North", the "International Transportation Hinge", an "Advanced Industrial Base", a "Modern Environmental City", and the "Center of Finance, Trade, and Tourism in Northeast Asia".[1]

The rapid growth of the city from a fishing village in the nineteenth century to a metropolis with a population of 5,000,000[2] has made Dalian a magnet for labor migrants. By 1998, the most conservative estimate placed the number of the floating population in Dalian at around 300,000.[3] Institutional – that is, household registration policy – and social discrimination force the vast majority of these migrants into the lowest rung of the labor market. Migrants commonly work as construction workers, garbage collectors, restaurant waitresses, domestic maids, factory workers, and bar hostesses.

A substantial fraction of female migrants find employment in Dalian's booming sex industry. Karaoke bars can be found almost every few steps throughout the whole city. Jian Ping, a reporter for the *New Weekly* magazine,[4] calls the whole city "a gigantic sauna salon or KTV bar".[5] According to one of the city's police chiefs, Dalian is currently home to 4,000 nightclubs, saunas, and KTV bars. This same police chief estimated that, as of 2001, 80 percent of the total population of migrant women works as hostesses in the nightclub industry.[6] The ratio provided by the police chief sounds astounding. He might be exaggerating a little, but his figure suggests that a high percentage of migrant women work as bar hostesses.

China's sex industry emerged in the wake of economic reforms. During the Mao era, prostitutes were sent to labor camps for education. In 1958, the CCP proudly declared to the world that prostitution had been eradicated, and this success was a symbol of China's transformation into a modern nation.[7] Since the economic reform of 1978, the state's more lenient stance has opened the way for the re-emergence of nightclubs and other leisure sites. In order to avoid any residual negative connotations left over from the Mao era, nightclubs in the current post-Mao period are referred to as karaoke bars, KTV plazas, or *liange ting* (literally, "singing practice halls"). Visitors to these bars are mainly middle-aged businessmen, male government officials, entrepreneurs, the nouveau riche, policemen, and foreign investors. Clients can partake of the services offered by the hostesses and at the same time cement social ties (*ying chou*) or *guanxi* (literally, relationships) with their business partners or government officials. Hostesses – mainly rural migrant women – play an indispensable role in the rituals of these male-centered worlds of business and politics.[8]

The companions or hostesses are referred to in Chinese as "sanpei xiaojie", literally young women who accompany men in three ways – generally understood to include varying combinations of alcohol consumption, dancing, singing, and sexual services. Generally between the ages of 17 and 23, these hostesses provide services that typically include drinking, singing, dancing, playing games, flirting, chatting, and caressing. Beyond the standard service package, some hostesses offer sexual services for an additional fee. Their monthly income ranges from the lowest of 6,000 yuan to tens of thousands of yuan. Hostesses first emerged in modest numbers at the end of the 1980s. Their numbers expanded rapidly in the mid-1990s as karaoke bars became favored sites, not just for male recreation, but also for networking between male businessmen and the local political elites.[9] It was roughly estimated that in 1991, more than 800,000 hostesses were involved in sex work.[10] Karaoke bars and the hostesses they employ are controlled and regulated by the state at the same time that they are used by the state and its agents, many of whom comprise the ranks of the karaoke-bar customer base.

Out of the 200 hostesses I worked with, only four were natives of Dalian. Most of the others came from rural villages in other parts of China, mainly from the northeast. During my research, I encountered several laid-off urban female workers who were married and in their thirties. It did not take them long to realize that they had entered a market too competitive for them. The younger rural women were much more favored by the clients. Seldom chosen by the clients, the urban laid-off women eventually disappeared. Rural migrant hostesses were extremely averse to exposing their rural origins. At the beginning of my field research, they reported that they were from large metropolitan cities, such as Dalian, Shanghai, and Anshan. It was only after we had become close friends that they confided to me that actually, they were from rural areas on the outskirts of these cities.

Erotic services take place in various establishments that include karaoke bars, hotels, saunas, hair salons, disco and other dance halls, small roadside restaurants, parks, movie houses, and video rooms. Among these establishments, karaoke bars demand the most stringent criteria for the women's height, facial beauty, figure, and such social skills as singing, dancing, flirting, drinking, and conversation. Unlike what is provided by many other establishments, where only intercourse is offered, karaoke-bar hostesses' services are far more encompassing. Only a few of the karaoke-bar hostesses would accept strangers' requests for intercourse, for which they charge twice as much as is charged in many other environments except for a few five-star hotels targeted at Japanese clients. Because only the beautiful and skilled can be chosen as company for the night, numerous young women could not survive in the karaoke bar and were thus forced to move to less desirable workplaces, such as sauna salons.

Karaoke-bar hostesses often expressed their contempt of women in other establishments whose work involves nothing but sex. At one time, when all sauna bars were closed in Dalian because of a local water shortage, sauna hostesses flocked to karaoke bars. The hostesses commented to each other in low voices, "Look at their gray faces! It's from daily sex work [*dapao*]". Sauna hostesses told me that they could not compete with the karaoke hostesses because "here clients are too particular about your looks and figure. It's different from sauna bars. In sauna bars, appearance is not that important because clients' goal is simply to have sex [*dapao*]". Karaoke-bar hostesses are aware of this difference. They rate their own status second only to foreign hostesses – French and Russian – in renowned hotels.

This chapter explores hostesses' material livelihood in the exploitative labor relations with violent gangs, abusive bosses, madams, and state agents, and the ways workers come to terms with their sex work. I argue that hostessing is these hostesses' only to bid for equal status with urbanites. It is their answer to, and an act of defiance against, the rural-urban dualistic society. This chapter unfolds in five parts. First, I discuss my fieldwork in Dalian. Second, I focus on the reasons for hostesses' entry into karaoke bars. Third, I contextualize hostesses' lived experiences in the material and power structures of the karaoke-bar sex industry. Fourth, I discuss hostesses' subjective understandings of sex work. In the last section, I conclude the chapter by exploring hostesses' future plans and aspirations.

Fieldwork

The argument developed in this chapter is based on some 20 months of fieldwork, between 1999 and 2002, in Dalian. My research sample includes approximately 200 bar hostesses in ten karaoke bars. However, I was intensively involved with three karaoke bars in particular, respectively categorized as high, middle, and lower class. The criterion of classification is based on the location of the bar, its organization and management, the level of the hostesses' physical attractiveness, and consumption standards. In this chapter, I mainly focus on the low-level karaoke bar, although I constantly draw on the other two karaoke bars as well. I was introduced to the karaoke bars by a friend who is an official. For a number of reasons, my initial attempt to interact with hostesses was not very successful. They did not have time to listen to me because their eyes were all fixated on each entering client, and they concentrated on the selection process (*shitai* – try the stage). Furthermore, my cultural style marked me as an outsider. They referred to me as "glasses" and "a college student". They ridiculed my student attire, my glasses, and my inability to understand or participate in their sex talk and jokes, and they refused to admit me to their circle. They did not believe in my ability to understand their lives, especially their inner turmoil, simply because I was not "in their shoes". They were also extremely wary of their own security from assaults by the police, hooligans, and others in their dangerous environment. They were also cautious in dealing with each other because any hostess might have some network with VIPs in the city that might harm them. For instance, some hostesses were kept as "spy hostesses" by some local police or officials for self-protection. They might report on other hostesses' prostitution and have these hostesses incarcerated or severely fined. Each hostess therefore used a fake name, a fake hometown, and a fake personal story. To overcome these barriers, I decided to spend more time with the hostesses. I handed in the rooming fees to the bar owner and lived with the hostesses in the karaoke bars. From then on, I was intensely involved in every aspect of their lives. A typical day in the field was as follows. We got up around three o'clock in the afternoon and ordered a light meal from a nearby restaurant. The remainder of the afternoon was free for shopping or visiting the beauty parlor. We ordered dinner at around six o'clock. Around that time, the first customers would begin to trickle into the bar. While waiting to be chosen, we sat in the bar lobby watching video compact disks (VCDs) or TV and chatting. Around midnight, we ordered breakfast and went to bed between two and three in the morning.

It was not my initial intention to research hostess–client dynamics by directly servicing clients as a hostess. However, objective circumstances mandated that I wait on clients. My personal profile fits within the range of hostesses' typical characteristics. I am Chinese and female. My fieldwork was conducted when I was 28 and 29 years old, which put me in the "autumn" years of a hostess's career path. This meant that a customer who saw me sitting in the KTV bar lounge would naturally assume that I was a hostess. I was also obliged to minimize the disruption of my research on the bar's normal business operations. According to KTV bar convention, a hostess can legitimately refuse to perform genital or oral sex acts with her customer. Although refusal can and often does spark conflicts between hostesses and clients, these incidents are considered a normal part of business. For a hostess to refuse to wait on a customer, however, is simply unheard of. This meant that if a customer chose me to wait on him, it would have been very difficult for me to refuse.

To avoid clashes with customers, I took certain precautions. I nevertheless became embroiled in several conflicts with customers. This was especially true during my fieldwork in a low-tier bar that is located in Dalian's crime-plagued red light district. Living in the karaoke bars, hostesses and I had to maintain constant vigilance against police raids and attacks by thugs from competing bars in the city – including other bar owners and some frequent clients. At night, three hostesses and I slept on the couches in one of the private rooms rented by customers during operating hours. Every morning before going to sleep, we pushed a couch against the door in case gangsters attempted to break in. At times of danger, we held our breath and turned down the lights, making the room look unoccupied. We escaped danger several times. Experience of common adversity gradually brought us together.

It took the combined efforts of bar owners, bouncers, and hostesses to keep me out of harm's way. I am indebted to them for their advice on safety measures and, at crucial moments, their direct intervention. To extricate me from precarious situations, owners and bouncers incurred the wrath of more than one irate customer, whose outbursts disturbed regular business operations. Hostesses also expended attention and energy that they would have otherwise spent on profit-making matters in order to look after my well-being. Without their sacrifices, my research in the bars would have been too dangerous to continue.

Entry into karaoke bar sex industry

Hostessing was by no means the first job for the hostesses. Many started out in factories, restaurants, and hotels as workers or waitresses. Some entered hostessing because late payment and severe deduction in wages put them in unbearable financial straits. Others went through the torture of abandonment and rape in the urban work environment. Most of them walked into the karaoke bars on their own initiative, but some were introduced by relatives or family members. Being a karaoke bar hostess did not demand any educational background. In my research sample, a majority of the hostesses graduated from elementary or junior high school. Only a handful went to high school and then failed the college entrance exam. All of them, however, had to meet four requirements: they had to have beautiful facial features and an attractive figure, be well dressed, be able to consume a great deal of alcohol, and be open to sexual variants. As I learned from the hostesses, each of them had to go through a transitional period at the beginning, when they spent all night crying before going to work with a smile. Wu said to me, "During the first week, I could not sleep. I spent night after night in tears. I started writing daily journals. I wrote down all the bitter feelings. I asked myself, if other people can do it [hostessing], why can't I? Is the money not good? [*qian bu hao hua ma*]?".

Wu migrated to a nearby city to work in a plastics factory. She found herself working three months without being paid. At the end of the third month, she could not afford to buy any food or drink. Later, she fell seriously ill and was hospitalized. She said, "Suffering from a high fever, I was given a transfusion in the hospital. I was by myself in the hospital, lying in bed. Nobody from work came to see me. I was holding the transfusion bottle with my left hand, trying to hang it onto the hook above my head. But I could not reach it. I was trying and trying, but still I could not reach it. How I wished someone were beside me – I did not ask for more. Just handing me a cup of water would have been more than enough! But there was nobody – only me. I was crying and crying. I was sick from work, yet nobody came to help me".

Because Wu was not paid a penny by the factory during these three months, she had to borrow money to pay her living expenses and her hospital bill. She finally walked into a karaoke bar. She said, "I have no other way to earn money but to make it from urban men". After working in the karaoke bar for a year, Wu not only helped pay her family back, but also sent over 5,000 yuan to cover her mother's hospital bill. When I visited Wu's home in Jilin province, Wu's mother told me, "Wu by herself has been sustaining the six-person family over these years". Wu knows that she would never have accomplished this feat if she had stayed at the factory that never paid her.

If hostessing is such a profitable profession, why is it young women's last choice? Why is it chosen only in the situation of greatest helplessness? What is it like to work in the karaoke bar sex industry? How is this money earned? The moment when they walk into the karaoke bars, what is waiting for the prospective hostesses? Once they are bar hostesses, what is their future? To answer these questions, we will have to start from the political history of the karaoke-bar sex industry in Dalian.

Karaoke bar industry

Anti-vice campaign

In 1984 the first dance hall appeared in Dalian. It featured a band of six singers and had a capacity of 300.[11] It was not until 1988 that the first karaoke bar emerged. Named "Tokyo 898", the bar was financed by a Japanese businessman and run as a Sino–Japanese joint venture. It is said that the bar's karaoke equipment was imported, brand-new, from Japan – an almost unheard-of extravagance at that time in China's economic development. Customers of the bar included foreign travelers and sailors, government officials, and the nouveaux riches.

After 1988, new karaoke bars mushroomed throughout the city. They have become the most fashionable male recreational and commercial activity. They are closely associated with Western audio and video technology, splendid exterior and interior furnishings, neon lights, high prices, and beautiful hostesses. Drastically different from the previous dance halls, which were organized by work unit, karaoke bars aroused tremendous social curiosity. They suit rich people's desire to experience a "modern" form of consumption, display their vocal talents, and display power and wealth. Patronizing luxurious karaoke bars became a lifestyle, a modern and prestigious symbol, often only afforded by such wealthy clients as foreigners, officials, and local nouveaux riche. Blue-collar urban men and migrant workers occasionally visit low-tier karaoke bars to imitate this life style.

Beginning in 1989, with the appearance of karaoke bars, the state launched periodical nationwide anti-vice campaigns to ensure "security and state control". The campaigns are aimed at "cultural purification" and "spiritual civilization". The "erotic company" of hostesses, pornographic TV shows, erotic performances, and prostitution within karaoke bars are condemned as "cultural trash" that "destabilize state rule and the socialist system". Restrictions stop short of an outright ban; rather, they intend to bring KTV bars into line with state-defined socialist culture. The government's charges against KTV bars are many.

First, KTV bars fail to live up to the standard of socialist business ethics. Unlike capitalism's exploitation of the working masses in the pursuit of riches, the driving force behind the socialist market is not the profit motive but rather dedication – to the party, nation, and people. Bar owners, however, are accused of ripping off customers by levying hidden costs and purposefully misrepresenting the price of goods and services. What is more, they use erotic services to prey on men's weaknesses and attract more business. All these behaviors exhibit an overemphasis on money making to the detriment of the socialist market's stability and development.

Second, the "erotic service" (*seqing peishi*) found in karaoke bars goes against "socialist spiritual civilization". The exchange of sexual services for money is an "ugly social phenomenon" associated with capitalism and should be wiped out to maintain a healthy socialist cultural environment and "civilized consumption".

Third, unlike the "healthy", collective recreational activities promoted by the government, karaoke-bar entertainment is centered on the individual. Karaoke is seen as the antithesis of healthy pastimes.

Four, the extravagance of karaoke bars clashes with the government's goal to downplay social difference. Since economic reforms, Chinese society has witnessed a tremendous growth in economic disparities. Karaoke bars highlight these trends by encouraging excessive and conspicuous consumption as way to show off wealth and social status.[12]

The main responsibility for administering state policy regarding karaoke bars is divided between the Bureau of Culture (BC) and the Public Security Bureau (PSB). These two agencies respectively represent the government's dual strategy of soft and hard administrative measures. The Bureau of Culture is responsible for ensuring that karaoke bars are managed according to socialist standards of civility and morality. It accomplishes this task through a variety of administrative and regulatory measures. First, BC maintains detailed records on bars' business location, name, proprietor, exterior and interior design, audio and video machines, and other information. Second, strict approval procedures were introduced to reduce the number of karaoke bars. Third, bar owners are required to attend monthly classes organized by the Bureau of Culture to study state policy and law. Those achieving high test-scores are awarded "Civilized Karaoke Bar" plaques that can be displayed inside their bars.[13] Fourth, karaoke bars should have "Chinese" and socialist characteristics. In particular, they should provide mainland Mandarin songs, "healthy and inspiring" revolutionary songs, Chinese-style wallpaper, Chinese paintings, Chinese-style bar names, and Chinese food and snacks. Lurking not far behind these regulations is a palpable sense of crisis induced by the idea that Western influences have begun to erode Chinese culture. As a BC official explained to me: "The imported Western culture in China is like an aircraft carrier – high quality, durable and powerful. Chinese culture, however, resembles a small sampan, only able to float a hundred miles. We need to develop a singing-and-dancing business with Chinese characteristics to attack the foreign cultural market in China".

PSB serves as an "Iron Great Wall" (*gangtie changcheng*), providing the muscle behind state policy. The main vehicle for PSB intervention is the anti-pornography campaign (*saohuang dafei*), itself a part of a wider comprehensive attack on social deviance known as "crackdowns" (*yanda* – literally, to strike severely). These campaigns last for spurts of three months at a time to be repeated three times a year, strategically centering on important holidays – National Day and Army Day – and events – the APEC conference. Crackdowns target a potpourri of social ills, ranging from unlicensed video game arcades – said to corrupt the minds of youth – to undocumented rural migrants – said to disrupt urban management.

The combination of prostitution and pornography is a mainstay in the list of crackdown targets. It covers pornographic media – magazines, laser discs – and performances – striptease. The behavior that receives the most organizational resources and manpower, however, is the "erotic services" conducted in KTV bars and other commercial establishments – saunas and hair salons. PSB employs a complex system of raids to attack karaoke bars. The techniques are self-described as "guerrilla warfare" (*da youji*) in reference to the heroic efforts of the Communist revolutionaries against the Japanese invaders and nationalists. Raids are divided into several types, including: "regular raids and shock raids, timed raids and random raids, systematic raids and block raids, daytime raids and night raids". Those PSB units and individuals that perform well – measured in the number of arrested hostesses and amount of fines levied – receive high honors and cash bonuses from their municipal government.

Impact on hostesses

Local officials

State policy is not unproblematically translated into reality. The complex interactions between sex industry participants on the one hand and state agents on the other lead to a gap between the "theory" of policy and the "practice" of enforcement. State policy is distorted and even derailed by the self-seeking behavior of local officials. Karaoke bars are an important source of extralegal income. As one PSB official candidly remarked, "Karaoke bars and hostesses are our sources of livelihood. We basically cannot live without them". Because these officials have the arbitrary power to arrest and fine the hostesses, hostesses are extremely apprehensive when they are chosen by an official. In such instances, they must obey the officials' demands, including sexual services.

Officials extract economic benefits from karaoke bars through a combination of bribes and fines. State policy is hijacked in the service of officials' personal economic interests, but local officials' exploitation of hostesses is not limited to economic benefits. PSB officials maintain a group of "spy hostesses" (*xiaojie jianxi*) who report on bar conditions as well as acting as these officials' personal harem. In exchange for their services, hostesses gain immunity from police sanctions. Hostesses allow corrupt officials to get rich, contribute to regional economic development, and enhance officials' political career advancement. There seems to be substantial pressures that push local government into at least tolerating if not absolutely embracing the karaoke-bar sex industry. I was told that a leader of a sub-region had turned the area into what became heralded as the "largest pornographic sub-region in the province". He built an extravagant mansion and hired hostesses to entertain visiting officials. His "brilliant achievements" eventually satisfied his superiors and gained him high awards, reputation, and promotion.

Bar owners

While local officials are manipulating state policy to exploit bar owners and hostesses for their personal gain, bar owners have their own strategies. The owners I worked for improvised creative maneuvers to counter local officials.

The owner of the upscale bar – one of three karaoke bars in which I conducted fieldwork – was a well-known local gangster. His karaoke bar opened in 1998 and since then, has been the most prosperous bar in the city of Dalian, housing over 100 hostesses. I came to this karaoke bar in June 1999. Just beginning my research, I did not know anything about the anti-vice campaign until July 1, the anniversary of the birth of the Communist Party. I went to work in the evening as usual. I was very surprised to find that all the hostesses' seats were unoccupied – only two hostesses came to work.[14] Not having the faintest idea what was going on, I was immediately led by the madam to the dressing room upstairs and advised to hide there instead of waiting in the hall downstairs. The madam told us to tell whoever saw us that we were salesladies selling beer here. Only after the madam left did I learn from the hostesses that an anti-vice campaign started in that month and that police would be raiding this place some time that night. Police raids meant that any hostesses in sight would be taken in and arrested. I was told that once you ended up in the police station, it took thousands of yuan to get out. The other two hostesses were in the same situation as I was – all newcomers and completely ignorant about this event. I was very frightened because I did not have a temporary-resident card, and my passport would definitely get me in trouble.[15] Luckily, when a couple of men – policemen wearing civilian clothes – came in and asked us a few questions that night, our answer that we were selling beer worked, to my surprise. Later I learned from the madam that our escape was due to the fact that the owner had paid off these policemen. During the last few days of the campaign months, I was living with another hostess. At midnight each night, when we took a taxi home from the bar, she instructed me to bend over and hide under the back seats to avoid being seen by policemen. She told me that during the campaign months, numerous policemen patrolled the streets looking for bar hostesses. In China, hostesses fall into a gray area – although the law does not clearly identify them as either illegal or legal, in everyday practice, it is recognized that "hostesses" are "sex workers" who provide illegal erotic services and hence, are the major object of anti-vice campaigns.

The bar owner, furious at the loss of business and local officials' restrictions, asked the madam to summon 130 hostesses to a meeting. He expressed his anger and antagonism toward the "unreasonable people working in the government" and listed his tactics to cope with the state policy. Angry as the bar owner was, he utilized non-confrontational maneuvers – that is, converting illegal bar hostesses into legal employees through shifts of title, dress, identity, work sections, and so on. Such a strategy not only left him some leverage at this critical point of the political campaign, but also allowed him to impose more severe regulations and discipline on the hostesses, who used to operate in a laissez-faire manner.

According to a city official, 1995 marked a change in relations between hostesses and bar owners from the contract system to an exploitative system. Before the police crackdown in 1995, hostesses were hired by the hundreds on contracts with bar bosses. According to the contract, hostesses received fees from the customers for their services. In addition, bar owners awarded them a percentage of the customers' bills. This contract system was brought to an end in 1995. To explain this change, we must start in the early 1980s.

With the rise in popularity of karaoke bars in Dalian, a red-light district sprang up in the center of the Zhongshan district. At some time around the end of the 1980s and in the early 1990s, a number of karaoke bars were opened on Stalin Road. By all indications, the scope of business must have been considerable. Hostesses were recruited by the hundreds. Every night they scoured the city's seaport for tourists and brought them back to the bars to engage them in sexual activities. During this period, bars and hostesses prospered.

One morning in 1994, a foreigner was seen running out of the area wearing only his underwear. A group of Chinese men followed him, shouting curses and flourishing clubs high in the air. It was said that the foreigner could not afford the tab for the previous night's sexual encounter. Managing to escape with his life, the foreigner subsequently brought charges against the bar's proprietor for exploiting him. The matter quickly escalated into an international conflict between the two affected embassies. The incident even made front-page headlines in the *Hong Kong Gazette* (*Ta Kung Pao*) in an article titled, "Dalian Red-Light District on Stalin Road".

Fearing that the image of the socialist regime would be tarnished by the scandal, the CCP Central Committee took immediate action by ordering that the area be cleaned up. After overcoming tremendous difficulties in breaking up patron–client ties between local officials and bar owners, the police finally cracked down in 1995.[16] To erase the global and national memory of the incident, the name of the street was changed from Stalin Road to People's Road.

This extreme police crackdown disrupted the previous system by which the bars operated and brought an end to the contract system and the percentage award from bar owners. Ever since, bar hostesses and owners have been under the strict control of local government. Owners view themselves no longer as dependents but as the saviors of the hostesses because they housed the hostesses for security and offered jobs. Since 1995, owners have required hostesses to turn in 10 percent of their fees to them.

In the particular upscale karaoke bar where I conducted research, during the anti-vice campaign, the owner extracted additional profit from the hostesses by charging more for their uniforms than they were actually worth. He also seized this chance to record every hostess' biological data. He asked all the hostesses to hand in their duplicate hometown IDs and Dalian temporary residence cards (TRC). He urged those who had not yet purchased or renewed their TRC to do so quickly. He claimed that he would compile a book with a record of their pictures, names, and photocopied TRCs, through which hostesses would be transformed into formal employees working as waitresses. He also effectively controlled their mobility and behaviors. Prior to the crackdown, hostesses were brought to any karaoke room for selection. After the crackdown, hostesses were grouped in tens and assigned to different sections of the bar – 10 karaoke rooms in each section. Instead of standing together in the entrance hall, hostesses now only gathered at their designated sections, waiting to be chosen. Every hostess was required to wear the uniform dress with a name card on her chest, in different colors for different sections. Hostesses had to report to the directors (madams) if they were going outside the bar (*chutai*: offer sexual services in hotels) with clients. They were ordered to be present at the bar at precisely 7:30 p.m. every day and not leave until 12 a.m. unless they went out with clients. Hostesses coming late or leaving early were fined 600 yuan. They had to request leave or a night off from the director, a request that, in principle, was not granted. The bar owner also demanded that hostesses' walking and speaking manner and singing skills be trained and disciplined. All these new demands, controls, and restrictions on hostesses were produced at this moment of conflict between bar owners and officials. The bar owner ensured the prosperity of his business by manipulating hostesses and maneuvering ways around state policy.

Local implementation of the state's anti-vice policy fails to reach the propagated objective of eliminating prostitution; it only aggravates hostesses' working conditions. Police raids of karaoke-bar hostesses make them legally and socially vulnerable. Hostesses' illegal identity forces them to face an exploitative, risky, and violent working environment. If some clients were to disclose their sexual services to the police, they would be subject to extreme humiliation, arrest, heavy fines, and incarceration. Because of this potentially horrifying outcome, hostesses do not disclose their real identity, and this ruse makes it easier for men to be violent towards them and even to murder them. It was reported that in the city of Shenyang, more than 100 hostesses were murdered in 1999.[17] In Dalian, murdered hostesses' bodies were found on the street, but the police could not identify them.[18] When I accompanied my best hostess friend, Wu, to her hometown, I asked her mother if she was worried about Wu's safety in Dalian. At my question, her mother's face sank with distress and torment. She kept silent for a long time before plucking up the strength to tell me that she had believed that Wu had been murdered in Dalian. She said, "I did not hear from her for three months. She did not call me. I did not have her phone number ... I really thought she was murdered. You know, it's so common in Dalian. I always heard the news about hostesses' dead bodies found there. I believed Wu was one of them. I was worried sick. I got so sick that I couldn't get up. I thought I was never going to see her again".

Violence

In the upscale bar, the main task of the security guards in green pseudo-military uniforms was to keep the hostesses from leaving before midnight, ensure that clients pay hostesses' tips, and maintain bar security. Occasionally, a team of security guards rushed upstairs like soldiers to quell fights in the karaoke rooms. The suppression of disturbances itself always involved violence and blood. Unarmed or armed – with beer bottles, knives, and glass – fights between drunken clients and between clients and hostesses were daily occurrences. At times, hostesses came downstairs, crying from their injuries: their legs, arms, and breasts black and blue from the hard pinches of some clients. Some hostesses chose to endure whatever abuse they are subjected to, but some opted to quit and, consequently, received no tips for the time they had put in. Those who clenched their teeth to see it through with big bright smiles held back their tears and complaints for later, when they sent off the clients and returned to the crowd of idle hostesses.

The low-class bar "Romance Dream" is located in the crime-plagued red-light district. The staff includes three multifunctional waiters – madams/doormen/janitors – two bar managers, approximately 27 hostesses, and a barkeep/security guard (*kan changzi de*). As with the high- and medium-level bars, blood ties link the bar proprietor and management into a relatively cohesive group. Each bar on this street has to hire a thug as the barkeep. This barkeep has to be a good fighter. Otherwise, the bar will be forced to close down as a consequence of harassment by roaming gangsters and thugs who roamed the streets. During my research in the bar, I witnessed numerous bloody fights between the barkeep, Bing, and bar waiters and gangsters, clients, and passers-by. I saw Bing and waiters throw heavy stones and chairs at clients and at the heads of some passers-by until blood streamed down their heads onto their faces. The bar owner told me that Bing, after having killed and severely injured many men in previous fights, was once sentenced to death. The bar owner spent a great deal of money finally to get Bing out of prison before hiring him as the bar guard. The mere presence of Bing in the bar kept many gangsters and thugs away. According to the owner, if Bing were not in the bar, it would definitely be a disaster: all of the hostesses would flee in fear, and everything would be plundered by gangsters. She entrusted me to Bing and the bar managers to look after my safety.

Gangsters and other bar owners often came to visit. They are all local. When they saw pretty hostesses, they dragged them upstairs and raped them. When they saw less pretty hostesses, they slapped their faces and beat them up. Hostesses were extremely apprehensive about some of the toughest gangsters and thugs. They would run as fast as they could to escape them. Once I fled along with the other hostesses. We escaped by climbing onto the overpass built over the bars, losing our shoes and cutting our feet in the process. It was a very unpleasant experience. Most of the bar hostesses have been raped at least once by gangsters. Twice the gangsters came in and started to pull me into a karaoke room. Luckily, they were stopped by Bing and the bar managers, who said, "She is not a hostess here. She is my friend". That assurance saved me from imminent danger, but the lingering fear remained.

To protect themselves, almost all the hostesses were connected with one or two street gangsters to gain protection. When a gangster came in, the hostess who was connected with him or to a thug in his group did not need to escape. My best friend, Wu, did not like the bar bouncer of a neighboring bar, but he favored her strongly. Wu had to develop a relationship with him. She told me, "In my home town, nobody dares to touch me because I have a wide network of friends. It's so different here. Here I don't have anyone. No one cares if I am bullied. He is a thug, and he is local. I have to be good to him. I need someone to turn to when I encounter trouble on this street". When Wu was harassed by someone in a different gangster group or by drunken clients, she would call the barkeep for help. On a couple of occasions, the barkeep, upon Wu's call, led a few gangsters into the bar to beat up the drunken client. Wu also hooked up with a bar owner in the city. She told me that these were the key people she turned to when she needed help. Like Wu, other hostesses were connected with a bar owner, a bouncer, or a skilled street fighter. They frequently joked, "We hostesses are relatives of the underworld".

An exploitative environment

Hostesses are expected to encourage customers in their consumption of beer, hard liquor, and snacks to boost bar revenues. Known as the minimum charge, these requirements create an onerous burden for hostesses. Hostesses are held responsible for ensuring that customers' expenditures reach the mandated level. To stimulate customers' consumption, hostesses themselves have to consume continuously, especially alcohol. This problem is especially pronounced in the upper-level bar, where the minimum charge is set at 400 yuan. The bathroom is always full of hostesses vomiting into the toilet before returning to their clients to continue drinking. Because of this daily alcohol overdose, most hostesses not only put on weight – which leads to other self-destructive weight-loss practices – but also develop stomach problems that, in severe cases, result in hospitalization.

Madam

In the upscale bar, three madams manage and discipline the hostesses. They treat hostesses violently. Once when I was sitting in the dressing room, a hostess came in to change into slacks because her client had been pinching her legs. While she was changing, a madam came in, looking furious. She slapped the young woman's face very hard and hit her in the head with her big interphone, yelling at her, "Don't you know that your client is looking for you? Why are you hiding here? I have looked for you everywhere! I am ordering you to go back to your client at once!". The poor girl tried to dodge the madam's blows as her face reddened from the madam's slaps. In an anguished voice, she agreed, "Sure, sure, I will go back right away". Fleeing the madam's blows and harsh words, she quickly slipped out of the room.

The three madams, ranging in age from 35 to 39 – "heads of the group" (*lingban*) – call on a team of hostesses and lead them into clients' karaoke rooms for selection by the client. The hostesses stated that the whole process depends on whether the madam presents you to the clients or not. Clients often look for a hostess who has a beautiful body and face, big breasts, who is able to drink, who can sing English songs, who is the best at singing and dancing, and so on. After inquiring about their preferences, the madams either strongly recommend several hostesses who "most closely fit their preferences" or directly push some hostesses to those clients' sides. It is therefore very important for a hostess to bribe one of the madams. Once I saw a hostess secretly handing 400 yuan to a madam at the entrance gate. The latter accepted it after feigning refusal several times. If the hostess does not bribe the madam, the madam will not call on that hostess nor recommend or promote her to the clients. Eventually the hostess is left with minimal chances to be chosen.

Each time hostesses "sit on the stage" (*shangtai* – selected by the clients as their companions of the night) they receive a minimum tip of 200 yuan from the clients, 20 yuan of which is paid to the bar as the "stage fee" (*taifei*). If hostesses go off stage (*chutai* – offer sexual services), the minimum tip is 400 yuan, and hostesses pay 50 yuan for the "out-of-the-stage fee". In each karaoke room, madams and waitresses each receive a tip of 100 yuan from the clients.

There is a certain degree of fluidity in the bar's division of labor. Madams and waitresses sometimes cross over occupational lines to serve as hostesses. For madams, acting as hostesses often reflects the abuse of power. Madams often use their gatekeeper role to reserve the best customers for themselves. During my research, I witnessed several times when the madams, instead of leading hostesses to karaoke rooms, volunteered to personally serve "good clients". A "good client" is defined by his high social status and more civilized manners, and he always comes for an hour at the most and gives larger tips. In such cases, hostesses suffer the least, for the shortest time, and for the highest tips. Madams use their power as gatekeeper to snatch up such clients for themselves, even going out of stage. Clients who are thus deprived of an opportunity to choose among hostesses must either awkwardly protest or settle for the madam. According to the bar owner, many of these clients never come back because they are irritated by the madams. Instead, they visit other bars to look for other hostesses.

Hostess Wu told me, "They [gangsters] beat us up any time they want! You think this [profession] is so easy to do? Who are we? Hostesses! The bar boss and managers belong to the upper class, and we belong to the lower class. I know that. Bing can rape us any time he wants, and you cannot utter a word! Sometimes I fought with Bing, but the other hostesses just tolerated him. I think if we could unite, together, we would be in a much better situation. However, some hostesses, like Lynn, fell in love with Bing and flatter him all the time! Because of that, they have more opportunities to be led to meet the clients by Bing and earn handsome tips every day".

Not only the hostesses' onstage fee but also their out-of-stage fee is exploited. The private room upstairs is prepared for clients to sleep with hostesses for a couple of hours or for a whole night (*baoye*). The price for a whole night is much higher than a couple of hours. However, it is always the barkeep, Bing, who talks to the clients and negotiates the price. Hostesses working the whole night only get half the tip (400 yuan) the following morning. The other half (400 yuan) is kept by Bing and the bar managers. No one dares to complain openly.

Hostesses' struggle

After a while, hostesses develop ways to cope with this inequity. When clients come to the bar looking for hostesses to go offstage, few hostesses consent. It leaves the outsiders with the false impression that few hostesses in this bar go offstage. In reality, however, almost all of the hostesses do, although behind the scenes, to save the entire tip for themselves. One hostess said, "Why should we earn the money for the bar managers? We have established a settled relationship with our clients. We schedule a time outside of the bar to do it. We keep the money in our own pockets. Who needs them as the mediators? Actually, everyone in our bar goes offstage, but secretly".

The bar managers and owner are stingy not only with the hostesses, but also with their steady clients. Wu told me, "Bar business should rely not only on us, but also on the steady clients. However, the bar managers exploit these clients even harder!". Aware of this situation, on the one hand hostesses face pressure to order more food and drinks in karaoke rooms, and, on the other hand, they secretly establish relationships with clients. As their connections are set up, hostesses request that their clients take them out for dinner. In such cases, they not only earn the tip of 100 yuan, but also help their clients save money from the bar overcharges.

Some hostesses sit on several stages at the same time (*cuantai*). For instance, Wu managed to sit on five stages at one time. She said, "The key is: Do not let yourself be seen by your clients when you are sitting on different stages. Once I heard that five of my steady clients were coming on the same night. I was sitting in the first client's karaoke room until it was time for the other clients to come. Then I said, 'I have been feeling really sick these days. I feel really uncomfortable now. Can you leave now and come back some other time?' He agreed and left, offering me a tip. Then, the other clients came one after another. I went into the second client's karaoke room and said, 'Look, my sister has just arrived here in Dalian with a friend. I really have to go to the train station to pick her up. It will take me about an hour or so. I will be back for sure'. Then I left and went into the third client's karaoke room and said, 'Look, my sister will come over to be a hostess. I need to rent her a room, buy her some clothes and merchandise for everyday use. When she starts working here, she will earn money and return the loan to me. Can you give me some money?'. He gave me 200 yuan. See, the tip is already in my hands. 'Thanks so much! I am sorry that I have to leave, but I will definitely be back in about forty-five minutes'. Then I repeated the same story in the other two karaoke rooms and promised to be back in, respectively, forty and thirty minutes. After that, I returned to the first karaoke room and said, 'Sorry I am back so late. Oh, I am feeling so exhausted and sick'. Then I stayed there for a few minutes before asking them to leave. They gave me the tip. Then I returned to the other three karaoke rooms, in turn, and repeated the same story."

Why hostessing?

One might ask, since the sex industry is so exploitative, dangerous, and violent, why would hostesses continue this work? What does their work bring them? How do they rationalize their work? What is their goal, and what are their aspirations? Does their work deteriorate or elevate their social status? Below, I will unravel two hostesses' stories to illustrate the reality that hostessing is their only venue to equal social status with urbanites.

Learned urban cultural styles

Karaoke bars, as flourishing new cultural spaces in the city, are the places where rural migrant women can achieve a certain degree of self-esteem through the sense of being accepted and desired by the urban men who choose them as companions for the night. The karaoke bar is also the place where these women can find secondary socialization by mingling with urban clients, where they feel "urban and cosmopolitan", both culturally and socially. Hostess Ying migrated to the city, and during the mid-1990s, she worked in a private factory, where she was even named the model worker. Eventually, the factory went bankrupt and closed down. Ying was laid off and left without financial sources. Her women friends took her to a dance hall to accompany men. To make a living, she followed them.

> I thought nobody would dance with me because of my low quality (*suzhi*) and rural origin. However, to my surprise, some urban men invited me. A man from the Labor Bureau even liked me a lot. Once, I ran into him on the street, and he asked me to have dinner with him in a restaurant. I refused his love but I did go to the restaurant with him. I was such a foolish cunt (*sha bi*) – I was completely ignorant of a restaurant, let alone of all the eating or talking etiquettes. I was such a foolish cunt, so stupid, you mother fucker. I did not know how to eat or talk. I was a peasant. When had I ever seen a restaurant? You know at that time [during the mid-1990s], nobody in my village had ever been to a restaurant. Very few had even heard about it. As a factory worker, I only earned 400 yuan a month. When on earth had I ever seen this amount of money and the atmosphere of the restaurant? After that event, I was so shocked by my incongruity with the urban people. I started working as a dancing companion. Two months later, I went back home with loads of money, several thousand. At that time it was a lot of money. Nobody had ever seen so much money before. The money I earned meant a lot to everyone.

For Ying, living an urban lifestyle affirms an equal status with urbanites; being chosen by urban clients in karaoke bars confirms her self-worth.

Independence

Hostesses' experience of rape and abandonment in the city teaches them not to be duped by men's romantic words and to embrace independence through hostessing. They commented, "Dalian men try to cheat both our bodies and our emotions. Without spending a cent, they get what they want from us". Hostess Guang served as a domestic maid in an urban family before hostessing. Within two months, she was raped three times by her male employer. Hostess Min worked as a restaurant waitress when she was raped and then abandoned by an urban customer. She said,

"Urban men take advantage of us both emotionally and physically. We cannot be too innocent (*tai chunjie*) or devoted; otherwise, we will be tricked, used and abandoned. Only women who are not pure can protect themselves".

Han worked as a hairdresser in the city. She lived with an urban man for three years in his home. During this time, she suffered from all kinds of physical and verbal abuse from his aunt and mother. For instance, they accused her of stealing their jewelry and associated her "thieving habits" with her rural background. All this abuse was targeted at her inferior rural background. Han exerted every effort to endure all this inhumane treatment. However, her urban boyfriend also worried that her rural family would become a bottomless pit, eventually draining all his money. He abruptly abandoned her, saying, "Our social status just doesn't match". Devastated, she believed that she would never find happiness unless she became the social and economic equal of the urbanites. She started working as a hostess. Five years later, she was very successful. She possessed two household registrations – one urban and one rural. She purchased two houses, one in her hometown for her parents and one in Dalian for her siblings. She supported her two younger sisters and a brother through school. She paid for the weddings of her four older brothers and sisters, and so on. She is now married to the financial director of a prestigious hotel chain.

Similarly, another hostess, Hong, broke up with her client boyfriend when failed to offer her the amount of money she expected. She commented, "I myself can earn 100,000 yuan a month from hostessing. To exchange this for his several thousand yuan – so little money – I have to obey everything he says. Who will do that? He thinks I am fresh from the countryside, so I can easily be cheated. With so little money, he wants me to be his second wife and control me as his possession by tying my arms and legs. That's impossible. I want to earn money for myself and spend it happily as I want. There is no way for me to spend his little money at the price of abiding by whatever he has to say".

If rural origin and cultural inferiority is the root of the hierarchical relationship between rural migrant women and urban men, then hostessing offers an opportunity to escape subordination. As paid work, hostessing represents an act of defiance against the misogynistic urban men who freely exploit the women's bodies and emotions. At the bar, men have to pay a high price to hostesses in exchange for even approaching them. This transaction transformed the situation that existed when migrant women were available to men as free dinner at the men's whim.

Hostessing allows the women to gain an economic profit and therefore independence from men. In the monetary transaction, hostesses attain a certain equality with the urban men by taking advantage of the men's resources. Having financial resources at their disposal brings the women power and confidence. Many hostesses who are married or are kept as second wives sneak out of the house to work. Setting up their own separate account allows them to spend their own money at will and secretly support their natal families. The economic power brought by hostessing earned Han and Hong a great degree of independence and equality in social and gender status in both familial and spousal relationship with urban partners.

Conclusion

This chapter focuses on layers of power relationship in the lived experiences of hostesses in the post-Mao urban karaoke-bar sex industry. The state's anti-vice policy is manipulated and usurped by local officials and bar owners for their own ends, leading to a violent working environment for the hostesses. Working amid such exploitative labor relations, hostesses struggle to reallocate male clients' socioeconomic resources into their own hands and subvert the urban–rural hierarchy. To them, hostessing is an expedient route to achieving a certain degree of social mobility. Hostessing is not a lifelong occupation. For the fortunate, opportunities for a better life lead them down other paths. The less fortunate are pushed into retirement as their increasing age puts them at a disadvantage in comparison with younger hostesses. Although some former hostesses stay on as madams and bar owners, most withdraw from the bars entirely. The hostesses' ideal exit strategies include marrying into an urban family, becoming the second wives (*ernai*) of wealthy businessmen or officials, and becoming independent businesswomen. These strategies are adopted with varying degrees of success. It is not uncommon for a hostess to exit and reenter hostess work multiple times before achieving "escape velocity".

Regardless of which exit strategy is adopted, a hostess's ability to extricate herself from the karaoke bars and start a new life with a new identity is burdened by the lingering shadow of her past occupation. Former hostesses live with the constant dread that their new lives will be destroyed by the exposure of their history of work in the karaoke bars. One former hostess, whose vending stall I helped to tend when she was ill, swore me to secrecy on several occasions about not "outing" her to the other vendors. Her anxiety is universally shared by former hostesses in all familial and occupational situations. Whether the wife of an urban man, a government official, or repatriated countryside entrepreneur, former hostesses must cover up their pasts at the risk of losing their hard-earned new lives.

Have hostesses attained upward mobility or reproduced social inequality? In the short run, the exit strategies of the hostesses carry the possibility that they are improving their social and economic condition. In the long run, however, former hostesses are always at risk of having their history as sex workers and their rural origins discovered and thereby losing whatever gains in status they have been able to achieve.

Acknowledgments

I extend my sincere gratitude to the editor, Ching Kwan Lee, and to Mark Selden for their incisive suggestions and criticisms. This chapter is based on my fieldwork, generously supported by the Yale Center for International and Area Studies and by the Yale Council of East Asian Studies.

Notes

1 Gu, Qiuping 2000 "Guoji Mingcheng Li Wo Men Hai You Duo Yuan" (Towards a famous city in the world) *Dalian Ribao* (Dalian Daily) May 25: C1.;   Zhang, Xiaozhao 2001 "Dalian Yaozuo Xiandaihua Shentai Chengshi" (Dalian as a Modern Environmental City) *Dalian Wanbao* (Dalian Evening Newspaper) 6 June: 1.

2 This is the official figure of the city's population (in the four central districts).

3 Zhang, Haibing 2001, *Xinjiapo Yu Dalian* (Singapore and Dalian) Shenyang: Liaoning Remin Chubanshe (Liaoning People's Publishing House): 142. Municipal officials interviewed estimated a floating population in Dalian of 1,000,000 people, from all over China.

4 Jian, Ping 2001 "Caifang Shouji: Jingyan Dalian" (Interview Memoirs in Dalian) *Xinzhoukan* (New Weekly), 10: 44.

5 Ibid.

6 Interview conducted in 2001.

7 See Hershatter, Gail , 1997, *Dangerous Pleasures: Prostitution and Modernity in Twentieth-Century Shanghai*, Berkeley: University of California Press.

8 Although karaoke bars are legal, they have always been one of the government's main "culture purging" targets. It is claimed that they work against the state's cultural logic in three aspects: (1) Socialist business should prioritize the needs of people and serve the people. It should be different from the commercial system, where the pure objective is to pursue and procure sudden huge profit. Many bar bosses operate their business by cheating customers and providing erotic services. (2) "Erotic company" (*seqing peishi*) is illegal and immoral and runs counter to socialist "spiritual civilization". Such "ugly phenomena" associated with capitalism should be wiped out to maintain the healthy and inspiring socialist cultural environment and "civilized consumption". (3) Juxtaposed against socialist recreations enjoyed by the masses, karaoke bars are more individually based, places where individuals pursue and express their "repulsive and hideous" desires to show off their performing talents and satisfy their sexual demands. In view of these reasons, karaoke bars regularly undergo a purging process to become part of "spiritual civilization". Frequent police raids are part of this process.

9 Male dominance of the business world in China is reinforced by the use of karaoke bars to entertain clients. While I heard that occasionally female businesswomen entertained male clients, I never witnessed such an arrangement myself.

10 See Pan, Suiming 1999, *Cun Zai Yu Hunag Niu: Zhong Guo Di Xia "Xing Chan Ye" Kao Cha* (Existence and Irony: A Scrutiny of Chinese Underground Sex Industry) Beijing: Qunyan Chubanshe (Qunyan Publishing House): 13–14.

11 Reconstructing the history of karaoke bars in Dalian proved to be exceedingly difficult. A combination of official denial and embarrassment has ensured that no publicly open records were kept on the subject, and the same attitude undoubtedly dissuaded any interested parties from prying. To piece together the story, I was therefore forced to rely entirely on the oral accounts of government officials in different divisions of the municipal Bureau of Culture.

12 See "Management Stipulations of Recreational Places", issued by the State Council, 1999.

13 This policy is designed to boost the bar owners' sense of pride as contributors to the socialist culture market. Inculcated with this new thought, bar owners will take the initiative to transform their bars into civilized spaces, where clients' lofty sentiments can be nurtured.

14 This is in the upscale karaoke bar where hostesses were not living in the bar. I lived with the hostesses in the low-tier karaoke bar in the red-light district.

15 After I received a visa to the United States, the government withdrew my ID card. The only ID left me was my passport. A passport without an ID card indicates that the person in question does not reside in China.

16 This information is taken from my interview with the political officials in the municipal government.

17 "Sanpei xiaojie de Falu Baohu Wenti" (Legal Protection of Hostesses), *Shenzhen Fazhi bao* (Shenzhen Law Newspaper), June 25, 2002.

18 Sun, Shaoguang, "Dalian E Mo Ba Xiaojie Fenshi Shiyi Kuai" (A Man in Dalian Divided a Hostess' Dead Body into Eleven Pieces), *Dongbei Xinwen Wang* (Northeastern News Net), December 12, 2003.

8 Rurality and labor process autonomy

The waged labor of domestic service[1]

Yan Hairong

When San Ba [March 8] Family Service Company, the first of its kind, emerged in Beijing in 1983, this event invited mixed comments. Some hailed it as a new window to show the world a new growth mark in the process of China's reform, while some others quietly wondered whether this new phenomenon would fit a socialist country. This is not to say that there had been no paid domestic service up to that time. What caused ambivalence in some people was not the phenomenon of paid domestic service *per se* but the reform strategy of formally commercializing and promoting it as a new normative service for consumption. When I interviewed him in 1999, the director of this company recalled the controversy as a product of the immature days of the reform. In the 1990s, people had already accepted it and no one would have found it remarkable, he said.

In the processes of general commercialization of social life in the post-Mao era, domestic service, purchased as wage labor, has indeed become a routine phenomenon in Chinese urban society. At this juncture, however, social contradiction and irony are embedded in domestic service: the reform has produced both greater social disparity and increased dependency of the affluent class on personal service, provided mostly by migrant domestic workers. Thus, while the newly emerging affluent class increasingly desires to keep a distance from the populace at large and wishes to maintain distinction and privacy in their domestic life, it depends on and becomes bound up with hired domestic labor in everyday life, requiring more and more domestic workers to live close to them under the same roof. This chapter examines the ways the wage labor of domestic service is articulated with China's transition to post-socialism.

During the Mao era, a small number of married rural women worked as domestic helpers in the city, where their stay varied from several years to decades. Their long-term employers were overwhelmingly members of the political and cultural elites, who held official positions in the state structure. In the fast expanding domestic-service labor market of the post-Mao era, affluent urban employers, profiting from a variety of occupations, overwhelmingly call for a supply of young rural migrant women as domestic workers, not only because they are cheaper, but also because they can be easily subjected to the employer's instruction, authority, supervision, and discipline. Hiring and firing occur at a much greater frequency. The existence of waged domestic service in the Mao era and the post-Mao era presents itself as a topic for comparison. On the one hand, the expansion of paid domestic service in the post-Mao era may seem like a logical continuity from the Mao era. If so, we might be tempted to explain the different experiences of these two cohorts as a function of the changing supply-and-demand market dynamics. On the other hand, another logic of comparison, centered on virtuous personhood, is often found among employers in China. Despite their overwhelming endorsement of the postsocialist reform, these employers often sing the virtues of older domestic workers of the Mao era and criticize a lack of these virtues among the younger domestic workers in the post-Mao era. What is at stake in making a comparison of paid domestic service between the two eras is how to draw connections and disconnections between Mao-era socialism and the post-Mao reform.

My basic thesis includes both a descriptive and an analytical argument. The descriptive argument is that while the essential tasks of domestic service seem to be the same in both the Mao era and the post-Mao era, migrant women's experiences of the labor process are significantly different. In the Mao era, migrant domestic workers had considerable autonomy in the labor process, while their younger counterparts in the post-Mao era are subjected to significant employer supervision and discipline during their work. The analytical argument proposes that it was the specific political cultures of the two eras – particularly different valuations of rurality – that underpin the labor experiences of domestic workers and shape the relationship between employers and domestic workers. "Rurality" here refers to rural subjectivity, habitus, and practices in relation to urbanity. Unlike many other social services, domestic service was unfortunately not transformed into socialized labor in the Mao era.[2] Thus it may not be the best site to showcase the radical postsocialist transformations in workers' experiences of labor relations. Yet it is my attempt to demonstrate that, even though domestic workers in both eras are employed as wage labor, there has nevertheless been a significant postsocialist transformation in how the meanings and social relations are articulated in the processes of domestic service. To draw connections and disconnections between the two eras in the wage labor of domestic service, I propose that migrant domestic workers' subsumption to wage labor was *formal* in the Mao era and *real* in the post-Mao era.

I borrow the pairing of formal vs. real subsumption from Marx, who analyzed the distinction between formal and real subsumption of labor to capital. In the process of formal subsumption of wage to capital, Marx observed that "capital subsumes the labor process as it finds it, that is to say, it takes over an existing labor process, developed by a different and more archaic mode of production".[3] Thus, by "formal" subsumption of labor under capital, Marx referred to "the takeover by capital of a mode of labor developed before the emergence of capitalist relations" (Marx 1977: 1021). The "real" subsumption of labor under capital, in contrast, enables extractions of relative surplus value in labor processes already radically transformed by the domination of capitalist relations. To illustrate the characteristic of the formal subsumption, Marx used two cases to show that, prior to achieving the formal subsumption, capital – in the form of usurers' capital and merchants' capital – could commission production for the sake of extracting surplus value, but did not intervene in the actual process of production itself (Marx 1977: 1023). The difference between the two subsumptions, therefore, is whether the labor process – hence, the actual relation between labor and capital – has been transformed to allow the characteristic capitalist extraction of surplus value. Marx conceptualized this distinction between "formal" and "real" subsumption as a means for grasping the particularity and specificity of the capitalist mode of production.

I use "formal" and "real" subsumption under wage labor to help me compare and conceptualize the ways in which paid domestic service has differed in the Mao and post-Mao eras. To avoid misunderstanding, I need to state four qualifications that apply to my borrowing. First, the subsumptions Marx analyzed were those of labor *under capital*, but here I examine subsumptions of domestic workers *under wage labor* in socialism and postsocialism. Mao-era socialism was a process of social experiments, trials and errors, contestations, and contradictions and had conflicting overlaps of old and new and of national political innovations and borrowings from the Soviet Union. Contract-based wage labor existed in this context of contested and struggling socialism, was introduced without the existence of private capital, was not always taken for granted, and was sometimes a contentious political issue, especially during the Cultural Revolution (1966–76).[4] Thus, second, the context of Marx's observation is the historically determined transition toward the capitalist mode of production. Formal subsumption, in Marx's analysis, is already the threshold – or initial process – of capitalist production. In my study here, I do not assume that socialism and postsocialism are locked into an historically determined transition, even though the assumption is widely held;[5] the transition from one epoch to the other was fraught with tensions, struggles, and indeterminacy. Third, by formal subsumption, Marx revealed that the labor process prior to capitalism continued in protocapitalism; but my study here does not argue for continuity in the labor process of domestic service between pre-socialism and socialism. Lastly, rather than focusing on surplus value extraction, the purpose of my study here is to understand the specific articulations of social relations embodied in the changed meanings and labor processes of paid domestic service.[6]

For my analysis, the concept of "subsumption to wage labor" is useful in two ways. On the one hand, it highlights commodification of labor and its inherent structural inequality as common conditions for domestic work in both eras. On the other hand, Marx's distinction between formal and real subsumption helps me to focus on the labor process as a site for examining and articulating the significant difference between the two epochs. In terms of labor process, commodification of labor means, in principle, that employers have the authority and the right to use, discipline, and supervise the worker in the way they see fit during the purchased labor time. But in the actual labor process in the Mao era, domestic workers' subsumption to wage labor was formal, meaning that employer authority and discipline did not so much bear upon or intervene in the details and organization of the labor process, and domestic workers had greater autonomy in their labor process and less disciplining of their rural personhood, thanks to the Mao-era structure of sociality, particularly its politicized valuation of rurality. In the post-Mao context of greater commodification of labor and relentless denigration of rurality, employer authority and discipline impresses itself much more strongly in the labor process, so that domestic workers have less autonomy in their work and in expressing their rural personhood.

Domestic service and rurality in the Mao era

Before the appearance of domestic service as wage labor in nineteenth-century China, servants were predominantly bondservants (*nubi*) who became indentured through birth, debt, or the human market.[7] Bondservants were subjected to specific legal classification, familial and clan rules, and patriarchal authority. More than two scores of terms for bondservants are found in Chinese historical documents, ranging from the beginning of the Qin dynasty (221 BC) to the end of the Qing dynasty (1644–1911). Bondservants, together with actors, prostitutes, and beggars, constitute a special class of people called *jianmin* – a low class of people – as opposed to *liangmin* which included literati, farmers, craftsmen, and merchants. Instances of land distribution policies in the Northern Wei Dynasty (386–534) and the Tang Dynasty (618–907) demonstrate that while actors, prostitutes, and beggars each had their own categories of household registration, bondservants were subsumed into the masters' households and were thus not entitled to land distribution.[8] On becoming bondservants, these persons would also most often lose their own family name and would be given a new name by their masters. Neither bondservants themselves nor even their descendants could take imperial exams, which was the common route to civil service. Legal codes not only differentiated between *jianmin* and *liangmin*, but also imposed different codes for masters and bondservants. Servants were most severely punished for offenses against their masters. In addition to these, there were varieties of rules upheld by local gentries to compel domestic discipline (*jiafa*) and clan conventions (*zugui*) that further subjugated bondservants. Chu has argued that the bondservant system (*nubi zhi*) was a form of mutated slavery linked with private land ownership and its highly elaborate social hierarchy.[9] The formal, caste-like servant system was officially abolished in the late Qing dynasty of the late nineteenth and early twentieth century, during which time servant labor came to be commodified as wage labor for hire.[10] The legacy of the bondservant system continued to exist, and in many places, the caste-like relationship existed as customs until the 1930s. Liang Qichao (1873–1929), the prominent late Qing reformer, reported that in his native place and its surroundings in Guangdong, there were *shipu*, families of certain lineage names that serviced families of other lineage names.[11] Lu Xun also reported that in his native place of Shaoxing in Zhejiang province, a similar class of people (*duomin*) had a subservient relationship with families of certain surnames and did not intermarry with others until the Republican Revolution.[12]

The long-standing social tradition of the bondservant system, already eroded by commodification of servant labor in the mid-nineteenth century, was resolutely swept away by the Communist Party-led social revolution in the first half of the twentieth century. Domestic service as wage labor continued to exist after the founding of the People's Republic in 1949. Domestic helpers were no longer called by any of the old terms. Instead, *ayi* (literally auntie) or alternatively, the classical term *baomu* or "protecting mother", originally referring to women in charge of protecting, nursing, and educating children in royal courts, became adopted as new categorical terms for all domestic workers regardless of their specific responsibilities.[13] The term *baomu* already came into use in communist rural bases in the 1940s, referring to both kindergarten nurses and rural women in surrounding areas who cared for children for communist cadres moving between battlefields. After the founding of the People's Republic in 1949, some of these cadres asked the rural women to come to the city with them to continue to look after their children. Some other cadres had one of their guards introduce them to a rural relative – almost always a woman – who was willing to work in the city. Some of these rural women then introduced some of their co-villagers to families that sought domestic service. A special stipend was included in the salaries of high-level cadres and intellectuals for the purpose of hiring domestic helpers, a supplement that was presumably justified by their unusual workload and responsibility. Ordinary urban families could and did employ domestic help, but often on a short-term basis, and they did not take it for granted as a long-term everyday practice. During the Cultural Revolution, the term *baomu* was considered to be denigrating, and only the term *ayi* was used.

In the Mao era, *baomu* were very few in number and were mostly illiterate or semiliterate married rural women. It is impossible today to estimate how many rural women worked in the city as *baomu* during the Mao era. Wuwei county of Anhui province was a base for Communist New Fourth Army, some of whose cadres entrusted their children to the care of local women. This connection opened the door for a sizable migration of women to the city in the Mao era as *baomu*. It was estimated by the county Women's Federation that 3000 to 4000 women from Wuwei worked in the city during the Mao era. When I asked why women migrated in that period, I was given the consistent answer that on the one hand, it was more difficult for men than women to find employment in the city, and on the other hand, since women generally earned fewer work points (*gong fen*) than men in farm work, it would be better for women to go to the city to work. However, among the migrants there were widows and married women who had disputes with their husbands or were domestically abused. Paid domestic labor, secured through village-based connections or through relatives working in the city, was the most common way that these rural women could separate from their husbands and earn an independent income in the city. The exodus of a small number of rural women to the city as *baomu*, as I have analyzed elsewhere, was pushed by a double underpricing of rural women's labor in the continued structure of rural patriarchy in conjunction with the state's specific modernization plans, which required hefty rural input into industrialization, in the context of the United States embargo and Cold War geopolitics.[14] The meaning of working as *baomu* carried a sense of shame, shaped by the power of local patriarchy and reinforced by the state's failure to socialize domestic service as public and socialist labor with due legitimacy, rights, and benefits.

The experiences of the 13 women I interviewed who had worked in the city as *baomu* during and at the end of the Mao era varied from family to family that they worked for, but there were numerous expressions of the *ku* (literally, bitterness) or hardships shared by these women. Rural life itself was *ku*. While they lived in the city, homesickness and particularly worry about their own children was by far the greatest *ku* for these women. Large workloads were a source of *ku*. Not eating at the same table or not having enough to eat at the home of the employers was *ku*. Not being trusted or respected by employers was *ku*. Grandma Four began to work in the city as a wet nurse in 1952. In the ensuing decades, until she settled back in the countryside in 1998, she worked for a number of families in the city as a domestic helper, and whenever she could, she worked for several families simultaneously. As she recalled her experiences:

> I had helped other [families] take good care of their children, but I left my own children at home. Then I missed my own children so bitterly. One time I dreamed that my third child fell into a pond and was drowned. Another time I dreamed that another child was drowned in the night-soil pit. I dreamed these and cried in my dreams, waking up in tears … *Ku*! Working at someone else's home was *ku*. There wasn't anyone looking after my children, but I had to take care of children for others …
>
> When dawn broke in the morning, I had to get up to buy groceries for the day and cook [for the primary employer family she lived with]. After lunch, I went to another family to wash clothes for them. After that, I went to the third family for two hours to wash clothes and mop the floor. Then I ate. In the evening I sometimes had to wait for the bus until eleven o'clock. If I didn't have to wait long for the bus, then I would get back past ten.

Aunt Lin Miao went to Beijing in 1976 and found a job taking care of an infant. She had to sleep with the baby at night and feed it from time to time. But the employers gave her food inferior to what they had for themselves. If they had wheat-flour noodles themselves, they would give her *wowotou* (corn flour bun). The grandmother in this family even watched her stealthily (*tou kan*) when Aunt Lin Miao prepared milk for the baby, worrying that Aunt Lin Miao might drink the milk herself. "They didn't give me good food, nor did they show me a good [friendly] face. It's *ku* for me". The second family she worked for was radically different.

> They were very nice to me. I ate together with them and had the same food as they did. When I was sick with a heart disease, the family wouldn't let me go back. The father in this family was the head of a hospital and asked me to get treatment in Beijing. I said I didn't want to burden them with this trouble. They were nice to me and I should think for their good by not burdening them. So I borrowed six hundred yuan from this family to get treatment in

my native place. Each of the six daughters in this family gave me fifteen yuan as a parting gift. I went back to this family before I was completely recovered, because I was concerned about the debt I owed them. I worked for them for two more years. They paid me the wage and I paid them back the six hundred yuan. They didn't let me do heavy work. They paid me thirty yuan a month.[15] The father of the family was an army doctor before and treated me very equally. All his daughters listened to me. In their home I managed everything and did everything.

When the experiences of the older *baomu* are compared with those of younger *baomu* today, two characteristics stand out: their autonomy in the actual labor process and their continued identity with rurality after their return. They all returned to rural life and rural labor without experiencing any of the subjectivity crises that younger migrants feel today. When I asked several women whether they could still fit into the life at home after their return, Aunt Lin Miao took the lead by answering, "Look, here I farm twenty mu of land. If I had changed, how would I have been able to do it?". Grandmother Four said, "To work outside is to eat bitterness. Why would I not be used to life at home?". In Wang Anyi's novel about *baomu* in the early Mao era, titled *Fu Ping*, the older *baomu* still plans to spend her retired life in her native place in rural Yangzhou, even though she has obtained a local household registration in Shanghai.[16] When commenting on how some migrant villagers have made money and now live in the county seat, and how new conflicts have emerged in the village, straining village and kin relationships, Grandmother said to her daughter and myself, "I worked all my life and never craved money. What is wrong with being poor? Poor people are good [*qiong ren hao*]!".

Comparatively speaking, the older cohort in the Mao era had significant autonomy in the employers' homes as a work place. None of the women I interviewed mentioned anything about their employers' supervision over the labor process itself. Granted, in some cases *baomu* had to receive instruction on how to make northern food for some of their employers, and two women complained that they were "stealthily watched" by members of their employers' families, but these women's word choice itself implies that they considered the supervision illicit and abnormal. Even those who watched these women might have shared the same view on their own act and thus watched "stealthily". Correspondingly, employers I interviewed who hired *baomu* in the Mao era also said that they entrusted housework to their *baomu*, but a few employers told me that they worried about or discovered their *baomu* stealing household food items, such as brown sugar. Yet employers' supervision and disciplining were largely absent in the daily labor process.

Employers of *baomu* in the earlier period often recalled how busy they were with work then and that they left the home and young children to the care of old *baomu*. In her seventies, Aunt Zhang recalled the *baomu* who helped her in the 1950s, after she and her husband volunteered to leave Beijing for the Anshan Steelworks in Northeast China. The children were very young, and Aunt Zhang was busy with her work for the propaganda department of the plant. Aunt Zhang detailed for me how the *baomu* carried the youngest one on her back to the kindergarten and, rather than buying shoes and clothes, she handmade cotton shoes and clothes, not only for herself but also for all the children, since it was a common self-reliant practice in a society where commodities were not always taken for granted. "Then I was particularly busy. I wouldn't come home for several days. Everything at home was taken care of by her [*baomu*]. So I didn't know anything about things at home. Then I just had no time, no energy [for home]. I was busy all day in the factory. Workers worked with tremendous enthusiasm [*re huo chao tian*]. Sometimes I came back and had to leave in the middle of the night. She would cook something for me. She was illiterate and also didn't know how to read a watch. She would use a pen to make an ink mark on the watch and then she would know when to wake me up … I still miss her now and all my kids miss her."

In the eyes of parents today, the parents of those days may seem like absentees or may appear absent-minded because of their dedication to work. Novelist Wang Anyi's *Fuping* more or less reflects a similar reality of "absent-minded" parents and the significant autonomy of the older *baomu* in the 1950s. The *baomu* in the story, called *nainai* (grandma), works for a couple who are former People's Liberation Army cadres. "Originally they had a supply system, living in public housing, eating in the cafeteria, and had their children watched over by *baomu* assigned by their unit. They did not have to worry about housework. Now they entrusted everything in the household to *nainai*" (Wang Anyi 2000: 15). Mr Nan, whose parents were in the army in the 1950s, similarly recalled *baomu* managing the home on his parents' behalf and sheltering the children from their parents' discipline. "Then we were very naughty. My parents were very strict. The *baomu* would protect us. She would hide us in her room and shut the door. She treated us as her own kids". It was not surprising that in those days, *baomu* sometimes could and did act as a "protecting mother" and intervened between the parents and the children. Child nurturing, certainly a parental responsibility in the Mao era, was more diffused and shared by a wider neighborhood and kin network. Neighbors could and did also shield children from their parents' wrath. In the post-Mao era, child nurturing has become intensified and concentrated within the parental authority and responsibility, which parents seldom care to share with others.

"Absent-mindedness" on the part of the employers facilitated the autonomy of domestic workers in the Mao era but is not a sufficient reason for it. I suggest that this seeming absent-mindedness, or lack of control of the domestic labor process by the employers, is underpinned by a valorization of rurality in Mao era social life. Rurality, associated with the legendary Yan'an spirit of the communist rural bases in Northwest China in the 1930s and 1940s and associated with progressiveness in the Cultural Revolution (1966–76), was given a revolutionary implication in Maoist socialism. Shortages in and simplicity of everyday consumption were given a politicized national ethos of "hard struggle and plain living" (*jianku pusu*) throughout the Mao era and had a significant impact on the transformation of urban life. It can be argued that during the Mao era, there was a considerable rustication of urban life. The majority of Mao era cadres were themselves from rural background or had been rusticated while working in communist rural areas prior to the founding of the People's Republic. The success of the revolution, the entry of communist cadres from the countryside to the city, and "hard work, plain living" as the dominant ethos of the era effected a rustication of urban life and mitigated the privilege and control by the urban bourgeois elite of the urban culture in general and of the sensibilities of domestic life in particular. In *Fuping*, it was *nainai*, the *baomu*, who taught her employers the Shanghai style of urban life. To be sure, privilege and hierarchy still existed and rebounded with the new bureaucracy, which contributed to igniting the Cultural Revolution, but the dominant ethos did indeed considerably weaken the political and cultural hegemony of the elites. During the Cultural Revolution, a large number of urban youth went to the countryside for rustication and tempering of their revolutionary spirit through learning from the experiences of "poor and lower-middle peasants" (*ping xia zhong nong*). In asserting the goodness of poor people, Grandmother Four was probably alluding to this general Maoist ideological context.

For rural women, working as *baomu*, the rustication of urban life meant a greatly lowered demand and scrutiny by employers of the quality of their everyday work, using elite standards. Instead, rural women's habit of frugality and their ability at bricolage were often appreciated by their employers. In Aunt Zhang's reminiscences, her children's wearing of old *baomu*'s hand-made shoes and clothes is a revealing and significant detail. It shows how fully the weaving and stitching of rurality into the fabric of everyday urban life was accepted. Along with the appreciation for the labor of making shoes and clothes, rurality itself was given an ideologically valued place in urban life. Incidentally, in the Cultural Revolution film "*Juelie*" (Breaking the Old Ideas), which was critical of elitism in education, one poignant detail was the scene of a college student in his dormitory room receiving a visit from his mother, who came from the countryside.[17] Clad in shining urban leather shoes, the student is profoundly embarrassed when he holds the hand-made cotton shoes his mother brought as gift. When the cotton shoes are passed from the hands of the mother to those of the son, the shoes change from an object of maternal affection that has crossed rural–urban distance to an object through which rural–urban distance and estrangement is made painfully obvious. The film used this detail to criticize this student's "revisionist" (bourgeois) estrangement from the rural masses and his denigration of manual labor.

Despite the household registration system that made rural-to-urban labor mobility very difficult in the Mao era, a great variety of interactions between the city and the countryside was evident during that time. One outstanding example is the practice of sending children from the city to the countryside for child care. In the Mao era, *baomu* worked in a general social environment in which assistance with child care by relatives and grandparents, who often lived in rural areas, was commonly mobilized. Young children were sent to the native place (*laojia*) to be raised by rural grandparents. Sometimes, grandparents were also asked to come to the city to help raise grandchildren. In the late 1960s and early 1970s, both my brother and I were raised by my grandparents and aunts in the countryside. This childhood rural experience is not uncommon for members of my generation or older people. In my interviews, I have also encountered cases in which intellectuals and cadres sent their children to be raised by working-class families in the city when they themselves were too busy with work or were sent down to the countryside. In the 1980s, the flow of children to the countryside largely disappeared when the post-Mao modernization drive compelled many urban parents to be intensely invested in developing a high *suzhi* (quality) for their single child, who must be prepared for China's opening to global competition.[18] Nowadays, parents would feel offended by the suggestion that they could send their child to the countryside. One male employer in his thirties who employed a *baomu* to provide child care commented to me, "In the countryside, they raise children just as they raise pigs and dogs". In line with the larger discourse of development, he invokes the image of primitive and stupefying rural nurturing, which seem to yield only pitiful beings, creatures on a low rung in the competitive process of social evolution. The animalistic image is employed to suggest that such children are deservedly condemned to a destiny as manual laborers. This representation of rural nurturing implicitly contrasts it with modern and high-value urban nurturing that actively pursues the development of the child's intellectual, artistic, and physical qualities. The halt to sending children to the countryside betrays a post-Mao belief that neither the competitive individual nor the national future can be entrusted to and nurtured in the countryside. Consigning children to valorized urban nurturing in the post-Mao era signifies a condemnation of rurality.

In the Mao era, *baomu* worked at a time when social mixing and interactions between the city and the countryside were considerable, with the countryside taking a high ground in socialist ideology. In addition to the migration of urban youth to the countryside for rustification, it was not unusual for urbanites in the city to form social or even familial relationships with people in the countryside. Speaking of my family's experience, because of my mother's work at a local government's agricultural bureau in the 1970s, she had a chance to meet a model laborer and was adopted as a *gan nüer* (dry daughter) by him and his large family in the countryside. My brother and I thus acquired many new uncles and aunts. There were many exchanges of visits and gifts between the two families until 1980, when my family moved to another city. Among the current employers of *baomu*, some also recalled for me their friendships with rural young people when they were in the countryside. Even in the 1980s, such relationships existed. An insurance agent who worked as a medical doctor in the 1980s remembered that a rural patient she treated was so grateful for her treatment that often when he came to the city, he brought her some of his home-grown produce; basically, he adopted her as a relative. By the 1990s, experiences such as these had become almost extinct and unimaginable.

Many critics have attacked the Mao-era policy of highly planned and controlled rural–urban mobility, considering them to constitute the greatest injustice against rural people, yet seldom is there any reflection on why there were numerous social exchanges and interactions between urban and rural residents in the Mao era, while there are so few of these in today's context of unrestricted labor mobility.

Exchanges today are dominated by the commercial interchange of wage for labor. One post-Mao migrant domestic worker whose family hosted an urban sent-down youth in the 1970s is indignant: the difference between the way her family treated the urban youth then and how she is treated in the city today is like heaven and earth. The structural subjection of the majority of migrants as nothing but cheap labor in the post-Mao market economy is little considered by the same critics who claim to be concerned with Mao-era injustice against rural people. The doctor-turned-insurance agent today hires a young *baomu* to assist her with housework. When the *baomu*'s mother wrote to invite this employer for a visit and offered her friendship and fictive kinship through the way she addressed her, this employer said that, although she enjoyed her previous experience of being adopted as kin by her rural patient, she did not want to be adopted as a kin by her *baomu*'s family because she needed to maintain a boundary for the sake of easier management of the employment relationship. In her eyes, the primary identity of the rural young woman working at her home is that of a wage worker. While this employer's anxiety to police the boundary is understandable in the larger structure of the market economy, her earlier engagement of urban–rural kinship and her rejection of it today indicate that the structuring forces of political economy reach deep into people's (in)ability and decision-making on forming non-commodified social relations across the rural-urban boundaries.

In short, a historical understanding of the conditions of labor for old *baomu* requires that we examine the terrain and fabric of sociality in the Mao era, during which rurality and rustication were given a moral-political value and in which the vision of modernity did not privilege urbanity to any considerable extent. The relative autonomy in the labor process for the old *baomu* was enabled in a society where rurality was woven into the urban body politic in a variety of ways – through the rustication of urban life, through ideological valuation of rurality, through social interactions between urban and rural families, and through the flow of young children to the countryside to be raised by rural kin. It is also important to note that it was a time when child care was not dominated by hired wage labor but involved caretakers from a variety of social backgrounds. When the care of urban children was carried out by a good mix of caretakers – kin and non-kin – and in multiple locations – spanning the countryside and city – the wage labor of domestic service did not distinctively mark the labor process itself. When urban child care is carried out predominantly by hired wage labor in post-Mao society, employers' authority has begun to bear upon the actual labor process itself in terms of detailed supervision and disciplining.

To stress domestic workers' autonomy in the labor process is not to belittle the class inequality relations between them and their employers in the Mao era. In the course of their narration, the older *baomu* I interviewed often remarked on the abundance of food available at the employers' homes and compared it with its scarcity in the countryside. The sources of *ku* and the various forms of hardships that they endured while working in the city for elite families made it understandable that, when the privilege of the political and intellectual elites was attacked during the Cultural Revolution, some *baomu* seized the opportunity and summoned up enough courage to speak against their employers and denounce them as members of the bourgeoisie in public.[19]

The changing meanings of *baomu*

Marketization in the post-Mao reform era has created a rapidly expanding domestic-service sector for urban households, drawing hundreds of thousands of rural migrant women into this labor force. In the current era, young rural migrant women constitute the main work force in paid domestic service, and these women are predominantly employed as live-in domestics. They are supplemented by middle-aged rural women, as well as urban women who are either retired or laid-off workers. Urban women, joined by some migrant women, are most often employed on an hourly basis. San Ba, the domestic-service company, requires that a domestic be employed to perform only one of three types of work: taking care of small children, looking after family elders, or performing general household work. But in practice, a domestic worker is often made to do any combination of these tasks or all of them. The actual number of *baomu* is very difficult to obtain regionally or nationally. According to the estimate of the China Home Service Association, the Chinese mainland has about 10 million domestic helpers.[20] In my interview with him in 1999, the director of the San Ba agency estimated the number of *baomu* in Beijing at 100,000. In a recent interview in 2004, he ventured that the figure for *baomu* in the city had reached 150,000.[21] Li Dajing, deputy head of the Beijing Municipal Home Economics Association, estimated in 2003 that about 200,000 households – some 7.6 percent – in all the eight urban districts of Beijing employed hired domestic workers,[22] while more than 10 percent of families in Shanghai now employ domestics.[23]

Migrant women become employed as domestic workers through two main channels. They may find employment through a kinship or native-place-based network. They may be recruited by township or county labor bureaux or the women's federation on behalf of companies such as San Ba that supply domestic workers to urban households. Domestic workers are addressed as *jiating fuwu yuan* (family service worker) in post-Mao official parlance, but they are still called *baomu* or (*xiao*) *ayi* in everyday vernacular and the popular media. Some employers told me that they take into consideration the self-respect (*zizunxin*) of domestic workers and introduce their domestic workers to their houseguests as their relatives (*qinqi*).

Given that almost all the young rural migrant women join the wage labor of domestic service as first-generation workers and are on the whole better educated than the small number of older *baomu* active during the Mao era, how do these young women see their subject position as *baomu*? While the specific history of the bondservant system may not be familiar to many Chinese growing up in post-1949 China, representations of servants, through widely known leftist literature of the 1930s and 40s, such as Cao Yu's literary debut *Lei Yu* (Thunder) and Ba Jin's *Jia* (Family), were very closely associated with the class injustice of traditional patriarchal society and have created some impressions among all those who grew up in post-1949 China. The revolutionary play *Bai Mao Nü* (White-Haired Girl), a dramatic story of the liberation of the peasant servant girl Xi'er from the persecution of her master-landlord, was widely popular in the communist-liberated areas in the 1940s and throughout the country after 1949. In this play, the experiences of exploitation and oppression are inscribed on the body of the servant girl and transform her from a youthful woman into a white-haired "ghost". It is in the figure and body of the peasant servant girl – the lowest of the low – that liberation is most powerfully signified. This context helps us to raise the question of what the term *baomu* means to migrant domestic workers today and what kinds of social relations the term suggests.

Almost all my interviewees who joined this work force in the 1980s and 1990s expressed discomfort with the term and found it *nanting* or *buhaoting* (does not sound good) at least, or more extremely, *zhenyaoming* (literally, drive someone to death). One married migrant woman complained, "*baomu* is particularly *nanting* … They should have addressed me by my name". Another also shook her head, "it [*baomu*] is worse than *ayi*. I prefer to be called *dagongmei* (literally, working sister)". Still another found it "*haochou* (very awkward, literally very ugly), not as good as *fuwuyuan* (service worker)". While a migrant woman reluctantly pointed out that to be a *baomu* is to be a *yongren* (servant), another returned migrant woman protested, "migrants in the city are like their [the city's] *yongren*".

Some educated rural young women expressed a deeper worry. Is the specter of the old oppressive society coming back today through domestic service? In 1996, Fang Lin became the first migrant woman to leave her village in Shanxi province for Beijing. When one of her older sisters informed her of the opportunity to work as a *baomu* in Beijing for a family that originally came from Shanxi, Fang Lin's first thought was "Why? This is like going back to the old society". She reminisced, "As soon as I heard that I would work as a *baomu*, I just couldn't accept it. My parents couldn't either. Now suddenly I was faced with this, I really couldn't take it. Neither could my parents". But Fang Lin eventually decided to work as a *baomu* in Beijing. As the system of "household responsibility" decollectivized rural agricultural production in the post-Mao era, the family had to swallow all the loss from the watermelon crop ruined by the weather that year. That summer Fang Ling needed to pay 4280 yuan to be enrolled in a technical school in the fall, and her crippled sister needed money to repeat the final year of high school in order to have a second chance at the national entrance examination for the university in the following year. Fang Lin knew that the family would not have money for both of them. Nobody told her what to do, but she knew. In order for her older sister to have another chance, Fang Lin decided to become a migrant to earn a living. Fang Lin thought hard about it and persuaded her parents that she could do it. "I told my parents that this [working as *baomu*] is nothing. Isn't it very common now? I read in the newspaper that even college students work as *baomu*".

While most urbanites care little about the terms such as *baomu*, *dagongmei*, *fuwuyuan* and take paid domestic service for granted in the context of the market economy, migrant women struggle with the ways these terms signify their class and gender subject positions in post-Mao society. The term *dagongmei* refers to rural migrant women working for service and manufacturing industries without any prospect of long-term contracts and benefits. Typically, they are employed by non-state-owned enterprises, which include domestic private enterprises, joint ventures, and transnational enterprises. While before 1949, the factory was considered a contaminating space, in which women were exposed to male gaze,[24] in both the Mao era and after, factory space has been considered a modern space of collectivity, discipline, and skill.[25]

Compared with the term *fuwuyuan*, which migrant women also prefer, it is not just the specter of the past that migrant women fear in the word *baomu*, but also the term's discursive power and the subjection it seems to suggest – a subjection that is an everyday reality for migrant women. Rong Guang became a migrant in 1992, when she was 17, and in 1999, she described her work experiences. "I was really not used to it and felt really down about myself. When I carried the baby out for fresh air, I always lowered my head and was afraid of raising it. I was really afraid of people saying, you are a *baomu* – this feeling was always with me. I'm especially against the word *baomu*. *Fuwuyuan* is better". The term *fuwuyuan* was created in the Mao era to refer to workers in the service sector, such as restaurant waitresses and hotel workers. From the Mao era context that everyone should *fuwu* (serve) the people (*wei renmin fuwu*), for some migrant women today, the term *fuwuyuan* still offers the comfort of a discursive legitimacy. In the documentary about migrant domestic workers, "*Yuan zai Beijing de jia*" (A Home Far Away from Home), there is a scene of one migrant woman, surrounded by her agitated colleagues, breaking down in tears in front of the camera and protesting, "Does not our work also serve the people?".[26] The subtext of invoking their work as "serving the people" is to assert the Mao era discourse of egalitarianism on the basis of the social – rather than economic – value of work, as a way to protest against their subjection today. For migrant domestic workers, to be addressed as *fuwuyuan* suggests that they are symbolically placed in a discursive context that can be linked to a modern egalitarian social relationship. Despite the fact that the term *baomu* came into circulation in the 1940s to displace the older terms for servants, today this term seems to many migrant women to recall the oppression of pre-1949 society and signifies an oppressive context that disciplines and regulates how they conduct their relationship with employers. The discomfort and fear for the term *baomu* comes from the way domestic workers today see in it the supposedly discredited episteme of the "old society" in which domestic workers as servants have no discursive power and recourse. This, I argue, is the main reason why many migrant domestic workers detest the term *baomu* and prefer the term *fuwuyuan*.

One may understand the problem with *baomu* as a bad word choice on the part of employers and urban society at large and deem the problem of its signification an unfortunate burden from the past. But this understanding is ahistorical, because it refuses to examine the historically-specific link between the term and current social relations that recall it. Such an understanding is also idealist, because it disavows the relationship between the sign and the social world in which it is embedded. If a sign signifies the past, the generative power to bring back the past is not in the sign itself but in the social relations that has brought history alive in the sign. As the current development of the city during the past two decades is served by a continuous fresh supply of young migrant labor, the exploitative relationship between the countryside and the city in some ways recalls the rural–urban relationship in China's semi-colonial history, analyzed in Fei Hsiao-tung's classic work.[27] The current rural–urban relationship and its implications for migrants is perceptively allegorized in a migrant woman's complaint that "migrants in the city are like their [the city's] *yongren* (servants)". Migrant domestic workers' problems and grievances against the term *baomu* and the analogous *yongren* are not about the past buried deeply in these signs but about the present that gives these signs a new lease on life.

Rurality and domestic service as a disciplining process

With the new vision and new strategy of post-Mao modernization plans, the city has increasingly monopolized the discourse of modernity and progress, both discursively and materially.[28] The elite imagination of post-Mao modernity, stimulated by the Open Door policy, stretches far beyond the framework of the nation-state and places Euro-America as the pinnacle of development and global modernity. With state investment increasingly concentrated in the city, making it the center for developing a commodity economy of scale, it becomes the central locale that represents modernity and progress. The countryside comes to be treated as a depository of backwardness, tradition, and low *suzhi*. Post-Mao schooling orients rural youth toward an urban-based modernity but frustrates their aspiration when the majority of them fail to pass national entrance exams for college admission. With rurality devalued, detested, or pitied as the moribund other of modernity and an obstacle to development, rural youth experience what can be called a "crisis of subjectivity". Gao Jialin, the protagonist in the well-known 1980s novel and film *Ren Sheng* (Human Life), is a rural youth who was devastated by his failure in the national entrance exam and the loss of his teaching position in a local school. To spare him from the hard physical labor of working in the fields, his mother sends him to sell home-made buns in the county seat. Intensely embarrassed by his own presence as a peddler in the farmer's market, he sneaks into the county library, where his thoughts take flight from reality as he turns the pages of magazines. He spends the entire day there without selling one single bun. The story is about this young intellectual's alienated relationship with post-Mao rurality and his frustrated efforts to locate his social position and agency. At the heart of the crisis of subjectivity is rural youth's estranged relationship with rurality as it is refracted through the dominant lens of modernity and thus the impasse they encounter in locating their social identity and agency in the countryside. Migration is the most common way for rural youth to "see the world" and to experience modernity. Migrants sometimes say to me, "We come to the city just like urbanites go to America", suggesting that we all pursue an experience of modernity elsewhere.

In this larger context, young migrants in the city are not only positioned as laborers, but also as apprentices of modernity. More specifically, "modernity" for young domestic workers is a new space of domesticity that demands their submission and a new set of tasks and protocols that discipline them in the labor process. One may argue that the matter of having or not having autonomy in the labor process is mainly related to the age profile of domestic workers. Older *baomu* in the Mao era had more autonomy because they were more experienced in housework, while the younger ones in the post-Mao era are supervised because they are inexperienced. But the fact of the matter is that employers in the post-Mao era often demand to be supplied with young domestic workers. Employers in their thirties and forties not only reject the experiences of older rural women as largely backward and unsuitable, but also find it harder for them to impress older migrants with their scientific reasoning and authority. Younger women are in demand because they are more malleable and submit more easily to their employers' instructions and authority.

In contrast to the rustication of urban life in the Mao era, urban life in the post-Mao era has been transformed by constantly renewed styles of consumption. The domestic space of the affluent has been particularly revolutionized in the process of the privatization of housing, the fever of apartment remodeling and refurnishing, and the mushrooming of high-end gated and guarded communities claimed to be of Italian, European, Californian, or some other style. The affluent urban home, showcasing great social disparity and cultural distinction, is an alien and alienating workspace for a rural young woman. Her experience with domestic work in the countryside is almost completely negated by the new environment. One domestic worker complained, "At home I also took care of my younger siblings, but this work is so demanding and complicated in the city. In the countryside, we think it normal that very young children sometimes fall or hurt themselves somewhere. Here it is a big deal, and I'm always the one who gets blamed. Employers also order me to feed the child different things by the clock, baby formula then, mashed fruits now, and so on. It makes my head spin". Employers find it amusing or unbelievable that migrant domestic workers do not know how to perform some "basic" household chores, such as ironing and cleaning hardwood floors. Or, as the most frequent and outraged complaint goes, migrant domestic workers are not even capable of seeing work: "She cannot see the dirt on the floor" or "She cannot see work with her own eyes" (*yan li mei huo'er*). In the new domestic space that embodies modernity, the young migrant domestic worker finds herself disoriented and subjected to a new material and symbolic order whose coding, alien and dominating, is programmed and commanded through the employer's authority and superior access to modernity. This is not unlike the way "luxury" disciplines hotel workers, as shown by Eileen Otis in this book. Her rural identity is highlighted as both awkward in and at odds with cosmopolitan domestic space, marking her as negative in value and identity. Marx wrote of the industrial worker: "The worker therefore only feels himself outside his work, and in his work feels outside himself. He is at home when he is not working, and when he is working he is not at home".[29] If the industrial worker has a space outside work to revive his own sense of being, the migrant domestic worker is in a doubly alienated situation: she is not at home even when she is home in the countryside; she is not at home when she is in the city working at someone else's home. As a young person, she often cannot help but negate herself through society's negation of rurality, but then she has no place to feel at home. With the double alienation and negation, she becomes – in the eyes of employers – a domestic wage worker without subjectivity. Many employers say, "They are like a blank slate". Thus, if the domestic worker cannot see work with her eyes, employers cannot see the subjectivity of the domestic worker, which provides justification for employers' pedagogical agency in training, molding, disciplining, and civilizing migrant domestic workers.

Employers do not just demand that housework is done, but they expect it to be carried out according to protocols that are efficient or appropriate to their relationship. The employers I interviewed often shared with me their acute and detailed observations of how migrant domestic workers carry out their work. Mr Nan, for example, was annoyed that his family's *baomu* did not have the "common sense" to know that she shouldn't touch the toothbrushes and face towels of the masters (*zhu ren de*). Sometimes, the failure of the domestic worker to comply with the expectation is attributed, not just to her lack of experience, but also to the quality of her thinking. As one employer observed, "*Baomu*'s educational level is usually low. They are rough (*cu fang xing*) laborers. Their thinking process proceeds on a single straight line (*zhi xian xing de*) and deals with one thing at a time. They do not know how to do things efficiently. For example, dishes that can be eaten cold should be cooked first, while dishes that must be eaten hot should be cooked last. While one prepares ingredients for one dish, one can have another dish cooking in the wok. But they don't do these things". When it comes to looking after small children, employers perceive a higher stake, such as that a disciplinarian needs to be present full-time to make sure that the right things are done in the right way. Whenever possible, employers ask their retired parent(s) to watch over the domestic worker when they go to work.

Underlying employers' stricter supervision and disciplining of migrant domestic workers today is the negative social value of rurality. If, in the post-Mao era, child care can no longer be entrusted to rural kin, can it be entrusted to a migrant domestic worker who embodies rurality? If "in the countryside they raise children just as they raise pigs and dogs", would employers entrust domestic work and child care to migrant domestic worker who were themselves raised like "pigs and dogs"? If rurality is to be rejected and overcome by post-Mao Chinese modernity, the migrant domestic worker should be supervised, disciplined, and civilized in the labor process "for her own good and for the good of everyone", as employers sometimes insist. With the value of rurality turning negative, it is no surprise that post-Mao migrant domestic workers working for urban households have less autonomy in their labor process.

What, in the post-Mao period, of young migrant women's relationship with rurality after their return? There is very little return to speak of. Unlike the older *baomu* in the Mao era, migrant domestic workers today rarely return to settle back in the countryside. Even when they return to get married and give birth, they know that they will go out again before long. When they do spend extended time in the countryside, they experience a body-mind disjunction. Veteran domestic worker Xiaohong, who has worked in Beijing since 1983 and has gone back and forth many times, is particularly articulate in her perceptions: "I felt that after going back, that heart of mine just couldn't settle down. I had never felt as if I would not go out again or I would like to stay at home. Absolutely not! I didn't have that peace of mind. I have always felt that I'll leave again after a short stay. One time, I didn't plan to come back out, thinking that Beijing is just so-so. But I came out again. I seem to feel that Beijing is especially bustling and boiling, like a whirlpool. At home, I feel especially lonesome, as if far away from life [*yuanli le shenghuo*]. After you return home, you find there is no change, no way out [*meiyou chulu*], and life is boring. So you come out again. Actually, in bustling Beijing, you only have this little room and you don't know people. But only here do you feel settled". To be in Beijing – as a stand-in for the city – is to be in the time-space of modernity, however much marginality, exploitation, and alienation a labor migrant experiences. Rather than taking Xiaohong's expression as a longing for universal modernity, I find her words helpful in problematizing how a specific post-Mao urban-monopolized modernity dominates the meaning of life itself, so much so that to be in the countryside is to be "far away from life".

The problem of return might be further illustrated in one somewhat extreme example related to me by Miss Lan in Hefei, the capital city of Anhui, about her family's young *baomu*. The young woman hired by Miss Lan's parents came to the city for the first time and was very homesick. A few times, she nagged Miss Lan's mother about letting her go back home for a visit. Lan's mother assured her that they would let her go back before January 15, the end of the lunar New Year. Indeed, Lan's mother found a temporary replacement and let her go for a week. But the *baomu* returned to Hefei after barely two days had gone by, saying that her home was too filthy for her to stay longer. The night she was at home, she did not sleep at all. Instead, she sat on the bed for the entire night because she found the bed too filthy to sleep in. The young rural woman's family noticed the change in her. Her grandfather said she had become *xiu* (bourgeois). *Xiu* is short for *xiu zheng zhu yi* (revisionism), a term that became prominent in Mao-era China during its decade-long ideological divergence from and debate with the Soviet Union (1956–66). The USSR, under the leadership of Khruschev, was criticized by China for having taken a bourgeois revisionist line of counter-revolutionary Marxism. That debate and the ensuing Cultural Revolution in China had circulated the term widely in Chinese society. The grandfather's criticism of this rural young woman's transformation as embourgeoisement harks back to a similar critique by the Cultural Revolution film *Juelie*, in which the young rural college student, clad in leather shoes, was embarrassed by his mother's cotton shoes as a sign of the rural. In these critiques, which are largely muted today, we discern a critique of a culture of modernity, not only for being exclusively urban, but also for being urban bourgeois.

Conclusion

While *baomu* in both the Mao era and the post-Mao era conducted their work in the form of wage labor and have been similarly subjected to structural inequality as domestic workers, significant differences exist in the relations and processes of labor in these two eras that bear out the political epistemic differences between the two eras. Central to my examination of *baomu*'s work experiences is whether domestic workers have autonomy in their labor process and what structural and ideological conditions enable or disable their autonomy. A critical enabling condition for domestic workers' autonomy is the valuation of rurality in the Mao era egalitarian ideology that allowed and encouraged rurality to be woven into the fabric of urban social and domestic life. This valorization of rurality, in the consciously politicized and radicalized Mao-era culture of modernity, is not external to the labor process but is the context that became expressed in the labor process itself. Rurality is fundamentally degraded in post-Mao modernity, which makes the city the hegemonic site of development and progress. This urban monopoly of modernity creates a crisis of subjectivity for rural youth. The relentless degradation and otherization of rurality in the post-Mao culture of modernity also becomes expressed in the labor process itself. Thus, the migrant domestic worker experiences dual subjection, as both a wageworker and a blank slate to the pedagogical and disciplinary authority of her employer in the labor process.

Notes

1 An earlier version of this chapter is published by the journal *Cultural Dynamics*, 18(1): 5–31. Many thanks are due to Chen Junjie, Zsuzsa Gilles, Eileen Otis, and Barry Sautman for their comments on earlier drafts of this chapter. I owe special thanks to Ching Kwan Lee, who has tirelessly read and responded to multiple revisions. Shortcomings of this chapter are all mine.
   Inspired by American women's mass revolt in textile and garment industries in New York in 1857, German socialist Klara Zetkin organized International Women's Day in 1911 and was supported by socialists in many European countries. In 1975, the United Nations endorsed the International Women's Day. The International Women's Day is an official holiday in China. Used in the name of this company, March 8 has becomes a gender code for women with little socialist content of gender equality. It ironically and completely naturalizes the association between women and domestic work.
2 A variety of service labor performed in hotels, cafeterias, restaurants, daycare centers, and the like became "socialized labor" in the Mao era, which means that such labor was socially and politically acknowledged to be in the public interests; labor planning and regulation were carried out by state or collective authorities, and most workers enjoyed employment guarantees and related benefits. On the failure to socialize domestic service, I give a more elaborate analysis of its relation to patriarchy in Chapter 2 of my book manuscript under submission, entitled *Belaboring Development: Migration, Subjectivity, and Domestic Labor in Post-Mao China*.
3 Karl Marx, *Capital, volume 1,* New York, NY: Vintage Books, 1977: 1021.
4 Tolerated and encouraged by Party leaders such as Liu Shaoqi and Deng Xiaoping, division and inequality existed in urban factories in the Mao era between permanent and regular work forces and the temporary and contract-based labor force recruited

from the countryside. During the Cultural Revolution, contract workers were agitators against the status quo. On the eve of the Cultural Revolution, Mao condemned "capitalist roaders" within the Party and state structure for "sucking the blood of the workers", turning into a bourgeois elements, and constituting a bureaucratic class in opposition to the interests of workers and peasants. See Maurice Meisner, *Mao's China and After*, 1999, New York, NY: Free Press: 306, 326.

5 The historically determined transition that I contest here refers to the view that Mao era socialism was a premature leap or an aberrant detraction from a normative trajectory of capitalist development and bourgeois enlightenment. Among intellectual elites, the post-Mao transformation was widely perceived as a historically destined transition that resumes a disrupted enlightenment project.

6 For discussions and debates on whether and how non-paid domestic labor performed by housewives creates surplus value, see, for example, Wally Seccombe, "The Housewife and Her Labour under Capitalism", (1974) 83 *New Left Review*: 3–24; "Domestic Labour – Reply to Critics", (1975) 94 *New Left Review*: 85–96; and Magaš Coulson and Hilary Wainwright, "'The Housewife and her Labor under Capitalism' – a Critique", (1975) 89 *New Left Review*: 59–71.

7 Chu Gansheng, *Nubi shi: zhongguo nubi wenti de lishi sikao* (A History of Servants: A Historical Examination of the Servant Question in China), Shanghai: Shanghai wenyi chubanshe, 1995; James Watson, "Transactions in People: The Chinese Market in Slaves, Servants, and Heirs", in *Asian and African Systems of Slavery*, James L. Watson (ed.), Oxford: Basil Blackwell, 1980: 223–50.

8 Chu, *Nubi shi*: 2.

9 Chu, *Nubi shi*: 130–6 also provides a fascinating account of servant resistance and uprisings. The largest uprising took place at the end of the Ming Dynasty (1364–1644) and swept over a dozen provinces and had a close relationship with the peasant uprising led by Li Zicheng that toppled the Ming Dynasty.

10 *Lu Deyang and Wang Naining, Shehui de youcichengmian: Zhongguo jindai nüyong* (Another Dimension of Society: Female Servants in China's Near-Modern Times), Shanghai: Xuelin chubanshe, 2004: 23–42.

11 Chu, *Nubi shi*: 147.

12 Ibid.: 148. A variety of servant categories existed in China before 1949, including bondservants. For writings on bonded servants in Hong Kong, see Rubie Watson, "Wives, Concubines, and Maids: Servitude and Kinship in the Hong Kong Region, 1900–1940", in Rubie Watson and Patricia Buckley Ebrey (eds), *Marriage and Inequality in Chinese Society*, Berkeley, CA: University of California Press, 1991: 231–55; and Maria Jaschok, *Concubines and Bondservants: The Social History of a Chinese Custom*, Hong Kong: Oxford University Press, 1988.

13 For the classical term *baomu*, see Lee Jen-Der, "Wet Nurses in Early Imperial China" (2000) 2(1) *Nan Nu*: 1–39.

14 Yan Hairong, "Spectralization of the Rural: Reinterpertion of Labor mobility of rural young women in the post-Mao era", (2003) 30(4) *American Ethnologist*: 578–96.

15 This is what a junior-to-mid-level urban worker might earn as a monthly salary in the 1970s.

16 Wang Anyi, *Fuping*, Changsha: Hunan wenyi chubanshe, 2000.

17 Li Wenhua, dir., *Juelie* (Breaking the Old Ideas), 1975.

18 Ann Anagnost, "A Surfeit of Bodies: Population and the Rationality of State in Post-Mao China", in *Conceiving the New World Order: Local/Global Intersections in the Politics of Reproduction*, Faye Ginsburg and Rayna Rapp (eds), Berkeley, CA: University of California Press, 1995: 22–41.

19 The older employers I interviewed all claimed to know of such cases, but all assured me that they were not criticized by their *baomu*. Be that as it may. Although there is little concrete record of how some *baomu* in the Cultural Revolution spoke in

public, the fact that they did speak is significant and should be remembered, however transient, momentary, and mediated their speech.

20 *South China Morning Post*, "Another 5 Million Domestic Helpers Needed, Says Group", February 17, 2004: A4.

21 See http://www.southcn.com/news/china/zgkx/200402110793.htm

22 Xinhua, "Beijing in Need of Housemaids", December 13, 2003.

23 *South China Morning Post*, "More Shanghai Families are Employing Maids", September 18, 2003: A6.

24 Lisa Rofel, *Other Modernities*, Berkeley, CA: University of California Press, 1999.

25 Ching Kwan Lee, *Gender and the South China Miracle: Two Worlds of Factory Women*, Berkeley, CA: University of California Press, 1998.

26 Chen Xiaoqing, dir., *Yuan zai Beijing de jia* (A Home Far Away from Home), Chinese Central Television and Anhui Provincial Television, 1993.

27 Fei Hsiao-tung, *China's Gentry: Essays in Rural-Urban Relations*, Chicago, IL: University of Chicago Press, 1953.

28 Yan Hairong, "Neo-Liberal Governmentality and Neo-Humanism: Organizing Value Flow Through Labor Recruitment Agencies",(2003) 18 (4) *Cultural Anthropology*: 493–523.

29 Robert C. Tucker, *The Marx-Engels Reader*, 2nd edition, New York, NY: W. W. Norton & Company, Inc., 1978: 74.

Part III

New professions and knowledge workers

9 The practice of law as an obstacle to justice

Chinese lawyers at work[1]

Ethan Michelson

MALE LAWYER 1 (L₁): How could you have signed this [labor] contract? Were you scatterbrained?

FEMALE CLIENT (C): Yes, at the time, I signed it with my eyes shut. I didn't read it at all.

L₁: Well, if you signed with your eyes shut, you should face the consequences alone. What were you thinking? … Are you divorced? Or is it possible you have other issues? You can't let go of problems. In your everyday life, do you often get into arguments with people? …

C: Why ask about my marriage?

L₁: I've already answered your legal question. Let's conclude this consultation here, okay?

C: I don't think you have any principles!

L₁: When someone asks you about your contract, do you have evidence? *Evidence! Evidence! Evidence! …*

MALE LAWYER 2: Let me tell you, you've passed the filing deadline; the labor arbitration committee will not arbitrate. The guy is right … I'm the lawyer, don't be so stubborn! … You have no chance! Get it? This is all I can say. If you still don't understand, seek the advice of someone wiser.

Labor dispute consultation at the BC Law Firm, Beijing, August 23, 2001

It has been accepted as a scholarly truism that access to justice cannot be reduced to access to courts. To answer questions about the overall accessibility of official justice, we must begin our analysis with the institutions that facilitate and limit the initial awareness of injuries and other violations, the escalation of these perceived transgressions to grievances, and the escalation of grievances to claims that may or may not end up in court.[2] Building on a research tradition in which lawyers are seen to "hold the keys that open or close the gates of the legal system",[3] this chapter scrutinizes the role of lawyers and law firms in these access-enhancing and access-depriving processes. My goal is to explain motive and mechanism in the case-screening process: why and how Chinese lawyers function as gatekeepers to justice by refusing to represent certain kinds of clients with certain kinds of problems. By showing how lawyers exercise power in the legal process through the control of meaning, this chapter explicitly links micro-level discourse to the macro-level issue of access to justice.

In the wake of China's economic reforms and restructuring of the state sector, the growing volume of labor disputes involving pensioners, laid-off workers, injured workers, and workers owed back wages has received both heightened scholarly as well as media attention.[4] Against this backdrop, observers of China sometimes assume that the rapidly expanding corps of lawyers and the rapid pace of legal reform serve to advance the interests of aggrieved workers.[5] To be sure, individuals are using the law – and using it successfully – with increasing frequency as a weapon to advance their rights and interests.[6] Yet, we must also consider the extent to which the law is a weapon lawyers use to refuse representation to, and therefore to undermine the rights and interests of, aggrieved citizens, as well as the reasons why they do so and the methods they employ in this effort.[7] As we will see in this chapter, lawyers serve as a gateway – which they frequently slam shut – to the legal system.

Researching Chinese lawyers in action

Observations of interactions between lawyers and clients at a Beijing law firm I will call the BC Law Firm serve as the primary source of data in support of my argument that lawyers are an obstacle to justice. Between March and August 2001, two Chinese undergraduates studying sociology at a major university in Beijing, hired and trained by me, observed 48 legal consultation sessions – representing 45 unique cases – at the BC Law Firm. They tape-recorded approximately half of all these consultation sessions; on the basis of notes taken by hand during the consultations, they were able to reconstruct each remaining session in its entirety. Five sessions were recounted after the fact by the attending lawyers. This research strategy allowed data to be collected without my presence as a foreign observer. The research assistants also conducted separate open-ended, semi-structured interviews with 35 of this firm's lawyers.

Of all 48 consultation sessions we observed, five – or almost 10 percent – involved labor disputes. Two of the sessions concerned wrongful termination and were pursued as labor-contract violations, one a pension dispute, one a dispute over wages owed, and the remainder representation in labor arbitration. Of all 48 sessions, nine had clients who could be identified as either migrants residing in Beijing or residents of locations outside Beijing. The clients in all labor consultations appeared to be Beijing residents. The consultations were split fairly evenly by gender, with 22 involving female clients, 17 male, and eight clients of both genders. There is no clear difference in the kinds of disputes brought by men and women. The estimated age of the client ranged from the mid-twenties to the early eighties, with the median age in the mid-forties. The only pattern with respect to age is that clients with housing-inheritance disputes tended to be older and those with economic disputes tend to be younger.

The 48 sessions I analyze involved a total of 27 lawyers. They were a very diverse group: some had worked only as lawyers, while some had held other careers prior to switching to law. Some had experience in other law firms. Some were from Beijing, some were from distant provinces. They were at different career stages: some were fully licensed lawyers, some were interning lawyers, and one was a partner. Only four were female. The average age was about 33; the oldest lawyer was in his mid-forties and the youngest were in their early twenties.[8] The names of all lawyers cited in this chapter are pseudonyms.

The plurality of the consultation sessions concerns housing disputes. This category includes nine disputes with other residents or tenants over property rights, many of which originated during the Cultural Revolution (1966–76) or earlier. Economic disputes, the second largest category, consist for the most part of debt and contract disputes. The administrative category includes a botched tubal ligation, a dispute over irregular fees levied by a local government office, and the case of an old man seeking reparations from the Japanese government for performing forced labor service in Japan during the Sino–Japanese War (1937–45). The police disputes include the assault of a woman by a police officer, a case of administrative detention, and a police shooting in which a teenage boy was killed. The criminal disputes include several serious assault cases and a case of incest.

I also marshal evidence from sources outside the BC Law Firm. I draw on additional data from 33 unstructured in-depth interviews I conducted alone with lawyers, legal scholars, government officials, and journalists in Beijing outside the firm (in 1999–2001 and 2004) and a survey of almost 1,000 lawyers in 25 cities across China conducted in the summer of 2000.[9]

The solo character and financial insecurity of Chinese lawyers

The financial success of lawyers in China's top corporate law firms working on international commercial transactions belies the grim reality that most Chinese lawyers are struggling for survival. At the root of this struggle is a model of organization giving rise to a life-and-death imperative to bill. We cannot understand why lawyers screen cases without understanding the pressure engendered by the organization of the Chinese law firm to generate legal fees.

Lawyers classify themselves according to their method of remuneration – salaried lawyers versus commission-based lawyers (E26).[10] Commission-based lawyers are typically called "lawyers who take a cut" (*ticheng lüshi*), but sometimes they also go by the name "cooperating lawyer" (*hezuo lüshi*), referring to a status more closely resembling that of loosely affiliated contract workers than that of stable, full-fledged firm members. While about half of all lawyers in Beijing in the summer of 2000 were paid exclusively on a commission basis,[11] almost all – 93 percent – of the lawyers I interviewed in the BC Law Firm reported getting paid this way. Larger firms organized in divisions handling larger, more complex commercial cases tend to employ more salaried lawyers, while the far more representative smaller firms handling run-of-the-mill civil cases tend to consist of more commission-based lawyers. In the smaller cities outside Beijing, with fewer large commercial transactions, 80 percent of lawyers are paid on a commission basis.[12] Salaried lawyers – who are called precisely this (*xinjin lüshi*), "lawyers that draw a salary" (*lingxin lüshi*), or "hired lawyers" (*pinyong lüshi*) – are found almost exclusively in the elite corporate law firms of China's big cities. They remain the exception to the rule. Commission-based lawyers, by contrast, account for the vast majority of Chinese lawyers.[13] Most Chinese lawyers "eat what they kill"; despite mandatory membership in a law firm containing at least three full-time lawyers,[14] they operate like solo practitioners, solely responsible for finding and representing clients from beginning to end. Indeed, a popular expression used to describe the life of commission-based lawyers is "fighting the battle alone" (*dan da du dou*).

The Darwinian struggle in the Chinese bar has been exacerbated by its rapid privatization.[15] Like China's small-scale private entrepreneurs, Chinese lawyers are autonomous, independent, and self-reliant. Known as *geti hu* (literally, "independent households"), these "[i]ndividual enterprisers are people who do not have formal positions at any state- or collective-owned work unit, but make their living solely from the market".[16] A popular professional nickname captures the plight of Chinese lawyers: "*geti hu* who know the law" (E14, E18, and I13). As one lawyer informant – who also worked as a journalist for a major national newspaper – summarized in 2001, "Lawyers are *geti hu*, just like those who set up stalls on the side of the road, like *geti hu* who sell fruit" (E14).

Privatization has aggravated not only lawyers' financial vulnerability, but also their institutional vulnerability *vis-à-vis* the state. In the wake of the privatization of the bar, lawyers' heightened autonomy from the state in their day-to-day work – the work of finding and managing clients and of investigating and processing cases – has ironically contributed to the persistence of their exposure to predatory harassment, intimidation, obstruction, and rent seeking from officials in various government agencies, including the police and procuracy. Owing to the professional, and even physical, dangers associated with their institutional marginalization, lawyers tend to screen out criminal defense, administrative litigation, and other cases that pit them directly against the interests of the state.[17] As a matter of selective adaptation to this hostile environment, an estimated one-fifth of lawyers surveyed in Beijing reported prior employment in the police, the procuracy, and the courts. Owing to the real measure of protection offered by their special "insider" connections to state actors, lawyers with such backgrounds are more likely than other lawyers to work in criminal defense and other politically risky fields of practice and less likely to report difficulty in their everyday professional practice.[18] Despite their salience in the screening process, these *political* pressures to avoid cases that could be construed as undermining the state's overriding goal to preserve social stability are beyond the scope of this chapter. Instead, the more limited focus of this chapter is on the effects of lawyers' *socioeconomic vulnerability*.

Given the difficulty most firms have in providing such basic resources as law libraries and computers, it should not be surprising that firms are even harder pressed to provide social security benefits. Among 283 law firms I surveyed in 25 cities across China in 2000, 30 percent failed to provide a single item from a list of five perks and fringe benefits, and only 13 percent provided at least two of the five items.[19] As might be expected, of 14 items lawyers were asked to rate in terms of their level of satisfaction, "social security benefits provided by my firm" rated far and away the lowest. The almost 1,000 lawyers I surveyed across China were twice as likely to say that they were "very unsatisfied" with their firms' provision of social-security items than they were with the item generating the second highest levels of dissatisfaction.[20]

Like many, if not most, Chinese law firms, the BC Law Firm imposes minimum annual billings quotas. In 1996 lawyers at BC were required to bill at least 15,000–20,000 yuan per year to stay in the firm; the firm collected these billings directly, and one-half then went back to the lawyer. Within a few years, minimum billing requirements had risen to 40,000 yuan. To put this in perspective, I estimate that in 2000, the median pre-tax, take-home income of lawyers in Beijing – above and beyond what their firms take from their gross billings – was 38,000 yuan.[21] In Beijing, a 50 percent rule governing lawyers' commissions – or fee retention – was the general policy across law firms, in accordance with Bureau of Justice regulations. Later, this policy was loosened to enhance law firms' discretion over lawyer remuneration, and some law firms increased commission rates to 60 percent to attract legal talent. Elsewhere, commissions have been as low as one-third of total billings (E25). At the BC Law Firm, the commission was still 50 percent in 2001 (I14).

Regardless of how lawyers are paid and the client is billed, legal fees are almost always paid from the client's own resources or from funds recovered or collected from the client's adversary in the dispute. In China, there is no norm or expectation of fee shifting; neither the English rule of two-way fee shifting – in which the loser unconditionally pays the winner's legal fees – nor the common American practice of one-way fee shifting – in which the loser pays the winner's legal fees if the loser is the defendant but not if the loser is the plaintiff – applies.[22] In contrast to American plaintiffs' lawyers, who survive on awards underwritten by insurance companies, the incipience of the liability insurance industry in China solidifies lawyers' dependence on clients rather than on an insurance payout. But even if lawyers could count on an insurance payout, the courts neither execute fee agreements nor withhold the fee from awards, but rather leave it to clients to adhere to such agreements on their own accord.[23] Consequently, lawyers experience great difficulty in collecting their fees, and they try to avoid "risky" clients.

The profound financial and social insecurity caused by these factors undermine the ability of lawyers to defend the rights and interests of the poor. Many lawyers echoed the sentiment that their first task is to ensure their own financial security (E02). "Lawyers are hunting and killing each other ... Lawyers are not like people think they are. They do not find justice ... Most lawyers consider only their basic survival" (I02).[24] The economic pressures produced by this remuneration and billing system overwhelm lawyers' ideals to represent aggrieved individuals. As Lawyer Mu described it, "When I first started working as a lawyer, I believed my interests and my clients' interests were united. At the time, if I lost a case I was devastated. Now I understand things better. My interests are not the same as my clients'. When I do my work, it's enough just to make some money" (I23).

Refusing cases with low fee potential

The consequences of lawyers' financial insecurity are not surprising. Cases with low fee potential, such as labor cases representing workers, are particularly undesirable. Yet they are advanced by clients for whom the small amount of money at stake is financially important. These matters are often about non-monetary issues, such as wrongful termination of employment and illegal working conditions. Sometimes claims are made on principle, to defend a sacred socialist entitlement. In the words of a retired cadre in his seventies who was fighting for a small retirement bonus promised to veterans of the Revolution, "I have over fifty years of Communist Party membership. How can I take this quietly? ... This is not about my one month's pension. I'm not short of money" (C31). Given the small sums of money involved, however, lawyers are rarely interested in cases of this sort.[25]

In the summer of 2004, the absolute minimum fee for legal representation was 2,000 yuan at a similar law firm (led by a former director of the BC Law Firm). Legal fees for criminal defense, especially for economic crimes, could be as high as 10,000 yuan. Legal fees for economic cases were typically charged on a sliding scale, according to the value of the object in dispute or the amount recovered or collected. The director explained that the firm's lawyers are inclined toward economic cases because of their potential to generate lucrative fees. As he put it, a labor case, by contrast, may involve recovering a month's salary, perhaps amounting to 2,000 yuan – a little more than employed workers' average monthly income in Beijing, and just enough to pay the firm's minimum fee. Under these circumstances, the lawyer lacks an incentive to accept the case; at the same time, the client lacks an incentive to hire the lawyer (E35).[26] In the field of labor disputes – representing workers – only work-related accidents, especially those involving dismemberment and wrongful death, offer the hope of a large award or settlement.[27]

Yet even lawyers who accept and win such cases report difficulty collecting fees. In addition, cases that are financially valuable on paper are not always convertible to cash. This is especially true for housing cases. Even if a housing property in dispute is of great value, the client may intend to live in it, in which case lawyers will tend to display only lukewarm interest at best. However, if the client intends to sell the property – or collect compensation from the property's occupant – or rent it out at market price, lawyers will tend to be far more enthusiastic. Lawyers are often interested in straightforward debt-collection cases, especially when the debtor has the financial means to pay his obligation. In short, whether or not the case involves recovering cash or convertible property is a critical determinant of the way it will be screened by a lawyer.

Among the 48 consultations we observed at the BC Law Firm, three-quarters of the economic cases – more than any other type of case – involved recovering cash or convertible property. At the same time, less than one-fifth of the housing disputes involved property that the client hoped to sell or use to earn cash. Not a single labor dispute involved collecting a significant amount of money or compensation.

Problems involving the recovery of cash or convertible property are far more likely to arouse lawyers' interest and enthusiasm. The way lawyers expressed interest in accepting a case was by: clearly indicating a desire to take it – making a sales pitch to promote his or her services – or discussing a fee – either a set amount or a contingency fee. According to this definition alone, attending lawyers expressed interest in 42 percent of all 48 consultation sessions. However, they expressed interest in 75 percent of the economic cases and in none of the labor cases. At the same time, while the attending lawyers explicitly refused the case in 21 percent of the 48 consultation sessions, they did so in 40 percent of the labor cases and in none of the economic cases.[28] The likelihood that a lawyer would express some interest in accepting a case was over three-and-a-half times greater if the problem involved recovering cash or convertible property – 92 percent versus 25 percent. While the attending lawyer explicitly refused the case in 28 percent of the consultation sessions that did not involve recovering cash or convertible property, he or she did not explicitly refuse any case that involved recovering cash or convertible property. In this small sample of consultations, the cases of aggrieved workers were screened out and economic cases were screened in. As we will see in the following section, however, economic considerations are sometimes trumped by cultural ones.

Refusing the high-risk client

In light of lawyers' dependence on clients to pay their legal fees out of their own accord and the client's weak incentive to pay, the lawyer–client relationship is antagonistic and adversarial. Lawyer Zhong, male, in his late thirties, and one of the more successful lawyers in the firm, says that lawyers need to treat their clients as their greatest enemy (I01). In another interview, the same lawyer reflects: "As a lawyer, you must conquer your client … The contradictions between lawyers and clients are the most concentrated. If the lawyer loses control, the lawyer will suffer the most harm of all … This is ten years of experience in a nutshell" (I39).

An important source of power that clients wield is the threat of non-payment. It is not uncommon for clients to refuse to pay lawyers' fees (I01).[29] The experience of Zhou Litai is instructive. Rising to domestic and international prominence thanks to his specialization in recovering compensation on behalf of migrant workers dismembered in industrial accidents, his celebrity has extended as far as *The New York Times, The Washington Post, Newsweek, USA Today,* and other foreign media outlets. Despite his tremendous success in representing over 800 migrant workers injured on the job, Zhou Litai has more recently proclaimed, undoubtedly with more than a tinge of hyperbole, "I have been judged China's most famous lawyer, but I am absolutely the poorest lawyer".[30] Asserting that 161 clients owe him a total of 5 million yuan – or US$605,000 – he has started filing law suits against clients who fled after collecting their awards.[31] This amount dwarfs those owed to the American divorce lawyers interviewed by Mather *et al.*, which ranged from US$30,000 to US$125,000.[32] Zhou Litai claims to lose 60 percent of the fees he bills.

Clients not only refuse to pay; they may also retaliate by suing their lawyers after an undesirable outcome.[33] According to an official in the Guangzhou Bureau of Justice, 60 percent to 70 percent of all administrative complaints against lawyers in the late 1990s were filed by clients who lost their cases and blamed their lawyers. In consultations with clients, lawyers are on the lookout for signs of implacable, uncooperative clients. The warning signs of a troublemaker include anger, ranting and raving, and "hysterical" outbursts couched in moralistic language about right and wrong, good and bad, and unfulfilled state obligations.

Although business clients may also cheat lawyers of their fee,[34] lawyers' overwhelming response has been to screen individual clients. Lawyer Mu gives serious consideration to all cases that he believes will generate fees, but he tries to avoid representing clients who are unreasonably demanding and who present unreasonable cases (I23). When explaining why they refuse clients, Chinese lawyers reported an aversion to: "clients of low quality [*suzhi di*]"; "clients with whom I have difficulty communicating"; "clients who try to direct my work"; "clients who have a foul moral character"; and "clients who won't stop pestering me".[35] The discourse of low quality also reflects a practice of "profiling" clients according to cultural stereotypes of workers and peasants with lower levels of education. As Zhou Litai states, "The critical problem is how to elevate the quality and cultivation of these people".[36]

A lawyer I interviewed used the term *diaomin* to characterize clients who fight their employers tooth and nail for wages and pensions, for example.[37] *Diaomin*, who are deemed more likely to challenge their employers and pursue labor grievances, are the most contentious and recalcitrant category of clients, precisely the troublemakers lawyers try to avoid. According to this lawyer, *diaomin* who challenge their employers are also more likely to challenge the lawyers they hire to do so and to demand a refund of their fees if their wishes are not completely fulfilled (E34). To be sure, lawyers "profile" prospective clients to some degree on the basis of experience; Lawyer Zhong's experience representing a client in a labor dispute seems to confirm the stereotype of the *diaomin*. After Lawyer Zhong applied for labor arbitration and wrote letters to the Deputy Party Secretary of the Beijing Municipal Party Committee and to leaders of the responsible enterprise, apparently to no avail, his client filed a formal complaint with the Beijing Lawyers Association, claiming that the legal fee was too steep (C19).

As we saw in the quotation that opened this chapter, lawyers even invoke and perpetuate stereotypes about the questionable moral quality of divorcees. In this particular example, by indicating that the client fit the profile of a divorcee, the lawyer effectively labeled her a "problem client". Divorcees in China continue to be evaluated as morally dubious, as troublemakers who have difficulty getting along with others, and as less fit to be good parents and productive citizens.[38] This, of course, is a cultural stereotype that becomes a reason and pretense for refusing representation.

Yet lawyers are not always stone-cold and heartless. Presenting their case in a way that elicits lawyers' sympathy is a major source of power wielded by clients. Some lawyers view such efforts to secure their sympathy as evidence of how crafty and emotionally manipulative clients can be. But other lawyers do try to help "deserving" clients in seemingly desperate circumstances, even if they are unable to pay the legal fee. This phenomenon is what Kritzer calls "de facto pro bono" work.[39]

In this section we have seen that economics sometimes trumps culture: lawyers like Zhou Litai accept cases with high fee potential even – indeed, exclusively – from "risky" clients. At the same time, however, we have also seen that culture sometimes trumps economics: lawyers not only report representing morally worthy clients even when their cases are unprofitable but, as we will continue to see in the following section, they also, and more typically, report refusing to represent clients who fit the profile of the *diaomin*, regardless of the fee potential of the case.

How lawyers use law as a weapon

The prior two sections concern the question of screening motive. Now I will turn to the question of mechanism. Refusing a case may be direct and explicit, but more often lawyers use methods to discourage clients that are less direct. Lawyers may quote excessively high fees: Lawyer Hou demanded 8,000 yuan for a case for which he would normally charge 3,000 yuan (I12). Another common technique is mis-educating and mis-informing the client in an effort to redefine the problem as one beyond the scope of the law. Legal discourse – what Sarat and Felstiner call "law talk" – is a strategic weapon lawyers use to control the situation and to placate and vanquish clients who themselves are trying to assert some degree of control over the legal process.[40] Lawyers invoke evidentiary issues, filing deadlines, a low probability of winning, and a high probability of court rejection as pretenses for denying the legal legitimacy of the case and for discouraging clients from pursuing redress by way of actual legal opportunities that may exist.

Clients talk about moral rights, justice, feelings and relationships, but for lawyers to gain full control, such discourse must be purged from consideration. Lawyers often contrast "feeling" with "reason" and "law"; they emphasize the need to separate what is reasonable from what is legally feasible and permissible. They use words like "rambling" and "annoying" to describe clients who try to gain their sympathy with long-winded sob stories. At best, lawyers deem these stories irrelevant blather, and they interrupt impatiently, demanding that the client stick to the relevant facts. At worst, lawyers view this discourse as an indication of a "problem client".

A client in a consultation session pleaded for help with a housing dispute that had eluded resolution for decades: "But he's so old and in poor health". To this Lawyer Ni replied, "The court doesn't care about feelings, the court cares only about evidence". About 10 minutes further on in the consultation, the client said, "My father took family very seriously". Lawyer Ni responded, "The court doesn't consider the goodness of people. For all those years, you didn't do anything. Why didn't you stand up for your rights? Frankly speaking, the court doesn't care about feelings". Earlier in this same consultation the lawyer said, "Evidence; the court doesn't care about feelings, it only cares about evidence" (C07).

When efforts to (mis)educate and "talk sense" into clients fail, lawyers display impatience, condescension, and exasperation. Lawyers' impatience with clients is a function of the financial potential of the case: The probability that the attending lawyer expressed impatience was more than three times greater if the case did not involve recovering cash or convertible property than if the case did involve recovering cash or convertible property – 25 percent versus 8 percent.[41]

The relationship between case screening and fee potential is often mediated by evaluations of the client's character of the client. A red flag for lawyers is raised when a client expresses anger and moral outrage.[42] As a consequence, lawyers aim to discourage such clients. While they are slightly more likely to refuse representation explicitly when clients express moral outrage – 25 percent when the discourse of moral outrage is present versus 20 percent when it is not present – lawyers are far more likely to use less direct tactics of discouragement to screen out cases they deem risky and undesirable: They are about half as likely to express interest in accepting the case – 25 percent versus 45 percent – more than three times as likely to display impatience – 50 percent versus 15 percent – and, consistent with the quotation that opened this chapter, almost three times as likely to invoke evidentiary problems or filing deadlines – 50 percent versus 18 percent. Importantly, even when the case entails recovering cash or convertible property, lawyers nonetheless send discouraging signals – disinterest, impatience, and ostensible evidentiary problems and filing deadlines – to clients who express moral outrage. When the case is not lucrative *and* the character of the client is undesirable, it is a virtual certainty that the lawyer will dodge representation.

The general empirical pattern is unambiguous: lawyers are more likely to turn away – both explicitly and indirectly – clients who bring cases that do not involve cash or convertible property and who are deemed potentially troublesome. Although the small number of observations prohibits definitive conclusions, the implications are clear: since labor cases typically involve small amounts of compensation pursued by urban China's most economically needy, this is precisely the category of disputes we would expect lawyers to shun the most. Of the four consultation sessions – among all 48 we observed – in which the attending lawyer invoked filing deadlines as a reason for refusing representation, three were labor disputes.[43] Institutional norms and legal doctrine do, to some degree, hinder lawyers from accepting labor disputes. But by obscuring the real opportunities to pursue labor disputes in the legal system, legal doctrine simultaneously serves as a tool for screening out these undesirable cases.

Discourse and deception

As we have seen, a common tactic deployed to refuse labor cases is to claim that a statutory 60-day filing deadline – stipulated by Article 82 of the 1995 Labor Law – has been exceeded. What lawyers do *not* say, however, is that this filing deadline is actually quite flexible. Article 85 of the Ministry of Labor's 1995 Opinion Regarding Some Problems in the Implementation and Enforcement of the Labor Law states, "'The date on which the labor dispute arose' shall mean the date on which a party knew or should have known that his rights had been infringed on".[44] The legal difficulties associated with establishing when a client "should have known" of a certain event introduces freedom and flexibility into the labor arbitration process.[45]

Furthermore, lawyers' discourse of the evidentiary imperative of litigation and of strict legal standards contradicts much of what we know about the actual operation of Chinese courts. Lawyers portray a legal system that is rigidly by-the-book and that offers little in the way of wiggle room for negotiation, persuasion, and informal influence. They deny the centrality of "sentiment and feelings" in a court system that, in fact, has been characterized as flexible, accommodating, and conciliatory.[46] Their discourse of the evidentiary imperative of litigation, their forceful negation of claims that "the law also considers sentiment and feelings", is part of an effort to strip cases of their legal significance and to negate the merit of clients' legal claims.

Such a conclusion can only emerge from a *constitutive* approach to sociolegal studies, in which law is treated not as a reified, stable, and transparent entity but rather as the product of a struggle between competing actors over naming the problem, over defining the problem as one that merits a legal solution, some other kind of solution, or no solution at all. Law is a fluid and contested process constituted by its actors, who imbue it with meaning and derive meaning from it through their actions, interactions, and struggles. In short, the power of law includes the power to obscure and obfuscate; law both reflects and reinforces power.[47] The practice of law is a confidence game in which "truth" and "reality" are manipulated for strategic purposes.[48]

Screening in comparative perspective

Chinese lawyers' motives and mechanisms for refusing representation reaffirm patterns observed elsewhere in the world, and in so doing contribute to the construction of a general theory of case screening. Research on lawyers in various Western contexts shows that lawyers can and do advance the interests of individuals with legal needs[49] and exhibit a widespread willingness both to represent the poor and the powerless[50] and to advance other "causes".[51] Nevertheless, contextually specific institutional conditions can produce countervailing economic pressures that overwhelm their ideals and altruism. In the American context, tort reform measures in most states, which impose caps on non-economic and/or punitive damages awarded by courts, have intensified competition and heightened the imperative in the American bar to adopt entrepreneurial strategies. These include the screening of prospective clients.[52] Not surprisingly, an estimated one-half to two-thirds of cases brought to contingency-fee lawyers are rejected.[53] Owing in part to economic disincentives produced by caps on awards and fees, rates of refusal are highest in the fields of medical malpractice and labor.[54]

In comparison to Chinese lawyers, American lawyers more commonly collect fees from insurance companies and from their clients' adversaries through fee-shifting. But when legal fees are paid directly by the client using the client's own resources, as is often the case in hourly- or fixed-fee arrangements, American lawyers, like their Chinese counterparts, become concerned about not getting paid.[55] Finally, American lawyers, too, are concerned about malpractice suits[56] and collecting legal fees. With respect to mechanisms, lawyers in the West have also been shown to put aside clients' discourse of everyday reason and feelings and to redefine clients' problems in strictly legal terms; Sarat and Felstiner call this strategy an "ideology of separate spheres".[57] After redefining the problem as a strictly technical-legal matter, lawyers can more easily exercise the power to "educate" the prospective client about legal "reality" – reality as defined by the lawyer to serve the lawyer's interests.[58] Mis-information and mis-education about the legal merit of the case become the basis for refusing or discouraging representation or for setting more "reasonable" and "realistic" goals and expectations for clients.[59]

Discussion and conclusions

As gatekeepers to justice, lawyers work to educate and to mis-educate people to the realities of legal institutions. By removing emotions and everyday reason and narrowing the scope of discussion to the relevant "legal" norms – as they variously define them – Chinese lawyers act as lawyers do elsewhere in time and place. Their use of rigidly legalistic discourse to deny the legal validity of claims advanced by clients is, to some degree, a function of institutional norms and legal doctrine, which privilege enterprise mediation committees and government labor arbitration committees. But this normative and doctrinal explanation is inconsistent with the reality that labor-dispute mediation within industrial enterprises has all but disappeared;[60] furthermore, it is also incongruent with the more flexible and more accommodating realities of the Chinese legal system as it operates on the ground. Legal doctrine is an important tool of obfuscation, wielded by lawyers to manage and screen out commercially undesirable cases brought by socially undesirable prospective clients.

Why do lawyers screen cases? Case screening is the manifestation neither of an inherent unwillingness to represent the poor and the powerless nor of a lack of social justice ideals. Rather, screening is the result of an institutional context in which lawyers, who are under enormous economic pressure, receive scant institutional support to protect the rights of the most vulnerable members of society. Yet lawyers' decisions do not adhere to an economic logic alone; the situation in China also reveals a clear cultural logic. By "profiling" prospective clients, lawyers reproduce social categories and thus reproduce social inequalities. Their use of cultural stereotypes to sort and filter cases brought by "undeserving" or "troublesome" clients reinforces barriers to justice and undermines the rights and interests of China's laborers by blocking access to the legal arsenal that has developed for the redress of their work-related grievances.

Yet clients are not hapless subjects. Taking labor disputes to lawyers in the first place is a reflection of the agency of aggrieved workers. The perverse irony is that, in their efforts to exercise agency, clients become agents of their own defeat by reinforcing lawyers' need to screen out potentially troublesome clients and their commercially undesirable cases. The state's paramount goal in China's legal reform is to preserve social stability by resolving popular grievances and complaints. Yet, insofar as the development of the Chinese bar serves systematically to deny justice to a potentially volatile segment of society, the present legal reforms may to some measure undermine this official goal.

Official efforts to improve access to justice for the poor have been concentrated in the legal aid system. China's legal aid system is developing slowly but surely in an attempt to fill the hole left by private legal practice,[61] especially following the 2003 enactment of the Regulations on Legal Aid. Although, in principle, legal aid lawyers are not supposed to refuse representation to qualifying clients, the very question of qualification is subject to the same discursive manipulation that occurs in the private bar. Indeed, in Katz's study of legal assistance offices in Chicago, lawyers not only rationalized screening out clients with whom they had difficulty communicating by labeling them "crazies", but also screened out clients perceived as shifty, of questionable moral character and credibility.[62] Anecdotal evidence from China suggests that, in practice, the same intolerance for and cultural stereotypes about "annoying" clients is even more prevalent among legal aid lawyers on the government payroll, for whom fee potential and fee collection are less relevant concerns than they are among commission-based private-sector lawyers, for whom the legal fee is the paramount concern.[63]

Consistent with previous research,[64] this chapter has shown that fee potential and fee arrangements are at the heart of case screening. Outside the legal aid system, courts sometimes waive litigation fees for the poor – on the basis of the 1989 Measures of the People's Court on Litigation Fees – and sometimes they shift litigation fees to the loser. However, there is less systematic, doctrinal flexibility with respect to *lawyers*' fees. On December 6, 2004, in recognition of the magnitude of the problem, the Ministry of Justice promulgated a directive calling on lawyers in the private bar to accept more cases from migrant workers trying to collect back wages and to reduce or waive legal fees when doing so.[65] The remission of legal fees in such cases remains voluntary, and while it is strongly encouraged, it has not been made mandatory.

Students of contemporary China have uncritically assumed that improving procedural and distributive justice in the courtroom improves justice writ large. This chapter points to a more useful research agenda: why are so few grievances transformed into legal claims? What is the role of lawyers in this transformation process? An additional direction for future research is to tease out more clearly the dialectical interplay between economics and culture, to specify more rigorously and definitively the relative importance of economic and cultural considerations. These effects, to be sure, are additive – and possibly multiplicative: clients who are both socially undesirable *and* whose cases are commercially undesirable are almost guaranteed to get screened out of the law firm. Under what circumstances does a desirable potential fee outweigh an undesirable cultural profile? Conversely, under what circumstances does a desirable cultural profile erase the disincentives brought by low fee potential? Such questions are not only among those awaiting future research, but also among those subject to policy influence.

Would any policy measures introduced in the private bar improve access to justice and the prospects for cause lawyering? There is currently a push to introduce a fee-shifting measure that would require the payment of lawyers' fees by the losing party[66] although superior courts have thus far stymied reform efforts.[67] At the same time, lawyers' incentives to represent aggrieved workers are likely to be greater if more law firms were to establish base salaries and pro bono systems to pay their lawyers for devoting some time to the protection of the legal rights of the poor and powerless.[68] Finally, lifting the ban on solo practice would hamper the widespread fleecing of affiliate lawyers by the owners of law firms and, concomitantly, would permit more lawyers to retain a greater share of their legal receipts. Any of these reforms, if adopted, would most probably help to reduce disincentives for lawyers to accept labor disputes and other cases of the poor. Even if adopted, however, such reforms would not address formidable *political* disincentives, a topic beyond the scope of this chapter, which must await more thorough treatment elsewhere.

Notes

1 This chapter is an abridged and re-edited version of an article of the same title originally published by Blackwell in (2006) 40 *Law & Society Review*, March: 1–38.
2 William L. F. Felstiner, Richard L. Abel, and Austin Sarat, "The Emergence and Transformation of Disputes: Naming, Blaming, Claiming ...", (1980–1981) 15 *Law & Society Review*: 631–54.
3 Herbert Jacob, *Law and Politics in the United States*, 2nd edition, New York, NY: HarperCollins College Publishers, 1995: 118, cited in Joanne Martin and Stephen Daniels, "Access Denied: 'Tort Reform' Rhetoric is Closing the Courthouse Door", (1997) 33 *Trial*: 26. Also see Herbert Kritzer, "Contingency Fee Lawyers as Gatekeepers in the American Civil Justice System", (1997) 81 *Judicature*: 22–9.
4 Publications on worker grievances and protest are too numerous to cite individually here. See Ching Kwan Lee's chapter in this book.
5 See Mary E. Gallagher, "'*Use the Law as Your Weapon!*' The Rule of Law and Labor Conflict in the PRC", in Neil J. Diamant, Stanley B. Lubman, and Kevin J. O'Brien (eds), *Engaging the Law in China: State, Society and Possibilities for Justice*, Stanford, CA: Stanford University Press, 2005: 54–83; Doug Guthrie, "The Transformation of Labor Relations in China's Emerging Market Economy", in Kevin T. Leicht (ed.), *Research in Social Stratification and Mobility*, Vol. 19 (*The Future of Market Transition*), Amsterdam: JAI Press, 2002: 139–70; Doug Guthrie, "The Evidence Is Clear: Foreign Investment Spurs Workplace Reform in China", (2000) 28 *Chronicle of Higher Education*: B11; Doug Guthrie, "The Quiet Revolution: The Emergence of Capitalism", (2003) 25 *Harvard International Review*: 48–53; Anita Chan, "Some Hope for Optimism for Chinese Labor", (2004) 13 *New Labor Forum*: 67–75.
6 Gallagher, "'Use the Law as Your Weapon'".
7 Austin T. Turk, "Law as a Weapon in Social Conflict", (1976) 23 *Social Problems*: 284; Pierre Bourdieu, "The Force of Law: Toward a Sociology of the Juridical Field", (1987) 38 *Hastings Law Journal*: 827, 835–6.
8 This approximates what we know about the true age and gender distributions of the Beijing bar. The mean age of Beijing's lawyers at the time was well below 40; at least three-quarters were younger than 40. About 30 percent were female. Ethan Michelson, "Unhooking from the State: Chinese Lawyers in Transition", PhD, Dissertation, University of Chicago, 2003: 41–2, 237.

9   See Michelson, "Unhooking from the State".

10 In the notation I use in this chapter for citing the primary data, "E" refers to interviews I conducted myself; "I" to interviews carried out by my research assistants; and "C" to the 48 lawyer–client consultation sessions. Thus, E18 (for example) refers to my interview number 18.

11 Michelson, "Unhooking from the State": 209–10.

12 Michelson, "Unhooking from the State": 191.

13 In Beijing, an estimated 12–17 percent of lawyers are paid a fixed salary and 30–39 percent a combination of base salary plus commission. Outside Beijing, only an estimated 3 percent of lawyers surveyed reported getting paid a fixed salary and 15 percent a combination of a base salary plus commission. Michelson, "Unhooking from the State": 43.

14 Although the general ban on solo practice remains in effect, in 2002, five solo-practice firms were established in Beijing on a trial basis. Michelson, "Unhooking from the State": 67.

15 Between 1993 and 2002, the proportion of state-owned law firms in Beijing shrank from 41% to zero. Across China as a whole, 23 percent of law firms were still state-owned in 2001, a precipitous drop from 65 percent in 1997. Michelson, "Unhooking from the State": 470–1.

16 Mayfair Mei-hui Yang, *Gifts, Favors, and Banquets: The Art of Social Relationships in China*, Ithaca, NY: Cornell University Press, 1994: 160.

17 Yongshun Cai and Songcai Yang, "State Power and Unbalanced Legal Development in China", (2005) 14 *Journal of Contemporary China*: 117–34; Ping Yu, "Glittery Promise vs. Dismal Reality: The Role of a Criminal Lawyer in the People's Republic of China after the 1996 Revision of the Criminal Procedure Law", (2002) 35 *Vanderbilt Journal of Transnational Law*: 827–64.

18 Michelson, "Unhooking from the State": 157, 162, Chapter 10.

19 These five items are: retirement pension, medical insurance, unemployment insurance, life insurance, and housing. Michelson, "Unhooking from the State": 219.

20 Michelson, "Unhooking from the State": 224.

21 Michelson, "Unhooking from the State": 336. In 2001 the official exchange rate was about 8.3 yuan per 1 United States dollar.

22 Herbert M. Kritzer, "Lawyer Fees and Lawyer Behavior in Litigation: What Does the Empirical Literature Really Say?", (2002) 80 *Texas Law Review*: 1943–83 for a helpful typology of fee arrangements and fee-shifting regimes; also see (1984) 47 *Law and Contemporary Problems*, special issue on "attorney fee shifting". Although the absence of fee shifting is the general rule in China, there are some important, albeit patchy, exceptions to this general rule.

23 To minimize losses and prevent working for nothing, commission-based lawyers typically charge an up-front base fee of 2,000 yuan to 3,000 yuan per case, plus some sort of commission, often 5 percent of the value of the case – the *biaodi*, the value of the object in dispute or the amount recovered or collected. However, it is important to emphasize the enormous variation with respect to the amount of both the base fee and the commission. Despite official fee standards set by the government, the general practice is to negotiate fees. Michelson, "Unhooking from the State": 200–1.

24 A lawyer I interviewed asserted that 90 percent of lawyers in Beijing are barely making a living. As he put it, "They don't know where their next meal is coming from", and they are "hustling for the sake of survival"; he estimates that only 9 percent enjoy high incomes (E19). According to my survey data, in Beijing, the top 20 percent of the bar earn 70 percent of total income, while the top 5 percent of the bar earn 39 percent. The bottom 60 percent earns only 15 percent of total income, while the bottom 80 percent earn only 30 percent Michelson, "Unhooking from the State": 338, a level of inequality even more extreme than that in the Chicago bar. John P. Heinz *et al.*, *Urban*

Lawyers: The New Social Structure of the Bar, Chicago, IL: University of Chicago Press, 2005: Chapter 7.

25 Indeed, it is the policy at many Shanghai law firms to prohibit their lawyers from representing workers in labor cases. Mary Gallagher. Personal email correspondence (August 23, 2004).

26 Yunqiu Zhang, "Law and Labor in Post-Mao China", (2005) 14 *Journal of Contemporary China*: 538–9.

27 See Joseph Kahn, "China's Workers Risk Limbs in Export Drive", *New York Times*, April 7, 2003: A3.

28 Examples of lawyers expressing interest by making a sales pitch for their legal services include: "I'll do my best to see that you get extra compensation. Now if you'll just sign this representation contract" (C30, a criminal assault); and "I can tell you're a morally upright individual"; "Pursuing justice through the law is better than any other method" (C37, a neighbor dispute). On a methodological note, I assigned a code of "1" when evidence of the respective characteristic is present – in this case, when evidence of "some interest in accepting the case" is present. The codes are conservative. For example, if a consultation session is assigned a code of "1" for "lawyer explicitly refused the case", we can be sure the lawyer refused the case. A code of "0," however, does not imply that the lawyer did not refuse the case, much less that the lawyer accepted the case, but indicates only that no evidence of explicitly refusing the case is present in the consultation transcript. Likewise, a code of "0" for "lawyer displayed impatience with client" implies not that the lawyer was gracious and polite, but only that no evidence to the contrary is present in the consultation transcript.

29 Wang Chenguang and Gao Qicai, "Lüshi Zhiye De Xianzhuang Diaocha: Wuhan Lüshi Fangtan Zongshu" (A Survey on the Current State of the Legal Profession: A Summary of Interviews from Wuhan), (2000) *Zhongguo Lüshi*, December: 7–8.

30 Li Gantu and Xun Qingju, "'Dagongzai Lüshi' Zhou Litai Xianzhuang Kundun" (The Weariness of the Workers' Lawyer, Zhou Litai), posted by the *Guangzhou Ribao*, December 8, 2003. Online: available at www.dayoo.com/content/2003-12/08/content_1318244.htm> (accessed September 26, 2005).

31 Yao Ying, "Legal 'Savior' Fighting For His Fees", *China Daily*, July 5, 2004. Online: available at www.chinadaily.com.cn/english/doc/2004-07/05/content_345478.htm> (accessed September 26, 2005).

32 Lynn Mather, Craig A. McEwen, and Richard J. Maiman, *Divorce Lawyers at Work: Varieties of Professionalism in Practice*, Oxford and New York, NY: Oxford University Press, 2001: 143.

33 Zhao Qiancheng, "Lüshi de 'Ku Shui' yu Duzhe de 'Wu Shui'" (A Lawyer's 'Bitter Water' and a Reader's 'Foggy Water'), *Beijing Qingnian Bao*, June 11, 2001: 8; Tian Lianfeng, "Shu le Guansi Gao Lüshi (Upon Losing a Law Suit the Lawyer is Sued), *Shenghuo Ribao*, September 20, 2002; Chen Min and Yang Gang, "Guansi Da Bu Ying Lüshi Cheng Beigao" (Upon Losing Law Suit Lawyer Becomes Defendant), *Yangzi Wanbao*, February 24, 2004.

34 See Bo Licheng "'Fengxian Daili' Hou Nan Shou Qian: Lüshisuo Gao Weitou Danwei Yaohui 40 Wan" (Collecting a Contingency Fee is Difficult: A Law Firm Sues an Organizational Client for 400,000 yuan), *Dianchi Zaobao*, September 25, 2004: 8; Zhou Mu, "Shui Lai Wei Lüshi Tao 'Gongqian?'" (Who Will Collect Back Wages on Behalf of Lawyers?), *Chengdu Wanbao*, December 13, 2004.

35 These are some of the verbatim responses written on questionnaires I administered in 25 cities in the summer of 2000.

36 Li and Xun, "'Dagongzai Lüshi' Zhou Litai Xianzhuang Kundun".

37 Kevin O'Brien and Lianjiang Li define the term *diaomin* as "shrewd and unyielding people" who mobilize legal resources to protect their rights and interests. See O'Brien and Li, "Villagers and Popular Resistance in Contemporary China", (1996) 22 *Modern China*: 30–1.

38 Xu Anqi, "One-Parent Family: Social Assistance for Marginal Groups", presented at Conference on Socioeconomic Rights in China, Dickinson College, April 16–18, 2004. On file with the author. Also see Emily Honig and Gail Hershatter, *Personal Voices: Chinese Women in the 1980s*, Stanford, CA: Stanford University Press, 1988: 212, 224, 237–9.

39 Kritzer, "Lawyer Fees and Lawyer Behavior in Litigation": 1945; also see Mather *et al.*, *Divorce Lawyers at Work*: 143.

40 Austin Sarat and William L. F. Felstiner, *Divorce Lawyers and Their Clients: Power and Meaning in the Legal Process*, New York and Oxford: New York University Press, 1995.

41 Impatience is manifested in different ways: lawyers may become patronizing and insulting, e.g. "You have serious problems!" (C35, a boyfriend/girlfriend problem). They may interrupt clients, e.g. "Let's stick to material issues!" (C31, a labor dispute). They also may raise their voices or rapidly and loudly tap their pens on their desks (C35).

42 Examples of emotionally charged language and moral outrage include: "It's just that I can't hold back my anger. This guy is just rotten" (C05, an economic dispute); and "Now good things do not come to good people. When I was still working, I was honest and pure, I was the stupid cow of society! Nowadays only the conniving get ahead in society, and the law protects these people!" (C14, a housing inheritance dispute). Although I found no evidence that a common discourse of "releasing anger" and "unjust treatment" varies by gender – either the gender of the client or the gender of the attending lawyer – the data do show clearly that older clients are more likely to invoke such emotionally charged, morally laden language.

43 Among all 48 consultation sessions we observed, evidentiary problems – including filing deadlines – were invoked as reasons for refusing representation in 11 – or 23 percent. Among the five consultations over labor disputes, however, evidentiary problems were invoked in three – or 60 percent.

44 *Chinese Law and Government*, 2002: 70.

45 Guangyu Li, "You Guan Laodong Zhengyi Chuli Wenti de Taolun" (A Discussion of the Issue of Handling Labor Disputes), (2004) 2 *Zhongguo Laodong*: 44.

46 Margaret Y. K. Woo, "Law and Discretion in the Contemporary Chinese Courts", (1999) *Pacific Rim Law and Policy*: 581–615; Isabelle Thireau and Linshan Hua, "Legal Disputes and the Debate about Legitimate Norms", in M. Brosseau, Kuan Hsin-chi, and Y.Y. Kueh (eds), *The China Review 1997*, Hong Kong: The Chinese University Press, 1997: 349–78; Lucie Cheng and Arthur Rosett, "Contract with a Chinese Face: Socially Embedded Factors in the Transformation from Hierarchy to Market, 1978–1989", (1991) 5 *Journal of Chinese Law*: 143–244; Li Su, *Song Fa Xia Xiang: Zhongguo Jiceng Fazhi Zhidu Yanjiu* (Bringing Law Down to the Countryside: Research on China's Grassroots Legal System), Beijing: Zhongguo Zhengfa Daxue Chubanshe, 2000.

47 See, for example, Lynn Mather and Barbara Yngvesson, "Language, Audience, and the Transformation of Disputes", (1980/1981) 15 *Law & Society Review*: 775–822; Bourdieu, "Force of Law"; Sally Engle Merry, *Getting Justice and Getting Even: Legal Consciousness Among Working-Class Americans*, Chicago, IL: The University of Chicago Press, 1990.

48 Abraham S. Blumberg, "The Practice of Law as a Confidence Game: Organizational Cooptation of a Profession", (1967) 1 *Law & Society Review*: 15–40; Carl J. Hosticka, "We Don't Care about What Happened, We Only Care about What is Going to Happen: Lawyer-Client Negotiations of Reality", (1979) 26 *Social Problems*: 599–610.

49 Maureen Cain, "The General Practice Lawyer and the Client: Towards a Radical Conception", (1979) 7 *International Journal of the Sociology of Law*: 331–54; Felstiner, Abel, and Sarat, "The Emergence and Transformation of Disputes"; Carroll Seron *et al.*, "The Impact of Legal Counsel on Outcomes for Poor Tenants in New

York City's Housing Courts: Results of a Randomized Experiment", (2001) 35 *Law & Society Review*: 419–34; Frank Munger, "Miners and Lawyers: Law Practice and Class Conflict in Appalachia, 1872–1920", in Maureen Cain and Christine B. Harrington, *Lawyers in a Postmodern World: Translation and Transgression*, Buckingham: Open University Press, 1994; Peter Karsten, "Enabling the Poor to Have Their Day in Court: The Sanctioning of Contingency Fee Contracts, A History tó 1940", (1997/1998) 47 *DePaul Law Review*: 231–60.

50 Louise G. Trubek, "Embedded Practices: Lawyers, Clients, and Social Change", (1996) 31 *Harvard Civil Rights-Civil Liberties Law Review*: 415–41; Douglas J. Besharov, *Legal Services for the Poor: Time for Reform*, Washington, DC: AEI Press, 1990; Jack Katz, *Poor People's Lawyers in Transition*, New Brunswick, NJ: Rutgers University Press, 1982; Rebecca L. Sandefur, "Organization of Lawyers' Pro-Bono Service and Poor People's Use of Lawyers for Civil Matters", presented at the Law and Society Association Annual Meeting, Chicago, May 27–30, 2004.

51 Austin Sarat and Stuart Scheingold (eds), *Cause Lawyering: Political Commitments and Professional Responsibilities*, New York, NY and Oxford: Oxford University Press, 1998; Sarat and Scheingold, *Cause Lawyering and the State in a Global Era*, New York, NY and Oxford: Oxford University Press, 2001; Stuart A. Scheingold and Austin Sarat, *Something to Believe In: Politics, Professionalism, and Cause Lawyering*, Stanford, CA: Stanford University Press, 2004.

52 Stephen Daniels and Joanne Martin, "'The Impact That It Has Had is between People's Ears': Tort Reform, Mass Culture, and Plaintiffs' Lawyers", (2000) 50 *DePaul Law Review*: 453–96; Daniels and Martin, "'We Live on the Edge of Extinction All the Time'", in Jerry Van Hoy (ed.), *Legal Professions: Work, Structure and Organization*, Amsterdam and London: JAI, 2001; Daniels and Martin, "It Was the Best of Times, It was the Worst of Times: The Precarious Nature of Plaintiffs' Practice in Texas", (2002) 80 *Texas Law Review*: 1781–828; Jerry Van Hoy, "Markets and Contingency: How Client Markets Influence the Work of Plaintiffs' Personal Injury Lawyers?", (1999) 6 *International Journal of the Legal Profession*: 345–66.

53 Kritzer, *Risks, Reputations, and Rewards*: 71; Kritzer, "Contingency Fee Lawyers": 24.

54 Martin and Daniels, "Access Denied": 28; Herbert M. Kritzer, *Legal Advocacy: Lawyers and Nonlawyers at Work*, Ann Arbor, MI: University of Michigan Press, 1998: 25; Kritzer, *Risks, Reputations, and Rewards*: 69.

55 Kritzer, *Legal Advocacy*: 117–18; Blumberg, "Lawyers with Convictions", in Abraham Blumberg (ed.), *The Scales of Justice*, New Brunswick, NJ: Transaction Books, 1973: 72–3; Blumberg, "The Practice of Law": 24-7; Mather *et al.*, *Divorce Lawyers at Work*: 142–3.

56 John Gibeaut, "Avoiding Trouble at the Mill", (1997) 83 *ABA Journal*: 48–54; Katja Kunzke, "The Hazard: Failure to Screen Cases", (1998) 84 *ABA Journal*: 57; Mary Beth S. Robinson, "Putting Clients to the Test: Careful Screening at Initial Interview Can Minimize Malpractice Risks", (1998) 80 *ABA Journal*: 80; Mark Bassingthwaighte, "Screen Clients to Avoid Trouble", *Virginia Lawyer's Weekly*, August 2003. Online: available at www.virginialaw.com/alpsva12.cfm (accessed September 26, 2005).

57 Sarat and Felstiner, *Divorce Lawyers*.

58 Carl J. Hosticka, "We Don't Care".

59 Mather *et al.*, *Divorce Lawyers*: 38, 93–4, 96–8; Kritzer, "Contingent-Fee Lawyers and their Clients: Settlement Expectations, Settlement Realities, and Issues of Control in the Lawyer-Client Relationship, (1998) 23 *Law and Social Inquiry*: 795–821; Sarat and Felstiner, *Divorce Lawyers*: 56; Douglas Rosenthal, *Lawyer and Client: Who's in Charge?*, New Brunswick, NJ: Transaction Books, 1974.

60 Fu and Choy, "From Mediation".

61 Benjamin Liebman, "Legal Aid and Public Interest Law in China", (1999) 34 *Texas International Law Journal*: 211–86.

62 Katz, *Poor People's Lawyers*: 29–32.
63 I am indebted to Sida Liu and Mary Gallagher, both of whom have participated in and extensively studied Chinese legal aid work, for contributing this point.
64 Kritzer, "Lawyer Fees and Lawyer Behavior"; Kritzer, *Risks, Reputations, and Rewards*.
65 The 2004 Circular on the Provision of Legal Services and Legal Aid to Resolve the Problem of Construction Fee Arrears in the Construction Industry and the Problem of Back Wages Owed to Migrant Workers (Ministry of Justice Document No. 159) was jointly promulgated with the Ministry of Construction for the purpose of implementing the 1993 Circular of the General Office of the State Council on Intently Resolving the Problem of Construction Fee Arrears in the Construction Industry (State Council Decree No. 94).
66 He Xin *et al.*, "Lüshi Daibiao Jianyi Shui Shu Guansi Shui Fu Lüshi Fei" (Lawyer Representative Suggests that the Losing Party in Litigation Pay Lawyer Fees), *Nanfang Ribao*, February 11, 2004; Liu Xianren and Chen Hong, "Lüshi Fei Daodi Gai Shui Chu?" (Who Ultimately Should Pay the Lawyer Fee?), *Guangzhou Ribao*, September 30, 2004.
67 Tian, "Shu le Guansi Gao Lüshi".
68 See Sandefur, "Organization of Lawyers' Pro-Bono Service".

10 Outsourcing as a way of life?

Knowledge transfer in the Yangtze Delta

Andrew Ross

Although it is the primary economic story of our time, the global liberalization of trade and investment was not considered a fit topic for discussion during the heated United States election season of 2003–4. Virtually the only form in which it surfaced was through the codeword "outsourcing", wielded by the challenger, John Kerry, as a rhetorical club with which to beat the incumbent. By any standards, the Bush administration, perceived to be highly vulnerable on its economic record, had made some spectacular blunders. For example, Bush's much ballyhooed appointee of a manufacturing-jobs czar had to be withdrawn when it was revealed that Tony Raimondo, the Nebraska businessman in line for the position, had laid off his own workers and was building a factory in China to replace them.[1] Shortly afterward, Bush's fund-raising and vote-seeking campaign was revealed to have outsourced its telephone solicitation contracts to call centers in the suburbs of New Delhi.[2] Nor did it help matters that his appointees at the Commerce Department routinely cosponsored high-profile conferences at such locations as the Waldorf-Astoria Hotel, which encouraged American companies to move their operations to China.[3] Indeed, whenever Bush or his appointees tried to address the public concern over outsourcing, they invariably blundered.

Spurred on by the public outcry over job losses, Americans displaced by outsourcing may have had reasons to blame their president, although they were more likely to criticize the company executives who ordered the overseas transfers. This disapproval drew on three decades of cumulative cynicism about the cold-heartedness of corporate America, from the first shockwave of factory closings in the 1970s through the increasing casualizing and downsizing of white-collar workers of the 1980s and 1990s. Inevitably, however, the strength of this sentiment carried over into disdain for the overseas workers who appeared to be benefiting from the job transfers. For some, it was easier to blame the faceless foreigners who took their jobs than to hold companies accountable for paying third-world wages and asking first-world prices.

Because the overseas workers were mostly Asians, they fit neatly into a century-old racist stereotype about foreigners from the East "stealing our jobs". In a slightly more genteel version of the Yellow Peril, almost every newspaper report about "the China threat" mentioned the 400,000 engineers who were turned out by Chinese universities every year. How could honest Americans compete with this colossal industrial army of skilled labor? The lives and attitudes of the Chinese employees in question were either taken for granted or, for want of further information, simply entrusted to the least tolerant sectors of the public imagination

While Americans have been fixated on domestic job losses, most are unaware that China has lost many more millions of jobs in the last decade than has the United States, whether from the closure, restructuring, or sale of state-owned enterprises or, more recently, from the pressure of WTO requirements on farmers.[4] In fact, Chinese job loss is just as much the result of corporate globalization and neo-liberal privatization as is United States job loss. In addition, the creation of a vast floating pool of unemployed – as many as 200 million, mostly farmers – poses the same kind of threat to the Chinese who are trying to hold on to their jobs as the threat of corporate offshoring does to United States employees. Because their prospects are now closely linked, the bread and butter of Americans is affected, not just by workers' opportunities in China's fully developed coastal cities, but also by the job hunger of underemployed peasants in the inland and western provinces, already earmarked as the next frontier for venturesome foreign corporations.

Neither armchair polemics nor deadline-pressured journalism can adequately capture the human dimensions of these offshore transfers. Yet these are the only means that United States combatants in the "outsourcing wars" have had at their disposal to respond to the latest round of corporate free trade policies. Labor ethnographers can fill the vacuum by helping to put a human face on the job traffic that is usually summed up in United States–China trade statistics or in the latest employment figures. We can offer a more complete picture of the aspirations, fears, and dispositions of the Chinese employees at the other end of the job transfers. Our fieldwork is also a singular resource for understanding the provisional labor markets that sustain the geography of work in China's transitional economy. Finally, given that the AFL-CIO has consistently refused to establish any official connection with the Chinese labor federation, there is a moral, if not a political, obligation for us to make the kinds of transnational connections that are crucial to combating corporate power.[5]

As outsourcing moves up the value chain, affecting more and more livelihoods in the highly-skilled sectors, some urgent issues need to be addressed. With ever more advanced technologies at their beck and call, and with their ever greater control over insecure, and non-unionized, workforces, it takes less and less time for corporate managers to submit skilled Asian workforces to the kinds of deskilling and dehumanizing that we have seen over the course of several decades in the West. Currently, however, their most strenuous efforts are focused on how to lessen the time it takes to transfer knowledge from one human resource to another in a cheaper part of the world. Charting and understanding this process requires our immediate attention and expertise, because it lies on the frontline of capital's effort to establish control over mental, or immaterial, labor.

My own research has focused on skilled Chinese employees and their managers in foreign-invested companies in Shanghai and the Yangtze Delta. Most of the firms I visited were located in the industrial corridor that runs from Shanghai's shiny new urban center of Pudong on the east coast to the ancient upriver cities of Suzhou and Wuxi.[6] For technology-driven companies, where I did most of my interviewing, the supply chain in this corridor is almost complete. The Lower Yangtze region is rapidly replacing the Pearl River Delta as the country's primary economic engine, and a much greater share of its foreign direct investment is flowing into higher-value production than into the predominantly labor-intensive factories of the south. Indeed, the Yangtze Delta economy is increasingly the high-tech core of China's claim to be the "world's factory". Shanghai's own booming service sector is spearheading China's less plausible aspiration to challenge India in becoming the "world's office".

Foreign investors are itching to transfer high-end manufacturing operations – such as product engineering, design, and research and development (R&D) – into the region as fast as they can. The chief barrier to accomplishing this "knowledge transfer" – the preferred corporate euphemism for outsourcing skilled, or high-value, jobs – is not the widely acknowledged concern about theft of intellectual property. The real obstacle, as I found out, has more to do with the difficulty of finding an adequate labor supply at the right price. Knowledge transfer rests on the ready availability of a pool of reasonably priced skilled Chinese employees with a few years of industrial experience. These are locals who speak adequate English, who are familiar with international business practices, and whose technical and managerial talents are sufficient to meet the demands of high-value occupations in foreign companies. Currently, the members of this group belong to the only labor pool in China that suffers from an acute shortage. Consequently, managers are wringing their hands over a labor market characterized by spiraling wage inflation and employee turnover rates of 20 percent to 30 percent – I found rates of up to 40 percent in some high-skill precincts.

If a surplus pool of talent materializes, and the current wage inflation is brought under control, the way will be clear for corporations to transfer more and more high-skill operations and ever greater quantities of high-value investment capital into China. The much-lamented United States job loss and capital flight of the last few years may well be seen as a trickle in comparison with the mass migration to come. "There's nothing anyone or anything can do to stop it", the regional director of a United States multinational firm assured me, casually citing a Shanghai joke he had heard recently: "Pretty soon, lawyers will be the only people left with jobs in America". Given the rate at which the work of paralegals and junior associates is being sent offshore, even this may turn out to be a generous estimate.

On the other side, in China, local and central government cadres are pulling every power lever at their disposal to ease the bottleneck and provide foreign investors with what they want. In early 2004, the Ministry of Education launched a drive to train an additional one million workers in occupations that labor authorities were beginning to officially label as "gray-collar".[7] Gray-collar is a rather broad category, covering everything from fashion designers to software engineers, from ad writers to numerical-control technicians. Recruits were expected to fill the gap between unskilled blue-collar jobs and the white-collar professional and managerial positions to which most college graduates aspired.[8] Some of the designated gray-collar occupations were the sweet ones, favored by every large city looking to promote its "creative sector", but the less glamorous ones were just as essential if China, courtesy of its foreign investors, was going to be able to sustain its long march up the value chain. Every offshore manufacturer in the Yangtze Delta needed skilled technicians, not just to maintain production levels, but also to upgrade plants from assembly and testing to accommodate operations of a higher grade. At the higher end, and especially in the semi-conductor industry, the shortfall was being addressed by importing Taiwanese engineers – a maneuver that added to the cross-Strait anxieties about a brain drain, which was claiming many of the island's best and brightest.

This massive effort at recruitment was a sobering addition to the list of favors that officials in developing countries have had to offer as part of what is misnamed free trade. Investors have come to expect a never-ending welcome parade of tax holidays and exemptions, acres of virtually free land, state-of-the-art infrastructure and telecommunications, discounts on utilities and other operating costs, and soft guarantees that labor laws and environmental regulations will never be seriously implemented. In the past, favors such as these have pandered to companies looking to manufacture cheaply. Now the model was being revised to suit the requirements of those investing higher up on the value chain.

It remains to be seen whether the result of this and other training efforts will ease the bottleneck. The restoration of an abundant labor supply may well bring down the high turnover rates and salaries. But the short-term crisis speaks to a phenomenon that is unlikely to disappear in the long run. The easy international mobility enjoyed by corporations and investors' capital is creating a workforce that responds in kind: employees who see no reason to be loyal. In their restless quest to seek out the cheapest and most dispensable employees, multinational corporations have made it clear that they will not honor any kind of job security. Hooked on the habit of job-hopping, it looks as if workers in China's transitional economy are simply returning the disrespect.

The footsoldiers

It was in information technology (IT) services, Shanghai's freshest industry, and one highly favored by the government, that I began my interviews inside companies. This is a sector in which offshore outsourcing from the United States, the European Union, and Japan has made some of its most visible inroads, and its employees are a new breed – urbane, aspiring, and none too patient. Although inexperienced, they are not absolute beginners. As I would discover, the attitudes they bring to the workplace have already been molded by several factors: their parents' and grandparents' career experiences during the socialist era; expectations about their own role as minor league pioneers of the nation's high-tech future; myths and business literature about market capitalism; and the steady pressure to forge their own way in a world without guarantees. Although their bosses would have preferred otherwise, they are not unformed, raw material, waiting to be processed into ideal corporate citizens.

One of the easiest, and most revealing, ways of seeing these new workers is to watch them eat together. On any day of the working week, the employee cafeteria at Shanghai Pudong Software Park (SPSP) – a high-tech zone at the pastoral edge of the new city – is a prime viewing site. The central dining hall seats about 1500 and is usually packed by 12.10 p.m. In the main canteen area, heads are quickly lowered over bowls with a sure sense of purpose. Mobile phones ring at every other table, and at some, there is a light conversational buzz, even a little hilarity. But the general goal is not to linger. By 12.45, the crowd is thinning rapidly. Most of the diners are at a courting age, but there is no flirting or cruising, indeed, very little socializing beyond the small groupings that enter and leave. Many of the workers wear ID badges around their necks, some wear the branded jackets of their companies. Clothing styles ran the spectrum from student scruffy to business casual. Quite a few of the young men wear suits, though this fashion decision is not necessarily a mark of corporate belonging – it is a common wardrobe choice among all of Shanghai's classes. Among the women, accessories, advanced hair care, dresses, and a distinctive fashion sense are few and far between, which puts these women in a category quite apart from the street-style standards famously associated with Shanghai women. Like techies anywhere, they have an air of being preoccupied and distracted from the world at hand.

If these are the footsoldiers of a new industrial army, their individual insecurities belie their collective presence and sense of discipline. At the time of my first visits to SPSP in early 2004, most of the 200 companies in the park had a small-to-medium payroll – the largest was Bearing Point's "global development center", with almost 400 employees. The products and services are customized for small, niche markets or clients with special needs. Consequently, the individuality of their skilled employees is a potential selling point. Yet the dining-hall experience is a stark reminder to employees that, while their new urban industry may still be in its infancy, it already has a seemingly populous labor supply. Shanghai's IT service sector is far from competing with India's, but the rate at which it is growing is comparable, and it has received lavish support from the central government. Even in this relatively bucolic spot, where the well-spaced buildings – far removed from Puxi's downtown throng – only reach four or five stories, the park's agglomerate workforce is 6,000 strong and ballooning by the month. "Every day", observed Emily Zhang, a programmer for a private Chinese company, "I look around and I can see hundreds of people who can take my place. China has no shortage of people, and IT is not really much different from a traditional industry. It puts a little more anxiety into my life, so I feel very lucky to have this job".

Zhang has a little more perspective on the matter than do her newly graduated peers. She has worked in various jobs before enrolling in college in her late twenties. By the time she graduated, a college degree was no longer an automatic meal ticket. Her graduating class of 2003, numbering 2.12 million students – 40 percent larger than the previous year's – took several months to find jobs. When they did, they found that average salaries, which had been climbing quite steadily since the mid-1990s, had dropped from the previous year. Also on the decline were the salaries of returnees, people who had studied abroad and had grown used to claiming a handsome reward for their English-language skills and exposure to Western ways. "The cost of human resources", concluded a salary survey by the global management consultancy Hewitt, "has peaked".[9]

This momentous news was toasted in corporate offices from one end of Shanghai to the other. When the 2004 results began to come in, the toasts continued. The national graduating class had swelled to 2.8 million – 3.4 million were expected in 2005 – and the monthly salaries of graduates had fallen even more, averaging from one-quarter to one-third less than the 2003 national figure of 1550 RMB – $187. One national survey reported that those who already held jobs saw their salaries drop by as much as 14.7 percent over the course of the year.[10] The official 2004 figures for Shanghai had fallen to 1,680 RMB – $203. Average starting salaries in multinational companies were a good deal higher. A new graduate could earn a 2003 average of 2650 RMB – $320 – in first-tier cities such as Shanghai, Beijing, Guangzhou, and Shenzhen, yet only slightly more in 2004, for a monthly average of 2,850 RMB – $344.[11] Wage inflation among skilled employees had been a standard complaint among those raising their glasses. Did these figures indicate that this problem was coming under control? Not exactly, and not yet.

For most foreign human-resource managers of operations in China, recruiting newly graduated students like Zhang is not the primary concern. They hardly need to consult statistics to know that the real difficulty lies with finding skilled employees who have a few years' experience. When they can find such workers, retaining them is the most important of their daily challenges. As Huan Benyin, a manager at the Chinese unit of Radiall, a French electronics company, lamented, "It's difficult to get the right people in the first place. But what really hurts is when you give them the benefit of training and then they leave for a better salary somewhere else".[12] So far, this charmed pool of employees seems unaffected by the downward wage pressure of China's vast oversupply of labor. Salary increases of 15 percent to 20 percent are typical, and the increase is even higher for key operational employees.[13] Engineers' ease of mobility, in particular, is a source of frustration to foreign firms itching to shift more of their technology-intensive business to China. Because of a severe shortage in their ranks, the bargaining power of these employees is not likely to peak until the graduate harvest of the last few years had seasoned.

Not surprisingly, Chinese employees in foreign firms are less sympathetic to the pains experienced by their counterparts in onshore regions, such as the United States, Europe, and such parts of East Asia as Singapore and Malaysia, the original location of their jobs. Unlike their parents, who were secure beneficiaries of the government's "iron rice bowl", these young people are beset by pressures on all sides to perform and achieve on their own. "We have to earn our life by ourselves", explained Emily Zhang. "My parents had a hard time in their lives, but not where they worked. That was the easiest part, they have never had to worry about that". [14] By contrast, her generation's urgent need to maximize short-term opportunities overrides most other considerations. The window for them to "earn their life" might not be open for too long, and they have seen it close for other East Asians. If they work in the burgeoning private sector, they are all too aware of how their employers can exploit the geography of work by playing workers off against each other in different regions of Asia, and within China itself.

In the IT industry, low-wage competition between India and China – the world's two largest countries – is already determining how and where white-collar jobs are finding their way to Asia. The going rate for engineers in the big Indian cities is lower than that earned by their counterparts in east China. This fact is not widely known, and the international business press, accustomed to seeing China in general as the lowest wage floor, regularly reports otherwise.[15] Even within the industry, knowledge about such wage comparisons is spread unevenly. However, India's trained workforce is not growing fast enough to keep up with the demand for all the back-office, call-center, and IT work brought to the sub-continent by the BPO (business process outsourcing). As a result, the major software companies in India have all set up shop in Shanghai, as support or to service the large Asian clientele or to gain a large portion of the massive growth forecast for Chinese IT. What pressure did this situation put on their respective workforces? In India, employees were told that they must work harder or they will lose their jobs, like everyone else, to China. In Indian IT companies operating in Shanghai, where I did many interviews, I found that employees are told that they must work harder because their Indian counterparts are paid less. Employers have long used such threats in labor-intensive industries. Now, it seems that the conditions are ripe for corporations to apply them to white-collar and highly skilled occupations.

Largely because he wanted to work with Indians who had experience in the software industry, Sean Chen – named for Sean Connery – took his first job at one of the Indian IT companies in SPSP. From the first day, he was made aware of the factors that drove the competition between these two low-wage countries: quality of infrastructure, costs of labor and social security, the potential of the China market, language and other skill sets, and clients' comfort level. "Chinese are cheap, but, in this case, not the cheapest labor", Chen quipped. "Knowing this makes a big difference to the way we do things in my workplace". Despite the pressure, he was not putting in the extra-long hours that were typical in the IT sector. In the Indian companies, employee time is flexible, but I found that employees were generally not expected to work more than an eight- or nine-hour day. Nevertheless, they told me that their minds were often preoccupied with "unsolved problems", even when they are not on the job. For knowledge workers, there is no escaping this occupational hazard. After a year, Chen's monthly salary was 3000 RMB – $363 – which is slightly below the IT market average in Shanghai, but he felt that he was getting training from the people with the best experience in the field.

Given that he was doing work that had previously been performed by an American, how did he feel about taking away the job? "Maybe this job would have been done in India", he replied rather evasively. When pressed, he acknowledged that Americans will have a hard time holding on to this kind of work: "They will have to retrain and find something with more value. They are more creative anyway. But I can do this kind of job just as well as an American. Even better, if I am dealing with Asian clients. These days, no one owns his job". Even so, he believes the comparison with India to be the more relevant one. His manager, a native of Mumbai, regularly tells him that the Chinese will never be able to match the IT advantage India has built up over the past 15 years. Chen is more optimistic about the prospects for his country: "We are fast learners, and we are desperate for work. Since we started later, we have to work harder to catch up. China will win in the end". Needless to say, IT managers in Shanghai are all too aware that appeals to the nationalism of such employees as Chen are an effective way of stimulating productivity.

Even with higher productivity, Shanghai would still be at a cost disadvantage with India. Chen's own manager sees a simple solution – outsource to inland locations. "My ideal business model", he declared, "would be to have one or two hundred engineers in Shanghai as a basic design workforce, and maybe two or three thousand in Chengdu to do the implementation – coding, programming, product development, testing, lower-level work". Eric Rongley, the managing director of Bluem, an IT startup with offices in downtown Shanghai, has more or less the same plan in mind: "What I see happening with my company is ending up with about fifty people in the States who are going around for different projects, about two hundred people here in Shanghai – project managers, business analysts, some teams – and then about two thousand people out there in Xian or Chengdu. I'm saving about half my costs right there".

As it happens, the names of these two cities are on the lips of most IT company managers in Shanghai. Their low labor costs, high-quality technology colleges and institutes, and existing software clusters make them a natural choice for job transfers. That they are thousands of miles from Shanghai matters no more or less than the distance from China to the United States. By the end of 2004, the region was beginning to reap results, in part thanks to the central government's Go West policy. In addition to an extensive software presence, spearheaded by such tech-industry leaders as Motorola, the Chengdu basin is able to boast several semi-conductor complexes; one in Leshan, run by On Semiconductor, and brand-new chip factories owned by Intel, Phillips, and SMIC. For more traditional heavy manufacturing, the preferred inland location is further up the Yangtze, in Chongqing, where such multinational names as BP, Honda, Visteon, Ford, Ericsson, B&S, and Suzuki have all set up shop so as to cut the costs of their coastal operations.

This geographical pressure exerts a different impact from China's already considerable demographic pressure, and it helps to explain the short-term perspective of many employees. Deprived of every reason to trust in government – trust being an entirely different matter from national pride – they have no more reason to be loyal to employers, who can move operations very rapidly to a cheaper labor market. As one Texan manager, in Suzhou – a Yangtze Delta city with the largest annual volume of foreign investment in China – put it to me, with a classic dose of native nonchalance, "We'll move on, just like the Old West. In China there will always be a better deal waiting in the next town". "All of these gleaming new factories are here today" – he languidly gestured around him – "but they could be brownfields tomorrow". Other managers like him assume that jobs will inevitably move westward. In China, by contrast, workers are accustomed to move eastward and southward, but even that exodus may change over time. Even if it does not, the uneven pattern of China's frenetic industrial development will continue to affect workers all around the world.

Working on the value chain gang

Employers are in a position to move jobs westward to better their profits. Their employees are not in a position to do the same, but whatever mobility they enjoy gives them leverage. Without a functional union to represent them – the few unions affiliated with the Chinese trade union federation I encountered in the foreign-invested firms are given such names as "staff club" or "welfare committee" to appease managerial fears – workers without skills have very few collective means to improve their conditions on site. Nevertheless, the volume of worker protests and wildcat strikes has risen "like a violent wind" – in the description of the Ministry of Public Security – since mass layoffs in the state sector began in 1997.[16]

For migrant workers, the most abused by far, the most effective form of leverage is to stay at home. In 2004, after the annual weeklong Spring Festival, more than 2 million migrants – 10 percent of Guangdong's workforce – failed to return to the Pearl River Delta's export processing factories in South China. Turnover always increases at this time of year, but these numbers were unprecedented. Given their net impact, this was one of the most massive, unorganized withdrawals of labor in recent times. Domestic commentators rushed to explain the phenomenon, pointing to deep discontent with decade-long stagnant wage levels, the rising cost of living on the coast, the absence of legal protection, and substandard workplace conditions, which are notoriously hazardous to workers' health.[17] Some cadres took the occasion to praise the government's recently implemented tax relief for farmers, which made the prospect of scratching out a living on the land preferable to staffing the sweatshops of Guangdong and Fujian.[18] The Ministry of Labor and Social Security interpreted the outcome as a collective act of resistance to the illegal factory conditions, and publicly called on South China's employers to heed the nation's labor laws. The region's export contractors, most of whom compete on razor-thin margins, were forced to recruit on the basis of the pathetic slogan, "Paying wages on time".[19] This promise is a response to China's biggest labor problem – the back wages owed to migrant workers.[20] Emboldened by seeing employers at a disadvantage, worker walkouts and wildcat strikes spread, and the aggrieved flocked to the legal-aid centers that are increasingly handling labor disputes as part of the country's rocky transition to a "rule of law".[21] Despite government efforts to alleviate the shortage, and increases in the minimum wage of up to 30 percent, the shortfall in 2005 was similar, if not worse, with many workers heading east toward the better conditions in Shanghai and its satellite cities.[22] As South China's multitude of small firms reacted to the crisis, the international business press raised the alarm. *BusinessWeek* asked, "Is China Running Out of Workers?".[23]

In the Yangtze Delta, unskilled workers have gained access to higher wages, and there is greater legal oversight of labor contracts. Nevertheless, turnover was especially high after the Spring Festival, and Suzhou wages rose accordingly. For skilled employees, the increases were much greater. A human-resources survey showed overall staff turnover in the city at 17.8 percent in 2003, as against Shanghai's labor change at 14.5 percent and China, as a whole, at 13.1 percent. Overall, salary increases, at 9.86 percent, were also higher than Shanghai's 8 percent, while the national figure was 7.5 percent.[24] For workers who have skills and experience, the ability to job-hop became a powerful bargaining tool. Gao Fenzhen is a machine-tool operator, without a university degree, who trained at Suzhou's Vocational Technology Institute. Promoted to technical lead after only 18 months at an American electronics company, he has a clear sense of that power. "I know I can get a better offer by signing with company X [a new semiconductor plant that was currently hiring nearby], and I am almost sure my boss will offer me more to keep me here". His confidence is magnified in Daniel Chou, a college-trained engineer in the same company, who put in his two years and wants to work with more advanced technology: "My career comes first, and I can tell my manager this. The response is up to him, but I don't think I will lose. Chinese like me have to put ourselves first. We don't have the advantage of time". Chou acknowledged that his harsh attitude was shaped, in large part, by the faithless conduct of employers. "Foreigners will leave when they find a cheaper environment", he observed matter-of-factly. "Right now, we are where Singapore was ten years ago, and they will leave as soon as we get to be too expensive".

While the bargaining power of such employees as Gao and Chou is always experienced individually, it is felt collectively as wage inflation by the human-resource managers. For some foreign-invested firms, this increase in labor costs has become a factor in whether they will stick around for very long. For most of the others, it affects the decision about the moment when they will decide to move higher-end operations to the region. This puts employees like Chou at the center of an industry-wide dilemma. His desire to work with more advanced technology can only be met by a company that transfers advanced operations from a more expensive location, either in the United States, Europe, or East Asia. Yet corporate executives will only transfer these units when Chinese skill sets are high enough to meet the challenges of management and innovation, when labor costs can be contained, and when they feel that their intellectual property will be secure from theft. Until those three conditions are met, overseas employees may be able to hold on to some of the jobs destined for transfer to Asia.

In the fully measured environment in which the Suzhou engineers operate, every task is subject to a cost–benefit analysis, weighed against its equivalent in several other locations around the world. Daniel Chou knows that what he can do and what he gets paid to do it are decisive pressure points in a global industrial chain. Neither the quality of his work nor the amount of his pay is exceptional in and of themselves. He just happens to be in the right place at the right time. His parents, also engineers, work in a factory that produces the first tractors in China, making way for the mechanization of the rural communes But, for all the local fame attached to the company's name, Chou's parents' own salaries and skills have no significance beyond the boundaries of their Henan township.

Given how closely they follow their employers' methods of pricing skills and location, it is no surprise that Chou and many others are already dreaming of starting their own companies. He imagines himself and his friends pooling resources and heading to the western provinces in a few years' time. "We would like to do something for ourselves", he shrugged. "In Suzhou, all the big decisions have already been made, by people far away".

While they give no evidence of placing great trust in their employers or their government, most of my interviewees were motivated by a sharp sense of national pride. One of Jacky Wu's primary tasks, as a process engineer, is to ensure that production lines are transferred smoothly from his company's plants in Penang and Bangkok. His job entails visits to these sites and close working relationships with the engineers whose knowledge is also being transferred. "It's not very high technology", he explained, "but we still have to prove that Chinese engineers are as good as Thai or Malaysian or Singaporean ones. If China wants to go further and actually create technology, our engineers have to be better, and maybe one day we can be as good as the Americans and Japanese. Then I can work with the really high-tech stuff". If you take his reasoning at face value, Wu's motivation on the job is, in part, driven by national pride. He knows, of course, that the jobs of the Thai and Malaysian engineers will be lost as a result. "I think they will have some problems", he noted soberly, "but China has also many people without jobs".

Wu's attitude is common among engineers who work close to assembly and testing operations. They tend to measure themselves against their counterparts in those Asian countries that hosted the first offshore sites for technology companies 10 or 20 years earlier. For product engineers, the comparison is with higher-level locations – Japan, Europe, and the United States – and it is more complicated by far. "Right now, it looks as if we are still twenty years behind", estimated Li Xiao Lin, who oversees a design division at an American electronics firm. "But the Chinese learn very quickly, and if we have good access to American knowledge, maybe my country can do it much more quickly. Right now, in my company, I think that Corporate would give us more control over design, but they are worried … not about China, but about whether we can retain our talent".

When such engineers as Li make comments of this kind, it is not always clear whether they are identifying with the interests of their employer or those of their nation. Company loyalty is scarce, but since most of the engineers want to work with higher technology, they are motivated to help their companies move offshore to the greatest technically possible extent. To that degree, their personal ambition coincides with the company's goals of further transfers. In fact, their morale would probably drop if the company failed to do so. Ultimately, however, they tend to view the greatest benefit as falling to China itself – a tendency discussed further by Dimitri Kessler in this book.

In the short term, foreign investors can profit from the nationalist sentiments of their Chinese employees. The zeal of engineers for bringing technical knowledge to

China coincides with the corporate need for a workforce that is enthusiastic about moving up the industrial value chain. If, in the minds of employees, their ultimate aim is to raise China out of its technological dependence on foreign expertise, the immediate impact is in complete harmony with the foreigners' local goal of reaping offshore profits before moving on to cheaper locations. Deng Xiaoping's famous dictum, "it makes no difference whether the cat is black or white, as long as it catches the mouse", works just as well – indeed, exactly as it was intended to work – for the foreign capitalist as for their patriotic employees.

Many of my interviewees noted the irony but saw no contradiction. "I am in favor of this direction", commented Li Xiao Lin, "and our government is doing the right things to keep us on this path. Things may change in ten years, but so far, it is win-win for both China and the West". In fact, the current situation was almost always described as win-win. But surely there must be some losers? "In some other countries, yes, I have heard things are not so good, they are losing their industries, and they sometimes blame China", Li added, "but China has had so many troubles, all of our families have suffered so much, and we have too many of our own people to take care of".

Pressed on this issue, Li acknowledged that he had personally witnessed some of the international friction generated by offshore transfers. At his company, where operations are about to be transferred from Singapore and the United States, some of his colleagues noted that their counterparts in these overseas sites had stopped responding to their queries about technical applications. "Maybe they are not happy about losing their jobs", one of them mused diplomatically, "and they don't want to help us anymore". "I can understand this behavior, maybe I will feel the same way", she added in anticipation of what she assumes is a probable occurrence. A Singaporean manager at an American disk-drive company, responsible for transferring production lines from Singapore, told me that his engineer colleagues over there had pleaded with him to go slowly, so that they could hold on to their jobs for a little longer. The "system", he explained to them, would not permit such a delaying tactic. Those who were assigned to come over to teach mainland engineers how to do their jobs were not at all happy. "But they are professionals", he observed, "and they know how to be responsible in their positions".

Earlier that same day, at Lilly, I interviewed a Chinese engineer whose previous job, at Trane, required him to be sent to La Crosse, Wisconsin, to learn the ropes as part of a planned production shift to China. "The American workers were very angry", he recalled, "and demanded that the managers send all the Chinese home. I would probably have felt the same way". But there was no personal animus, he added. "Outside of the workplace, in the bars, they were very friendly to us. We had to go to the Denver plant for our training, and then, for one reason or another, the production line was not moved to China". The difference in response between the militant American workers who resisted the plant transfer and the Singaporean engineers who aided the transfer because of their "professionalism" was not just a difference of class; regional location was a big factor Singaporeans have come to accept their lot as a way station in the global production chain. Twenty years ago, they had seen the jobs come, and so they are more stoical about seeing them go

By contrast, the workers in Wisconsin have not yet got the message – resistance is futile – that employers want to send.

But their resistance will not amount to much in the long run if they cannot communicate effectively and meaningfully with their counterparts in Singapore and Suzhou. Acting together on their combined knowledge may help to establish some control over their mutually shared livelihoods. It may even prove more useful to them than shoring up the job know-how, which their employers are trying to shift from one workforce to another. In the period of national industrialization, workers in many countries have been able to forge this kind of common solidarity. As a result, they are able to push for strong labor unions, progressive taxation, and a sheltering raft of employee benefits that are the prerequisite for a relatively equal and humane society. Workers in the new corporate free-trade economy – where employers are able to operate runaway shops on a global scale – are having to start all over again, building up the international connections and mutual trust that will bring justice for all.

Managerial chutzpah

Employees like Li, Wu, and Chou came of age at a time when free-trade agreements allowed corporations to be as flighty as they pleased, so that managers were hardly in a position to expect any different conduct from workers whom they considered expendable in the long run. In addition to creating a working class wherever it goes, capital also engenders new forms of workers' resistance. High turnover is not just an effect of the labor market, it is also a reflection of the inconsistency of investors. The restless mobility of workers who see no reason to be loyal is a good example of corporations reaping what they sowed

Even so, the lack of employees' loyalty is a frequent complaint among foreign managers, and in technology-driven industries it is harshly combined with the expectation that employees will steal the company's technology. Especially guaranteed to dismay managers are the inflated aspirations of college graduates. No one, they lament, is content to commit to a stable career track at the technical end. Such craft professionals as engineers are unwilling to apply their occupational skills for long. They all want short work contracts and expect quick promotions, steep salary upgrades, and managerial responsibilities well before their time. Billy Yep, operations manager at Bearing Point, suggested that China is going through its version of the Me Generation – and pointed to the nation's one-child policy as a contributing factor. "The whole culture expects a single child to show improvements and attainments every year. So everyone wants to be a project manager in at least two years". He has seen job-hopping in SPSP escalate to a rate of every two months in some cases, a turnover that contrasts sharply with the stability of the staff he worked with in his native Singapore. Melding such self-seeking individuals into a team is his daily challenge. James Jasper, an HR manager at a United States software firm, pointed out that "these kids have never seen a downturn, they will be spoiled until it comes along".

Yep's and Jasper's comments reflect a consensus view shared by human-resource managers of foreign firms in Shanghai, who bewail the work mentality of the city's Brat Generation. In rapidly changing economic times, generational complaints such as these are not uncommon. In this case, the youthful offenders appear to have acquired their bad habits from Shanghai's boomtown culture. Because of all the new career opportunities, the city's pampered youth has lost its chance to learn the kind of work ethic – distinguished by patience and loyalty – that is favored by most employers. But what has triggered this environment of rampant personal gain? Who, exactly, has spoiled the crop? Almost certainly, some of the causes lie with opportunistic investments on the part of those same foreign companies. Their managers are reaping a harvest sowed, in part, by corporate adventurism. The disloyal mindset of their job-hopping employees, always on the lookout for the main chance, cannot easily be distinguished from the ravening mentality of the investor, always on the lookout for the best returns.

When it comes to finding employees with just the right fit, managers are seldom happy with what they get. As often as I heard the complaint about the excessive individualism of Shanghainese youth, I also heard managers bemoaning the lack of personal initiative. Mark Cavicchia, managing director of e-verse, a Los Angeles-based software developer with offshore sites in SPSP and in Bangalore, offered a common perspective: "The Chinese think collectively. They have no concept of personal space. They are not into individual-type thinking". For the kind of position that requires analytical skills, this shortcoming can be a real obstacle. Ramesh Govindan, a technology manager at a United States multinational, whose job is to effect knowledge transfer to local employees, assessed the consequences: "They also are not up to 'thinking outside the box', which is not good in the IT industry. You tell them to do something, and they will do a good job, but they are not likely to deviate from those instructions. In high tech, you are supposed to exploit the technology, to stretch the limit. You need to say, 'It's taking me ten steps to do this, can I do it in five steps?'. You probably don't see that happening in Chinese technicians".

An even greater source of managerial frustration is something that they experience as an opaque communication style on the part of their Chinese employees. Govindan put it this way: "There is a difference between what they mean and what they say. When you tell them something, they nod the head and say, 'Yes, we understood', when they haven't. So I ask them to say it in their own words to see if they really understood". Even worse, in his view, "Chinese technicians may also know what is being asked, but they don't want to tell you the answer – they know, but they won't tell you". His comment reflects the general perception of foreigners that mainland Chinese people are not in the habit of speaking directly, especially to their bosses. Chris Grocock, a regional director for a British headhunting firm, offered a precise diagnosis: "Culturally, Chinese don't like to be bringers of bad news, or they don't like to say no. So the common answer to questions is either to skirt them or answer a different question … Or they pretend they didn't hear the question at all".

Govindan, Grocock, and Cavicchia were echoing the opinions of at least 50 managers whom I interviewed for this chapter, whether in IT services or in manufacturing. For each of them, what they saw as "Chinese characteristics" was an obstacle to rational corporate conduct, and a frustrating challenge for the would-be managerial reformer.[25] These characteristics can be summed up as follows:

1 Mainland Chinese obey whatever a boss tells them, but they are at a loss when asked to think for themselves.
2 Because of the pervasive influence of "face" in the culture at large, they will not risk bringing shame on others, especially bosses, by pointing out errors.
3 They learn quickly, but only if they are shown how.
4 China's educational system is top-heavy on drill and routine, making it necessary to retrain them rigorously to think and act in a creative fashion.
5 If they revert to "the boss is always right" conditioning when they become managers, they are more likely to train sycophants than to direct them to become good performers.
6 They have little sense of loyalty and are liable to walk out with corporate intellectual property (IP).
7 The single-child policy, in which they have been unduly pampered, has made them self-centered and incapable of relating to others in teamwork.

Nearly all my interviewees expressed similar views about the work mentality of mainland Chinese employees. Most of them seemed comfortable about offering such sweeping generalizations, even those who had only been in China for a matter of months. This arrogance was compounded by the fact that non-Chinese-speaking foreign managers usually communicated with employees through a local middle manager, in a relationship not unlike that of the compradores of Old Shanghai. After a while, I began to suspect that they had all read the same book in the airport lounge. Indeed, the most popular business literature around town is aimed at preparing foreigners for the cultural differences they are likely to encounter. Volumes of such tips sport titles such as the corporate consultant Laurence Brahm's *When Yes Means No*.[26] Because these books have absorbed several centuries of Orientalism, they often offer updated versions of old Western stereotypes of Asian behavior, masquerading as insider information from such old China hands as Brahm. Like all such trading in stereotypes, these books leave the reader believing that seemingly contradictory perceptions are, in fact, just the flip sides of the same mentality. In this way, the "Oriental" is both obscure and transparent to the Western eye, both exotic and all too knowable, not "like us" and yet also capable of conforming to our ways.

The managers I interviewed accept the notion that mainland Chinese think and act in lockstep and that individualism is an alien property of the culture, whether from several centuries of the dynastic "horde", or from decades of socialist collectivism. Drawing on a long legacy of Western distrust of the Chinese, they also believe that their employees, given half a chance, will take advantage of any cross-cultural confusion to further their own self-interest. The first belief explains their employees' aversion to risk as if it were a culture-bound condition of blind Confucian obedience. The second explains their employees' minor acts of enterprise as a reflection of their ethical blindness. If the two beliefs seem contradictory, they can always be rationalized in the following way. The former distills the worst of "Asian despotism" – mass conformity with authority. The latter extracts the worst of "Western individualism" – go for oneself.

In truth, however, when managers made such comments, they were not describing their Chinese employees at all. They were justifying to themselves the reasons why they did not have a workforce of ideal corporate employees who would be all things to them, and who would also come at a discount price. The inability to access such employees at will is the real source of their discontent. It is one of the reasons, for example, why human-resource managers take such an interest in personality tests for aptitude in local employees. Several Shanghai IT firms are developing software programs responsive to cross-cultural differences, which will aid in recruiting the most suitable Chinese employees.[27]

Some of the managerial frustration comes from the additional pressure to perform placed on offshore sites. In IT services, there are many occupational tasks that merely require employees to follow a process laid down in a manual or a template provided by a project manager. Indeed, for many BPO tasks, the process has to be written down in this way to ensure seamless communication between the client and the offshore site worker. To complete such tasks barely requires any more mental variation than does an assembly line or data-entry job. Work moves along mechanically, with each phase of product delivery guaranteed by a streamlined process. In addition, however, other tasks can only be accomplished through individual problem-solving, and they require some degree of personal initiative. In traditional companies, with a workforce of scale, tasks may be broken down and allocated to different divisions with different pay scales. But increasingly, managers, especially in the knowledge industry, demand more flexibility from employees, who are expected to switch in and out of roles as required, regardless of their salary level. This is particularly true of smaller firms that eke out profit margins from a limited human-resource pool, but it is no less the case in multinationals hoping that the cost savings from offshore sites could be spread across more and more of their operations.

How do employees respond to these multiple demands? Lu Shilun, an engineer at one of SPSP's American multinationals, used a digital metaphor to describe the result: "It's just like opening different programs or applications in your brain. The one you use for half the day is only for input, and the other one is more interactive, where you feel you are competing against the program, like in a game, or that you are making up new rules to make the program compete for you". Lu explained that the general manager had told her that the goal in IT is to "work smarter, not harder", but she confessed that it was often quite difficult to interpret exactly what her boss wanted, other than that "we're not supposed to overrun on the project schedule or go over budget". Even her project manager admitted that he had given up listening very closely to his superior, who often issued contradictory requests. Some employees, especially those with experience of both Chinese and Western companies, are quick to acknowledge that the cultural differences do not always help matters. Lu's housemate Albert Chang, a programmer at an Indian company, explained: "At a Chinese company, the boss is usually always right, and so there is no confusion. I prefer the foreign style, where you can have open speech and participate in decisions. But this means that my manager is also more open about what he wants". "Sometimes", he added, with precise diplomacy, "I think he wants a little too much".

From the perspective of their Chinese employees, the foreign managers are the ones who are difficult to read. Their demands are more likely to be enigmatic, especially since they are trying to translate a distant corporate policy into directives for an inexperienced local staff. Most offshore sites were established initially to cut the costs of low-skill operations. But because they are the cheapest link in the chain, the pressure to expand them by taking on higher-value operations kicks in quickly. When local wages rise – and in Shanghai's IT industry, that has been the case – managers have to deliver better profit and productivity figures, often while using more or less the same workforce. Consequently, the demands made on employees multiply and they are asked to take on many different kinds of tasks. Under such circumstances, communications deteriorate, and employees have one more reason to jump ship for some more lucrative opportunity or for one that involves less pressure. The resulting high turnover bequeaths additional burdens on those left behind.

Circumstances in manufacturing industries differ, but my interviews with employees showed a similar pattern. Friction in the workplace is interpreted by managers as primarily attributable to the "cultural burden" of mainland Chinese, while employees find it easier to distinguish between the cultural otherness of their managers and the often contradictory demands placed upon them by people who are not likely to be their bosses for very long. Cultural differences are real enough, but miscommunication has just as much to do with the contentious nature of workplace relationships in a new industrial environment, where the rules of work are not yet determined. What managers expect and what employees are willing to give is by no means a settled matter. It is fair to say that the outcome of this informal bargaining is not just a concern for Chinese seeking a humane workplace or for foreign managers seeking a compliant local workforce. It has consequences for employees all around the world, whose jobs potentially hang in the balance.

Overcoming obstacles

The longer that foreign managers stay, the more their views harden around the bottom line. Among the older China hands, who have been in Shanghai since the late 1980s, I found that there is very little left of their idealism, misplaced or otherwise. "I guess one of our disappointments", one of them mused to me wistfully, "has been around the expectation that China would prove a cheap place for us to be". He was referring to several factors: the disastrous era of joint-ventures – when a majority of foreign investments failed; the ever-elusive

"China market" – which Westerners have been chasing for several centuries; the most recent inflationary boom in east China; and the transfer onto wholly-owned foreign enterprises of social security and other benefits hitherto borne by the state – a fiscal load that can amount to as much as 44 percent of labor costs.[28] Even so, no one should shed a tear. For the profit-hungry, no rate of return can ever be enough.

But for the domestic labor movement in outsourcing countries to respond in a roundly informed manner, we need to learn much more about labor conditions on the ground in China. In the United States the AFL-CIO's vestigial Cold War mindset is a huge obstacle to progress. It is difficult to see who, if anyone, benefits from the persistent use of China as a whipping boy for the woes of American union members. Anti-immigrant, anti-foreign sentiment has often accompanied expressions of economic nationalism in United States history,[29] and China-bashing still has its uses within the AFL-CIO, just as it does for factions of the Democratic and Republican establishment. Most of the major trade-union movements in Europe, Africa, Asia, and Latin America have established ties to China's labor federation. By contrast, the AFL-CIO's continuing embargo on any formal relations with the All-China Federation of Trade Unions (ACFTU) has meant that workers in both countries have no contact with one another, while corporations increasingly have as much access and exchange as they could wish for. At this stage in the game of free trade, such an imbalance is a clear impediment to the international cause of workers' rights.

Aside from the legacy of Cold War intransigence, there are at least two other mindsets that stand in the way of our further understanding of China's transitional economy. First, it is fair to say that China-watchers are often predisposed to be stunned by the sheer size and scope of China's problems and ambitions. In the reform era, this attitude has mutated into stupefaction at the velocity and scale of China's industrial development. The result has encouraged us to imagine that we can be little more than passive spectators, dumbfounded before the unfolding of an epic, unauthored narrative. A second obstacle is an overconfident presumption that we already know how predatory capitalism works in colonizing new markets – a reaction that feeds the detached smugness of the armchair leftist. From this perspective, China has already sold its soul, and the relentless logic of accumulation will reap the results. No less than the first, this view reinforces passivity, this time in the face of a spectacle fully authored and underwritten by global investors.

Ethnographers have little use for either awe or certitude. That is why our field work can be especially helpful, not only in contributing to a history of the present, but also in preparing for a future that is by no means guaranteed. Since its liberation from foreign occupation, China's path toward modernization has been resolutely unique, and the latest phase of the reform period is no exception. Labor researchers and educators have a special role to play in fully documenting this singular expression of economic civilization.

Notes

1   "Bush Pick Bows out after Dem Criticism", *Houston Chronicle*, March 12, 2004.
2   "Bush Campaign Ran from Noida Call Center", *Hindustan Times*, May 16, 2004.
3   Louis Uchitelle, "In Business, Washington Pursues Two China Policies," *International Herald Tribune,* December 11, 2003.
4   One survey, from the Conference Board, in conjunction with The National Bureau of Statistics of China, estimates that, between 1995 and 2002, China lost 15 million manufacturing jobs overall, compared with 2 million in the United States. The biggest losses were in textile manufacturing, steel processing, machinery, and non-metal mineral products. For that same period, China's industrial labor productivity growth exploded at a 17 percent annual rate. The Conference Board, Report R-1352, *China's Experience with Productivity and Jobs: Benefits and Costs of Change,* www. conference-board.org. After the State-Owned Assets Supervision and Administration Commission announced in 2003 that it would concentrate on retaining and restructuring less than 200 of the large state-owned enterprises, plans were set in motion to sell more than 190,000 state companies to private investors. Allen Cheng, "Labor Unrest is Growing in China", *International Herald Tribune*, October 27, 2004. As for the number of peasants released from farm labor in the last decade, estimates range as high as 150 million. The numbers are likely to be augmented by WTO compliance rules that eliminate crop subsidies and open the domestic market to foreign imports.
5   Gregory Mantsios, "Tea for Two: Chinese and U.S. Labor: A Report from China", (2002) 11 *New Labor Forum*, Fall/Winter: 61–73; Ken T. Wong, "Blaming it All on China", (2004) 13 *New Labor Forum*, Fall: 90–5; Anita Chan, "Labor in Waiting", (2002) 11 *New Labor Forum*, Fall/Winter: 54–9.
6   The firms I visited ranged, in size and scale, from Chinese start-ups to top brand multinationals. I interviewed employees at global corporations including GM, GE, Lucent, Lilly, IBM, DuPont, Nokia, Phillips, Maxtor, Hewitt, Bearing Point, AMD, Cadence, Motorola, Fluor, Kulicke & Soffa, National Semiconductor, and Fairchild, as well as smaller companies, both local and foreign, in the private sector. The three main sites for my interviews in the Yangtze Delta region were Shanghai Pudong Software Park, where IT and software service firms are clustered; Zhangjiang High-Tech Park, where microchip fabs (fabrication plants) and R&D centers are located; and Suzhou Industrial Park, the biggest magnet for foreign investment in China, which hosts a range of high tech and precision manufacturing plants. In addition, I conducted interviews in industrial parks in Wuxi and, in the west of China, in Chongqing and Sichuan. In Taiwan, my visits were to Hsinchu Science-Based Park and high-tech environs. In central Shanghai, my interviews were conducted among the membership of the American Chamber of Commerce and at selected service-sector companies, primarily foreign-invested.
7   Short-term training would also be offered to 3 million technician-level students as part of a national program involving more than 500 Chinese professional training schools and 1,400 companies and enterprises. "China Badly Needs 'Gray-Collars' for Manufacturing", *China Daily*, March 21, 2004.
8   "Bright Prospects Ahead for Technicians", *China Daily*, April 2, 2004.
9   Yan Zhen, "Locals Better Paid in Yangtze Delta", *Shanghai Daily*, March 23, 2004: 3.
10 "Graduates' Hopes Dampened by Salary Fall", *China Daily*, June 15, 2004.
11 The figures for multinationals are from the Shanghai Hewitt office. Shanghai saw more than 100,000 university students graduate in 2004, an increase of 20,000 over the previous year. Because of the glut, many graduates had to look for jobs outside the city. "Graduates Find Work But Many Leave the City", *Shanghai Daily*, June 7, 2004.

12 Peter Marsh, "World's Manufacturers March into China", *Financial Times*, June 22, 2004.

13 HR surveys in Shanghai show an annual rise of 7 percent in professional salaries for foreign-invested firms in 2003 and 2004 and 11 percent for hot fields such as engineering, IT, sales and marketing, business development, and mid-to-upper-level management. Barbara Koh, "China's New Labor Shortage", *AmChat*, October 2004: 22–3.

14 For essays that document the change from the traditional work unit, see Malcolm Warner (ed.), *Changing Workplace Relations in the Chinese Economy*, London: Macmillan, 2000.

15 Some organs, like the business-oriented *Shanghai Daily*, had a local incentive to promote this factoid. Thus, a September 20, 2003, headline story on the software boom ("City Rises as Hub for Software") reported that companies paid $3000 to $4000 for an Indian engineer and only $2000 to $3000 for the Chinese counterpart.

16 Dorothy Solinger, "Workers of China Unite in a Paradox for Communism", *Straits Times*, February 14, 2005. Ching Kwan Lee, "Pathways of Labor Insurgency", in Elizabeth Perry and Mark Selden (eds), *Chinese Society: Change, Conflict and Resistance*, New York, NY: Routledge, 2000: 41–61.

17 Liu Weifeng, "Labour Shortage Puzzles Experts", *China Daily*, August 25, 2004; "Migrant Worker Shortage Affects Enterprises As Well As Society", *Gongren ribao* (Worker's Daily), September 14, 2004; "Some Chinese Cities Run Short of Migrant Workers", *Straits Times*, August 6, 2004; Yao Yuan, "China, Land of 1.3 Billion, is Short of Labor", *Asia Times*, August 16, 2004; "China's Factories Face Labour Shortage", *Straits Times*, September 9, 2004; Fan Ren, "Drought of Migrant Labour", *Beijing Review*, August 5, 2004; Tim Johnson, "Chinese Factory Workers Begin Protesting Low Wages, Poor Conditions", *Monterey Herald*, September 7, 2004.

18 Faced with rising protests over the gap between rural and urban incomes, Hu Jintao's government took steps, beginning in 2003, to reduce the burden of rural taxation, and to phase out the agricultural tax by 2006. The State Statistical Bureau reported that farmers' per capita income increased in 2004 by 12 percent to 2,936 RMB ($387), which, adjusted for inflation, showed a 6.8 percent increase. The tax burden on peasants dropped by 44.3 percent. "Farmers' Per Capita Income Stands at 2,936 Yuan", *China Daily*, February 2, 2005.

19 Many municipalities in the region raised their minimum-wage levels. Government officials in the Guangdong township of Xiaolan took the opportunity to welcome only those investors willing to pay 600 RMB ($75), well above the minimum wage of 450 RMB ($56). Alexandra Harney, "Guangzhou and Shanghai Slug it Out", *Financial Times*, December 7, 2004: 5.

20 "Migrant Workers Learn to Say 'No' to the Market", *Sina.com*, September 21, 2004. In 2003, as much as 41.7 billion yuan (over $5 billion) in late wages was owed to 8.5 million of the country's 100 million migrant workers. "Rules Mapped Out to Protect Workers' Rights", http://china.org.cn/english/2004/Dec/113778.htm.

21 For an analysis of workers' increasing use of legal channels, see Mary Gallagher, "'Use the Law as Your Weapon!' Institutional Change and Legal Mobilization in China", in Neil Diamant, Stanley Lubman, Kevin O'Brien (eds), *Engaging Chinese Law*, Stanford, CA: Stanford University Press, 2005. Also see Anita Chan, "Some Hope for Optimism for Chinese Labor", (2004) 13 *New Labor Forum*, Fall: 67–75.

22 To alleviate the shortage, the government lifted a decade-long ban on hiring fresh migrant workers in Guangdong after the Lunar Year festival. But the numbers were down again in 2005, and railway authorities in Anhui noted a 20 percent decrease in traffic to Guangdong, and a 30 percent increase to the Yangtze Delta, where labor conditions were better. Olivia Chung, "Guangdong Labor Lures Not Working", *The Standard*, February 25, 2005; "South China Feels Acute Labor Shortage", Xinhua News Agency, March 3, 2005.

23 Dexter Roberts, "Is China Running Out of Workers?", *BusinessWeek*, October 25, 2004: 60. Jim Yardley and David Barboza, "Help Wanted: China Finds Itself with a Labor Shortage", *New York Times*, April 3, 2005. Thomas Fuller, "China Feels a Labor Pinch", *International Herald Tribune*, April 20, 2005.

24 The findings of the survey (*Work China Employee Survey: The Keys to Commitment in China*), by the HR consultancy Watson Wyatt, were presented at a meeting organized by AmCham's Human Resources Committee on Employee Recruitment and Retention in Suzhou (September 22, 2004). The figures for China (13.1 percent) were the highest in the Asia–Pacific region. Thailand came second, with 11.8 percent, and Malaysia came last, with a turnover rate of 5.5 percent.

25 See Aihwa Ong, "Re-engineering the 'Chinese Soul' in Shanghai", Chapter 14 of *Re-Engineering Citizenship*, Durham, NC: Duke University Press, forthcoming.

    The exact cultural origin of Chinese social customs, such as the all-important *guanxi* (interpersonal connections), is the object of much scholarly debate. See Thomas Gold, Doug Guthrie, and David Wank (eds), *Social Connections in China: Institutions, Culture, and the Changing Nature of Guanxi*, New York, NY: Cambridge University Press, 2002.

26 Laurence Brahm, *When Yes Means No (or Yes or Maybe): How To Negotiate a Deal in China*, Hong Kong: Tuttle, 2003.

27 Several Shanghai firms (Shanghai HRO Consulting, Professional Way, Xunda Professional Services) were developing HR software or personality tests specifically for the Chinese labor market.

28 In Shanghai, for example, a typical social-benefits load for which an employer is liable includes 22 percent for pension costs, 2 percent for unemployment, 12 percent for medical, 7 percent for housing, and 1.6 percent for disability insurance. These figures are from a service breakdown provided by Shanghai Foreign Service Co. Ltd (SFSC), a company providing HR services to foreign-invested representative offices, joint ventures, SOEs and privately owned enterprises in China. The lowest contribution in the Yangtze Delta was in Suzhou Industrial Park, where employers paid only 22%. Employees contributed the same percentage, both sums going to a central Provident Fund modeled on the welfare system in Singapore.

29 Dana Frank gives the best account of this history in *Buy American: The Untold Story of Economic Nationalism*, Boston, MA: Beacon Press, 1999.

11 Nationalism, theft, and management strategies in the information industry of mainland China

Dimitri Kessler

What are the strategies managers deploy to control the work of knowledge workers in China? How do engineers respond to these tactics, and what are the consequences? How does economic reform affect this play of management strategies and worker adaptation? I discovered that the complexities of economic reform in post-Communist China have led to a rather unique dynamic. Multinational managers are convinced that Chinese engineers are nationalistic and that, because of this nationalism, engineers refuse long-term commitments to foreign firms. What is more, managers tell stories of engineers who work for foreign firms in order to appropriate advanced technologies, to benefit the greater good of China. These stories leave managers with a heightened sense of the risk of technological theft, and this sense of vulnerability drives efforts to routinize work aimed at diminishing the technological access of engineers in China.

This chapter draws on 100 qualitative interviews of engineers, entrepreneurs, and government officials in the information industry of Taipei, Taiwan, and Beijing and Shanghai, China, which I conducted from 2001 to 2003. In addition, I had casual conversations with engineers in Cambridge, Britain, Geneva, Switzerland, and Madison, Wisconsin, in the United States that further refined this project. Interviews were designed to draw out information regarding company rivalries and their influence on tech transfers to China.

Engineering salaries

The salaries of engineers in China depend on whether engineers work for the government or private enterprise, for domestic or foreign firms. Although the influence of private and foreign firms is growing, government-owned enterprises employ the greatest number of engineers in China. Most of these government ventures set the salaries of engineers according to government guidelines. In 1999, government enterprises paid engineers $4,500 to $6,500 a year. At that time, salaries paid by domestic private enterprises averaged $8,000 a year, although noteworthy exceptions to this average exist. Engineers with a doctoral degree from Huawei, for instance, have earned as much as $25,000 a year. Foreign firms paid engineers $10,000 a year or more, depending on their experience.[1] Of course, private enterprises do not provide the housing and medical services that government employers do. However, wages in the private sector still pressure government enterprises to raise salaries. In 1999, ministries, including the Ministry of Finance, announced that they would raise the salaries of engineers by 50 percent. A 2004 survey of electronics engineers in China notes that engineers with doctoral degrees are earning average salaries of $10,685, a 12 percent increase over salaries paid the previous year. Those with a bachelor's degree earned $7,104 in 2004, a gain of 8 percent over the previous year.[2]

These salaries are dramatically lower than those in advanced industrialized nations. A 2004 survey of the *Electronic Engineering Times* notes that the yearly salaries of engineers in Europe averaged $64,200. The figure for the United States was $100,500 and that for Silicon Valley, $114,575. Even engineers with the modest responsibilities of staff engineers in the United States earned $96,000 on average in salaries and benefits.[3]

Not only are the salaries of Chinese engineers low, the number of engineers available in China is on the rise. Since the earliest economic reforms, Chinese universities went from graduating engineers at a third the rate of universities in the United States to graduating engineers at about equivalent rates. University degrees are not a good gauge of engineering abilities. For instance, programmers tend to depend on a portfolio of programs, rather than on university training, to find employment. University degrees are more significant for the future of engineers in the semiconductor sector, although even for semi-conductor engineers, it is work experience that defines the abilities of engineers and differentiates their value to employers. While such multinationals as Microsoft and Intel offer training to certify engineers in niche technologies, engineers tend to depend more heavily on employment experience, not on the routine of formal qualifications. Nevertheless, the number of engineers graduating from Chinese universities identifies a transformation of the field of Chinese engineering.

We would expect this tide of low-cost engineers to shift at least a portion of other nations' employment. A *BusinessWeek* article, for instance, quotes the CEO of one of the most prominent electronics manufacturers, Flextronics, noting that the Chinese have "enormously talented engineers, and they all want to work … I understand why US electronics companies are worried".[d]

Interestingly, the number of engineers from mainland China is growing in and outside China. Of the 183,000 doctoral degrees in science and engineering awarded to foreigners over a decade and a half in the United States, mainland Chinese earned 26,500 degrees. Over that time, students from Europe earned 16,000 degrees; and the Taiwanese, close to 15,500.[5]

The shortage of engineers

A shortage of engineers in China exists, despite the graduation rates noted above. Among other things limiting the availability of labor in the information industry in China is that multinationals avoid older workers. The oldest of the Chinese engineers I interviewed, even those at the top of the managerial ranks, were in their middle thirties. One engineer expressed the view that a lack of flexibility in instruction at universities in China contributed to the youth of mainland Chinese engineers. He explained that multinationals were not willing to transfer research and development activities to China until:

Table 11.1 Science and engineering first university degrees

	Number of degrees in selected nations			
	China	United States	Japan	Germany
1984	115,287	331,900	246,689	37,171
1985	127,405	331,526	247,258	37,468
1986	138,724	327,174	249,377	38,336
1987	157,893	322,821	252,688	39,153
1988	175,584	330,248	252,294	40,620
1989	173,681	337,675	247,643	45,081
1990	181,771	351,855	263,985	47,520
1991	190,805	366,035	284,617	51,402
1992	193,088	372,092	292,085	51,538
1993	223,447	378,148	295,743	54,686
1994	235,313	381,411	307,159	57,910
1995	216,555	384,674	330,210	61,223
1996	281,245	386,578	341,792	64,640
1997	296,723	388,482	348,897	68,116
1998	322,769	390,618	352,289	64,931
1999	359,478	394,620	350,535	57,987
2000	330,061	398,622	353,465	54,184

Source: *National Science Board. Science and Engineering Indicators 2004*, Arlington, VA: National Science Foundation, 2004.

We started getting good Chinese available. There was no Chinese programming industry, and the Chinese, the Chinese, the level of the people, the technical level was backward. You had people working on way out-of-date PCs. And, you know Chinese education. You study with your professor. Your professor tells you, well, the professors knew nothing about computers. So until you had this trickle down, Chinese technical abilities ... [weighted pause].

The youth of mainland engineers is at least partly the result of the hiring practices of multinationals in mainland China. In China, age is a function of the varying political climate. Older Chinese are associated with the politicized inefficiencies of communism, while the youth are associated with the greater pragmatism of marketization. Accordingly, multinationals actively recruit engineers according to their age – a practice that contributes to the stratification of Chinese society. In a nation where millions are out of work, multinationals in the information industry complain that the market for engineers is tight.

One of the older foreign engineers I interviewed, a man who worked for IBM and had worked in China longer than most foreigners have, said of IBM that "their research institutes are all kids". According to this engineer, IBM will not hire anyone over the age of 25. He remarked that:

the industry is new, and anybody who was around before the industry started is worthless. Anybody who worked in a Chinese work unit is worthless ... People, the first job they go to, if it is a place where the requirements are really low and the other workers are not really good, they just do not develop. You learn what level is acceptable, and if what's acceptable is really low, you go somewhere else, and it's really tough to pick it up.

The head of the United States Information Technology Organization[6] (USITO) reiterated this idea in a different fashion. He remarked,

> There are very few very experienced people in the industry here. Quite honestly, I mean, who has twenty years of experience working in a computer company in China? Nobody. Because twenty years ago, there was nobody here. Twenty years ago, there were very few college graduates in this market. 1982, you know, the first wave of graduates after the Cultural Revolution. And you know, your work experience in 1982 to 1992 was not exactly, you know, shall we say ... what corporate headquarters would expect corporate experience to be ... You know? So that experience does not quite count. So there's really only like five or ten years' work experience in a lot of these people.

The rapid rise of expectations

Hiring practices that restrict the pool of the potential applicants and the dismantling of the isolation of the Chinese economy are contributing to the tremendous rise of engineers' salaries. When foreign enterprises first arrived in mainland China, barriers to competition in China allowed foreign firms to pay engineers a fraction of the market value of their productivity outside China. Government enterprises dominated the employment of engineers in China, and the wages of engineers at these enterprises were fixed and relatively low. Even emerging private enterprises could pay lower wages, since the fixed wages of government enterprises limited the choices open to engineers. The growth of private enterprise and the influx of foreign firms transformed this situation. At a time when few foreign firms were well established in China, there was less competition. As a result, although multinationals paid engineers salaries above those of alternative positions with Chinese government and private enterprises, the salaries of engineers in Chinese enterprises and foreign firms showed greater similarity.

In the 1980s, 90 percent of the salaries of engineers *at foreign firms* went to the government in the form of taxes. Multinationals tried to circumvent the high tax rate by qualifying most of engineers' pay as cost-of-living allowances. Since it was expected that the cost of living would not vary with the responsibilities of workers, secretaries and engineers received equivalent allowances for the cost of living. Multinational representatives I interviewed complained that, in this context, it was difficult to offer economic incentives to workers to promote above-average accomplishments: with tax rates above 90 percent, workers received a negligible part of whatever raises they were offered. Thus, raises were not a cost-effective way to motivate workers. One of the only motivational awards that multinationals had to offer engineers was training opportunities. At the time, the Chinese economy was closed to commodities from outside China, and the opportunity to train in Hong Kong was highly prized, since that stay allowed workers to purchase commodities that were not available in mainland China.

This changed in the 1990s, when the government allowed multinationals greater freedom to adjust the wages of their employees. It is worth noting that these reforms have met resistance even among the youth of the Chinese information industry. I interviewed the founder of a multinational that had had 8,000 applications of the most highly qualified programmers in China for 50 positions. In the interview, he complained that the turnover of engineers at that multinational had at times approached 200 percent in a single year. According to this interviewee:

The mistake we made: we hired top notch people, and when they came in, they were highly paid. In that climate, it's very difficult, actually, to give engineers additional encouragement, a bonus or a raise of wages. So that's a mistake.
And they find higher salaries elsewhere?
No.
Why leave?
It's not that they find higher salaries elsewhere. They compare to each other.[7] That's the killer … If salaries elsewhere are one thousand lower, but they find they're fifty renminbi lower than the fellow sitting next to them, they will leave. They will think it's not fair. They will complain. They will do something to harm our company, which I hate.

Accounts of resistance aside, economic reforms have radically altered the ability of multinational managers to adjust wages. The flood of foreign investment in the 1990s intensified the competition between foreign firms and led to dramatic wage increases. One foreign engineer who worked in China 15 years ago and again recently, reported:

I was making about the same as twenty Chinese employees … and probably worth thirty in that position. Now I'm making about the same as probably two or two and a half Chinese employees … Figure in another few years, I'll be one and a half or so. At that point, I won't be priced that far out of the industry. On the other hand, at that point, I won't have such a skills advantage over the people who are here.

A representative of USITO, with a wider perspective on the information industry, commented on wage increases:

At the beginning of 1992, 1993, average increases of foreign invested enterprise salaries were around 30 percent, 25 percent a year. And it's been dropping. Twenty-three, nineteen, seventeen, sixteen, steadily. Still, this year, I think it was like nine. You know, 9 percent salary increases. You know, people around here are like, 'sucks, you know. I only got a 10 percent raise last year'. And in the United States, Hong Kong or anywhere in the world, you get a 3 percent raise, and you're like … So it's … The expectations are skewed.

Turnover

Competition for the pool of potential applicants sought by multinationals motivates many multinationals to poach the engineers currently working for competitors. Since this practice is widespread, rising salaries reflect the fact that engineers are moving from firm to firm, not that workers are getting pay increases from their current employer. The USITO representative I interviewed mentioned: "Retention in China. There is no loyalty, I mean, here. It makes Silicon Valley look like a hot bed of loyalty. It's crazy. I mean, if you spend two years in a job, people here question what you are doing. And nowhere is retention so low, turnover so high as in hightech companies". A foreign engineer remarked:

> If someone is worth 120,000 a year, and they're being paid 30,000 a year, then DEC is going to try to take them from Sun, Sun's going to take them back from DEC, and people aren't stupid. If they're not going to be getting 40 percent a year raises from wherever they are, then they are going to go to the places that offer them 40 percent more.

Anecdotes about engineers pitting multinationals against one another to raise their salaries are everywhere. I talked with one engineer in his mid-twenties who had recently completed a two-year training program at one multinational. The program was part of the requirements for taking a more advanced position within the same firm. Just after finishing the program, however, this engineer took a higher-paid position at another multinational, which, my interviewee joked, gained a worker with sensitive knowledge about the technologies of its competitor. Another interviewee from a United States semi-conductor enterprise echoed the comments of the USITO representative, remarking that there was a general expectation that people would transfer to a new firm on a biannual basis. My interviewee was approaching a two-year anniversary at a multinational, and she was looking for a position elsewhere because she believed that others would look askance at her abilities if she were not able to find another position. I talked with one engineer who, when applying for work at a multinational, noticed that the interviewer was wearing a watch from a competitor. He discovered that the interviewer had arrived two weeks earlier after working for the competitor although, evidently, he was already hiring others for the corporation that had convinced him to leave.

The link between rising salaries and turnover is not unique to China. Researchers have noted the high mobility of engineers in California,[8] where the turnover rates of engineers appear to be higher than those elsewhere in the United States, even when the size of firms is taken into account.[9] And yet, as I noted above, the salaries of engineers in California are far greater relative to salaries elsewhere in the United States and Europe. These dynamics are counterintuitive, since we expect higher salaries to raise the willingness of workers to commit to a firm.[10]

It is difficult to determine the extent to which rates of turnover in China are higher than those elsewhere. A few interviewees from the United States explicitly compared China negatively to California. A few Taiwanese interviewees expressed considerable concern about the turnover of engineers in mainland China. Other Taiwanese believed that engineers in mainland China were acting exactly as Taiwanese engineers had acted when the information industry was first established in Taiwan, although this view affirms that engineers in mainland China are more likely to leave their firms than do the Taiwanese of today. It is worth noting that I was told that engineers in China consider two years a long time at one firm, while Prasad mentions that engineers in India and California consider twice that time to be a long time.[11] However, the extent to which salaries are rising more quickly in China than elsewhere is not the most important aspect to note. What matters most is that managers have a unique explanation for what is otherwise a *pervasive* experience.

Nationalism and theft

The government is still a prominent source of engineering employment in China and actively recruits engineers through universities and engineering associations. I myself met engineers that the Chinese government recruited through associations of ethnic Chinese engineers in California. Government engineering projects are often organized with the aim of developing domestic alternatives to foreign technologies, and participation in these projects often implies a degree of nationalism and antagonism to foreigners. For instance, one engineer I knew of was a student with a pronounced talent for engineering; he also had all the ties to the government he needed to have a bright future in China. When he decided to seek a doctoral degree in Europe, however, his professors refused to write the necessary letters of reference in the attempt to prevent him from going to a university overseas.

Nevertheless, engineers have *relatively* few ties to the propaganda and organizational dynamics ordinarily associated with nationalism in mainland China. Engineers tend to articulate a rhetoric of economic rationality and science, and they are relatively free from the influence of Chinese communism. Science students are, for instance, exempted from a Marxist political examination that gauges the political thought of students.[12] Frequently engineers have lived abroad in academic and professional settings. Even those who have not left mainland China are likely to have employment opportunities in foreign firms and with private Chinese enterprises.

Nonetheless, the managers of multinationals are vocal about the nationalism of engineers in China, and many managers believe that nationalism explains the turnover rates among Chinese engineers. One of my interviewees had designed employee retention packages for foreign enterprises in mainland China. Following the theme of a lack of loyalty of the Chinese to their enterprise, he told me:

> Ordinarily, people don't stay or leave because of salary. It's just kind of expected that you will make a ton of money once you rise to a certain position. You need to have other things, things like leadership, culture, purpose. What is my company doing for China? I know a lot of people who are like, x x company, they do not understand China ... Quite often, what we'll see is, you

know, you will go through three or four, what I've seen is that you go through three or four major high level postings at foreign enterprises, and then you'll take, you'll either start your own company, or you'll take a very low paying job at a state owned enterprise or something like that to help the country. Very nationalistic. Patriotic. Help develop the country, or work as an advisor to the government.

Most notably, multinational managers believe that the nationalism of Chinese engineers contributes to theft. Managers told stories of nationalism motivating engineers to reengineer foreign technologies in Chinese-controlled form for the benefit of China. A management interviewee told the story of a programmer who was considered a national idol after he wrote a book expressing the view that property rights in the information industry are a modern form of imperialism and that theft is a just method of fighting the influence of foreign firms in China. A Chinese engineer/entrepreneur raised in Sweden and employed by a Swedish firm told me the story of a nationalistic engineer who worked at the same enterprise. This engineer would work for foreign enterprises to gain access to more advanced technologies. After a period, he would leave the foreign enterprise, register his own enterprise, and work "for friends" for little remuneration until he was "bankrupt". After this, he would look again for work in a foreign enterprise, and he had apparently moved through this cycle nine times!

Engineers themselves tell these stories of nationalism. The most striking anecdote was of a Chinese engineer I interviewed with experience at a long-established semi-conductor multinational in the United States. He said that his position at the United States multinational was ideal. The work he was doing was cutting-edge and allowed him to register 20 or more patents. He was highly paid, the pace of work gave him ample time to relax, and he and other engineers at the multinational expected the firm to guarantee their position for the rest of their lives.

My interviewee, however, met the founder of a semiconductor enterprise in mainland China. This "convincing and charismatic" person asked him, "What are you doing [in the United States], where you are discriminated against, when you could be in China, contributing to your country, working for the Chinese people?". Months later, my interviewee left his highly paid, comfortable position for a job working with the man who had asked him this question. He was expressly committed to transferring sensitive foreign technologies to the Chinese, and he mentioned that he was worried that I might inform authorities in the United States about his activities in China.

In China, my interviewee was paid a third of his former salary. Apparently, he was bitter about this reduction because he was had been told that differences in the cost of living would render the wage differential negligible, and that was not true. Unlike the pace of work he had experienced in the United States, he said, he now worked almost without rest. There were few other experienced engineers at the firm, and this lack intensified the demands on my interviewee. He had no time for vacations and was telephoned throughout the night by the other engineers, who did not want to make even the least significant decisions without him for fear of physical reprisal. He explained, "They will be beaten if they make a mistake". My interviewee mentioned that there was a limit to how long he could accept these conditions and that he was thinking about moving on. However, nationalism and the opportunity to contribute to the advancement of the Chinese people had motivated this interviewee to leave the relative ease he had been guaranteed in the United States and persuaded him to persevere for a time.

I interviewed one mainland Chinese engineer who worked for a private enterprise in the United States. This engineer was in China to sell the technologies of the United States firm to the Chinese. I was astonished to learn that the Chinese government had also appointed this interviewee to oversee a government organization that was a potential purchaser of the technologies he was selling. I asked, politely, if my interviewee felt that it might be a conflict of interest to hold the two positions. He replied: "Yea, actually, that's true. Yea, that's a very hard thing to me. I'm Chinese. We have a technology. This firm. I have to protect. I have to work for this firm, try to sell our technology to Chinese parties". For this interviewee, selling foreign technologies in China was difficult because he was *Chinese*, and as a Chinese citizen, the interviewee identified with the government's aim of developing alternatives to foreign technologies. Throughout the interview, he explained why China is developing alternative technologies to avoid the manipulation of foreign firms. Thus, what was difficult for this engineer was defending the interests of a foreign firm in China, not the obvious conflict of interest as the negotiator of both the buyer and seller of sensitive technologies.

When I spoke with a couple of Chinese engineers about nationalism, they said that they preferred to work with Chinese equipment and programs if the cost to them of doing so was reasonable. However, if there were too many negative consequences to not having the more cutting edge equipment and programs of foreign firms, they would not buy exclusively Chinese. There was a limit to their willingness to sacrifice themselves on the basis of nationalism. After stating that they would not work at a loss with Chinese enterprises, however, they told me that they tried to avoid Japanese firms except when there were no alternatives.

It seems worth noting here that anti-Japanese propaganda is a critical part of Communist efforts to promote Chinese nationalism. Tourist parks dedicated to relating stories of Japanese aggression in China were part of the campaign to raise patriotism among the youth and quiet criticism of the communists after the Tiananmen demonstration.[13] Outside of formal interviews, I spoke with many mainland Chinese who voiced antagonistic and prejudiced remarks at the mention of the Japanese. Thus, there is no need to wonder at the findings of a Japanese journal that interviewed university graduates in mainland China about the jobs they most preferred. Nine of the ten most preferred firms were in the information industry. Although Japanese enterprises are a prominent force of the information industry in China, and Japanese enterprises have established joint ventures with Chinese enterprises that have transferred sensitive technologies to China, only two Japanese firms were among the 50 most preferred corporations – ranked thirty-second and forty-sixth.[14]

The limits of management control

Managers and engineers themselves circulate stories of engineers whose thievery is motivated by nationalism. These stories reflect and exaggerate management fears of technological theft and motivate a variety of management strategies to protect against this practice. But since engineers require access to sensitive technologies to fulfill their day-to-day activities, it becomes all the more difficult for managers to restrict access. For instance, Chinese engineers do not need to work at foreign firms in order to have access to sensitive technologies. Foreign firms have to negotiate access even with the engineers of Chinese enterprises to which they outsource low-value-added activities.

Two interviewees at Chinese enterprises mentioned that they argue with their foreign allies about the degree of access their engineers require. One Chinese enterprise was developing the Chinese version of a program designed for the United States. This kind of programming is ordinarily a low-value-added activity and requires less engineering expertise. My interviewee, however, explained that at times, programmers have to add new functionalities to the existing program. This addition requires that they have access to the source code of the program, and thus, a conflict of interest arises:

> If you give away, if you're a foreign firm, and you give away too much of your source code, you lose control of the program. So that's a bit of a battle between who holds the source code. So they [the foreign firm], every time we [the Chinese enterprise] want to add functionality, you have to work with them to get them to add the functionality [themselves] or give you the tools to develop it.

Thus, even when Chinese engineers are merely fulfilling their responsibilities, multinationals resist so as to protect themselves from theft. Engineering requires access to sensitive technologies, and managers are less able to limit the number of engineers having access to sensitive technologies when engineers move frequently from firm to firm. Thus, the turnover of Chinese engineers is associated with the perceived likelihood that mainland Chinese engineers are technological thieves.

I talked with entrepreneurs at a few foreign enterprises who considered moving engineering activities to mainland China. They thought seriously about the move because their competitors were already established in China and because they believed that the market is available potential there is tremendous. However, they also felt that mainland Chinese engineers pose too great a risk to their proprietary technologies, and they decided against moving to China.

Is turnover good for firms?

The majority of my managerial interviewees talked about turnover in the information industry as a threat. Some interviewees expressed the view that turnover threatened the foundations of innovation itself. Other interviewees thought that turnover, though regrettable, was natural to high-tech industries. Still others believed that turnover, whatever its cause, could not be avoided.

Academic authors, too, have questioned whether turnover and technological theft have overall negative effects on innovation in the information industry. Although there are those who believe that turnover impedes the development of more effective research teams,[15] others stress that turnover and theft promote the wider spread of specialized skills.[16] A handful of managers I interviewed talked about turnover in positive terms, and their views are worth mentioning.

Two of the managers to articulate this alternative perspective worked for two of the largest programming multinationals in the world. These interviewees mentioned that they make most of their profits from platform technologies – servers and operating systems. Their competitors are other multinationals platform providers, not the modest enterprises that restrict their programming to a few applications. Platform programming requires more extensive expertise, greater organization and investment. The complexity and cost of the technologies involved minimizes the threat of individual acts of theft. What is more, even when engineers leave one of these firms with sensitive technologies, they tend to try to establish smaller enterprises and develop programming with more modest requirements. For smaller enterprises – what one interviewee referred to as "onehorse carriages" to describe the restrictions of their expertise – the threat of theft is more serious, since engineers, through individual theft, could walk away with the technology that gives the enterprise its edge in the market.

Furthermore, engineers who work at firms that develop platform technologies tailor their programming to the requirements of the platform of *that* firm. Since training in the requirements of alternative platforms takes time, even after engineers establish new enterprises, they tend to write programs for the platform of the firm they walked away from. Thus, even if engineers write application programs that compete with those of a multinational they worked for in the past, those programs are likely to be built for the platform requirements of that multinational. For multinationals that make their profits from platform programming, the turnover of engineers out of their ranks actually contributes to the growth of a population of programmers who make the particular multinational's platform more attractive by writing application programs dedicated to it.

The only two other interviewees to talk about the benefits of turnover were semi-conductor engineers. They expressed the view that turnover facilitates the transfer of technology from firm to firm and that the costs and benefits to any individual firm are negligible. Firms suffer the theft of their secrets while simultaneously gaining access to the secrets of others. Although this perspective is interesting, the fact that most entrepreneurs I interviewed fretted about the turnover of engineers indicates that they consider the outflow of their secrets to be more important than their learning the secrets of others.[17] It is further worth noting that one of these two interviewees was the head of a manufacturer utilizing more mature technologies. Their manufacturing relied on 10-year-old technologies that were often embedded in "equipment recipes". This enterprise was likely to gain more *from* others than what their engineers could offer *to* other firms.

Representatives of firms on the cutting edge of semi-conductor technologies were much stricter about access to their technologies and more nervous about the turnover of their engineers. One interviewee at Intel associated the tight control of knowledge Intel tries to maintain with "the military". Two other Intel engineers were forced to refuse to talk to me after their manager found out their plans to meet with me in a coffee house after hours. Two cutting-edge Taiwanese enterprises, SMIC and TSMC, have benefited from the turnover of engineers from other firms. Yet they, too, are known to try to maintain tight control over the *out*flow of their own engineers. TSMC, in particular, is known to have filed suit against its own engineers for exporting techniques to mainland China.

Controlling creativity

Entrepreneurs in those corporations that make the move to China mentioned anticipating the theft of engineering secrets as one of the most important factors that influences their management practices in mainland China. To protect themselves against theft, managers institute two distinct practices. First, firms restrict engineers' access to their technologies and isolate engineers in narrow specializations to make it more difficult for engineers to reengineer the technologies they work with. Furthermore, managers force engineers to organize and document their work in ways that make it easier for others to continue the work of one engineer once that engineer leaves the firm.

To restrict the access of engineers, for instance, one engineer/entrepreneur I interviewed used hardware to embed key programs – programs that engineers would not ordinarily embed in hardware – in such a way that they could not be copied or transferred out of the hardware via the internet. He could control the access of the engineers who worked for him by controlling their access to the room where the hardware was housed. A New Zealand entrepreneur explained the technique for narrowing the expertise of engineers in the following way. He founded a programming firm with a Chinese engineer to whom he gave the following advice on how to protect their program from theft: "What I told him was, keep one developer, one programmer, he just works on this area. He doesn't learn about the, the client. And the person developing the client, he doesn't learn about the … yea".

Large enterprises tend to require engineers with a greater variety of expertise, and as a result, are better able to manipulate the organization of work to keep engineers from achieving the understanding that might allow them to duplicate the technologies they work with. Engineers working in different specializations for a large enterprise often work at different facilities, and this circumstance makes it easier for managers to control the communication between engineers. Often, engineers access the technologies they work with through computer networks. One foreign engineer I interviewed with work experience in China and the United States for one of the largest semi-conductor enterprises reported that, in China, he could not access networks sites that had been available to him in the United States. He asked for an explanation and was told that the information from those sites was too valuable to be viewed by Chinese engineers.

Enterprises that require fewer engineers and less variety of expertise have a diminished ability to organize work into specializations to make it difficult for engineers to understand the duplication of a product. Thus, they resort to more drastic measures to protect their intellectual property. One enterprise where I interviewed gave the most important tasks to one engineer, leaving four or five other engineers to work only on less demanding programming tasks. In another enterprise where I interviewed, two of the founders selected one Chinese engineer among the 50 qualified engineers who worked there. After cultivating ties to this engineer to guarantee his loyalty, the founders secretly rented a villa in the mountains and, together with that one engineer, disappeared for a month of work to write one of their most important programs. To date, no one apart from the founders and that one engineer were allowed to view the program.

These strategies to narrow the skills of engineers have their intended effect. One interviewee mentioned that the Chinese government is aware of and tries to profit from the mobility of engineers. He noted that Huahong, a government semi-conductor enterprise, is offering 6 million yuan to anyone who will provide the company with .25-micron wafer manufacturing technologies. My interviewee explained that, although the money was attracting a lot of attention, no one engineer could ever provide the asked-for technologies. The expertise of engineers is too specialized to allow one engineer to know all the requirements of this process.

Regardless of efforts to isolate engineers in specializations, engineers maintain leverage over their managers through their creativity. From this circumstance stem management strategies to routinize engineering work. One of my interviewees talked of "code cowboys" to refer to the independence of more eccentric engineers. Programmers and managers share a mythology of eccentric and elite programmers who work independently and disdain the formalities and organizational requirements of large enterprises. Although it strains their organizational arrangements, large companies seek out these programmers since they are thought to write the most innovative programs. Managers, however, caution that these loners are able to write programs that other engineers are neither able to understand nor improve on. Managers love and fear these eccentric programmers. While their innovations have great market potential, firms must adjust their programs from time to time. If only one engineer understands a program, managers depend on only one engineer to develop that program throughout its evolution. This arrangement becomes a disaster for a firm if a program developer decides to leave. One interviewee remarked that the solution "is to design something not just so that it works, but so that it works and can be understood by whoever takes over your position after you leave".

Thus, the managers I interviewed expressed the need for engineers to work according to established norms that allow other engineers to develop a program even after the original programmer is no longer at the firm. One of my interviewees explained the need for engineers to document their work in this way: "If you just sell someone software, it could take, I could figure out how to change it. If you have the source code, you have to go in there and, line by line, teach yourself how the entire thing works ... If you have the documentation, you can read it ... and teach yourself much faster".

I found that other multinationals express related concerns regarding how to coordinate the efforts of their engineers. Consider, for instance, the words of a manager from IBM who designed a training program to *discipline* programmers:

Few [programmers] have been taught effective programming principles, and fewer still know how to plan or track their work. They rarely document their designs before they build them, and they rely on compilers and debugging aids to fix the defects they inject while designing and implementing their products.[18]

The software community has had a long history that sort of honors the hacker mentality. Software people are very bright and they have done marvelous work but they are loners. They sort of produce things themselves. They are proud of debugging and all that sort of thing and that is inherently limited … [T]he software business is essentially paralyzed by debugs. We spend half our time debugging codes.[19]

In China, since management strategies to routinize work are a reaction to nationalism and the threat of theft, they take a form that differs from efforts to routinize work to lower wages. The salaries of Chinese engineers, though rising, are a fraction of wages elsewhere. Therefore, managers are motivated to routinize the skills of engineers to protect themselves against theft in China, not to diminish the skills of Chinese engineers to prevent them from negotiating raises in their salaries. This is especially true since the greater skills of Chinese engineers give multinationals greater leverage to undermine the salaries of engineers in developed nations. Isolating engineers in specializations does keep them from developing a conception of the overall design of a product to prevent theft. Yet it does not deprive them of creativity and conception within their specializations. Managers want to prevent engineers from gaining control of *products*, not of all innovative skill. In addition, efforts to force engineers to document their work routinize engineering in the sense that they allow firms to more easily substitute one engineer for another. In and of itself, however, documentation does not affect the creativity of the work and in this sense, it does not give management incentives to institute coercive forms of discipline that could inhibit innovation. Thus, these strategies of routinizing work represent the extension of management control over engineers' creativity, not the automation or degradation of the quality of work itself.[20]

The motives and institutions of theft

The effects of stiffer competition for engineers, turnover, and theft are not restricted to foreign firms. A management interviewee at a Chinese enterprise had heard of competitors offering engineers pay increases of 50 percent to move from their current firm to another, and he thought turnover in the information industry in China was 30 percent a year. A manager at a different enterprise mentioned to me that his firm was forced to institute a new management regime after a few engineers took positions at other enterprises. The new organization divided the responsibilities of engineers in order to lower the value of the expertise any engineer could take away. To maintain the smooth functioning of the firm, engineers were required to keep records of their work in great detail. The ideal was to organize work so that "anyone could walk away" without affecting the firm.[21]

Although interviewees at Chinese enterprises talked of theft, they did not connect it with nationalism. Of course, Chinese-on-Chinese theft does not look like nationalism. Still, the comments of interviewees at Chinese enterprises were quite different from those made by people I interviewed at foreign firms, who stressed the effects of nationalism on the motives of Chinese engineers. Others talked about the lure of money. Still others tied theft to negative aspects of Chinese culture. These themes all tended to frame theft in terms of a propensity on the part of Chinese engineers to steal.

One Japanese interviewee, for instance, made a distinction between the Taiwanese and the Chinese. He admitted that Taiwanese enterprises violate patent protections all the time, and he associated these violations with a common Chinese culture of *guanxi* that resists the rule of law. He commented: "In Japan, the Taiwanese, Hong Kong, and the Chinese, we call Chinese. Actually, the people of these three areas are ... completely different people ... They have different ideas, different cultures and a different business mind. We recognize. In Taiwan, business is different [from mainland China]. The Taiwanese always stress, the Chinese government is governed by people, not governed by the law. For the Taiwanese, it is easy to move to China". Interestingly, a mainland Chinese engineer raised in the United States also tied theft to Chinese culture. Telling stories of engineering theft and fraud, he commented: "I'm not used to the people here. Though I'm changing as well ... I hate the way I'm changing ... I remember, my aunt in Philadelphia, she told me. How to do business in China mumbo jumbo. I did not believe it ... I believed the western way will work in China ... We have to adapt. We have to adapt to survive".

Even Taiwanese interviewees tied theft to Chinese culture. A researcher I interviewed mentioned Taiwanese policies to promote the travel of engineers from India to Taiwan. He explained that the policies were intended to circumvent the need to hire Chinese engineers, since they are thought more likely to thieve. On the topic of these policies, a subsequent interviewee observed that the Taiwanese prefer engineers from India because "the culture of India is different" from that of mainland China.

While interviewees at Chinese enterprises seemed to agree with foreigners that engineering theft is common in China, they linked this to the deficiencies of Chinese institutions, not the propensity of the Chinese to thieve. They stressed two themes: the need for greater management experience, and the difficulties of effectively enforcing consequences on thieves.

For instance, two Chinese investors believed that theft in China reflected the quality of management in Chinese enterprises. They were confident that incidents of theft would lessen as Chinese entrepreneurs gain greater management experience. Quite a few interviewees expected that Chinese entrepreneurs will gain this management experience from foreign firms. One Chinese enterprise where I interviewed was working with a firm from India to import "modern management strategies" to improve their control of new technologies. In addition, I interviewed a Chinese engineer who was a star of sorts in the Chinese information industry. He confessed that he needed management experience to *profit* from the skills he possessed. His contributions to Chinese programming were widely applauded and widely pirated. As a result, he decided to work as a manager at a foreign firm to gain experience with the management strategies foreign firms employ to control their technologies. A manager I talked to expressed the view that the transfer of foreign management techniques was essential to the competitiveness of Chinese enterprises, more so than the transfer of engineering expertise.

I also interviewed one man who mentioned that firms selling stolen technologies in China often disappear after a few negotiations. Just finding a firm against which to file a complaint is difficult. A Chinese entrepreneur mentioned a parallel experience, one illustrating the difficulty of seeking restitution from employees. He discovered that a few employees had committed theft, and he tried to discipline them. However, they disappeared, and the firm was unable to find them. These entrepreneurs conceded that engineering theft is common to the Chinese environment. However, they tied theft in China to institutional arrangements, not to the motives of Chinese engineers.

Conclusion

This chapter tries to illustrate a unique dynamic in management strategies that emerges from the complexities of Chinese economic reform. Engineers moving from firm to firm in order to obtain salary increases are less likely to develop long-term commitments to the enterprises that employ them. Managers anticipate this situation and organize engineering responsibilities so as to protect their firms from theft. Once engineers find that opportunities within a firm are restricted, they are even more strongly motivated to move from firm to firm to acquire new experience. This process generates a self-perpetuating cycle of tension and movement.

Engineers I interviewed in the United Kingdom and the United States identified with this volatile atmosphere. A few commented that these conditions – the youth of engineers, rising salaries, turnover, theft, and the organization of work in anticipation of theft – are common to the information industry all over the world. Tension concerning the control of sensitive technologies is far from unique to China, and many of the dynamics discussed here have parallels elsewhere. National identities, too, have a demonstrated effect on other global workplaces in the information industry.[22]

Nevertheless, in China, the owners of advanced technologies and their apprentices negotiate their interests in a climate in which their differences are racially marked. This atmosphere aggravates conflicts of interest between the Chinese, the multinationals, and their foreign managers. The effects of this are profound and make negotiations of technological apprenticeship in China quite different from those in Silicon Valley.

It is not my intention to measure what proportion of engineers in mainland China is nationalistic, or the extent to which they are. No doubt, engineers involved in the information industry ordinarily have or are seeking experience with foreign enterprises, and many have traveled to further their expertise. Many have entrepreneurial aspirations, few are politically radical, and all are aware that their livelihood depends on deepening economic reform. Nonetheless, even if the more dramatic accounts of nationalism are rare, their visibility attests to their importance. Even engineers for whom nationalism is not a critical motivation will pass on the stories of those for whom it is. Listening to these stories, the managers of foreign firms come to hold more extreme views of the Chinese.

The highest-ranking multinational managers are ordinarily not from mainland China and understand that the nationalistic climate in China sets them apart. It contributes to their sense that the Chinese will take advantage of foreign enterprises. Often, foreigners, confronted with accounts of Chinese nationalism, come to anticipate a very antagonistic variety of nationalism from all Chinese. Thus, multinational managers in China tend to attribute turnover to the lack of loyalty of Chinese engineers, not to their own wage policies. If multinational managers think that Chinese engineers are nationalistic and lack loyalty to foreign enterprises, it aggravates the antagonism and threat that multinational managers feel in mainland China. This climate accelerates the efforts of managers to organize work to deprive Chinese engineers of sensitive expertise.

This situation affirms the nationalism of those Chinese who anticipate that foreigners will not risk their control of sensitive technologies for fear of its passing to the Chinese. Thus, Chinese engineers are making their choices to move from firm to firm in a climate that radicalizes the meaning of national origin. Multinational managers talk about protecting themselves from theft in mainland China as protecting themselves from the Chinese. Chinese engineers identify with China, not only because the Chinese communists have taught them to, but also because foreigners anticipate and affirm that identity. If the rhetoric of multinational managers affirms that mainland Chinese are a threat, it reaffirms the notion of a conflict of interest between Chinese and foreigners in the minds of the Chinese.

Interestingly, it appears that Chinese enterprises are adopting the management strategies of foreign firms. However, Chinese enterprises experience a form of foreign management that is tailored to the perception that the Chinese are most probably thieves. To the extent that prejudice affects foreigners' perceptions, and to the extent that foreign management strategies achieve their aim of restricting the development of engineers, Chinese enterprises contribute to the system that extends foreign control of sensitive technologies into mainland China.

A methodological appendix

I discovered in the field that Chinese and foreign firms alike are wary of allowing people from outside the firm to enter their facilities in China, though they are relatively at ease with one-on-one interviews. Adapting to these obstacles, I designed a project of one-on-one interviews with a wider variety of firms than I had initially planned. At the outset, the nationalism of Chinese engineers was not a prominent theme of my interviews. Since I had at most three interviews at any one firm, I paid more attention to rivalries between firms than to the dynamics within firms. However, my questions about firm rivalries and their influence on tech transfers between Chinese and foreign firms prompted interviewee after interviewee to talk about the control of knowledge and of knowledge workers within the firm. Thus, the theme of the nationalism of engineers in mainland China emerged in my thoughts.

Of course, my nationality affected comments on the topic of nationalism. Foreigners in China, for instance, tend to think of people in terms of the Chinese on the one hand and everyone else on the other. Since foreigners expect other foreigners – including myself – to agree, foreign interviewees were more comfortable criticizing the Chinese and voicing their national chauvinism to me.

Conversely, I felt that the Chinese kept their chauvinism more to themselves. For many mainland Chinese, foreigners inspire a degree of antagonism. I sensed that my Chinese interviewees softened expressions of nationalism out of politeness and the desire to avoid the appearance of a confrontation. Interestingly, for a few Chinese, I was less threatening than some other foreigners because I immigrated to the United States from Europe. This effect was heightened since, without fail, the Chinese ask foreigners where they are from. In a more obvious manifestation of this habit, after I explained to a taxi driver that I was from Switzerland, he was moved to tell me that we – and here, he was referring to the rest of the world – could overcome the United States in war if we joined forces. This is not the kind of thing that the Chinese express directly to foreigners from the United States. In contrast, the Taiwanese tended to prefer reminiscing on time they spent in the United States and were silent on the subject of my immigration. I gathered that this attitude reflects the prominence of the United States in the Taiwanese imagination.

Gender also affected my interviewees. Apart from a dozen people, all my interviewees were men. Although I conducted a few interviews in office settings, most of my interviewees preferred to talk in less professional settings, where gender effects were more prominent. In China, both foreigners and Chinese are wary of inviting a researcher into their affairs without a *friend* to introduce them. Matters went relatively smoothly with the right *friends*. Where I had no ties, I sought out interviewees where they were most comfortable. That meant attending a variety of gatherings, cocktail parties, and a couple of times, a bath house. This manner of establishing interviews, of course, contributed to the fact that I interviewed far more men and far more managers than I would have otherwise liked.

Male camaraderie had everything to do with obtaining information in these settings, and it was all the easier for me to negotiate this through my familiarity with my own masculinity. On the other hand, a man in this environment is expected to enjoy enormous quantities of alcohol and to visit prostitutes. I know that a few interviewees were more reticent with me after they realized that I was not responsive to lewd suggestions. I remember feeling relief when one interviewee asked me whether I wanted tea or alcohol at a meal. I realized only after I committed the offense of asking for tea that he had asked me out of politeness and was not going to trust anyone who would not drink alcohol. Even a female interviewee tried to insist that I interview her in a spa setting, and she offered to purchase a swimsuit for me when I steered the interview toward a coffee house. Navigating gender was a matter of access to information.

Since most of my interviewees were men, I lack a comparison to gauge the effect of gender on the interviews. One interesting exception to this was the following: I asked interviewees in mainland China what effects they felt from the system of household registration. I thought that the need to register would do what it was designed to do – restrict the mobility of workers from outside cities to privileged positions. With one exception, interviewees replied that the need to register their household had no effect on their lives. Managers commented that they could import whomever they wished to the cities, and that firms involved in sensitive technologies are often able to register their employees with few restrictions. Managers mentioned that they often sought out students from nearby universities and that most students are able to register through the universities. Of course, managers were not likely to discuss with me the migrants without papers who work at their factories, and engineers I interviewed were either residents or gave the appearance of having papers that were in order.

In one interviewee, however, I was speaking with two mainland Chinese programmers at once. One engineer was in his twenties and the other, in his thirties. When I asked about *hukou* (household registration), the more youthful one quickly replied that no, *hukou* had no effect whatever on him. At this point, the more experienced engineer chided the other man. He explained that he was beginning to think about *hukou* differently with age. As a youth, he commented, he was relatively free to move without applying for the privileges of a Beijing resident. If he ever had a family, however, he thought the fact that he was a migrant to Beijing would affect what schools his children could attend. From that interview, I gather that the fact that my interviewees were mostly men, and that my mainland Chinese interviewees were mostly men in their twenties to mid-thirties profoundly affected what my interviewees were thinking about, and their replies to my questions.

Notes

1 Sunray Liu, "China increases wages, incentives to engineers", *Electronic Engineering Times*, www.eet.com/salarysurvey/1999/chinaview.html.
2 "Salaries, benefits are up for Chinese engineers", *IT News Australia*, September 16, 2004, www.itnews.com.au/storycontent.asp?ID=5&Art_ID=21616.
3 Robert Bellinger, "Mean wages edge closer to six-figure mark", *Electronic Engineering Times*, August 25, 2004, www.eet.com/showArticle.jhtml?articleID=30900112.
4 "High Tech in China: Is it a threat to Silicon Valley?", *BusinessWeek*, October 28, 2002, www.businessweek.com/magazine/content/02_43/b3805001.htm.
5 National Science Board, *Science and Engineering Indicators 2004*, Arlington, VA: National Science Foundation, 2004.
6 This organization once received money from the government of the United States to represent the interests of United States firms in China. The organization no longer receives financial aid from the government and primarily represents the interests of the largest multinationals in the information industries.
7 Apparently, engineers were even hacking into the accounting programs of this multinational to compare their wages with those of their fellows.
8 A. Pakes and S. Nitzan, "Optimum Contracts for Research Personnel, Research Employment, and the Establishment of Rival Enterprises", (1983) 1 *Journal of Labor*

Economics: 345–65; E. Rogers and J. Larsen, *Silicon Valley Fever*, New York, NY: Basic Books, 1984; Paul Almeida and Bruce Kogut, "Localization of Knowledge and the Mobility of Engineers in Regional Networks", (1999) 45(7) *Management Science*, July: 905–17.

9 David Angel, "The Labor Market for Engineers in the U.S. Semiconductor Industry", (1989) 65(2) *Economic Geography*, April: 99–112.

10 David Hachen, "Industrial Characteristics and Job Mobility Rates", (1992) 57(1) *American Sociological Review*, February: 39–55.

11 Monica Prasad, "International Capital on 'Silicon Plateau': Work and Control in India's Computer Industry", (1998) 77(2) *Social Forces*, December: 429–52.

12 Suisheng Zhao, "A State Led Nationalism: The Patriotic Education Campaign in Post-Tiananmen China", (1998) 31(3) *Communist and Post-Communist Studies*: 293.

13 Suisheng Zhao, A State Led Nationalism: 295.

14 "IT chanye wei dalu daxue biyesheng diyi jiuye xuanze, *Digitimes*, September 24, 2003.

15 R. Florida and P. Kenney, "High Technology Restructuring in the USA and Japan", (1990) 22 *Environment and Planning*, February: 233–52.

16 David Angel, The Labor Market for Engineers: 99–112; AnnaLee Saxenian, *Regional Advantage*, Cambridge, MA: Harvard University Press, 1994.

17 Although, in addition, this would seem to reflect the reticence of my managerial interviewees to talk about their strategies to pilfer the secrets and engineers of other firms.

18 Watts Humphrey, *Managing Technical People: Innovation, Teamwork, and the Software Process*, Boston, MA: Addison Wesley, 1997.

19 *Dataquest*, 1–15 March 1995 in Monica Prasad, International Capital on 'Silicon Plateau': 440–1.

20 For insightful discussion of this, see Stephen Marglin, "What Do Bosses Do? The Origins and Functions of Hierarchy in Capitalist Production", (1974) 6(2) *Review of Radical Political Economy*: 60–112.

21 Renhe ren shi keyi queshi de, dou keyi zou.

22 Ailon-Souday, Galit and Kunda, Gideon. "The Local Selves of Global Workers: The Social Construction of National Identity in the Face of Organizational Globalization", (2003) 24(7) *Organization Studies*: 1073–96.

12 Honing the desired attitude

Ideological work on insurance sales agents

Cheris Shun-ching Chan

> We know that we are being exploited by capitalists. But we prefer to be
> exploited by capitalists to being exploited by our state, as in the past.
>
> An insurance sales agent in Shanghai, August 2000

Commercial life insurance as an industry is emerging in China at the intersection
of the country's transformation from a socialist to a market economy and the
global expansion of the insurance industry to developing countries. It was introduced to the People's Republic of China (PRC) in 1992 by an American insurance
company, American International Assurance Company Limited (AIA), a subsidiary
of American International Group, Inc. (AIG). Local life-insurance companies
emerged in 1994–5, and a number of Sino–foreign joint ventures were established
from 1996 onwards. Many of the insurers began their business in Shanghai.
Because of its particular logic of estimating the monetary value of human lives,
commercial life insurance always faces strong cultural resistance whenever it is
introduced to a new population.[1] Life-insurance companies everywhere rely for
success on active solicitations by insurance sales agents; this is particularly the
case in societies that lack a tradition of personal insurance. While life insurance is
sales-driven and sales agents are indispensable to the development of the industry,
selling life insurance belongs to the category of "dirty work".[2] In China, selling
life insurance is a new way to make a living. In 2001, over 40,000 people were
working as life-insurance sales agents in Shanghai.[3] The national sales force
is estimated at about 1 million.[4] Chinese sales agents go door to door to sell
something the local people generally do not want or have even thought about;
every day, the agents face not only rejection but also contempt, disrespect, and
frustration. Why are they drawn to this new occupation? How can they engage in
this job and keep up their morale?

The institutional dilemmas intrinsic to the life-insurance industry call for the
development of specific psychological attitudes in the sales agents. Such attitudes
are brought about by orchestrating the desired psychological outlook within
the insurance corporations and the adoption of such an attitude by the agents
themselves. Honing the desired attitude allows the sales agents to feel empowered
even as exploitation in the sales process is legitimized and neutralized.

This chapter draws on the ethnographic data I collected in Shanghai between 2000 and 2004. I spent more than 14 months conducting participant observation in four different life-insurance companies in Shanghai: a foreign insurer (AIA), a domestic company (Ping An), and two joint ventures (Pacific-Aetna and Allianz-Dazhong). I spent two to three months in each company on a daily basis, attending training sessions for agents and regularly joining their morning assemblies. With their consent, I observed some agents' sales routines and interactions with their prospects. A total of 120 sales agents, 50 managerial staff, 96 life-insurance clients, and 35 prospects were interviewed. In addition, I conducted informal interviews with more than 20 local residents with whom I interacted regularly, such as newspaper sellers, restaurant waiters and waitresses, taxi drivers, shopkeepers and gym members. More than half these people had purchased life insurance of some kind.

Labor market, gender, and the workplace

Given the difficulties of selling life insurance, why do some people enter this occupation in the first place? A scrutiny of why people choose such a job is indicative of changes in the workplaces in China. Although the Shanghai sales agents gave various reasons for their choice, a few common factors can be identified at different periods of time. These factors are related to the social organization of the Chinese labor market in the reform era.[5]

When AIA pioneered the personal-sales method for marketing life insurance, this American company started with an ideal model of insurance sales. It recruited young degree holders, most of them males, for the sales force. As one of the few large foreign corporations in Shanghai in the early 1990s, AIA was appealing to young educated people. It successfully convinced these young, ambitious men and women that the Chinese insurance industry would experience rapid growth and that they would be entering on a promising and lucrative career. Those who joined AIA in the early years were optimistic about the future of the insurance industry, though many of them did not have a clear idea about the exact nature of insurance. Shan Hui Fan, who joined AIA in 1992, described what drove him to become an insurance agent:

> I majored in business management and I wanted to work for a foreign company … . As a young man, I wanted to establish my career and make a good income. I knew that AIA was an international brand name. At that time, the insurance industry in China was not yet developed. I believed that it had a huge potential. I was optimistic about this industry.[6]

Shan was one of the many young graduates who sought to work for foreign companies and were optimistic about the prospects of the life-insurance industry.

AIA endeavored to present its sales agents as professionals. In the first two years, it recruited more males than females into its sales force. According to some senior agents, AIA did not screen out females but targeted both sexes, judging only on the basis of ambition and eagerness. It was pure coincidence that more men than women were drawn to this new industry. Since 1994, a greater number of females have joined the company. Chu Siujuan, who joined AIA right after she received her bachelor's degree, recounted why she was interested in this occupation:

> I just finished school and I wanted to have a career. I saw that AIA was a large American corporation. I attended the recruitment talk and was convinced that the potential market for life insurance in China was gigantic. I believed that I could establish my career through insurance sales.[7]

Chu's reason for joining AIA was similar to Shan's. In the course of my research period in 2000–2, I saw a rather balanced ratio of male to female sales agents in AIA.

When Ping An joined the life-insurance market in Shanghai in July 1994, it imitated AIA in recruiting young, educated adults. Nevertheless, Ping An soon found that selling protective forms of life insurance and presenting the sales agents as professionals did not work effectively in China. This domestic insurer then adopted a new marketing strategy called "the tactics of the human sea" (*renhai zhanshu*) and invented some life insurance products that were more appealing to the local population.[8] Since it needed to augment the sales team within a short period, Ping An could no longer be selective in recruiting agents. A large number of laid-off workers from former state-owned enterprises (SOEs), mostly women in their mid-forties, became sales agents for Ping An. Ping An deployed a recruitment strategy similar to that of a direct-sales organization. Agents were encouraged to recruit other agents to work under them to become their downline agents. More women were drawn to the company because of the opportunity to work part time,[9] and as a result, in 1995–6, there were salient differences between the sales force of AIA and that of Ping An. The agents of AIA were better educated and presented themselves in a professional manner, whereas the agents of Ping An were derogatorily described as being like housewives.

To the surprise of AIA and its agents, in 1996, the "housewives" were earning more than the "professionals" at AIA. But the difference arose chiefly because the products Ping An offered were better received by the locals and Ping An offered relatively high commission rates to its agents. In 1996–7, when some young agents realized that higher earnings could be realized at Ping An, they left AIA for the Chinese company. Thus, AIA lost a certain percentage of its sales force to Ping An, and to replace the lost agents and to expand its sales team to compete with Ping An, AIA was forced to be less selective in its recruiting. The differences between the sales agents of AIA and those of Ping An became less striking, though many young men and women tend to join foreign or joint-venture insurers.

Ping An's initial success drew attention to the work of insurance sales. Some, bored by the working environment of the SOEs and collective enterprises, quit their jobs to join the insurance industry. The majority of these people had been engaged in middle management, where they had earned stable and adequate incomes. Most of them were in their early thirties and had worked for the SOEs or collective enterprises for about 10 years. They disliked their former workplaces for the paternalistic organization and complex collegial relationships. They wanted greater autonomy and flexibility in their working hours and interactions with colleagues. They were among those who "jumped to the sea" (*xiahai*) to seek not only better pay but also a sense of achievement and satisfaction from work. Xu Fei, a woman in her early thirties, became an agent for AIA after having worked for an SOE for years.

> I found my former work unit too old-fashioned. The interpersonal relationships there were too complicated. Those at the top were very controlling, and you had to be careful when you interacted with those above you. I felt suffocated … I wanted to do something else. I wanted to have more autonomy and freedom. I like to work more independently and individualistically. I like the simple collegial relationship here. Everyone focuses on their own sales activities, and no one comes to bother you.[10]

Interestingly, quite a large number of women in their early thirties quit their former jobs to join the insurance sales force for reasons similar to those cited by Xu.

After 1997, another factor became more noticeable when the problem of *xiagang* (on-the-job layoff) from SOEs and collective enterprises threw a large number of people into insurance – an industry they joined mainly because there were no other options. For the most part, these are men and women in their mid-forties to mid-fifties, but younger people in their early to mid-thirties are also found in this category. Chang Leihan and her former colleague, both women in their mid-forties, joined Ping An because:

> [Sigh!] We have no better choice. How to say it … we are the victims. People in our generation are the victims of this country's political campaigns in the past and economic reforms at present. When we were at school ages, we couldn't go to school because of the Cultural Revolution. Now with the economic changes, we were laid off. We don't have any specific knowledge and skills to compete with others for a decent job. We actually don't think that the insurance sales job is for us. But we have no other options. What else can we do?[11]

The emergence of large numbers of laid-off workers further shaped the gender composition of the insurance sales forces. Citing a survey from 1996, Thomas Rawski reports that 59.2 percent of the laid-off workers at the national level were women, and the proportion of women in the laid-off pool in Shanghai was as high as 68.9 percent.[12] The life-insurance industry absorbed a segment of these workers, and consequently more women were found in insurance sales.

Thus, in contrast to Robbin Leidner's finding that in the United States, more men than women are drawn to the insurance industry, in Shanghai, more females than males are engaged in insurance sales.[13] Furthermore, different proportions of men and women are found in different insurance companies. Among the four sales teams I researched, only the team of the Sino–German insurer, Allianz-Dazhong, had a greater number of male agents. The sales team of AIA had a virtually balanced ratio of men and women, whereas Pacific-Aetna and Ping An employed a greater number of women than men. The differences in the gender composition among different insurers follow a pattern. More women worked for the domestic Ping An and the highly localized Pacific-Aetna, while more men worked for the least localized company, Allianz-Dazhong. AIA seemed to have a relatively equal proportion of male and female agents. This pattern can be attributed to the differences in the various insurance companies' public images and their variations on organizing their sales teams. Although Pacific-Aetna and Allianz-Dazhong were both Sino–foreign joint ventures, the former had many more female agents, whereas the latter employed a greater number of men. Pacific-Aetna presented itself as a caring institution, while Allianz-Dazhong presented itself as an "unconquerable institution". In its advertisements, Pacific-Aetna used the logo of a baby angel to symbolize its mission, whereas Allianz-Dazhong used the top of a bridge as its logo. Women and men were drawn to different insurance companies in part responding to their gender roles and identities. More women than men were found in both Ping An and Pacific-Aetna, both of which used a direct-sales strategy.[14] In these two agencies, individual agents were systematically and tightly organized into groups. On the other hand, agents in AIA and Allianz-Dazhong worked more individually and independently. It is likely that women feel more comfortable working in groups, whereas men prefer to work more independently.

In short, the novelty of work in the insurance industry attracted both men and women from diverse backgrounds. More young men are drawn to the foreign, or less localized, joint-venture companies; whereas more middle-aged women are interested in the local, or highly localized, joint-venture companies. This pattern of gender and age differentiation is primarily shaped by the organizational images the companies seek to project and the management they practice. As an entity, life-insurance companies employ a greater number of females than males as sales agents; this disparity is caused by Ping An's domination of the market. However, gender identities do not appear to be a prominent strategy of labor control. As the following sections will show, all insurers endeavor to control the agents, regardless of their gender and age, through a psychological means to hone a desired psychological attitude.

Institutional dilemmas and the need for ideological work

Viviana Zelizer suggests that the utilitarian association of money with death results in a negative evaluation of life-insurance companies and their agents.[15] Additionally, the occupational stigma that clings to life-insurance agents comes from the institutional dilemma of life insurance as operating somewhere between commerce and altruism. As front-line practitioners who actively seek out prospective buyers and talk to the public about life, death, and money, insurance agents involuntarily bear the stigma of "dirty work". To perform the "dirty work" and be productive, the sales agents are required to hold certain psychological concepts conducive to their work. While I agree with Zelizer on the commercialism-altruism ambiguity of life insurance, I find that two additional institutional dilemmas are generic to the life-insurance industry, and these necessitate ideological work on insurance sales agents.

First, the operation of life insurance is based on two essential forms of rationality – a probabilistic calculation of risks and a commensurate evaluation of human life.[16] Paradoxically, this most rational institution requires various non-rational practices, such as selling a pessimistic future, impulse buying, and believing in the sacred functions of life insurance.[17] Second is the question of risk management. People who most need life insurance are normally the same people who face greater risks. Nonetheless, insurance corporations will have difficulty remaining in business if most of their clients are at high risk.[18] In addition, people at high risk tend to be financially less well off and therefore less able to afford insurance premiums. Therefore, as a commercial institution, insurance companies have to target the least risk-prone population as their customer base. In other words, sales agents have to sell life insurance to those who are young and healthy and have the least need of life insurance.

These institutional dilemmas of life insurance require agents to acquire a mindset that serves to ignore selectively some characteristics of insurance and magnify others. In China, the need for such a mindset is even more pressing. Commercial life insurance is not only a new commodity but also a new concept to the local population. The cultural taboo on talking and thinking about premature death and the existence of alternative risk-management practices in China have made selling life insurance extremely difficult.[19] Dealing with a reluctant clientele is, not surprisingly, an unpleasant and frustrating undertaking. In addition, the commission-based income system – introduced by AIA – that is commonly adopted by insurance companies is new to the Chinese workplace. Commissions, the universal practice in the insurance industry, are the principal source of income for insurance agents. They are structured to decrease over the life of a policy, so that in order to make a decent living, an agent must continually sell new policies.[20] Annual incomes of sales agents vary widely, from less than 12,000 RMB (US$1,446) to 120,000 RMB (US$14,460).[21] The majority of agents earned less than 24,000 RMB (US$2,892) in the years 2001–2, a sum that was slightly less than the average income in Shanghai.[22] Furthermore, in China, sales agents are categorized as self-employed. They are required to sign "agent contracts" designed by the insurance companies they work for. The contracts vary from company to company, though they are all worded so as to protect the interests of the companies. In Shanghai, employers are required by law to provide "four basic fringe benefits" to their regular employees – pension, medical insurance, unemployment insurance, and a housing allowance; however, the "self-employed" status of the agents deprives them of these benefits. The lack of a steady and assured income, as well as the absence of basic benefits, eventually reduces the attraction of this occupation. The dropout rate among sales agents is always high.

According to a number of agents and agency development managers in Shanghai, the annual dropout rate of insurance agents in 2000–2 was as high as 70 percent to 80 percent.[23] All life insurers are constantly exploring means to retain their existing sales agents and to recruit new ones.

On the one hand, a commission-based income system pressures the sales staff to work hard for survival; on the other hand, such a system allows greater leeway for the agents to decide how much they want to earn and how hard they want to work. Not all the agents who stay in this business meet the sales targets set by the company. One of the common complaints by the in-house managers of the transnational insurance firms is that the agents are "too passive" and "too contented".

> One of the major problems of our agents is being too passive. They lack self-motivation! They still carry a socialist mentality. And they are impeded by their old habits ... Some complained that no one ever took them out to show them how to deal with resistant prospects. You see? They are still waiting for someone to give them instruction or guidance ... When their first year commission (FYC) for the month has reached 1500 yuan or so, they are contented. They ease up and go home!.[24]

As the sales agents live on commissions, the working hours also depend on the individual's self-discipline and motivation.[25] If the agents do not have a boundless desire for money and for professional success, the insurance company is doomed to have a low sales volume. Insurers must therefore transform the sales agents' character into one that is ambitious, aggressive, competitive, and with a mindset of "gotta win".[26]

The psychological barriers of sales agents

To be an insurance agent, using one's personal relationships and social connections in an effective way is almost inevitable. Against the common notion that personal and business relationships are always conflated in Chinese society, many agents, especially new ones, experience an uneasy struggle of transforming personal relationships into business relationships. One new agent expressed a typically uneasy feeling:

> [The senior agents] taught me to hold an old schoolmate reunion in order to sell them insurance. I don't know what to do ... I can't be pushy; otherwise, they will think that I want to make money off them. Making money out of a friend's pocket is not a good feeling. It will make me feel like I am too instrumental in using friendship.[27]

While *guanxi* (interpersonal relations) plays a significant role in the business world in China, at best, a personal relationship does not involve money issues.[28] A person may connect a friend with another friend for business, but it is best not to become involved in any direct monetary exchange with that friend. The closer the relationship, the greater is the taboo that attaches to money. As the income of insurance agents comes directly from the sales, the agents feel embarrassed when they sell to their close friends and relatives.

Moreover, sales jobs, especially personal sales, are traditionally not considered a respectable occupation in Chinese society. The inherently low social status of sales persons and the commission-based income system further burden the morale and productivity of sales agents in China. The agents cannot help feeling uneasy when they sense that the prospects – especially when the prospects are their good friends or relatives – might be judging their motive for selling insurance and look down on them. For example, a new agent of AIA, Xin Yanming, stayed home for several days, without any motivation to go out after a negative encounter with Deng, a prospect who was her friend. Xin dressed the way AIA had told her to and closely followed the selling steps and the sales talks she had learned in her training. However, Deng was not interested. Instead, she asked Xin a question, which badly upset Xin: "Hey, what made you work with insurance? This is not an easy job. I've never imagined that you would want to do this kind of work". Although Deng sounded very sincere and sorry for Xin, her comment that she had never imagined Xin to take up the work of selling insurance clearly expressed disapproval of this occupation. Two weeks later, I had a chance to ask Xin what she had felt at that moment. She said:

> I already felt uneasy when I was presenting the product to her. You know, we were schoolmates. We were supposed to be equal. But I felt like I was asking her a favor … She knew that my income came from commission. It's embarrassing … She asked me why I had to be an agent … Being an insurance agent was as if you had nothing else to do. I didn't go out for several days. I felt so reluctant to.[29]

Many new agents, who had worked for less than six months, usually face the same psychological complications of "making money out of friends' pockets" and the feeling of being looked down on by friends. "People say selling insurance is like begging for rice!". Some agents said with an ironic laugh.

Life-insurance sales represent a case of not only "emotional labor" but also "relational labor".[30] Insurance agents must use their existing relationships and create new relationships for achieving economic transactions. In exploiting the existing relationships for economic benefit, they have to deal with the dilemmas and boundaries between altruism and utilitarianism. To blur the boundary between a monetary and a personal relationship and to overcome the low status of sales work, insurance agents must internalize a belief that they are doing something that is of benefit to the buyers, not simply making money off them. At the same time, they must learn to feel good rather than embarrassed and uneasy when they urge their friends to buy insurance. In other words, they need to acquire specific framing and feeling rules to legitimize their sales work.[31]

The orchestration of the desired attitude

What is the desired attitude?

Both Robin Leidner and Guy Oakes observe that insurers in the United States use various social-psychological techniques to mold their sales agents' attitudes and ways of thinking.[32] Insurance agents receive training in maintaining a positive mental attitude so as to prepare them to deal with the emotional challenges of the selling process. Leidner finds that the agents hand over to the company the right to reshape many aspects of their personalities, including their emotions, values, and ways of thinking, in order to do their job effectively.[33]

In Shanghai, in everyday conversations among insurance sales agents, one can always hear mention of *xintai* (psychological attitude). Having a "good" psychological attitude distinguishes the top sales agents from the rest; and having a good psychological attitude in a particular circumstance distinguishes a successful sale from a failure. Some agents engage in a "good" psychological attitude often, as if it were an intrinsic part of their personality, whereas some other agents adopt such an attitude only in particular circumstances, when it becomes necessary to bring a sale to a successful conclusion. Thus, a good psychological attitude can be a disposition or it can be a conscious effort. It is vaguely defined as containing a range of framing and feeling rules that organize and enable the sales agents' professional activities. In addition, these rules shape the agents' way of life to facilitate and maximize insurance sales. The ideal sales agent as portrayed by the insurers is someone who "embeds insurance in daily life and daily life in insurance" (*shenghuo baoxian hua; baoxian shenghuo hua*). In other words, agents should make use of every occasion in their daily life to sell insurance and at the same time put selling insurance at the center of their life and organize their life accordingly.

In various training sessions and morning assemblies the sales agents have been taught a number of sales strategies and sales talks. A substantial number of the training sessions are dedicated to teaching the agents how to handle rejection and turn it into acceptance. To move those who refuse insurance, the agents must genuinely believe that the products they are selling are good and are absolutely necessary for the prospects. They have to perceive themselves as saviors performing a missionary role, and they should not take rejection and disrespect personally. They have to believe that the prospects reject life insurance solely out of ignorance, and the agents have a duty to teach the prospects the importance of life insurance. However, when the prospects are willing to listen to their presentation, they should avoid going into the details of the products. The reason is that the more the prospects know about the details, the more questions they will have and the less likely they will be to buy. Alternately, the prospects might calculate the pros and cons of the products meticulously and decide not to buy. Therefore it is very important for the agents to close the sale as quickly as possible. In other words, the agents should try to induce the prospects to buy on impulse rather than after rational calculation. A trainer uses the term "cruel and merciless" (*xinhenshoula*) to describe how the agents should be in order to close a sale promptly. They cannot be too considerate. This seemingly "irresponsible" deed of soliciting impulsive decisions should nevertheless be understood as doing the prospects a favor. If a prospect has shown a slight interest in buying the product(s) but the agent fails to close the sale, the agent will have to bear the guilt in case this prospect should subsequently encounter an accident or serious illness without insurance protection. Or the agent will sorely regret it if the prospect eventually buys an insurance policy from someone else.

How do agents change their attitude?

Life-insurance companies attempt to shape the psychological attitude of their sales agents through a series of training sessions. However, very few agents can transform their psychological attitude without the aid of various kinds of collective dynamics. Small-group interactions and large-scale collective assemblies are necessary to challenge the agents' existing framing and feeling rules and socializing them into new ones.[34]

All insurers require their agents to attend morning assemblies, or what AIA calls morning calls, at which some companies require the agents to chant slogans and sing the company songs to boost their morale. Pacific-Aetna leads its agents in physical exercises in the morning to refresh their bodies and to relax them before going out into the field. Both insurers and sales agents in Shanghai describe the insurance market as a battlefield and the agents as warriors. These metaphors validly reflect the everyday life of the sales agents. In a battlefield, they can always get hurt psychologically, if not physically.

Insurers use group dynamics to manage and channel sales agents' psychological attitudes, though variations exist. The more an insurer is localized, the more group processes are adopted. Ping An and Pacific-Aetna are among all most group-oriented in managing their sales agents. AIA and Allianz-Dazhong also encourage agents to share and discuss problems with their fellow agents, but they are less active in organizing and promoting group dynamics. Agents of Ping An and Pacific-Aetna are organized into small groups to vent their frustrations, to comfort each other, and more importantly, to make sense of their experiences and to give meaning to their job. For example, a senior agent of Ping An, Dai Hong, held a group sharing meeting with her 13 downline agents every day right after the morning assembly. The following extract from my field notes illustrates how the group meeting could help to forge the desired attitude.

> In the morning assembly, the agents were told that the growing unpopularity of a Ping An investment insurance product, *unit-link*, was in part due to AIA's attack on the product through the media. Dai's agents look dispirited. Dai is anxious to comfort them and enliven their morale. She says, "I'm also angry at AIA ... My sales volume dropped recently. However, I'm maintaining a good psychological attitude. I firmly believe that our *unit-link* is a good product. Our clients are just too ignorant ... Don't think that you are making money off the prospects. Even if they don't buy any from you, they would

buy some from others". Chang Xu Qiu, who has been an agent for almost a year, responds, "Yes, It's better not to think that we are earning money from them". Dai says, "Yes, you better forget about the commissions. Don't think of the commission rates when you are selling".[35]

Dai was leading her group to believe that there was no inherent problem with their product. AIA's attack and prospects' ignorance were believed to be the real problems. The above dialogue among the agents demonstrates that the desired psychological attitude is indeed full of paradoxes. The agents must legitimize their unstructural commercial practice on the one hand and convince themselves that they are not unstructural and commercial on the other. While the agents are aware of their low status in an increasingly stratified society, they must constantly convince themselves that they are respectable.

The morning assemblies and sharing meetings are, on the whole, more effective in transforming the framing rules of the agents. Some occasional collective gatherings, such as ceremonies, annual meetings, parties, retreats, and group excursions, are more powerful in commanding excitement and emotive responses. Pacific-Aetna is most effective among insurers in mobilizing its sales agents' emotions. The highest level in-house managers, who came from Taiwan, brought with them some specific techniques to please the agents and to create a familial working environment. First of all, they disparaged their own status to the agents to make them feel flattered. The general manager and other high-level managerial staff addressed their sales agents as "partners" (*huoban*) in the daily routine. In ceremonial activities, they called the agents "my bosses" and explicitly said that their incomes depended on the agents' sales. In its Annual Awards Presentation Ceremony (AAP) in May 2002, the company invited a famous Taiwanese singer, Zhou Huajian, to perform.[36] The highest level managers told the agents that they spent US$100,000 to invite Zhou for no other reason than to make them happy. In addition, the AAP general managers and a number of high-level managers dressed up to entertain the agents. The general manager played Snow White while the head of the sales and agency development manager wore a miniskirt and danced the hula. All these efforts elicited joyful screams and laughter from the agents.[37] These feelings of joy, empowerment, and indebtedness channel the agents to wholeheartedly follow the framing rules imposed by the insurers.

Given the less localized organizational characteristics of AIA and Allianz-Dazhong, these two insurers tended to use more rational discourses in an attempt to change their agents' attitudes. Instead of eliciting the agents' emotions, AIA and Allianz-Dazhong used story-telling techniques to guide the agents into believing that what they were doing was "meaningful", and that "meaningful" work was routinely associated with tough obstacles. For example, the agents were repeatedly told stories of how someone or a team survived in a desert without water. The stories were supposed to boost the agents' faith in themselves and in the insurance industry. Compared to group dynamics, story-telling is less effective in orchestrating the agents' attitudes. Very often, the stories come from the training materials, which were imported from America or Germany.

They are out of context and irrelevant to the local agents. When the agents do not have strong feelings about the stories – in other words, when the agents' emotions are not mobilized – it is difficult to imagine that they would change their psychological attitudes.

Three mechanisms of ideological work

Honing the desired psychological attitude amounts to ideological work because the successful construction of such an attitude conceals the institutional dilemmas and legitimizes the institutional structure of life insurance. However, as the desired psychological attitude has always to be produced and reproduced, and can never be fully actualized, ideological work is always a work in progress. In Shanghai, I found three mechanisms at the core of such ideological work. They are, first, a sacralization of money and insurance that eulogizes the meaning of insurance and redefines monetary and intimate relationships; second, an allocation of blame on individuals that conceals the dilemmas of life insurance; and third, a celebration of the new logic of labor that condemns a socialist mentality and socialist habits.

Sacralization of money and insurance

In socialist China, there was strong disapproval of money-oriented behavior and ideas that indicate capitalist practices and ethics. Nor was there any need to be money-oriented, since all basic needs were provided by government redistribution. Money and personal relations were separate. Although using personal and social relations are crucial in life-insurance sales, the sales agents feel ambivalent when they attempt to sell an insurance policy directly to their good friends. There still exists a distinction between a monetary, business relationship and a non-monetary, personal relationship. In dealing with the boundary between personal and monetarily relations, insurers and their sales agents seek to sacralize money and insurance. The sacralization of money and insurance is also necessary in dealing with the public's resistance to putting a price on a human life. Nevertheless, the sacralization of money is possible only in a particular capitalist context, where widows and orphans cannot survive without the large lump sums provided by insurers and in a situation where premature death implies "an unnecessary waste of money".[38]

There is no doubt that urban China, especially Shanghai, is becoming more money-oriented with increasing privatization and marketization of the economy. In this context, a lump sum paid by an insurance company indeed serves a significant function. Life insurers and their agents who are guided by a good psychological attitude magnify the function of money by sacralizing life insurance and the work of selling insurance. For example, a senior agent of AIA eloquently depicted selling insurance as a philanthropic work in a lecture he gave to new agents:

What is selling insurance? Selling insurance is indeed selling money. Now we take a little bit of money from our customers but give them a lot in case they need that. Yes, this is insurance! We are selling money. And we are selling time. The compensation paid by an insurance company can sustain one's life. We are selling time and money to our customers. Can you say that insurance is not about love and humanity?.

The sacralization of money and insurance is an ideological attempt to resolve the dilemma of commerce and altruism and the problem of putting a price on human life. It is also an attempt to legitimize the insurance agents' encouragement of impulse buying. Since insurance is good and valuable, even an impulse purchase is seen as ultimately beneficial to the clients.

Allocation of blame

One of the cultural and political implications of the economic transformation from a socialist to a market economy is the transfer of the locus of responsibility and blame from the state or other collective bodies to individuals. The sales discourse of life insurance eulogizes self-reliance and individual responsibility for one's own well-being. It strongly condemns not only the residual socialist mentality of relying on the state but also any tendency to seek help from neighbors, colleagues, friends, relatives, and family members. Individuals are the locus not only glory and fame but also of blame and guilt.

The life insurers in Shanghai, especially the foreign and joint-venture companies, noticeably glorify self-reliance and deplore dependence. In effect, the sales agents attribute the difficulty of selling life insurance to the problem of the prospects. They blame the prospects for being ignorant, dependent, irresponsible, and selfish. A senior agent of Pacific-Aetna, Xu Jing, described how she releases her anger on the resistant prospects in order to keep a psychological balance:

When I am too frustrated by the stubbornness of the prospects, I will give them a lesson. This helps me to keep a psychological balance … Once I met a prospect … I patiently educated him to the proper concept of insurance … He was just not listening to me. He said he already had a pension and some health insurance from his work unit. He said if he ran into an accident, the relatives would give a helping hand to his wife and child. He even said the children's home would take care of his child in the worst case … I was so pissed off. This guy was so selfish! I scolded him, "You are such a selfish idiot! How can you still have such an outmoded attitude? I bet your wife and your child will leave you and ignore you one day. You will regret [your decision] and recall what I told you today!". Then, I left immediately. I felt good! I felt I did a right thing … I told my downline agents that it's all right to scold their prospects occasionally to keep their psychological balance.[39]

Putting the blame on the prospects quite effectively obscures the inherent contradiction between defining insurance as an instrument of risk management and selling insurance to those who have low-risk profiles. At the same time, it is an individualization process of shifting all the blame and guilt to individuals. It is possible that once commercial insurance becomes a preferred mode of risk management, informal means of mutual help will become socially less acceptable – a reality that Carol Heimer finds in the the United States.[40]

Celebration of the new labor logic

The smashing of the iron rice bowl and the decline of the *danwei* (work unit) culture mark an era of new labor logic in China. Uneven payments, extended working hours and competition replace the egalitarian principle of the workplace. A celebration of this new labor logic is found in the workplace of life insurance.

In China, resistance to change from socialist to capitalist workplaces can be found. Ching Kwan Lee has written about workers' nostalgia for socialism that underlies protests among the unemployed in northern China. She demonstrates that workers are critical of the new labor logic of unbridled competition.[41] Workers in Shanghai are comparatively more contented with the capitalist principle and the accompanying labor logic. Nonetheless, nostalgia for socialism is found among the losers of the economic reforms. Zhu Yin, a 50-year-old agent who joined Allianz-Dazhong after he was asked to retire early from an SOE, expresses his ambivalent feelings about the transition:

> Our economy has changed too much and too fast. We are better off when it comes to material things. And we have more products to choose from … But life is not as easy as before. In the past, we were all under the same roof. We were secure and protected by the state. You didn't feel that you were above someone but you didn't feel that you were under, or of less value of, someone … Everyone was … more or less the same. Life was simpler and easier. Now it's different.[42]

Zhu's ambivalence about the economic changes in China is typical among the agents who join the occupation as a result of the lack of other employment opportunities. These agents are less likely to fully adopt the psychological attitude desired by the insurers.

The highest-selling agents of various insurers and many of the agents of Pacific-Aetna have nevertheless celebrated the new labor logic. In describing the pressure associated with working as an agent, a junior agent of Pacific-Aetna, Wang Ganyan, justified the new labor logic:

> After I became a sales agent, my life changed radically. I was a supervisor in my former work unit. I went to work in the morning and back home in the late afternoon. I spent Saturdays and Sundays with my family. Now I work much more. I make phone calls at night to the prospects and to my downline agents.

I visit prospects on Saturdays and Sundays. I work seven days a week and over twelve hours a day. We know that we are being exploited by capitalists. But we prefer to be exploited by capitalists than being exploited by our state, as in the past.[43]

When asked why he and his fellows were willing to be exploited by capitalists, Wang emphasized that they were materially better off by working for capitalists. "Even the bathrooms in this office are cleaner than those in the SOEs", she said. "This gives us a better sense of ourselves". Thus, workers in post-socialist economies are probably more aware of class exploitation than workers in societies that have always been capitalist. To them, the improved material life in comparison to the materially deprived condition under the socialist regime has justified the exploitation.

Furthermore, the insurance agents in Shanghai have been collectively engaged in giving meaning to their new working life. In a workshop designed to raise morale for the sales agents of AIA, agents with high sales volumes were invited to share their experience with others. Many of these agents were making sense of their new working life. A senior male agent of AIA, over 40, was very proud of his distinction from his neighbors:

Ten years ago, I wore gray clothes and a pair of shabby sandals. I earned 36 yuan per month. My neighbors wore the same and earned the same, 36 yuan. I was no different from them. Today, I am wearing a Western suit and tie. I am earning thousands a month. I am confident every day when I walk out the door of my home. When my neighbors are back home and rest in the evenings, I am still working. But now my pocket has a different amount of money from theirs. My value as a person is different from theirs![44]

The new labor logic of unequal payment based on differential labor values is being legitimized through the commission-based system of insurance sales and the consequential practices and social constructs of meaning. Endless material and symbolic desires are celebrated, and contentment is deplored. This labor logic does not only mask the institutional dilemmas of life insurance, it also legitimizes and buttresses the institutional structure and the exploitative mechanism.

Conclusion

I suggest that the institutional dilemmas of commercial life insurance necessitate ideological work by the sales agents. This ideological work is brought about by orchestration of a particular attitude that is conducive to sales productivity. Three elements of the desired psychological attitude serve an ideological function. First, the sacralization of money and insurance partly eases the problem of putting a price on human life and partly resolves the dilemma of commerce and altruism. Second, the allocation of blame to individuals conceals the dilemmas and signifies a process toward individualism. Third, the new labor logic shapes a new workplace culture and conceals class exploitation. I find that the formation of the desired psychological attitude in China is, in a way, very similar to what Robin Leidner and Guy Oakes have found in the case of the United States but also more complicated. Apart from companies' training and structured routines, sales agents rely on group dynamics to alter their framing and feeling rules. Both the local insurers and the highly localized joint ventures are most eager to use group dynamics to control and manage the agents. These insurers are in general more effective in shaping their agents' psychological attitude than are the others. Pacific-Aetna, which was especially good at mobilizing the agents' emotions, was most effective in channeling their agents' psychological attitudes. Thus, the effectiveness of the ideological work on sales agents varies among insurance companies depending on the strategies and techniques the in-house managers apply. Furthermore, variations are found among individual agents within the same company. Converting the psychological attitude of the agents who join the industry involuntarily is extremely difficult. On the other hand, the agents who quit their former jobs to join the industry are most receptive to adjusting their psychological attitude to achieve the desired outlook. They are more willing to make this adjustment, not because in this way they encounter fewer frustrations and fewer difficulties in selling insurance but because they need the desired attitude to empower themselves and justify the termination of their former employment. Since these agents chose to give up jobs with a steady income, the cost to them of failing in insurance sales is especially high. To prove that they have made a "correct" decision, they are the most ready to shape their psychological attitude in a way to facilitate their sales performance. They are the sales agents who are most willing to work for long hours to strive for career achievement. Therefore, agents' career history and initial motivation for joining the industry explain their different receptivity to the demand for ideological work. Ironically, the agents who feel most empowered through the work of insurance sales are those who work around the clock, every day of the week, and are most aggressive in exploiting their personal relationships in financial transactions.

Notes

1 For cultural resistance to commercial life insurance in the United States, see Viviana Zelizer, *Morals and Markets: The Development of Life Insurance in the United States*, New York, NY: Columbia University Press, 1979.
2 Ibid.: 119–47.
3 *Almanac of Shanghai Insurance 2002*, Shanghai: Shanghai Insurance Institute, 2002: 26–9.
4 The estimate is made by Stephan Binder, Tab Bowers, and Winston Yung in "Selling Life Insurance to China", (2004) *The McKinsey Quarterly: China Today*, Special Edition: 83–7.
5 For a substantial discussion of the transformation of the social organization of the labor market in China, see Ching Kwan Lee, *Gender and the South China Miracle: Two Worlds of Factory Women*, Berkeley, CA: University of California Press, 1998.
6 Participant observation, Shanghai, February 2002. In a company setting, Shan Hui Fan shared his views about his career path in AIA with other sales agents.

7 Interview, Shanghai, October 2001.

8 Life insurance and property insurance are the two major categories of insurance available in China. Life insurance includes not only term life and whole life policies but also endowment, investment insurance, personal accident insurance, hospitalizing insurance, and critical diseases insurance. All other types of insurance, such as auto insurance, liability insurance, and fire insurance, belong to property insurance.

9 A small number of young, educated agents joined Ping An because they believed that this new company would provide them with greater opportunity to establish their careers. Nonetheless, these educated agents were the minority in Ping An's sales force.

10 Interview, Shanghai, January 2002.

11 Interview, Shanghai, March 2002.

12 Thomas Rawski, *China: Prospects for Full Employment*, Employment and Training Papers, 47, Geneva: International Labour Office, 1999: 8.

13 Robin Leidner, *Fast Food, Fast Talk: Services Work and the Routinization of Everyday Life*, Berkeley, CA: University of California Press, 1993.

14 For a discussion of why women were drawn to direct-sales organizations in the United States, see Nicole Biggart, *Charismatic Capitalism: Direct Selling Organizations in America*, Chicago, IL: University of Chicago Press, 1989.

15 Viviana Zelizer, *Morals and Markets*: 41–89.

16 Wendy Espeland and Mitchell Stevens, "Commensuration as a Social Process", (1998) 24 *Annual Review of Sociology*: 313–43.

17 Viviana Zelizer, "Human Values and the Market: The Case of Life Insurance and Death in 19th Century America", (1978) 84 *American Journal of Sociology*:591–610; see also Robin Leidner, *Fast Food, Fast Talk*.

18 The concept of risk I adopt here is a realistic approach following Ulrich Beck and Anthony Giddens' discussion of the risks of the modern society. See Ulrich Beck, *Risk Society: Towards a New Modernity*, Thousand Oaks, CA: Sage Publications, 1992; Anthony Giddens, *The Consequences of Modernity*, Stanford, CA: Stanford University Press, 1990. For a social construction perspective on risk, see Mary Douglas and Aaron Wildavsky, *Risk and Culture: An Essay on the Selection of Technical and Environmental Dangers*, Berkeley, CA: University of California Press, 1982. For a Focaultian perspective, see Francois Ewald, "Insurance and Risk", in Graham Burchell, Colin Gordon and Peter Miller (eds), *The Foucault Effect: Studies in Governmentality*, Chicago, IL: University of Chicago Press, 1991.

19 Cheris Shun-ching Chan, "Making Insurance a Way of Life in China: How Culture Matters in Creating a Market", doctoral dissertation, Department of Sociology, Northwestern University, 2004.

20 Commission rates vary among products and payment duration. Typically, an agent receives a First-Year Commission (FYC) of 32–40 percent of the First-Year-Premium (FYP) of a whole life policy with an endowment element. The commission rate for the product sold is substantively reduced to 8–15 percent in the second year, 3–8 percent in the third and fourth year, and 1–3 percent in the fifth year. Normally, no commission is given after the fifth year.

21 The references of the US dollar in the entire text are calculated on the rate of US$1=8.3 RMB as of June 2004.

22 The figures are estimates made by the author from her interviews with informants. The average annual income in Shanghai city in 2001 was 26,169 RMB (US$3,152) and in 2002 was 24,078 RMB (US$2,900). Sources come from *China City Statistical Yearbook*, 2002 and 2003, Beijing: China Statistics Press.

23 This figure is actually comparable to the dropout rate of insurance sales agents in the United States. According to Leidner, the average retention rate for agents in the insurance industry after five years was only 18 percent. See Robin Leidner, *Fast Food, Fast Talk*: 95.

24 Interview, Shanghai, April 2002.
25 Gary Alan Fine, "Organizational Time: Temporal Demands and the Experience of Work in Restaurant Kitchens", (1990) 69 *Social Forces*: 95–114.
26 Robin Leidner, *Fast Food, Fast Talk*: 86–124.
27 Interview, Shanghai, April 2002.
28 For an excellent thesis on the non-neutrality of money and the social and cultural embedding of the uses of money, see Viviana Zelizer, *The Social Meaning of Money*, New York, NY: Basic Books, 1994.
29 A casual chat with the informant, January 2002.
30 For the concept of "emotional labor", see Arlie Russell Hochschild, *Managed Hearts: Commercialization of Human Feeling*, Berkeley, CA: University of California Press, 1983.
31 For an insightful discussion of how "feeling rules" work, see Arlie Russell Hochschild, "Emotion Work, Feeling Rules, and Social Structure", (1979) 85 *American Journal of Sociology*: 551–75.
32 Robin Leidner, *Fast Food, Fast Talk*; Guy Oakes, *The Soul of the Saleman*.
33 Robin, Leidner, *Fast Food, Fast Talk*.
34 For the role of small-group interactions in creating a group culture, see Gary Alan Fine, "Small Group and Culture Creation: The Idioculture of Little League Baseball Teams", (1979) 44 *American Sociological Review*: 733–45; for the role of large-scale collective assemblies in eliciting emotions, see James Jasper, *The Art of Moral Protest*, Chicago, IL: University of Chicago Press, 1997.
35 Participant observation, Shanghai, March 2002.
36 Zhou Huajian is indeed a very popular singer in Taiwan, Hong Kong, and parts of China.
37 I did not have a chance personally to take part in AAP activities. I watched the video tape that recorded the AAP, read the details of the ceremony in the monthly magazine of Pacific-Aetna, and interviewed the agents who attended the ceremony.
38 Viviana Zelizer, "Human Values and the Market": 604.
39 Interview, Shanghai, July 2002.
40 Carol Heimer, *Sharing Risks: The Institutional Division of Labor in the Management of Risk*, American Bar Foundation Working Paper, #9803, Chicago, IL: American Bar Foundation.
41 Ching Kwan Lee, "From the Specter of Mao to the Spirit of Law: Labor Insurgency in China", (2002) 31 *Theory and Society*: 189–228.
42 Interview, Shanghai, April 2002.
43 Interview, Shanghai, August 2000.
44 Participation observation, Shanghai, May 2002.

Index

AIA (insurance company) 230–1, 232, 233, 234, 236, 238, 239, 240, 243
Allianz-Dazhong 230, 233, 238, 239, 242

baomu (carers of children) 149–50, 156–9, 163
Beijing Transluxury Hotel *see* hotel sector

cellular activism 17–18, 19–26, 35; background 19; and different interest groups 25; and intra-company divisions 25; and intra-family hostility 25; and localization of interests 25–6; logic, potential, limit of 29; payment arrears 22–4; pensioner protests 19–21; and workplace specificity 24–5
census 2000 40–1, 54–5
Chinese Communist Party (CCP) 104
community 9–10, *see also* neighborhoods

danwei (work units) 2; demise of 10, 41–2; and destruction of family 42; enduring practice of 87–94; and interior design 51–2; and neighborhood transitions post-*danwei* 47–8; and provision of employee facilities 52; and public housing 48; and social position 42, 48, 54; and suicide 41–2
demonstrations/protests 10, 196; and cellular activism 17–18, 19–26; and fear of police repression 23; and insurgent identities 18; and keeping within the law 22–3; reasons for 17; road blockages 19–21; size/number of 17; success of 21; and working-class rebellion 26–9, *see also* Liaoyang protests
department stores, contrasting labor regimes in 95; threatening slogan in

77, *see also* factory-in-the-department store; Harbin No.X Department Store; Sunshine Department Store
domestic service 8–9; as alienating experience 160–1; and autonomy of workers 152–3, 155, 163; background 145–6; and bondservants 148–9, 164(n12); and categories of servant 148–9; changing meanings of *baomu* 156–9; and class inequality 155; and denouncing of employers 156, 164–5(n19); as disciplining process 159–62; and dual subjection 163; expansion in 145–6; experiences of *baomu* 149–54; formal vs real subsumption to wage labor 146–8; Mao/post-Mao comparison 145–6; and marketization of post-Mao reform era 155, 156; non-paid 147, 164(n6); representations through literature 156–7; and rurality in Mao era 148–56; and sending of city children to countryside 153–4; and socialized labor 146, 163(n2); and specter of old oppressive society 157; and urban affluence 160

economic restructuring 3–4
employment *see* labor
engineers, age of 211–12; and controlling creativity 220–2; and economic reforms 213; and firm rivalries 225–6; and gender 226–7; and government as source of employment 215; and growth of private enterprises 212; and high tax rate 212; and limits of management control 218; and male camaraderie 226; motives/institutions of theft 222–4; and multinationals 212–13; nationalism of

An environmentally friendly book printed and bound in England by www.printondemand-worldwide.com

PEFC Certified

This product is
from sustainably
managed forests
and controlled
sources

www.pefc.org

PEFC/16-33-415

MIX

Paper from
responsible sources

FSC® C004959

This book is made entirely of chain-of-custody materials; FSC materials for the cover and PEFC materials for the text pages

#0259 - 221112 - C0 - 234/156/14 - PB